RIFLE GUIDE

R. A. Steindler

Stoeger Publishing Company

Copyright © 1978 by R. A. Steindler

All rights reserved. No part of this book may be reproduced or transmitted in any form or by any means, electronic or mechanical, including photocopying, recording, or by any information storage and retrieval system, without permission in writing from the Publisher.

Published by the Stoeger Publishing Company
55 Ruta Court, South Hackensack, N.J. 07606

Library of Congress Catalog Card No.: 78-13800

ISBN: 0-88317-092-2

Manufactured in the United States of America

Distributed to the book trade by Follett Publishing Company and to the sporting goods trade by Stoeger Industries. In Canada, distributed to the book trade and to the sporting goods trade by Stoeger Trading Company, 900 Ontario Street East, Montreal, Quebec H2L 1P4.

On the front cover: Winchester Model 94 lever-action carbine. On the back cover, from the top: Browning BAR semiautomatic rifle, standard grade 300 Winchester Magnum; Sako A111 Deluxe bolt-action rifle, 30-06 caliber; Remington Model 760 BDL custom deluxe pump-action rifle, 30-06 caliber; and Marlin Model 336-C lever-action carbine, 35 Remington caliber. Cover photographs by Raymond Wells and Robert Koumjian.

RIFLE
GUIDE

Contents

About the Author	8
Introduction	9
1. In the Beginning	13
2. Where the Action Is	31
3. A Look at Today's Rifles	55
4. Playing the Numbers	85
5. Rifle Ballistics	101
6. Handloading	119
7. This Thing Called Accuracy	139
8. Sights	165
9. Rifle Care and Tinkering	187
10. Military Rifles	219
11. Hints for Riflemen	231
12. Reading for Riflemen	247
Appendices	253
Good Starting Loads	255
Cartridge Specifications	288
Graphs	298
Index	303

About the Author

A shooter for nearly half a century, and a hunter for almost as long, R. A. Steindler's interest in rifles extends from designing them to testifying about them in courts of law. A competitive shooter for many years, he has also designed a number of wildcats, has written extensively about rifles and is a consultant to the firearms industry.

His hunts have taken him to Europe, the United States and Canada, as well as parts of South America. Between hunting trips and writing books and articles, he also finds time to do most of his own gunsmithing work and to continue his work as firearms expert in court cases. He maintains a complete forensic firearms laboratory and travels extensively in connection with his private practice.

Bob Steindler has been an avid black powder shooter since the first of the replica guns were imported, is also a handgunner with a special interest in handgun hunting and competitive shooting, while his shotgunning and training of gun dogs is limited to upland game due to lack of time.

Steindler is also the author of RELOADER'S GUIDE, STANDARD DIRECTORY OF PROOF MARKS, SHOOTING THE MUZZLE LOADERS, HOME GUNSMITHING DIGEST, MODERN ABC'S OF GUNS, and FIREARMS DICTIONARY.

Introduction

If I were to follow tradition, I'd recall here what my first rifle was and how much I paid for it. The truth is that I paid nothing for my first rifle. The first rifle I ever fired and which I used that long-ago summer, was a rimfire bolt-action rifle that belonged to my cousin, and we spent most of the summer burning up ammunition. That fall, my uncle handed me a rifle and invited me to go hunting for roe buck. I collected my buck with one shot from a 7 x 57 Mannlicher rifle, and if memory serves me, I was not quite 11 years old. I got a nice rack mount and that rifle for a combined birthday and Christmas gift.

Since then I have fired many, many rifles: in hunting fields, on target ranges and in plain plinking and professional gun testing. Over the years, I have also collected a fair library, with many of the books having the word "rifle" in the title. In reading these volumes, I noted that each author had a special area of interest in the rifle field: the match shooter, the Africa hunter and the rifleman who sought his target high in the mountains. Thus, each brought to his pages some likes and some pet peeves and dislikes and, more often than not, somehow glossed over points which he knew but forgot that others did not know.

Not that this book is totally free of prejudices or pre-conceived notions and ideas—but I did try to stay clear of them. I tried to bring the novice rifleman something that would serve him in getting the basics under his belt and perhaps get him interested in some other areas as well, such as hobby gun tinkering, handloading or perhaps developing a better wildcat cartridge.

In my collection of 300 or so rifles, I have some very handsome ones, some which should be restocked and reblued and there are even one or two which should be junked. But as long as they shoot where I aim them and deliver good accuracy, I am content. To me, a rifle is to be used, not something with an intrinsic value or perhaps a dollar value which is to be looked at but not touched.

This is not a highly technical volume. And because of this, I hope that more budding riflemen will get something out of it, even if I did not cover the width of the lands and grooves on each type of rifling and every rifle. It's important, but not that important when you shoulder that rifle and settle the sights on the target.

Good shooting, and I hope, good reading.

—R. A. Steindler

Chapter One
In the Beginning

Chapter One
In the Beginning

Only the firearms historian is particularly interested in pinpointing precisely the place and the year in which gun powder was discovered. Once the behavior of gun powder was known and understood and sundry means of using it had been developed, the smoothbored cannon was the first gun or weapon to be used widely.

It was not until around 1450 that the rifled barrel appeared, with some historians crediting a Viennese gunsmith, Gaspard Kollner, with rifling the first barrel, and others claiming that it was August Kotter of Nürnberg who invented the rifled barrel. It took another 150 years before the military accepted that new-fangled idea but, by 1631, the Hessians had several companies equipped with carbines that had rifled barrels.

Some early crossbows, which apparently antedate both Kollner and Kotter, had a rifled tube mounted atop the crossbow; the bolt was propelled through the tube. Archers, of course, had long known that a rotating or spinning arrow was far more accurate and deadly than a nonrotating one, so it is not at all surprising to learn that riflemen hurriedly got out of the way of expert bowmen and crossbow shooters.

The conical projectile of the black powder guns is vastly superior to the round ball, and rifling a barrel made the projectile that was fired through such a barrel a great deal more accurate, hence also more efficient. Rate of twist of the rifling is usually given as one turn per so many inches (e.g.: 1:10), and in some respects this twist governs the weight and even the length of the bullet that can be fired through it so that the bullet will be stabilized during its flight to the target.

The Swiss, to whom rifle shooting has always been a way of life, found it necessary in 1563 to legislate against the use of rifled guns in matches in which non-rifled guns competed. Henceforth riflemen had to compete against riflemen, and the government even awarded special trophies for shooters using a rifled bar-

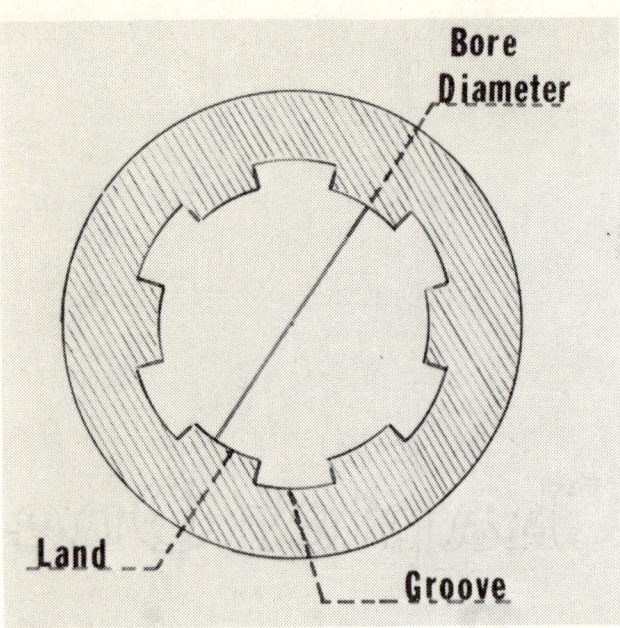

Bore diameter is measured between opposing lands. The lands in the barrel, of course, cause the grooves to be made in the fired bullet.

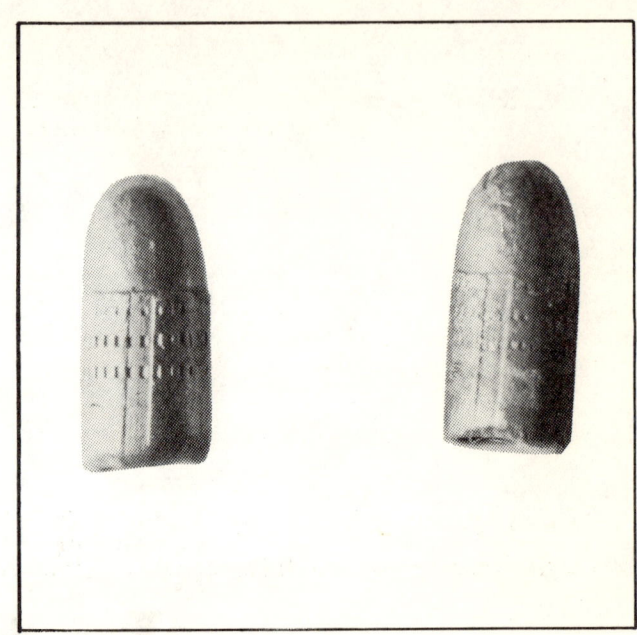

Lead bullets recovered from bullet recovery box show details of rifling.

rel. The British were a bit slower to accept the idea that rifling was essential for better accuracy, and a number of different riflings were tried. The Metford rifling was developed in 1865, and consisted of a shallow segmental rifling of five very shallow grooves which were slightly rounded. Tests conducted with a 450-caliber rifle, firing a paper-patched bullet, produced some very fine groups. The Whitworth rifling was hexagonal and called for a hexagonal bullet that weighed 530 grains and was 1.375-inches long. Another rifling experiment — this one resulting in an oval rifling — was the Lancaster two-groove rifling.

As smokeless powder replaced black powder and as the self-contained cartridge became more popular, harder steels were required for the higher pressures created by the burning smokeless powder. This, in turn, made it necessary to make better and longer-lasting rifling cutters. Basically, there are a number of ways of cutting the rifling into the hole drilled through the steel rod. Harry Pope's gain twist rifling, with its slightly rounded edge of the grooves and narrower than usual lands, and its left-hand twist where the bore diameter tapers toward the muzzle, was designed for lead bullets. To this day,

Pope barrels, if they have been properly cared for, have maintained their famed accuracy.

Currently, several rifling methods are being used. The oldest method which is still in use is the cut rifling where a cutter is pushed through the pre-drilled hole in the steel rod that eventually will become the barrel. Hook rifling calls for the cutter to be pulled through the future barrel. Broach-type rifling calls for a special cutting tool with teeth. Early broaches were pulled through, whereas current manufacturing practices call for the broach to be pushed through. This type of rifling is found most often in handgun barrels. Button rifling calls for a mandrel to be forced through the barrel, and, in contrast to the other methods of cutting rifling, button rifling is considered to be a swaging process. Another swaging process is hammer rifling, in which a steel mandrel is inserted into the hole in the steel rod, and the future barrel is then hammered until the inside of the bore conforms fully to the mandrel.

The ultimate accuracy of a rifle depends on many things: the barrel, the bedding of the action and barrel in the stock, the ammunition, the type of sight used, and, of course, the shooter. Each barrel, and thus each rifle, is a law

Moving at about 4000 feet per second, a 25-grain bullet hits an egg. Note in this series of ten photos that total destruction of the raw egg does not occur until bullet has moved well out of the picture.

IN THE BEGINNING

16

RIFLE GUIDE

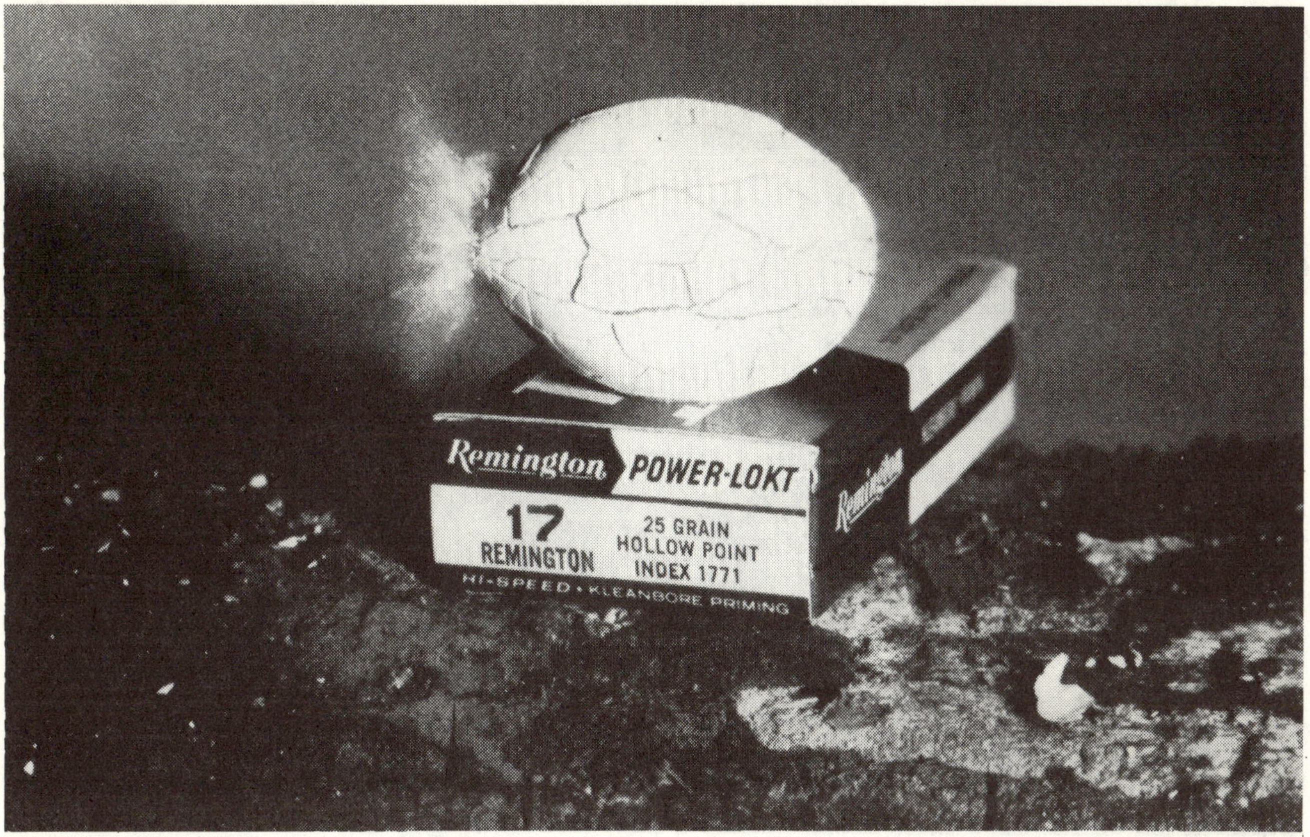

IN THE BEGINNING 17

RIFLE GUIDE

IN THE BEGINNING

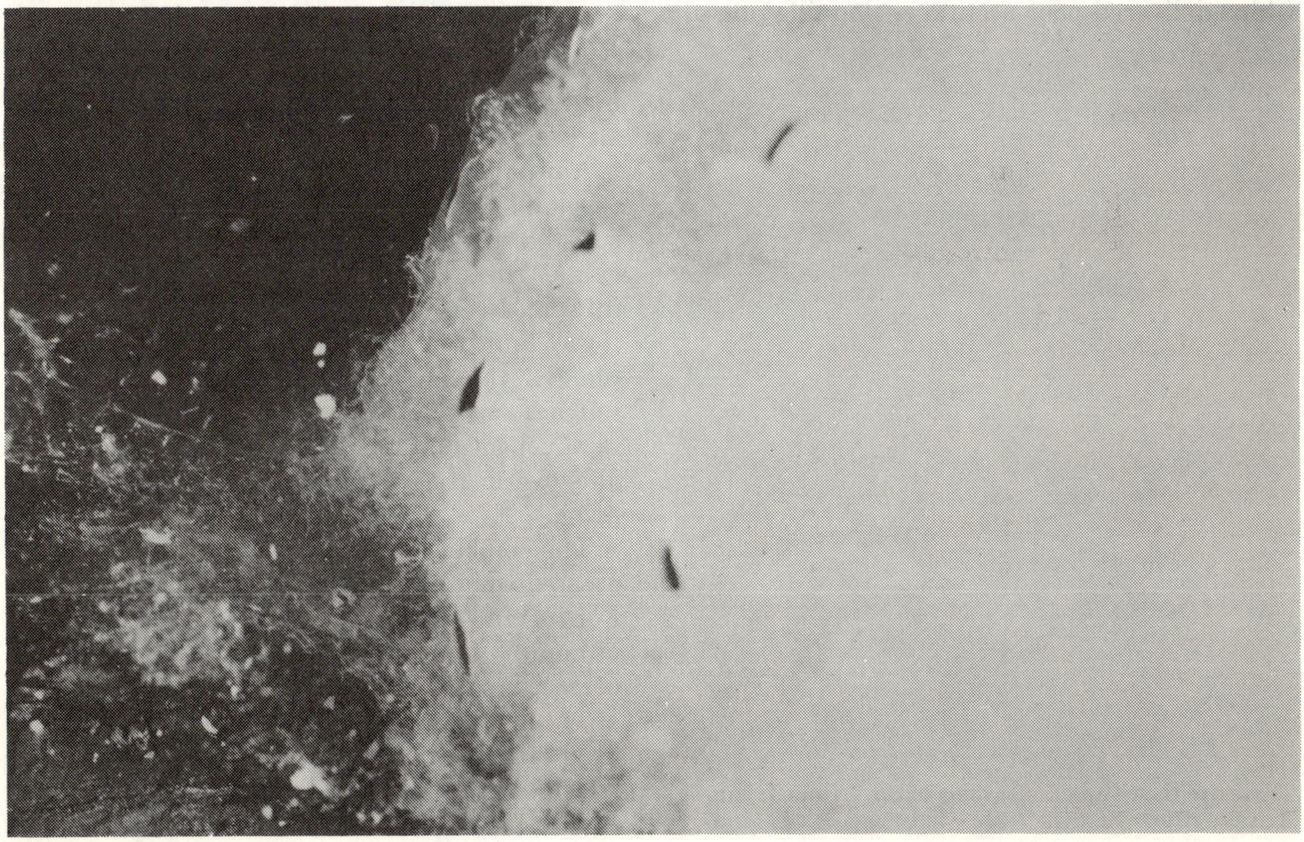

unto itself. This explains why one shooter will get excellent groups with a given rifle and one brand of ammo, while another shooter, using another rifle of like model and manufacture and the same brand of ammunition, has trouble keeping all his shots on the paper.

Some ten years ago an R&D engineer of one of the major gun makers and I conducted some tests which were rather revealing: As it comes from the mill, the barrel steel is in the form of steel rods. The forklift truck moving a bundle of these rods puts extra stress on some of the rods as the bundle is being lifted. We marked two such rods, later had them rifled on the same machine by the same man, and then attached an action to one of these barrels and fired it from the machine rest with precision-loaded ammunition.

We then unscrewed the action, threaded it onto the other barrel and repeated our shooting tests. As a control we had also taken one unstressed barrel blank and this, too, was rifled by the same man and on the same machine as the other two barrels. The unstressed barrel was much more accurate than the stressed barrels, which delivered poor accuracy. Bending one of

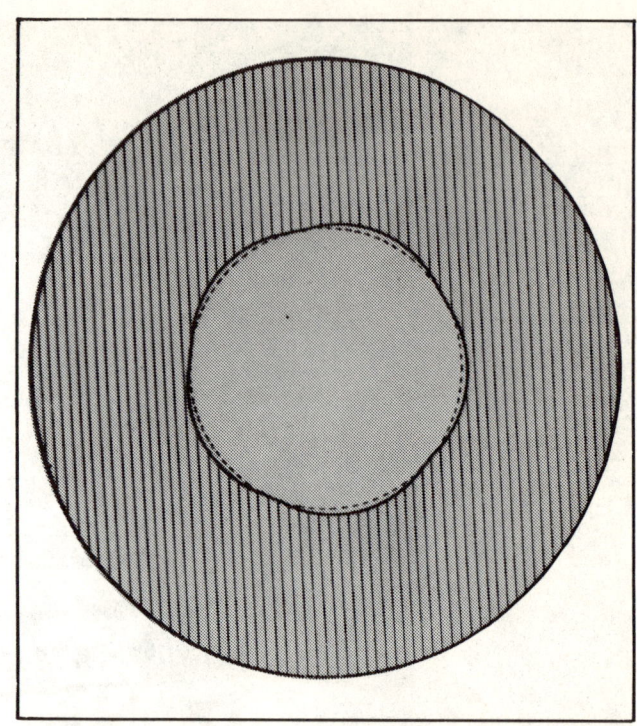

The Newton rifling was created by Harry Pope, who had charge of the barrel shop. Pope insisted on an odd number of grooves so that the rifling cutter would be supported by a land as it cut each groove.

these barrels—a process known as barrel straightening, still practiced by expert barrel makers—improved the performance of the stressed barrel to some degree.

A number of different steels are used in barrels, and some rifles even come with a stainless steel barrel. Barrels destined to be used for 22-caliber rimfire rifles are not exposed to the same internal stresses and strains as a barrel destined for a 7mm Remington Magnum rifle, for example. In the latter barrel, the steel must be tougher so it can withstand the friction of the high velocity bullet, higher barrel temperatures and overheating of the steel due to too-rapid firing.

The smokeless powders of 20 or 30 years ago created what can be called cartridge monsters. For instance, the 220 Swift got the reputation of being hard on barrels. It was claimed, and correctly so, that barrels were shot out, often after only 500 rounds of ammunition had been fired through a barrel. This barrel-life problem is still with us, but in a much more limited way than it was 30 years ago when cartridges were

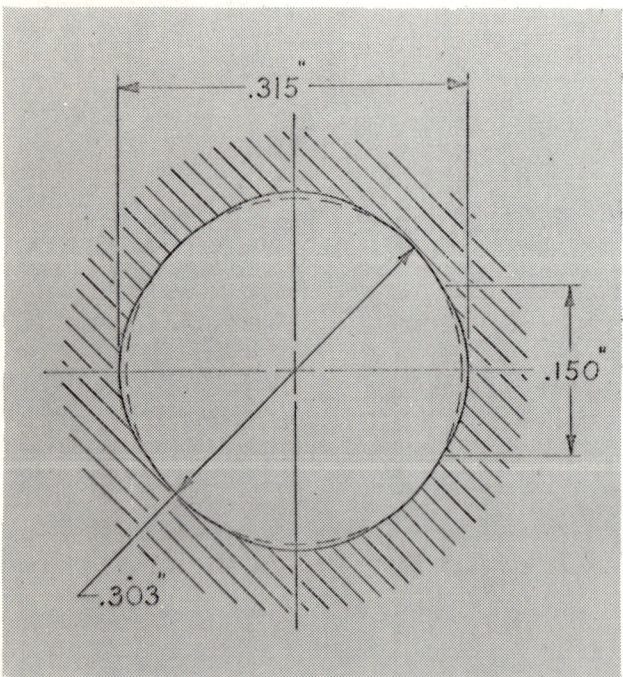

These are the rifling dimensions of the 7.7mm Japanese Arisaka rifle.

sometimes classified as being "hard" or "easy" on barrels.

Stainless steel is, of course, one answer for such barrel burners, but because it is harder to machine, one must expect to pay a higher price for a rifle with such a barrel. A rifle wholly made from stainless steel was manufactured on a custom basis for a short period, but cost and production problems finally forced the company to drop it.

Wear and tear on the rifling is due to several factors. Ultrahigh-velocity cartridges generate very high temperatures in the chamber, and hot gases then move up the barrel. The friction of a tight-fitting bullet is another cause of barrel wear. The slightest unevenness in the barrel also leads to excessive wear and tear on the barrel. Despite regular cleaning, one of my early 17-caliber rifles had to be scrapped — a burr in the bore opened the bullet jackets like banana peels, and the bullet fragments never even reached the 50-yard target to which I finally moved.

Shooting large quantities of steel-jacketed bullets, mostly of the military salvage type, is foolish since the low cost of the bullets seldom even comes close to offsetting the cost of a new barrel plus the gunsmithing charges for installing it. Barrel heating, which invariably leads to barrel or heat erosion, also invariably opens up groups.

Barrel wear, or shooting out a barrel, is a gradual process, and it seldom comes as a surprise. When it was new and for some years thereafter, my first 7mm Remington Magnum shot excellent groups with ease and cleanly took more than 20 big-game animals, including moose and caribou. Then, after almost 5000 rounds, I noticed that the groups were beginning to open up; when I got tumbling or keyholing bullets, I knew it was time to hang a new barrel on that action.

Making rifle barrels, even with the most modern production methods, is a tricky job. If you consider that one starts with a solid rod of steel about two inches in diameter which has to have a straight hole drilled through it; and then perhaps that hole is enlarged with another passage of the deep-hole drill; and finally there is rifling — which can mean a chattering reamer and clogged cutting teeth which don't cut properly. Remember that additionally there is stressed steel, plus the numerous other problems which crop up in barrel making, and you can understand why guns vary in performance.

Air gaging of barrels was considered to be the ultimate test for checking the perfectness of a new barrel, but in essence, air gaging seems to serve no better purpose than to see if the air gage works properly. This means of checking a barrel was designed not only for checking the straightness of the barrel and the bore, but also for checking the evenness of the rifling.

If you have a chance, look at the rifling in the barrel of a current production black powder

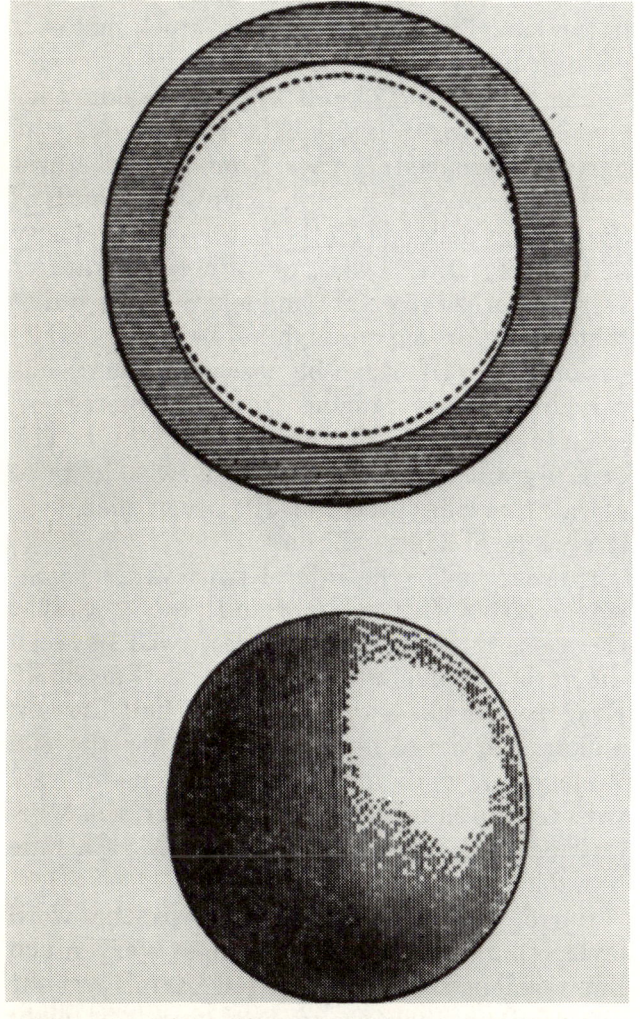

Rifling and bullet of the Lancaster rifling. The oval bullet moved spirally toward the muzzle thanks to the oval rifling.

IN THE BEGINNING 21

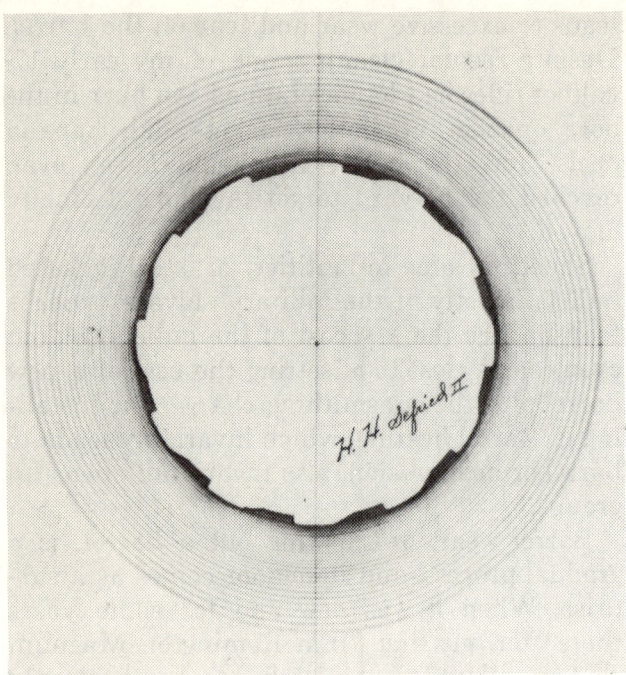

Coltsman rifling consists of 12 lands and 12 shallow grooves. In this rifling, designed by Harry Sefried who is now with Sturm, Ruger and Co., the driving edge of the land is sharp and at right angles to the bore. The trailing edge blends away to avoid an unnecessary sharp corner. Rifling was designed to give rifling a positive grip on bullet without too much displacement of bullet jacket-metal, and this in turn gave bullet better flight characteristics.

rifle or musket. It is shallow so that the pure lead projectile can easily engage, and since black powder projectiles don't move very fast, the rifling does not need to be very deep.

Barrel steel must be flexible, but just how flexible barrel steel really is was brought to my attention some 15 years ago. I had purchased one of the better-known magnum rifles in early spring, shot 200 rounds of factory ammo, partly to sight the rifle in and to get some practice, and partly so that I could reload the brass. Because I anticipated some long-range shots, I practiced getting into shooting position and popping distant targets until I felt that the rifle was simply an extension of my arm.

Then came a hot and humid summer, a couple of rush projects, and, before I knew it, it was almost time to pack up and head west for my annual big-game trip. It turned out that the once-accurate rifle was not even printing on a two-foot x two-foot target! Examination showed that the barrel channel wood had not been waterproofed, which permitted moisture to enter. This warped the wood, which, in turn, exerted considerable pressure on the barrel, resulting in groups that were really not groups but bullet patterns.

The question as to which part of the rifle is the most important is like asking, "What came first, the chicken or the egg?" The rifled barrel houses the chamber in the rear end where the live cartridge rests before it is fired. It is the place where the needed gas pressures build up that finally give the bullet the required push to its intended target. The rifling in the barrel gives the bullet the gyrational spin it needs to make it fly true. The action, containing the firing system and perhaps the cartridge magazine or clip, is essential to start things happening in the barrel's chamber, and the stock makes it possible to hang on to the whole works.

The width and depth of grooves, or conversely, the width and height of the lands (the parts not grooved), varies from manufacturer to manufacturer. To some extent, the depth of the grooves depends on the anticipated velocity of the projectile. Twist, or rather the rate of twist, governs the weight and length of the bullet that can be driven through a given barrel. The various 6mm rifles can be used with handloads carrying bullets ranging from the Sierra 60-grain to the Speer 105 grain bullet. Why no 115- or 120-grain bullet? Because the twist in most of the 6mm rifles precludes the use of such relatively long and heavy bullets.

However, even the rate of twist varies somewhat, partly with calibers and partly because there is a variation in the rate of twist between the various barrel and gun makers. The 30-40 Krag usually has a 1:10 twist, and half the gun makers use the same rate of twist for the 308 Winchester, while at least as many use a 1:12 twist for the same cartridge. However, the Marlin Model 62, chambered for the 30 M1 Carbine round has a 1:20 twist.

Barrel configuration, or perhaps the word style is more applicable, changes very much like fashions in clothes. Round barrels are the standard, but there are tapered barrels, straight and bull barrels, and round barrels with various steps machined into the exterior. The bull bar-

Barrel boring in a British barrel plant. Greener, in various editions of his *The Gun and Its Development* states that the drawing was made in his plant, then, in still another edition, that it was made in another barrel factory.

rels, better dissipate the heat of firing, have less barrel whip, and therefore are stiffer and more accurate. Octagonal barrels, hexagonal barrels and half-round/half-octagonal barrels show up too. The original idea behind the octagonal barrel was that the flat surfaces offered more area for the heat to dissipate, but these days, anything but a round barrel is a rather unusual feature. It may serve as a cosmetic addition, or the special barrel configuration may have been used because someone wanted it that way, or the barrel maker simply felt like making one. Many shooters find that such barrels have a lot of eye appeal, but when it comes down to it, the tapered round barrel is the one most hunters and shooters buy, even when given a choice.

What about barrels for 22 rimfire rifles? Since the 22s in their various shapes fire relatively low velocity bullets and the powder charge in the cases is minimal — just enough to get the bullet moving first through and then outside the barrel, barrel wear is not a problem. Many 22-caliber rimfire rifles which are 30 or more years old still shoot to point of aim. The older barrels which have worn out were originally fired with corrosive ammo; it was not so much friction that ruined these barrels, but the chemical process of corrosion.

IN THE BEGINNING

Note how current Marlin rifling shows the same basic idea as the Colt rifling shown earlier.

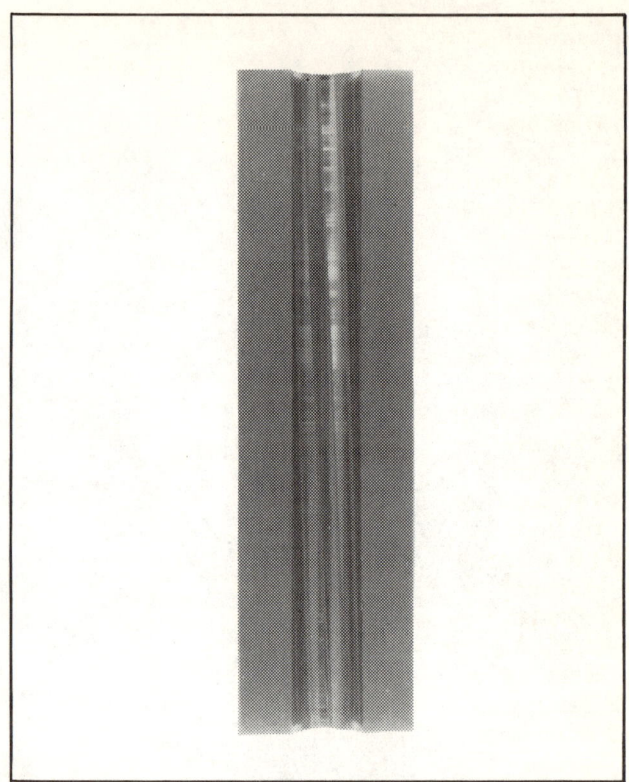

Section of a handgun barrel showing the rifling.

The worst enemy of the 22 rimfire rifle is the cleaning rod. Devoted target shooters will become furious if someone admits to having scrubbed a barrel clean, not because fouling is good for the scores, but because the careless use of a cleaning rod, applied either from the breech or the muzzle end, is almost certain to damage the rifling.

TWIST FOR MOST COMMON CARTRIDGES

Caliber	Most Common	Also Used
17 Remington	1:9"	
22 Hornet	1:16"	
219 Zipper	1:14"	
222 Remington	1:14"	1:16"
222 Remington Magnum	1:14"	1:12"
223 Remington (5x5.6)	1:12"	1:10" and 1:14"
224 Weatherby	1:14"	
225 Winchester	1:14"	
22-250 Remington	1:14"	1:12"
220 Swift	1:14"	
220 Weatherby Rocket	1:14"	
243 Winchester	1:10"	1:9"
244 Remington	1:10"	1:12"
6mm Remington	1:10"	1:9"
6mm International (6x47)	1:12"	
256 Winchester Magnum	1:14"	
250-3000 Savage	1:10"	
257 Roberts	1:10"	
25-06 Remington	1:10"	
257 Weatherby	1:12"	
6.5x54 M-S	1:8¼"	
6.5x55	1.8"	1:8¼" and 1:9"
6.5 Remington Magnum	1:9"	
264 Winchester Magnum	1:9"	1:10"
270 Winchester	1:10"	1:9" and 1:9½"
270 Weatherby Magnum	1:12"	
7x57, 7mm Mauser	1:10" U.S.A.	1:8.66" (22 cm) Europe
280 Remington	1:9¼"	1:9½"
284 Winchester	1:9½"	1:10"
7x61 S&H	1:10"	

RIFLE GUIDE

Caliber	Twist	Alt. Twist
7mm Remington Magnum	1:10″	1:9″ and 1:9½″
7mm Weatherby Magnum	1:12″ (since 1965)	1:10″ (prior to 1965)
30 M1 Carbine	1:20″	
30-30 Winchester	1:12″	1:10″
30 Remington	1:12″	
300 Savage	1:12″	
30-40 Krag	1:10″	
308 Winchester (7.62 NATO)	1:10″	1:12″
30-06	1:10″	1:12″
300 H&H Magnum	1:10″	
308 Norma Magnum	1:12″	1:10″
300 Winchester Magnum	1:10″	1:12″
300 Weatherby Magnum	1:12″	
303 British	1:10″	
8mm Remington Magnum	1:12″	
32 Remington	1:14″	
32 Winchester Special	1:16″	
8x68S	1:10″	
338 Winchester Magnum	1:10″	1:12″
340 Weatherby Magnum	1:10″	
348 Winchester	1:12″	
35 Remington	1:16″	
350 Remington Magnum	1:16″	
358 Winchester	1:12″	1:10″
358 Norma Magnum	1:12″	
375 H&H Magnum	1:12″	1:14″
375 Weatherby Magnum	1:12″	
44 Magnum	1:38″	
444 Marlin	1:38″	
45-70	1:20″	
458 Winchester Magnum	1:14″	1:15″, 1:16½″ and 1:18″
460 Weatherby Magnum	1:16″	

Here's a guide to twist: the longer the bullet, the faster the twist must be. Because the European twist for the 7mm Mauser is 1:8.66 and that the barrel makers here use the slower 1:10 twist, the European barrel is the better choice if a longer bullet is to be used. Also, if a bullet is to be driven at a lower than normal velocity for a given caliber, the twist of the rifling should be faster to help stabilize the bullet.

The depth of the rifling varies with gun makers, and even with standard calibers, not all gun makers use the same twist for the same caliber. Similarly, the width of the lands and grooves, as well as the number of lands and grooves, vary a great deal from barrel maker to barrel maker, each of them being totally convinced that his is the only reliable way of doing the job.

In a comparison of two barrels chambered for the same caliber, where one has a somewhat faster twist than the other, extensive shooting tests have shown that the slower twist tube requires more precisely made ammunition, and that the chambering must also be more precise. On the other hand, quick-twist barrels produce more friction and therefore more heat, and such barrels will wear out sooner than those with a slower twist.

The shallow rifling seen in the barrels for black powder rifles and handguns is needed so that there will be as little lead fouling as possible; because of the shallow rifling, only the purest soft lead should be used to make balls or bullets for such guns. The deeper rifling found in centerfire as well as rimfire rifle barrels is needed so that the jacketed bullets, or those cast or swaged from lead alloys will accept the rifling once the bullet enters the bore.

Keyholing, or tumbling of bullets, occurs when the rifling is imperfect, or in some cases, when an uneven spot in the rifling tears open the jacket of a fast-moving bullet. Some experimenters still maintain that nearly all bullets begin to tumble sooner or later, and that this occurs at the extreme ranges where the shooter cannot observe bullet impact or behavior. The occasional flyer — a shot not near the other bullet holes in the target — is probably due to an imperfect bullet. This theory is given credence by the fact that those wonderful fussbudgets, the benchrest shooters, not only weigh and mike each bullet, but also check its concentricity before loading it.

Over the years, since the importance of rifling and twist was realized, a great many different rifling methods have been tried. The gain twist, where the rifling starts with a slow twist at the breech and becomes faster as it nears the muzzle, is one of the more lasting notions about rifling. Although research in this area has been slowed somewhat, it seems likely that some day we will have newer and harder steels for barrels. This, in turn, may not only require different methods of rifling, but perhaps also a new concept in the rifling itself.

Riflemen are a different breed of shooter when compared to the handgunner or the smoothbore shooter. Not only do we have blank spaces in our knowledge of how rifling affects a bullet at the extreme ranges, but also of how the width and the depth of the lands and grooves may play a role that has not been explored to any degree. Bullet jackets and bullet design, as well as manufacturing methods, have changed considerably in the last ten years. Perhaps a better bullet jacket is just around the corner — and this might require a new rifling system. Riflemen are inveterate experimenters and most of today's commercial cartridges are the result of a rifleman's labor in some basement or on the range. And that is the name of the game, as long as care and caution are used at all times.

Cold swaging or hammer forging barrels is said by some to create less strain on barrel steel than does the cutting of the steel from inside the bore.

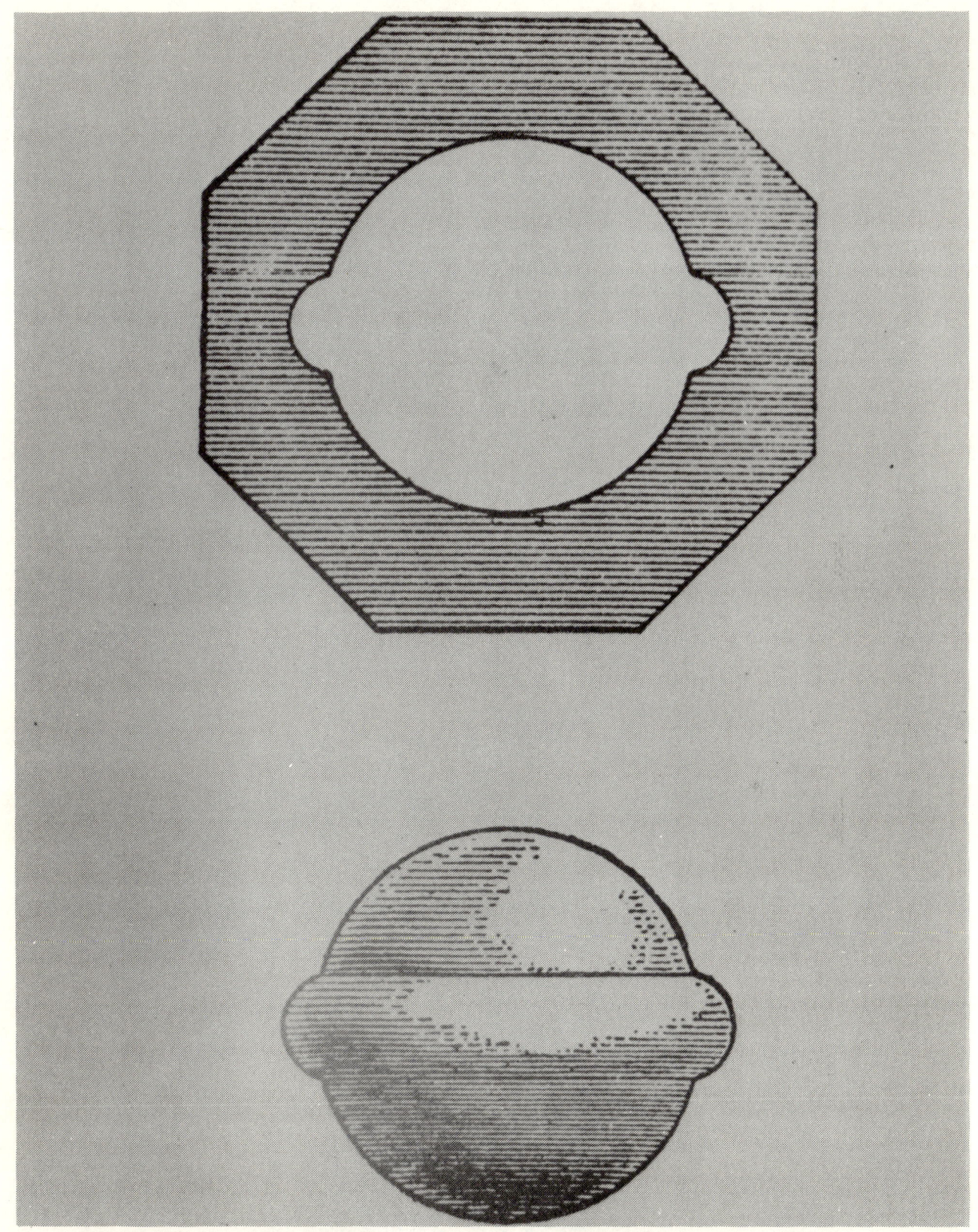
The rifling and the bullet of the Brunswick rifle. The belted round ball fits the two rifling grooves mechanically instead of relying on the seating of the bullet by gas pressure.

Chapter Two
Where the Action Is

Chapter Two
Where the Action Is

Although multi-shot black powder rifles were in use before the self-contained cartridge was introduced, the majority of these guns were muzzle loaders. The introduction of the early self-contained cartridges produced the first of the breech-loading guns, and these were designed to function as single-shot rifles. From the single-shot rifle in which one cartridge was chambered, fired, the case extracted or ejected, and a fresh round loaded to continue the cycle, came the idea to store a few extra rounds of ammunition in the action so that the shooting speed of the gun could be increased.

The design of the single-shot action is varied, and there are as many different action designs as there are commercially produced rifle calibers, and perhaps even more. The Burnside, the Sharps, the Remington Rolling Block, the Winchester High-Wall and the Low-Wall, the Stevens and the Peabody are perhaps the best known of the American actions. In Europe, the Aydt, Deeley and Edge, the Farquharson, the Flobert, the two Martini designs, as well as the German Schuetzen actions are the most readily recognized actions.

The lagging interest in single-shot actions and rifles after World War II was reversed when returning GIs brought liberated European rifles home, and when the Australian 310 Cadet Martini rifles were sold here as surplus. Since ammunition in this caliber was not available, these little rifles were rechambered to 357 Magnum. This conversion became so popular that the supply of the original Australian Cadet rifles was soon exhausted, and shooters began to look for other actions that could be restored, repaired or rebarreled. The Remington Rolling Block was widely revived until the supply of these actions became scarce, and from then on, the development and production of new American single-shot rifles proceeded full speed ahead.

The revival of the single-shot rifle and its wide acceptance among shooters was so great that a number of "new" single-shot actions were designed. The Ruger single shots, the ill-fated Colt-Sharps, the Harrington & Richardson Topper top-break series, and the reintroduced Trapdoor Springfield, the Wickliffe '76, and a number of semi-custom actions are the best known of the new single-shot designs.

Why single shots in this day and age of the semiautomatic and the bolt-action rifle? Most shooters who use single shots feel that the challenge of the hunt is much greater with such a rifle than with a multi-shot rifle. If you don't hit the target with the first shot from a bolt, lever, pump or autoloading rifle, you always have a second or third shot ready within a fraction of a second; with the single shot, the first shot must be the telling one.

Another often-heard reason for the switch to the one-shot gun comes from the older shooters who recall that their dads or granddads used to collect the winter venison with some old single shot, and now they want to try their skills afield the same way. For some, it was a nostalgia trip, and for others, it was a quest for a more leisurely way of shooting and hunting. And since most of the new single-shot rifles are every bit as accurate as any other action design rifle, the varmint hunter has also turned to the single-shot rifle.

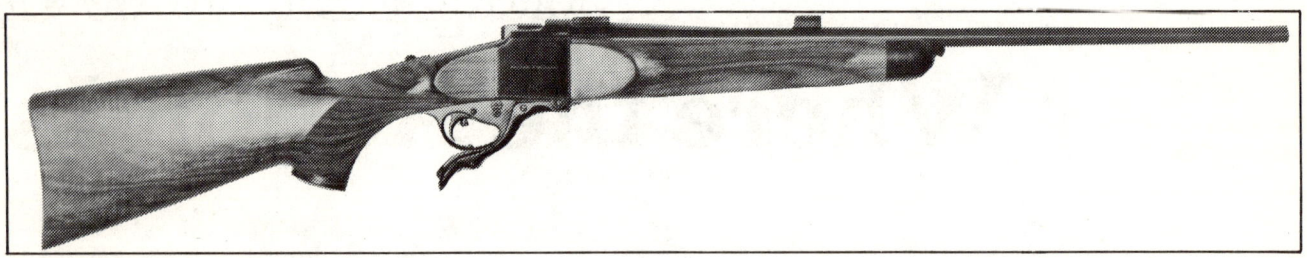

This restocked and rebarreled Farquahrson is chambered for the 243 Krag which is almost identical to the 243 Winchester. Stock by Shellhamer, barrel and action work done by RCBS for Fred Huntington of RCBS.

From bottom: A restocked BSA Martini rechambered for the 357 Magnum round; a Winchester High-Wall restocked with Oregon myrtle wood and now chambered for the 6mm/303 British Improved; and another High-Wall also restocked and chambered for the now obsolete 219 Zipper.

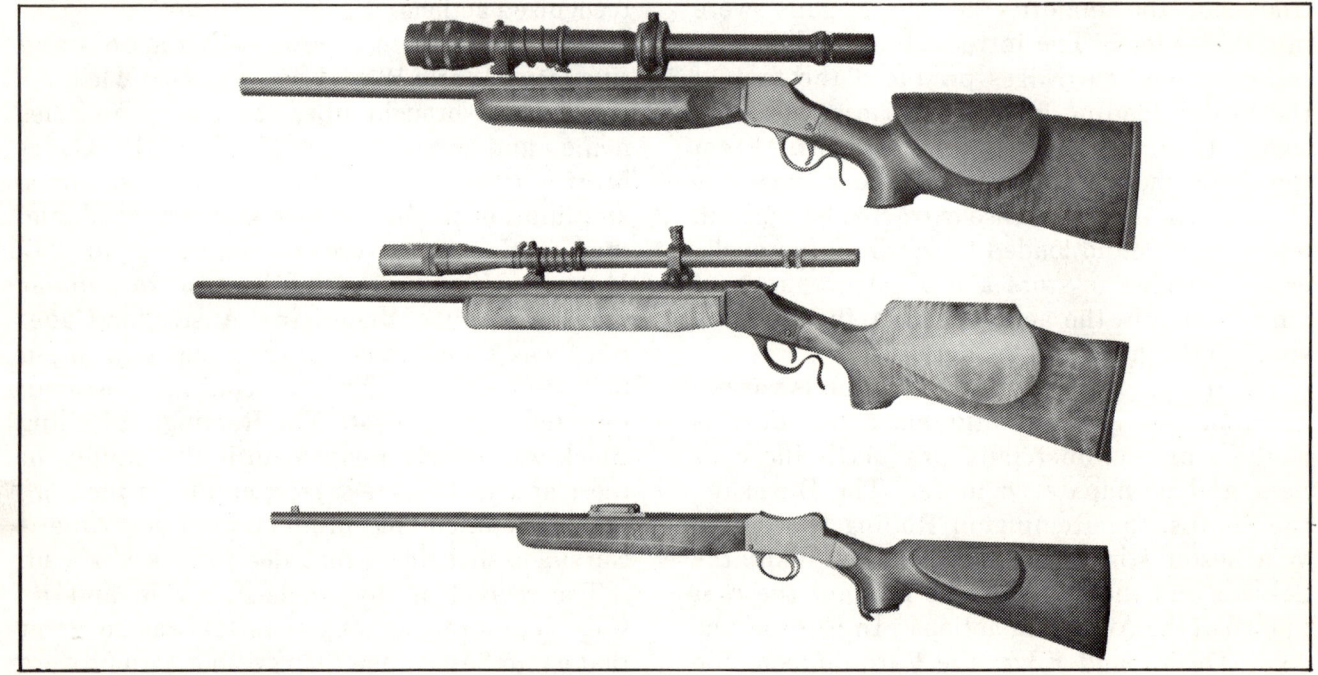

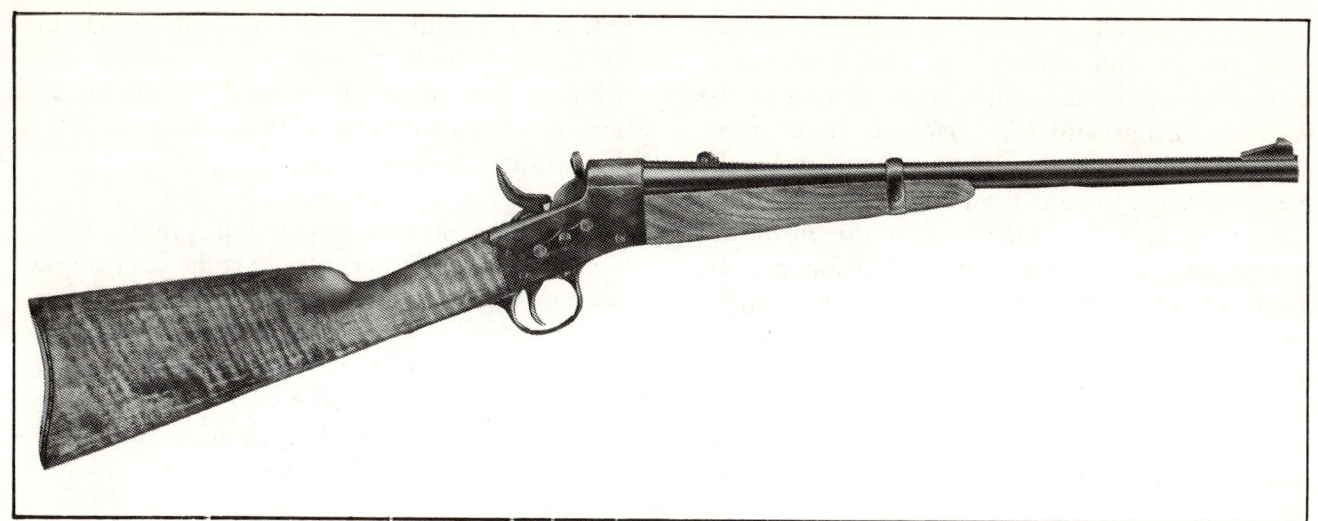

One of the numerous reproductions of the Remington Rolling Block—copying the original design of the rolling block; rifles as well as handguns are now offered with this action.

Bill Ruger's single-shot rifle was one of the first of the new single shots that, when introduced, signalled the healthy revival of the single-shot rifle.

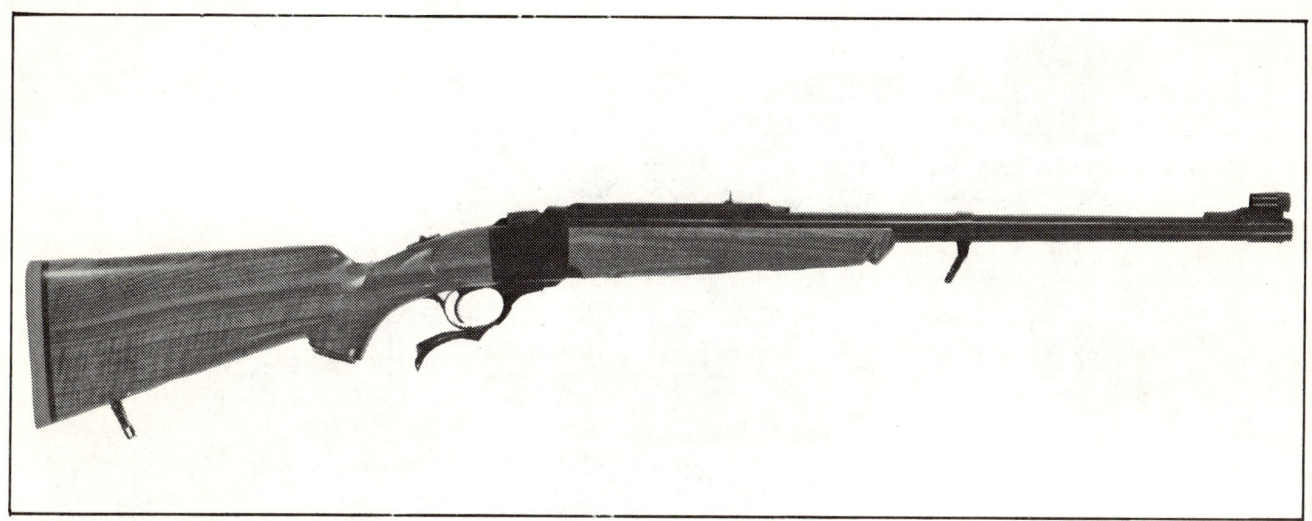

Many of the match rifles are also single shot, although in this case the action is based on the bolt-action design. In this type of rifle, the machined cut in the action that normally holds the magazine or clip is omitted, as is the magazine itself. The cartridge simply is placed on a smooth steel block so that the bolt, as it moves forward, chambers the round.

While the basic single-shot design is based on a solid steel block that moves downward when the action is opened, all of the other action designs are based on a solid steel bolt that moves forward to lock the action and rearward for ejecting the fired cartridge case and for chambering a fresh round. The British double rifles are of the top-break type, similar in design and function to the actions seen on side-by-side shotguns, while the German and Austrian double rifles are patterned after the over-and-under shotgun designs.

The bolt-action rifle is undoubtedly the most popular type of action, with the lever action holding down the second place, and the autoloading and pump-action rifles rounding out the

WHERE THE ACTION IS

picture. The bolt-action rifle is undoubtedly the most trouble-free rifle design, and this is confirmed by the military rifles of the armies of the world. Until assault rifles became the primary service weapon, the bolt-action rifle was the weapon issued to most troops.

The bolt-action design is also the most accurate design, if such a generalization can be made validly. The minimum of working parts, the solidity of the action, and the fact that the one-piece stock acts as support for action and barrel all contribute to the inherent accuracy of this rifle action. The design also permits repairs, should they be required, without too many tools and without too much trouble. Cleaning of the bolt-action rifle is simple since the bolt can be removed and the action and bore can then be cleaned from the rear rather than from the muzzle.

At one time, takedown rifles were popular, but interest in this design has almost disappeared. Interchangeable barrels in different calibers were offered for a while, such barrels being fastened in the same action and stock. However, shooting tests showed that the design lacked accuracy, and the cost of this Mauser rifle was so high that the shooter could have bought two rifles for the same money.

The Wickliffe '76, a modified version of the old Stevens 44½, is the newest of the single-shot rifles to be produced in large numbers.

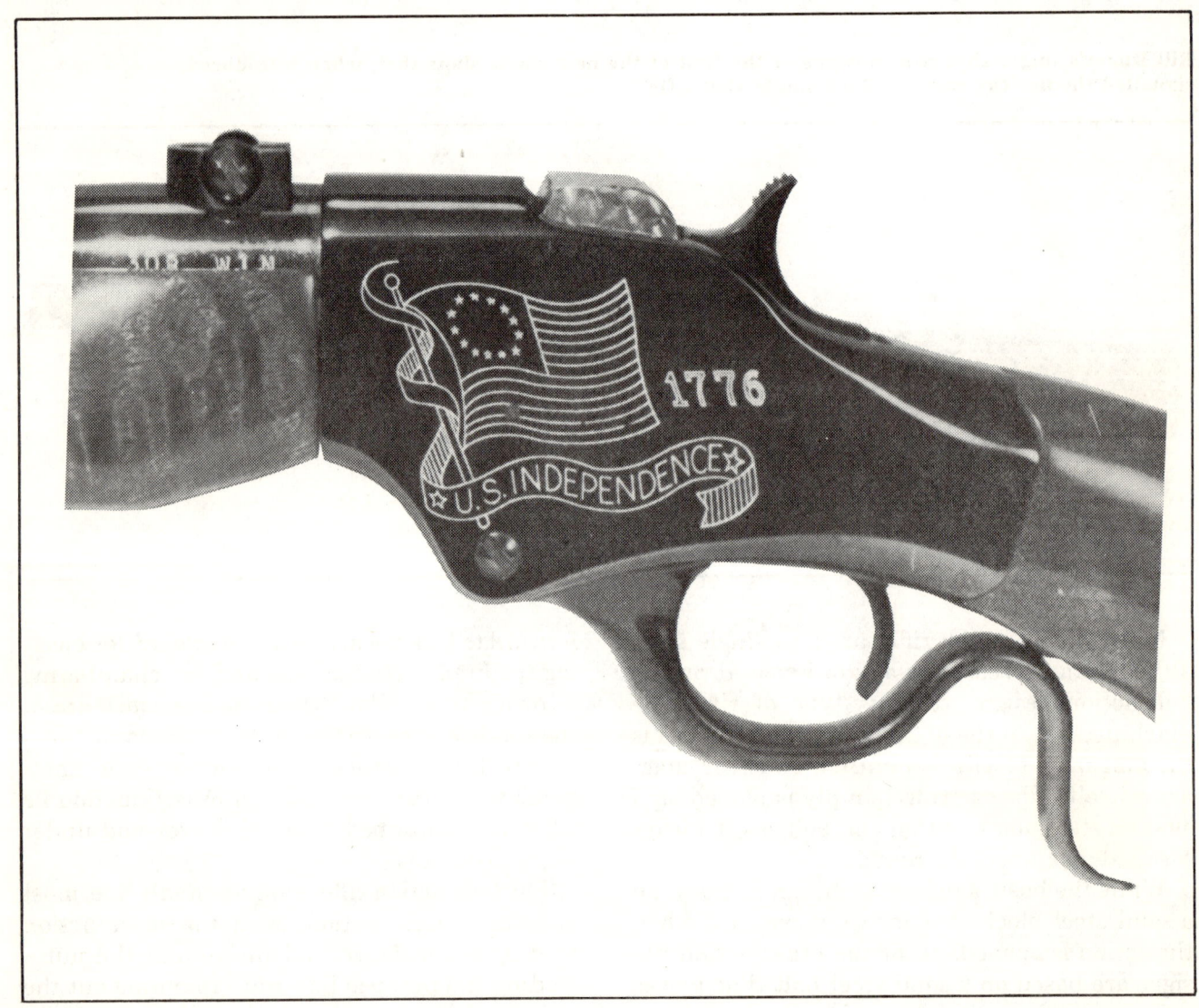

Single-shot bolt-action target rifle. Rimfire single shots are ideal choices for the training of youngsters, while more sophisticated rifles such as the match guns are nearly all single shots based on the bolt-action design.

Traditional bolt-action design of the Ruger Model 77 shows the classic lines of this type of rifle. Most of today's bolt actions are based to some extent on the Mauser design.

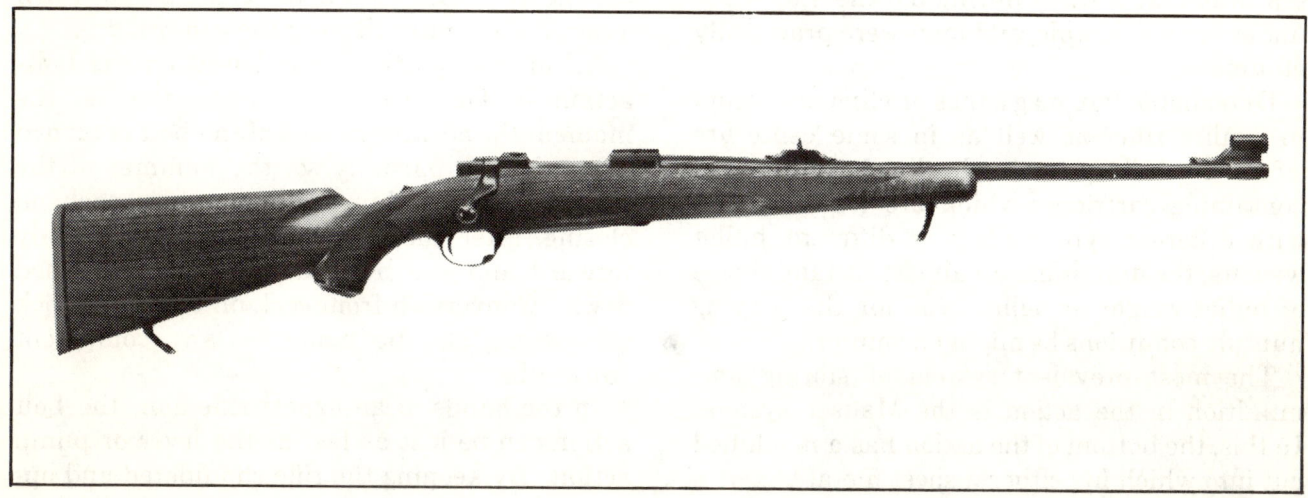

WHERE THE ACTION IS

Remington Model 4 takedown, rolling-block rifle was one of the first of the takedown rifles. Although practical, rifles with interchangeable barrels never become overly popular except for some single-shot rifles.

The design of the cartridge container has changed over the years. One of the first military bolt-action rifles, the Kropatschek rifle, used a tubular magazine that was fastened to the action underneath the barrel. This design is still being used in lever actions, while the detachable box magazine or clip is used in several action designs. Stripper clips—small spring-loaded metal strips which held a number of live cartridges in a row so that all of them could be fed into the magazine with one motion—were in extensive use in military rifles. After the ammunition was seated in the magazine, the stripper clips were discarded. The advantage of this system was that loading during darkness or while under fire was simple, and jams were practically eliminated.

Detachable box magazines or clips are found in rimfire rifles as well as in some centerfire rifles. By having two such clips or magazines containing cartridges which are loaded either with different type bullets or different bullet weights, the hunter has an almost instant choice of bullet weight or bullet type for the varying hunting conditions he might encounter.

The most prevalent system of storing ammunition in the action is the Mauser system. In this, the bottom of the action has a machined cut into which fits either a sheet metal box or a steel box welded to the action. Closed on the bottom and containing a spring and a follower, the box magazine stores the cartridges which are pushed upward by the action of the spring. The cover on the bottom of the magazine may be omitted and instead of the magazine going through the stock, the magazine bottoms into the stock; in this case it is referred to as a blind box magazine. If the magazine goes through the stock, the cover may be hinged and spring-loaded so that removal of the ammunition can be accomplished by simply opening the magazine floor plate. When emptying such a magazine by running each round through the action, care must be taken not to touch the trigger when a round is chambered since the gun will fire.

All of the sporting rifles based on the bolt-action system cock on opening—that is, the moment the cocking handle of the bolt is turned upward, even partially so, the hammer of the gun is cocked. Many military rifles cock on closing, after the bolt has been moved fully forward and the bolt handle is being turned down. Conversion from cock on closing to cock on opening can be made by any competent gunsmith.

In the hands of an expert rifleman, the bolt action can be just as fast as the lever or pump action. By keeping the rifle shouldered and operating the bolt with the palm of the right hand, the expert shooter can extract, eject and feed a new cartridge into the chamber while the left hand remains clasped around the forend, bringing the gun back out of recoil and re-aligning the sight with the target. Most of the companies making bolt-action rifles also offer southpaw versions of their most popular bolt-action rifles.

The lever-action rifle with its tubular magazine is the traditional western rifle or carbine. The Savage Model 99 and the Browning BLR do not use the tubular magazine; the Savage contains a magazine similar to the rotary magazine of the Mannlicher design, while the Browning rifle incorporates a detachable box magazine. Instead of moving the bolt back and forth by means of a bolt handle, the lever-action design incorporates a finger lever that is moved up and toward the shooter to close and lock the action, and is pushed forward to open the action. The Marlin family of lever-action rifles and carbines has side ejection of the fired cases, as does Mossberg's Model 472, while the Winchester

From left: **A military stripper clip, a detachable rotating magazine from a Mannlicher-Schoenauer rifle, a detachable magazine for a centerfire rifle, and a clip magazine from a 22-caliber rimfire rifle.**

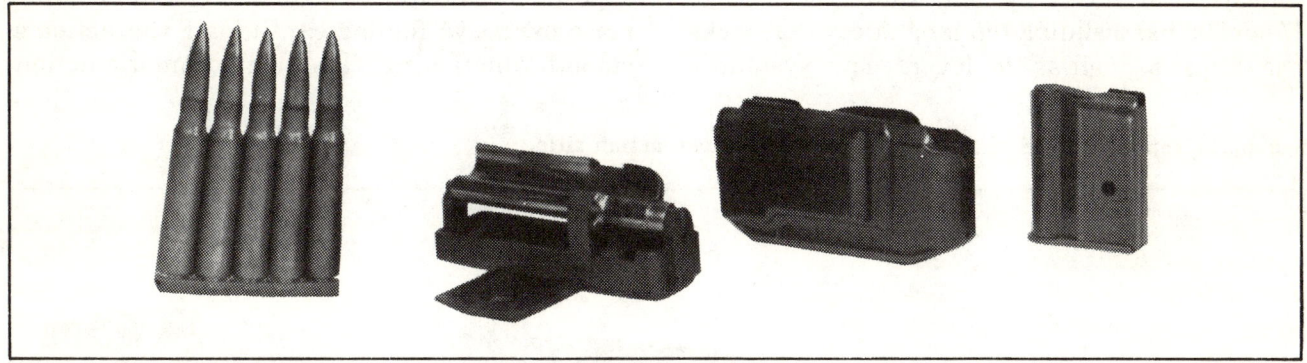

At top, a Remington Model 600 which has a non-functioning magazine floorplate. This is sometimes called a blind magazine. At bottom, the more-often-seen hinged magazine floorplate.

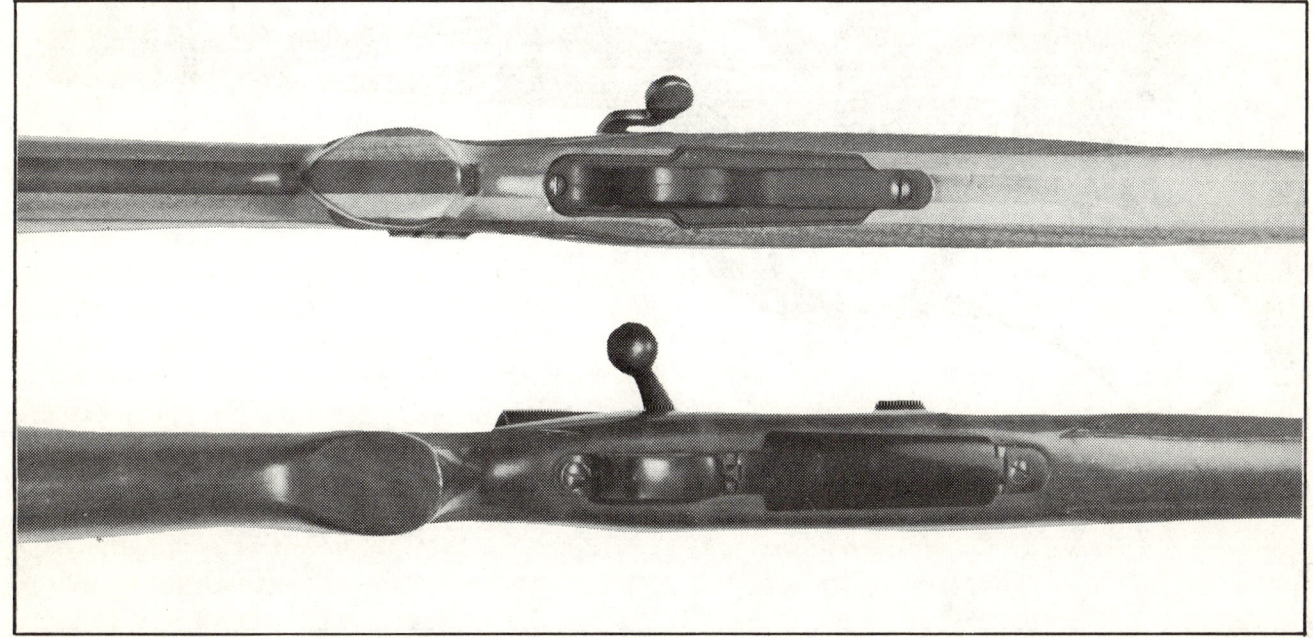

WHERE THE ACTION IS

Model 94 ejects fired cases upward from the top of the action. The Savage and Browning rifles also have side ejection, while the various replicas of the Winchester Model 1873 are also top-ejectors. Scope mounting is only complicated on the Winchester lever actions, and in this case a side mount rather than a top mount is the answer to the problem of scope mounting on a top-ejector.

Most of the lever-action rifles and carbines are chambered for the traditional deer or brush cartridges, with the 30-30 Winchester being the most popular caliber. Although trigger pull in bolt-action rifles is often easily adjusted by the shooter, this is not the case with the lever actions. Some of them rely on the half-cock as the only type of safety system, while the Savage Model 99 has a sliding-top tang safety that locks the trigger as well as the lever. This system is similar to the safety system seen in bolt-action rifles where the safety locks the trigger, and may or may not also lock the bolt. The typical western rifle or carbine comes with a straight stock (Browning, Marlin, Savage, and Winchester), but Marlin and Savage also offer their lever-action guns with pistol-grip stocks. When rifles with their various actions are compared, the traditional lever action is the flattest one. This explains why it was and still is *the* saddle scabbard gun in the West.

The semiautomatic action has been refined to such a degree that you can now get such a rifle in a wide variety of calibers, from the 223 Remington (5.56mm) to the 30-30, the 44 Magnum, and the 308 Winchester or 7.62 NATO. This type of action requires regular care and cleaning since excessive fouling can impair the action's smooth functioning. The semiautomatic action

Schematic representation of the Savage Model 99 lever-action rifle.

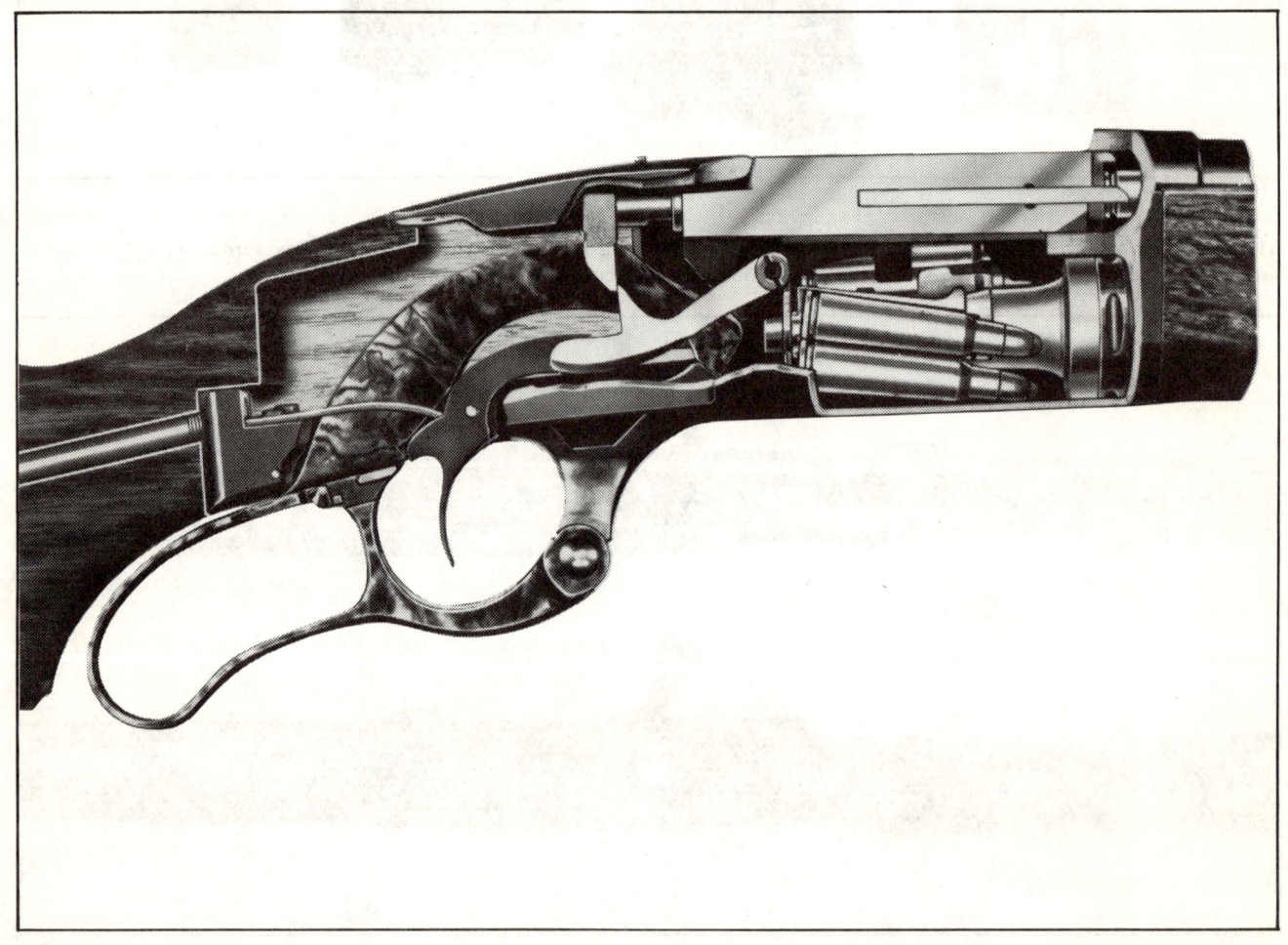

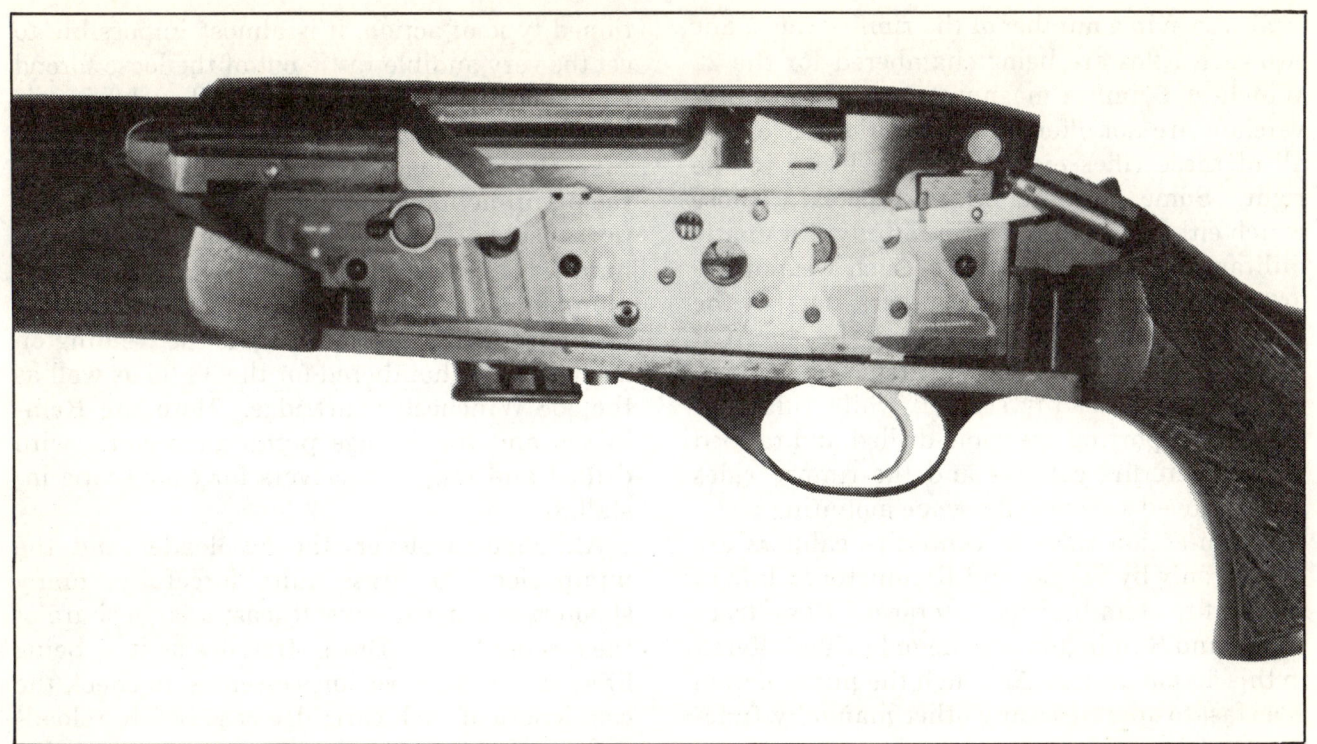

Cutaway model of the Weatherby 22LR semiautomatic rifle.

At top, a Mannlicher bolt-action rifle with double triggers. Note butterknife bolt handle and pistol grip. Compare this with rifle below it, a Browning lever-action 22 with straight grip or Western-style stock.

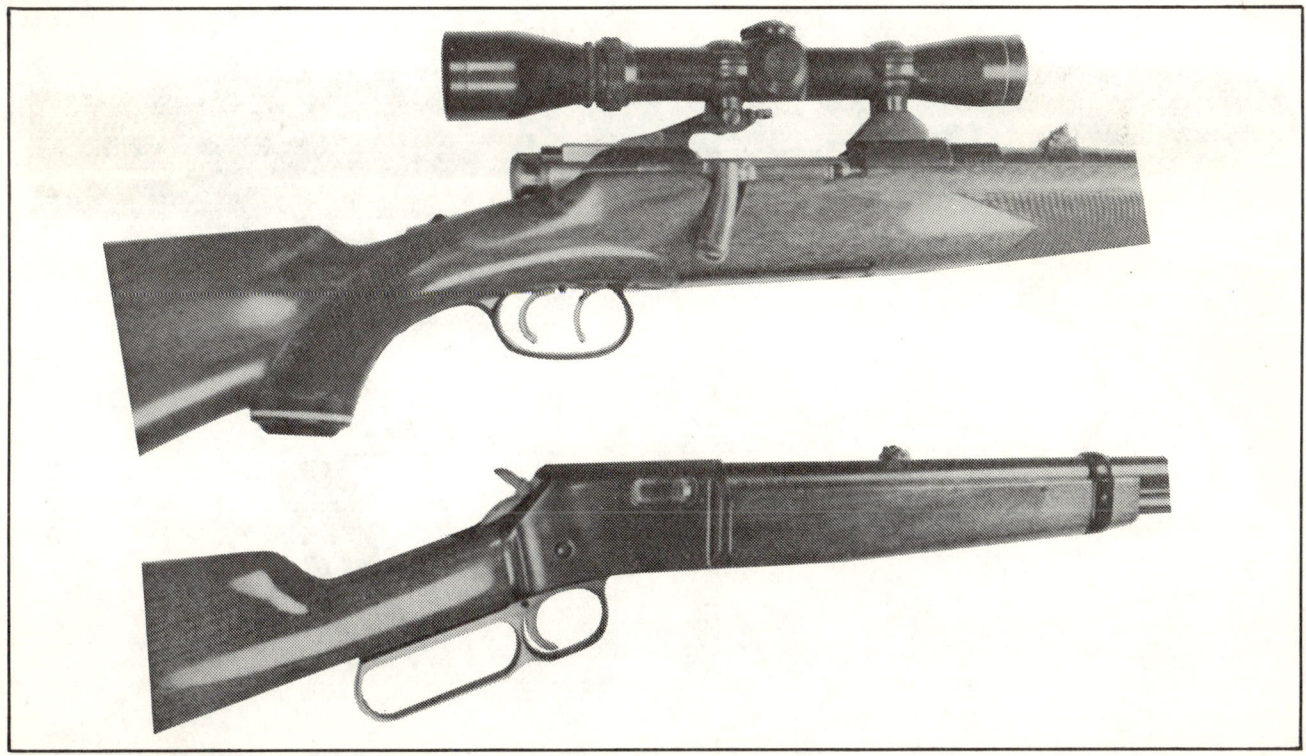

WHERE THE ACTION IS

39

is also seen in a number of the rimfire rifles, and two such rifles are being chambered for the 22 Winchester rimfire magnum round. Southpaw versions are not offered in this action style, and all of these rifles eject the spent brass to the right. Some of these rifles — especially those which either had their origin in fully automatic military rifles or are copies of such weapons — are also offered in handgun calibers, notably the 9mm Parabellum or Luger, and the 45 ACP round. Rifles of military persuasion on the whole are not readily scoped, while rifles designed for sporting use come drilled and tapped in the centerfire calibers and the rimfire rifles have grooved receivers for scope mounting.

Pump-action rifles in centerfire calibers are offered only by Savage and Remington, while in the rimfire chamberings. Interarms' Rossi from Brazil and Remington are the only rifles offered in this action design. Although the pump action is as fast to operate as any other manually functioned type of action, it is almost impossible to get the very audible rattle out of the loose forend which acts as pump handle — and such a rattle is a dead giveaway when you are stalking game. Like the autoloaders or semiautomatic rifles, the pump-action guns also eject the spent brass to the right. Despite this obvious drawback, a number of left-handed shooters have made the pump models their field guns, from chuck hunting to deer and other game, since the Remington Model 760 is chambered for the 30-06 as well as the 308 Winchester cartridge. Both the Remington and the Savage pump guns come with drilled and tapped receivers for easy scope installation.

Although the lever, the autoloader and the pump eject the brass quite forcefully, many shooters manage to save at least a large share of the ejected brass. Brass stretches as it is being fired; it therefore becomes essential to check the case length of each cartridge case before reload-

Action of the Harrington & Richardson semiautomatic 22 rimfire magnum with detachable clip or magazine. Bolt is locked in rearward position here, and the safety button at right rear of action is on the safe position.

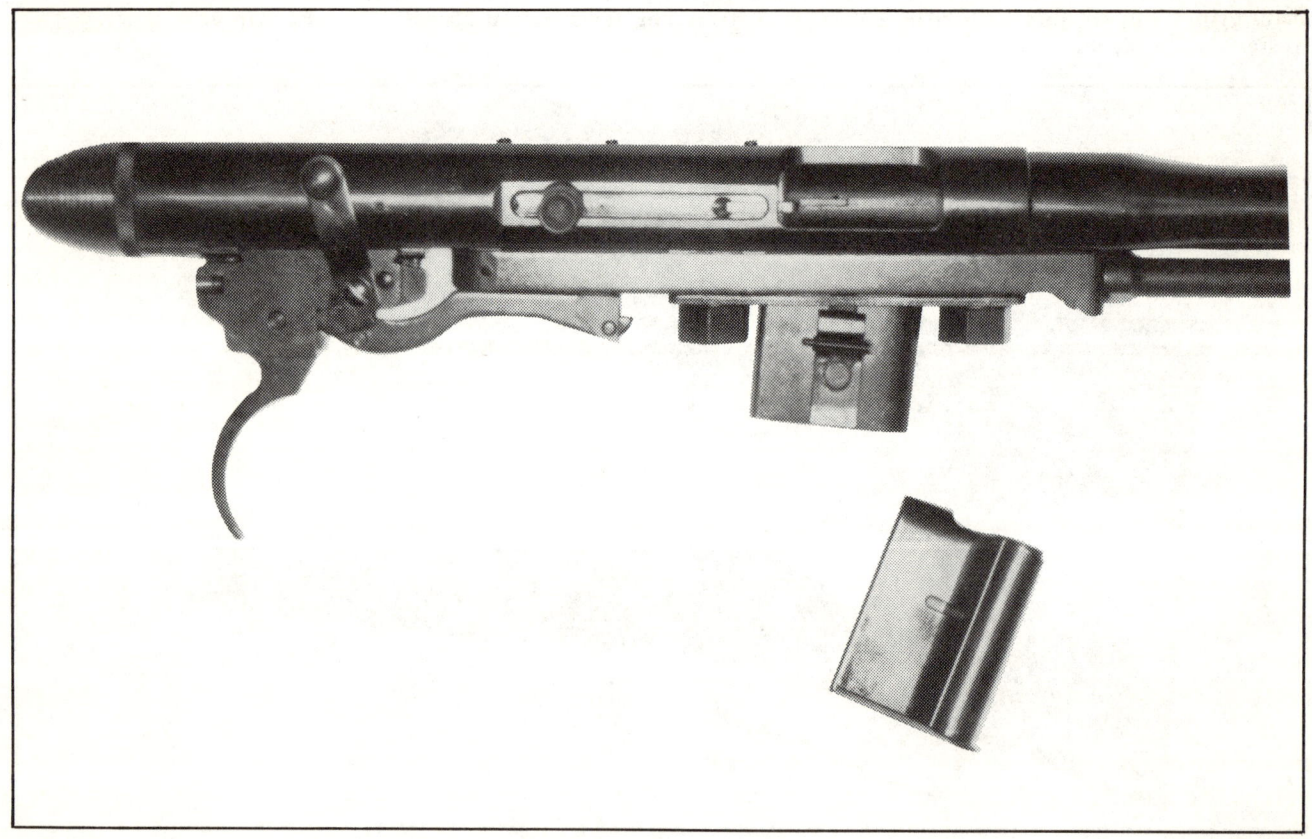

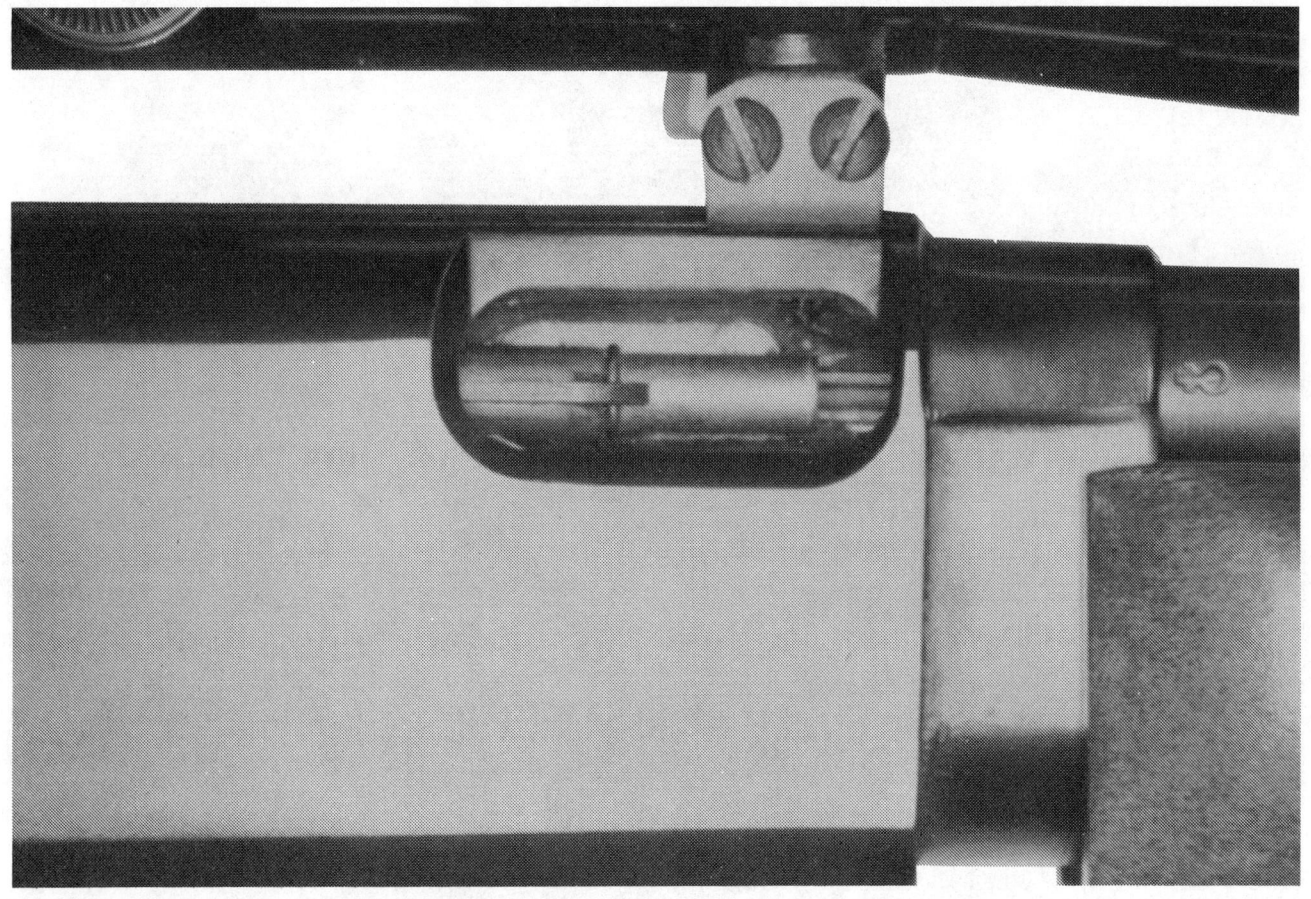

High-speed photograph of 22LR Remington pump gun—the rifle has been fired and the forend is being pushed back. The case has been extracted from the chamber, is just about to be flipped out of the ejection port.

ing it. Cases that have stretched beyond the factory specs must be trimmed, especially when the cases are being reloaded for any of these three action types. It must be stressed, too, that loading tables usually indicate the type of gun used to test the loads. Pump actions, autoloaders and lever actions must be loaded with somewhat lighter loads than the bolt-action rifles. When seating bullets, be certain that the overall length of the finished handloaded cartridge does not exceed the specs given for the factory round.

Rifles with tubular magazines must never be loaded with cartridges which are topped off with spitzer bullets. Use only flat-nosed bullets for such loads. When the loads in the tubular magazine are moved back and forth with the recoil of the gun, the pointed bullet can detonate the primer in the cartridge ahead of it.

Combination guns originated in Germany and Austria, where bird and big-game seasons overlap and the hunter must be ready to take a shot at antlered game and birds without being encumbered by two different guns. In contrast to other countries where carrying a firearm afield during the closed season is prohibited, the German hunter always carries a rifle afield for use on vermin or sick game. From this demand for versatility came the combination gun.

In our domestic hunting conditions, a number of instances where a combination gun comes in handy can be cited. For example, consider the turkey hunter. Although he is permitted to use either shot or bullets in most areas, it always seems to happen that, he will have a rifle along when he needs a shotgun or will have the shotgun handy when he is in dire need of a bullet. On a hunt in Texas, using a Krieghoff Drilling I

With scope in place, this highly versatile drilling downed a Sitka buck on the Y-O ranch.

An hour later, and with the scope removed, the shotgun barrels of the drilling took this gobbler.

shot blue quail, turkey, javelina and a whitetail deer, plus a rattler.

The combination of two shotgun barrels with one rifle barrel is known as the Drilling, while the Vierling has two smoothbore barrels plus two rifle barrels, the upper one usually chambered for a rimfire cartridge, the lower one usually chambered for a centerfire cartridge. Drillings and Vierlings are quite expensive, but are also a pure joy to use, especially when the gun is equipped with quick-detachable claw mounts for the scope giving the rifle barrel or barrels much greater versatility. Should you ever fall heir to a Drilling or Vierling, be sure to use suitable ammunition, this being marked on the barrel flats, along with the proof marks.

The most widely known combination gun is the Savage Model 24 in its many chamberings and styles. Here, a smoothbored and a rifled barrel have been combined, with the most prevalent chambering being a .410-gauge barrel in combination with one chambered for one of the rimfire cartridges. This, with the 30-30/20-gauge chambering, makes a fine combination gun for the squirrel and turkey hunter and for the upland game and deer hunter respectively. Other combination guns, usually of the over-and-under type, have made their appearance on the scene, but the relatively high costs of the imports make them prohibitively expensive by the time they reach the consumer.

The Garcia Bronco was somewhat similar to the Savage M24, except that it had a skeletonized metal buttstock, and therefore weighed only 3½ pounds. Harrington & Richardson have long been offering their Model 158 which, in a sense, is also a combination gun. A top-break action gun, the Combination Topper is offered with two barrels, one a 20 gauge smoothbore, the other chambered for either the 30-30 Winchester or the 22 Hornet round. Takedown is simple and quick, and although it is not usually feasible to take along that extra accessory barrel, the gun has great versatility.

In selecting a rifle, the choice of action may be dictated by the caliber. Because of their case design, some cartridges can only be used in bolt-action rifles and in single-shot rifles. The bolt- and the lever-action guns do not require as much care as do the autoloaders and the pump actions, while the single-shot rifles are singularly free of functioning trouble since the major malfunctions usually occur in the magazine and cartridge feed system. The bolt-action rifle is inherently the most accurate of the multi-shot actions, and it is also the strongest as far as chamber pressure is concerned.

The hunter seeking his buck in brush will need a smoothly functioning rifle that is compactly made — one which has a relatively short barrel. In contrast to this hunter, the sheep or goat hunter or the one who hunts plains game such as antelope, will exclusively want a rifle that will deliver maximum accuracy and velocity. This, of course, means a longer barrel, perhaps 24 inches, or even 26 inches. In brushy country, the autoloader, the pump and the lever action have the mechanical advantage, while plains game is best hunted with a bolt-action rifle. Thus, the ultimate use of the rifle will, in some ways, dictate the action choice once you have made your caliber selection.

Remington and Winchester, the major producers of sporting guns and ammunition, are also the primary sources for new calibers. Some of these calibers simply never become popular, and after a few years rifles were no longer

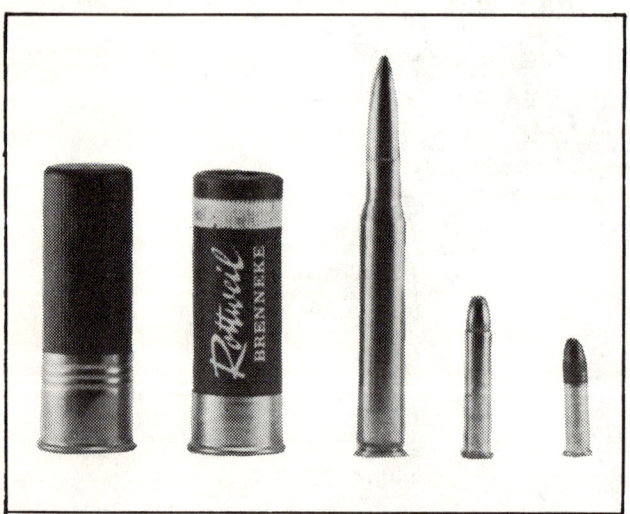

Two shotgun barrels give a hunter the instant choice of shot or slug, plus of course the rifled tube. With chamber inserts, such as furnished on special order with Krieghoff drilling, the hunter has the additional choice of using either the 22 Winchester Magnum round or the standard 22LR cartridge.

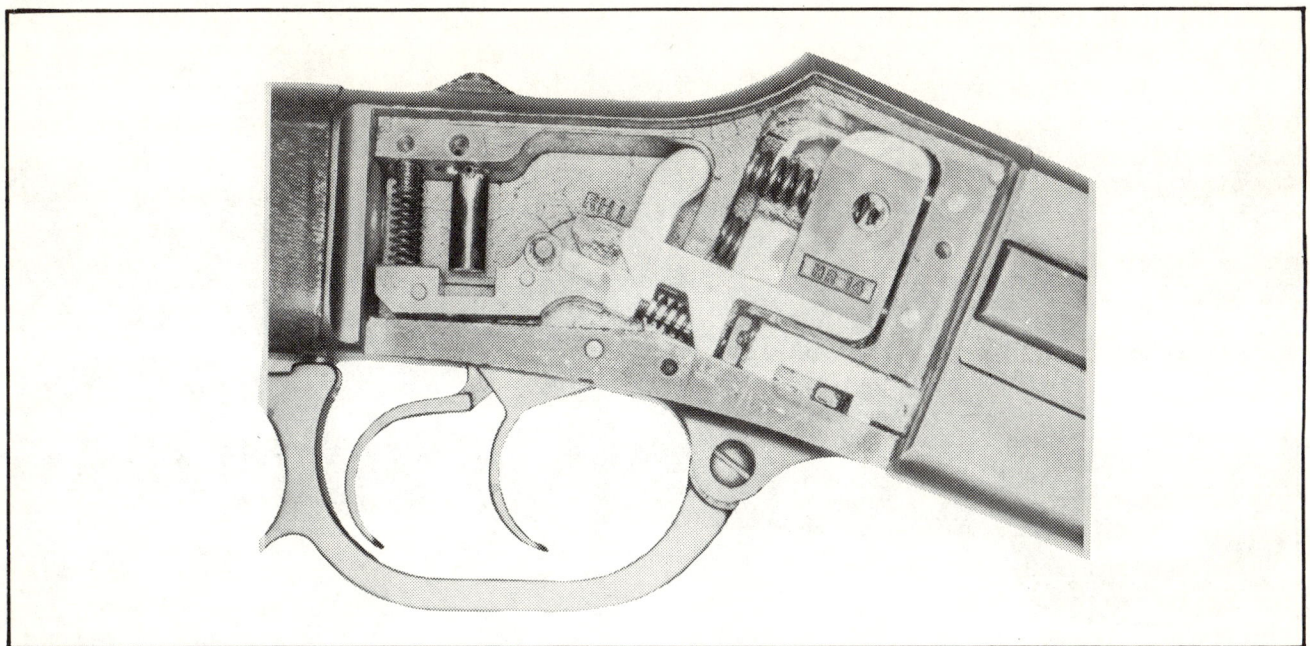

Action details of a rifle-shotgun combination gun based on the lever-action design. Lack of demand and relatively high cost, plus some mechanical problems, ended the short but unhappy life of the Staggs-built combination gun.

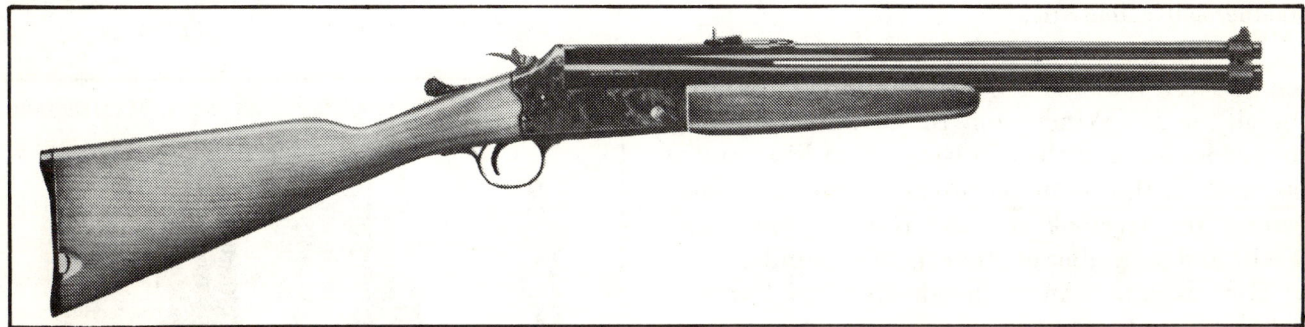

The Savage Model 24, here shown in the Camper model, is one of the most widely seen and used combination guns. Rugged and priced within the reach of most, the gun is offered in a wide variety of chamberings.

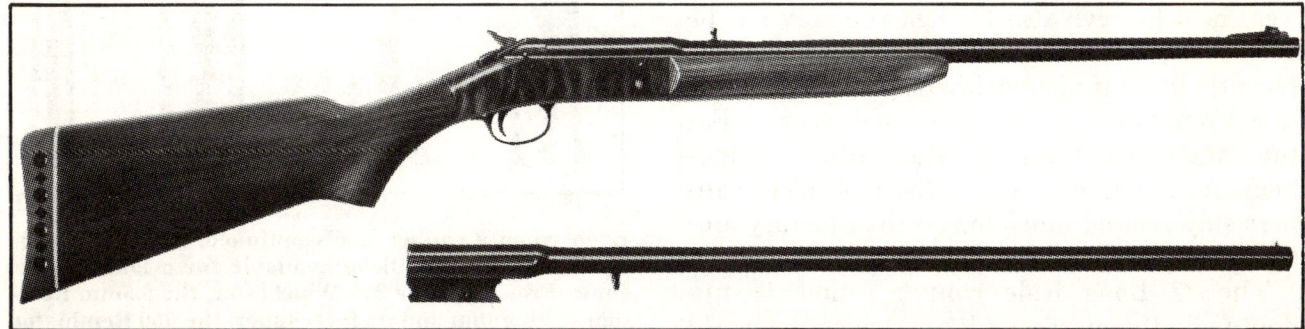

Harrington & Richardson's Model 158, the Topper, can be considered to be a single-shot rifle with interchangeable shotgun barrel, or a shotgun with interchangeable rifle barrel.

This 7.7mm Japanese Arisaka rifle was blown up on purpose. A similar load literally disintegrated another bolt-action rifle.

chambered for such a "new" caliber. This fate befell the 225 Winchester, the 6.5mm Remington Magnum and the 350 Remington Magnum, as well as the 5mm Remington rimfire. The same fate overtook the 257 Roberts, the 220 Swift and a number of other factory rounds.

How does this affect the shooter and hunter who is not a handloader, or how might it affect the handloader two, four or six years from now? Since the ammunition factories continue to produce ammunition in the discontinued calibers, the Roberts and the Swift rounds underwent healthy revivals. Though you may not be able to buy rifles chambered for some of the recently discontinued calibers, you will be able to get ammunition for quite a few years. For the handloader, brass cases and other components for reloading some of these obsolete calibers stay around much longer than factory ammunition.

The 22 Long Rifle rimfire round is undoubtedly the most popular cartridge the world over. It is used on target ranges everywhere. Unquestionably it sees more use than any other

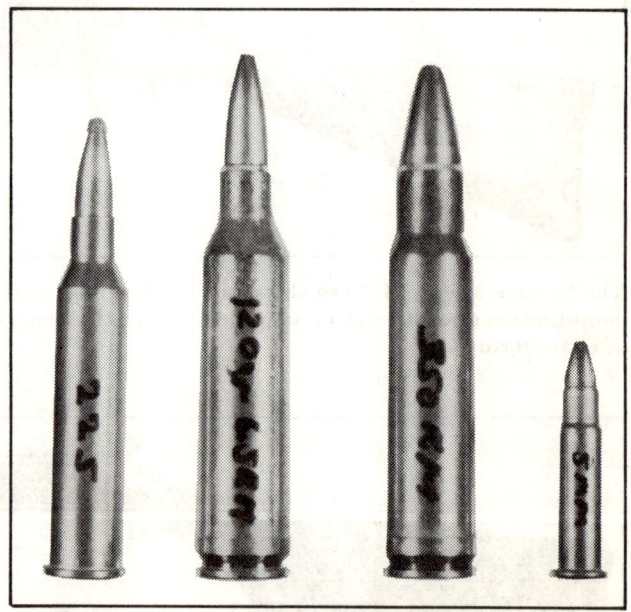

Even when a caliber is discontinued, ammo for some of these calibers will be available for a long time to come. From left: the 225 Winchester, the 6.5mm Remington Magnum and its forerunner, the 350 Remington Magnum and the 5mm Remington rimfire round—all introduced within the last 15 years and all dropped shortly after introduction.

cartridge as a plinking round and for training shooters. Even the military has used and still uses the 22 rimfire as a training round — and its a small-game cartridge within a limited range. More rifles and handguns are chambered for the rimfire round than for any other cartridge, and cost per shot fired is still low enough to allow widespread and continued use.

The 22 Short is primarily used in ISU target events, and the Long Rifle round is used not only in International matches, but also in the Olympics, in Camp Perry during the National matches, and on ranges from Maine to Washington. Match ammunition is superbly accurate and should be used only in matches. For plinking, the lead bullet round or the copper-coated bullet round will suffice, while the hollow-point load remains a good game load. However, the hollow-point load might spoil more meat than the regular round when the shot is not properly placed.

The 22 caliber Winchester Magnum round is meant for small-game hunting and pest control, and has a maximum effective range in most instances out to about 100 yards, give or take 25 yards. It is a little too expensive for plinking and it also develops a bit more blast, so that it is not the ideal training round. The now-defunct 5mm Remington Magnum, a true 20 caliber, had a shade better ballistics than the Winchester round but could only be found in a Remington bolt-action rifle.

In the centerfire calibers there is quite a lot of overlapping so far as use is concerned. The 17 in its various shapes and forms would obviously have to be a varmint round, but it seems that more game has been taken with that little bullet than with the 220 Swift and its cousins. The 22 caliber centerfires are basically varmint rounds and were widely used until some game departments clamped down on the use of the 22 caliber centerfire loads as deer and antelope

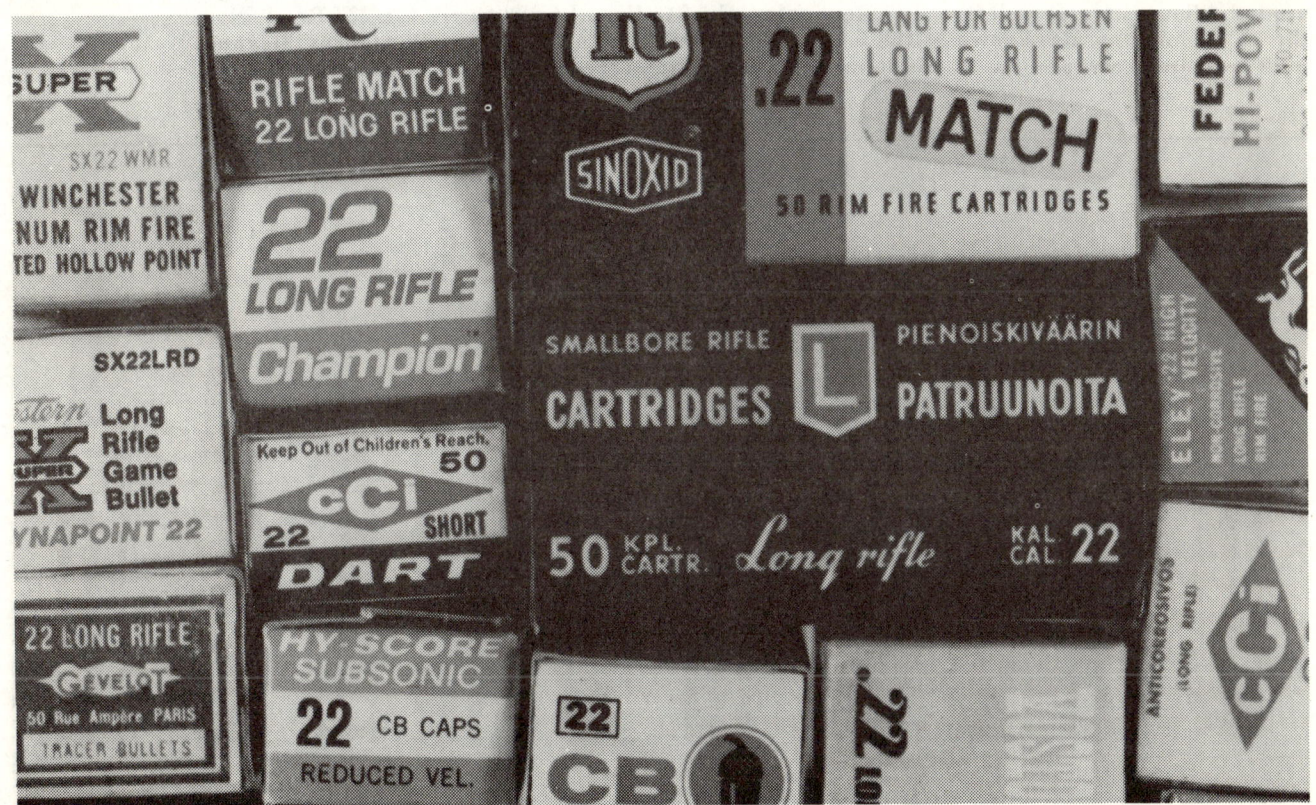

There can be little doubt about the worldwide popularity of the 22 rimfire cartridge. Shown here are only a few of the better known makes of this ammo, including French, British, Russian, German, Mexican, Australian, and U.S.

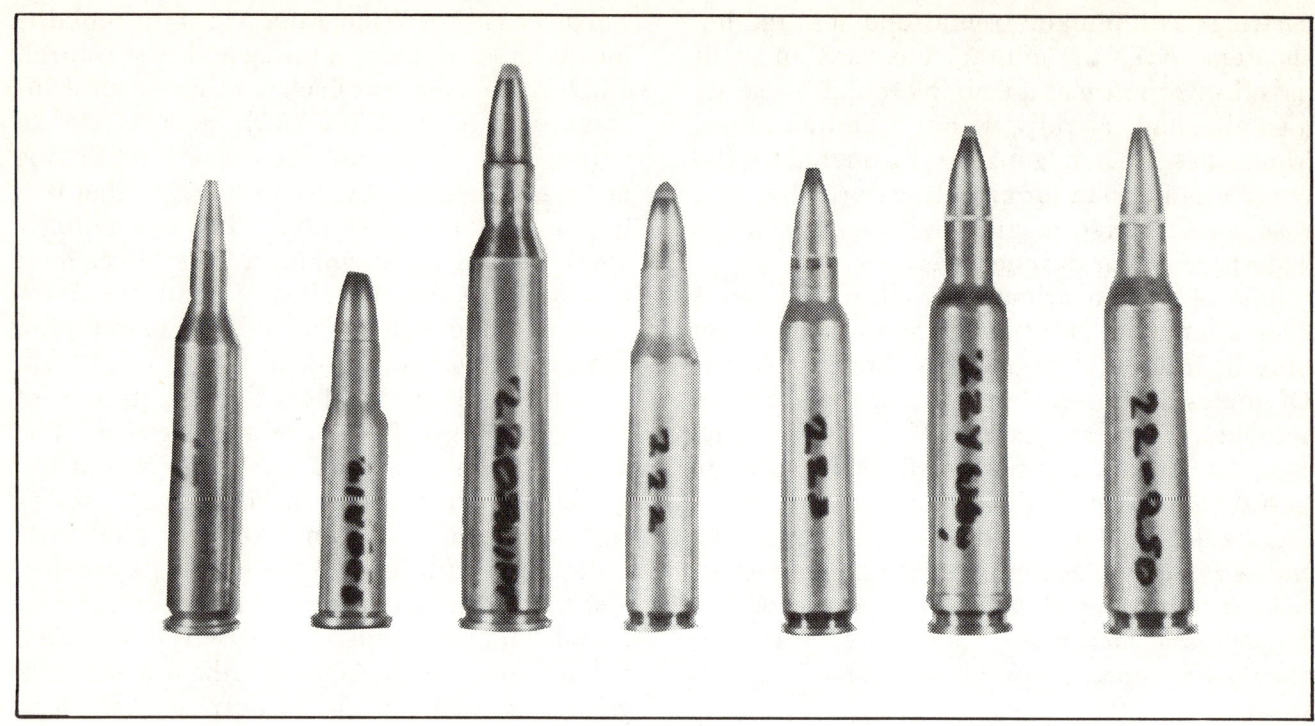

Not counting some of the more exotic wildcats, there are at least ten popular varmint cartridges around. Shown here, from left: the 17 Remington, the 218 Bee, the 220 Swift, the 222 Remington, the 223 Remington also known as the 5.56mm in its military form, the 224 Weatherby Magnum with its belted case, and the 22-250 Remington, which for years was a wildcat number.

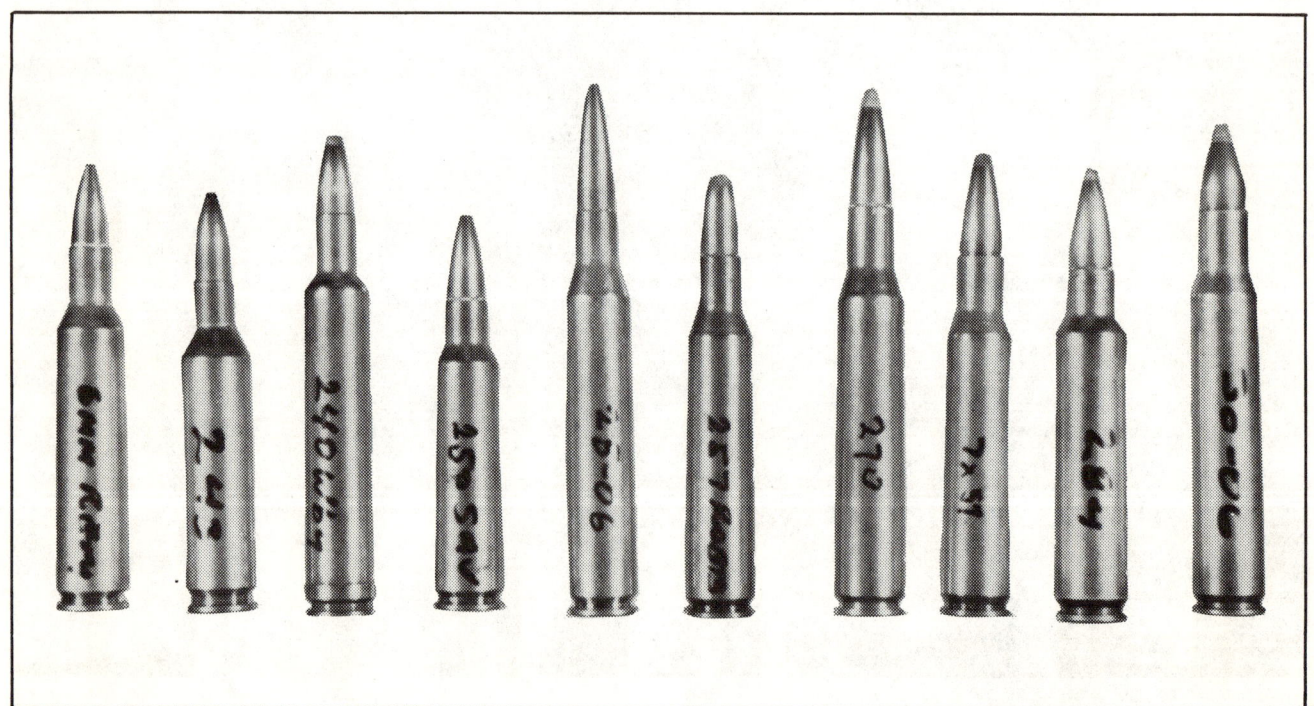

Some of the better-known medium-game cartridges. The 6mm Remington and the 243 Winchester at far left, the 240 Weatherby Magnum, the 250 Savage, also known as the 250-3000, the 25-06, the 257 Roberts, the 270, the 7x57 or 7mm Mauser round, the 284 and an old favorite—the 30-06.

rounds. Of course, this required good shot placement; because many hunters were not able to place their shots accurately, and too much game was wounded, the 22 centerfire rounds are now outlawed as medium-game cartridges. Contrast this with Australia, for instance, where the 22 rimfire and centerfire rounds are used widely for game control and pest shooting. The 17-caliber round capabilities on game were tested at game preserves, as well as in some states where the caliber restrictions were not in effect at the time of the testing.

The various 6mms fill a dual role — a great varmint caliber and a medium-game cartridge at the longer ranges. The 25s, though capable of good accuracy for varmint hunting, have a greater following in the fraternities of deer and antelope hunters, as well as sheep and goat hunters. The 270 Winchester round is another excellent medium-game load that has also seen considerable use on the larger species, including elk, caribou and black bear. The 6.5mm or 264, in some loadings, is just a little below the performance level of the 270, while the 264 Winchester Magnum is a shade below the big 7mm Magnums in performance.

The various 280s and the larger editions, the 7mm Remington Magnum and the Weatherby round, are belted rounds, as is the 8mm Remington Magnum, a true 323-caliber cartridge. The 30-caliber cartridges fill the gap between the 7mms and the 8mms, and here the range extends from the 30-30, the 30-40 Krag and the 300 Savage to the 30-caliber magnum rounds such as the 308 Norma, the 300 Winchester and the 300 Weatherby Magnums, and the now almost-forgotten 300 H&H Magnum. In the middle of this class is, naturally, that old favorite, the 30-06 and its counterpart, the 308 Winchester, also known as the 7.62 NATO round.

The 303 British, the 7.7 Japanese, the 8mm Mauser (also known as the 8x57), and the 8mm Remington Magnum are next in size. The 8mms are good big-game calibers, with the 8mm Remington Magnum being the counterpart of Winchester's 338 Magnum and Weatherby's 340 Magnum. The 303 British, the Japanese service round and the 7.65 Argentine Mauser are akin to the 30-06 in performance, especially with the heavier bullet loads in the '06.

In the biggest of big calibers, the 375 H&H Magnum is the undisputed choice for big and often dangerous bears. The 44s — the 44 Magnum and the 444 Marlin — make good deer rounds in thick brush, and the revival of the 45-70 has given the deer hunter yet another brush cartridge. The 458 Winchester Magnum and the 460 Weatherby Magnum are the largest

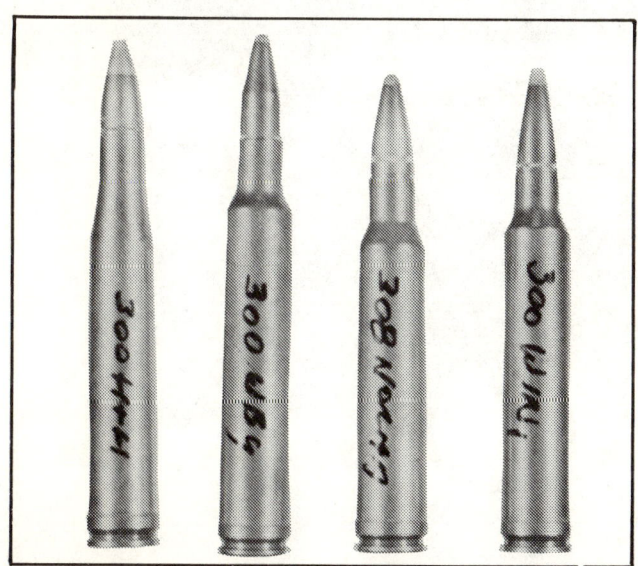

In the 30-caliber magnum class, the old 300 H&H Magnum, the 300 Weatherby Magnum, the 308 Norma Magnum, and the 300 Winchester Magnum rounds.

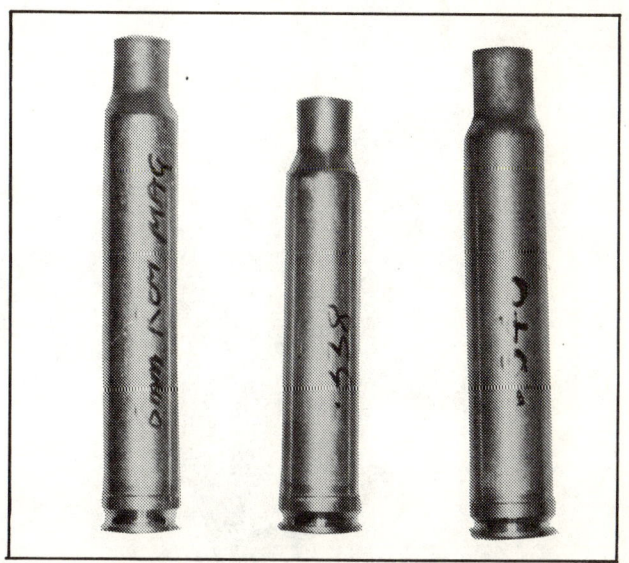

Shown here are the leading three 32-33 caliber cases — the 8mm Remington Magnum, the 338 Winchester Magnum and the 340 Weatherby Magnum.

Selected walnut stock shows fine line checkering. Although finer checkering is available on a custom basis and has a lot of eye appeal, its practical value when too fine can be questioned.

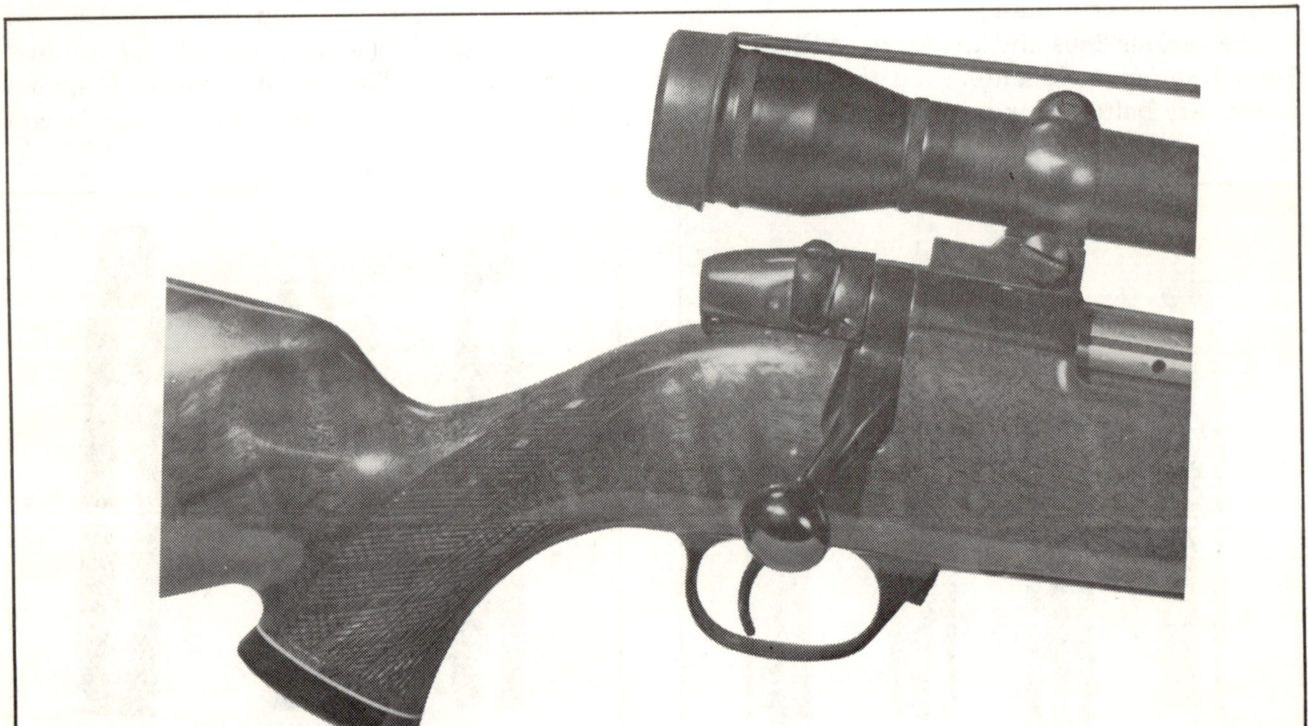

Skipline checkering, originally first produced by German stockmakers, has eye appeal and practicality, plus being fairly easy to produce.

of the domestic rounds and are excellent bets for elephant — a critter you are not very likely to encounter either in Maine or Wyoming.

Most of the rifle stocks made today are of walnut, with Claro walnut being the primary source for factory stocks. A rifle is too often judged by its stock rather than by its performance. A nicely shaped stock made from some exotic wood, hand-checkered to perfection, will not allow the rifle to shoot one bit better than if the rifle were stocked with a piece of ordinary hardwood — as long as the inletting and bedding is done with the same care in each case. Some years ago, hand-cut checkering became so costly that factories began to use impressed checkering, which was neither good looking nor very serviceable. Checkering tends to prevent slippage of the hand off the smoothly finished wood. It also has eye appeal if done well, but poor checkering is worse than none at all.

Some gun tinkerers develop into highly skilled wood workers, and many of them do their own checkering. The indication of the degree of fineness of checkering is usually given in lines per inch, with 22-to 24-lines per inch usually being the finest, while 14 lines-per-inch checkering is quite coarse. Checkering is usually seen on the pistol grip of a rifle stock, but checkering on and around the forend is not unusual. Skipline checkering is said to have had its beginnings in France; others claim it is of German origin. It is seen mostly on imported rifles and a few custom stocks.

Benchrest stocks and some target stocks are quite flat on the bottom to make resting them on supports easier. In designing the stock for my custom 458 Winchester rifle, I was aware that recoil with this cartridge is considerable. Beginning with a flat base on the forend, I added a feature usually seen on the stocks of trap or skeet guns: finger grooves. Being endowed with fairly large hands, I need the flat forend and the finger grooves or rails to help me in keeping the rifle steady while firing offhand, but also to speed sight recovery after coming out of recoil.

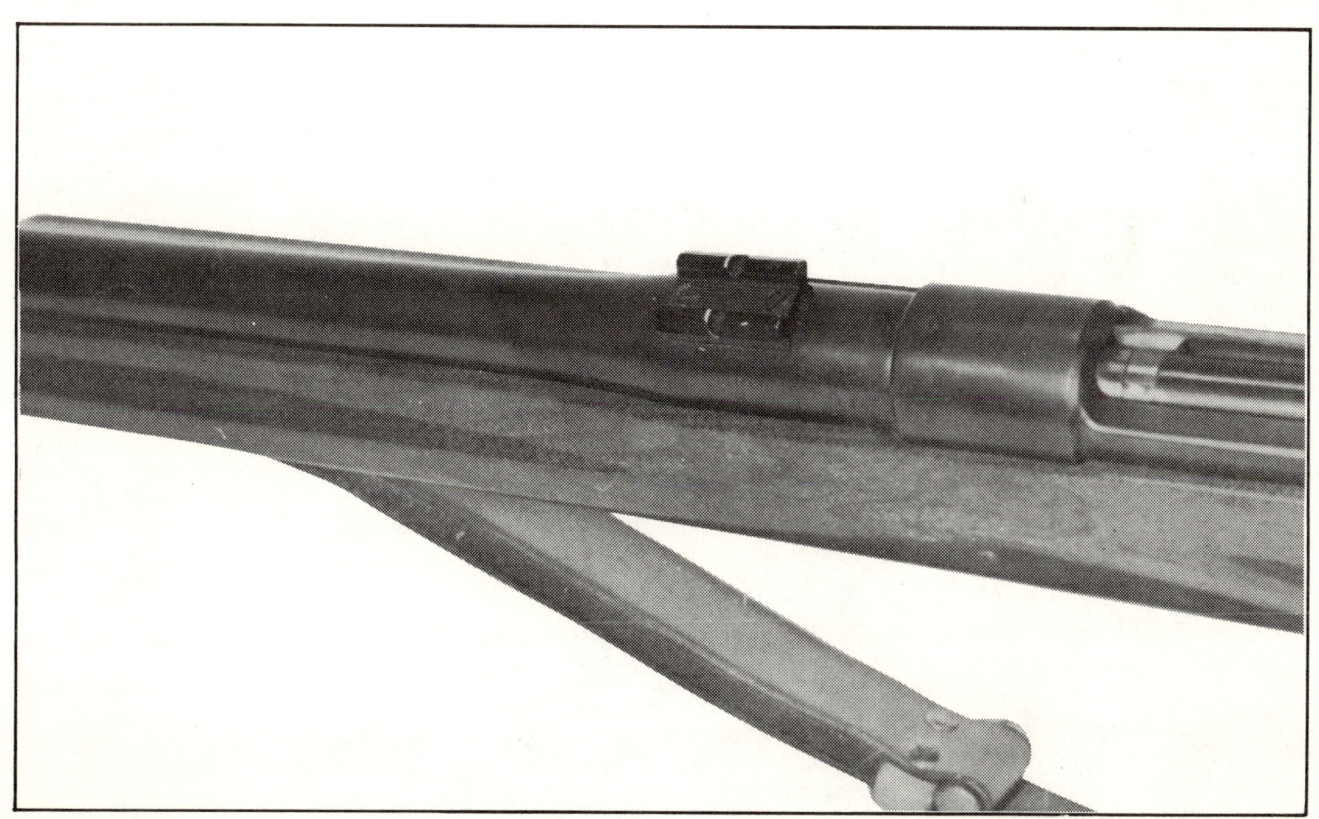

Fingerrail designed for stock of author's custom 458 Magnum permits faster sight-picture recovery, also gives stock a custom look.

Chapter Three
A Look at Today's Rifles

Chapter Three
A Look at Today's Rifles

Guns in general and rifles in particular are traditionally made from wood and steel. Every so often, a rifle comes along that does not quite fit the pattern. A few of these non-conforming rifles find acceptance by shooters, but most of them fall by the wayside. Two examples which have found acceptance are the Charter Arms AR-7, the gun that could be referred to as "the gun that stores itself in the butt, and also floats," and the autoloading rimfire rifle made by Remington, known as the Model 66 or the Nylon 66.

Plinking, or informal target practice, is best done with a rifle that chambers the 22 Long Rifle cartridge, but you can plink with any rifle, centerfire or rimfire, small bore or large bore. And if you are a glutton for punishment, you can even use a 458 Winchester Magnum or a 375 H&H Magnum for punching holes in targets. A light rifle such as the Remington 66 is a fine all-around choice for hunting and plinking; though quite accurate as a rule, it does not qualify as a target rifle.

No matter from what position target rifles are fired — that is, offhand, prone or from the bench — they are heavier than the sporting rifles. The weight lies in the barrel which usually is heavier and non-tapered, and is commonly referred to as target or bull barrel. Such a barrel gives greater accuracy, and the stock is especially designed for this type of shooting. The greater weight of the gun means greater stability. This, in turn, translates into a steadier sight picture, and a steady sight picture means that it becomes easier to place that bullet right in the bullseye.

The rimfire rifles are undoubtedly the best choice for the beginning shooter, since neither recoil, muzzle blast nor even the cost of ammunition will hurt anyone. Finely tuned match rifles are the most accurate rifles produced anywhere; for small-game hunting and varmint shooting at limited ranges, the 22 Long Rifle cartridge or the 22 Winchester Magnum round will be more than adequate.

In the centerfire lineup, the 17-caliber rifles

created a relatively long-lived excitement, but are now fading from popularity. Some 30 or more years ago when there were fewer calibers on the market, the specialized rifle — the gun designed specifically for woodchuck shooting or antelope hunting or elephant hunting — was not yet in vogue. The hunter used his one and only rifle for popping chucks, for collecting his venison and for ending the career of a chicken-stealing fox.

For many years, the 30-06 was considered as the most versatile caliber, and more than one article has been devoted to extolling the virtues of this all-around caliber. Commercial loadings with bullets weighing only 110 grains to bullets weighing twice that much are widely available, even in some of the most remote areas. With the light bullet, the varmint hunter can be happy — providing he sights in his rifle with the light bullet loads or remembers his ballistics well enough to hold over or under as the need arises and as he switches from light to heavy load or vice versa.

That the '06 is alive and kicking is demonstrated by Remington and the Accelerator round. Introduced in 1977, this cartridge consists of a standard 30-06 cartridge case, a 55-grain 22-caliber (.224") pointed soft-point bullet which rides in a plastic sabot, the sabot being seated in the case mouth and neck of the '06 case. The bullet has a muzzle velocity of 4080 feet-per-second, has a flat trajectory which is ideally suited for varmint hunting, and recoil is mild; about what could be expected from a 22-caliber centerfire rifle. (The plastic sabot falls away from the moving bullet after the projectile leaves the muzzle.) Although accuracy in most rifles is not in the same class as could be expected from a regular varmint rifle, this cartridge should do the job it was intended for if the range is not stretched too much beyond the 100-yard mark. The Accelerator functions normally in single-shot, bolt-action and pump-action rifles, but will not operate the mechanism of a semiautomatic rifle, where it must be manually fed and ejected.

In recent years, some of the arms makers and importers have become more aware of what shooters and hunters want in a rifle. Now, recoil pads, sling swivels and even special scope bases are furnished with some rifles. Of course, on major items such as scope bases and rings, you pay for the item, but at a slightly reduced price.

Somewhat more intangible is the claim that such-and-such a rifle has the fastest lock time of its breed. Lock time is defined as the time interval required from completing the trigger pull until the firing pin or striker hits the primer, thereby igniting the priming compound within it. A short or fast lock time is highly desirable in target rifles, but is of relatively little value in a hunting rifle. A reduction of the lock time can be brought about by shortening firing-pin travel or hammer fall, by increasing the weight of the firing pin or hammer, or by installing a somewhat stronger mainspring.

Inasmuch as most shooters know which type of action they prefer when shopping for a new rifle, the following listing is by types of action, with the rimfire rifles being listed first.

RIMFIRE RIFLES

SEMIAUTOMATIC & PUMP ACTION

BROWNING

BAR-22 AUTO RIFLE
15-shot tubular magazine, 22 LR only, 20¼-inch barrel, 38¼ inches, about 6¼ lb. Pistol grip and forend decorated with cut checkering, French walnut stock. Gold bead front and folding leaf rear sight, cross-bolt safety, receiver grooved for scope mounting.

AUTOLOADING RIFLE
11-shot tubular magazine in butt stock, 22 LR only, 19¼-inch barrel, 37 inches overall, about 4¾ lb. Checkered walnut stock with semi-beavertail forend. Gold bead front, folding leaf rear sight. Engraved receiver is grooved for scope mounting. Offered in Grades I, II and III, with Grade I also available in 22 Short chambering.

BPR-22 PUMP RIFLE

Tubular magazine, rifle offered in 22 LR (15 shots) and 22 Magnum (11 shots), 20¼-inch barrel, 38¼ inches overall, about 6¼ lb. Pistol grip and forend carry cut checkering, French walnut stock. Short stroke pump action, gold bead front and folding leaf rear sight, cross-bolt safety, receiver grooved for scope mounting.

CHARTER ARMS

AR-7 EXPLORER CARBINE

8-shot clip, 22 LR only, takedown with 16-inch barrel with barrel liner. Assembled 34½ inches long; when taken down, 16½ inches. Barrel and action store in plastic butt stock with rubber recoil pad acting as water-tight closure. Square blade front, rear peep sight adjustable for elevation only. Weight 2¾ lb.

Browning BAR-22 Auto Rifle

Browning Autoloading Rifle

Browning BPR-22 Pump Rifle

Charter Arms AR-7 Explorer Carbine

HARRINGTON & RICHARDSON

MODEL 700 AUTO RIFLE

5-shot clip for 22 Magnum, 22-inch barrel, 42½ inches overall, about 6½ lb. Walnut stock with Monte Carlo, pistol grip, composition butt plate with white spacer. Blade front and folding leaf rear sight, action drilled and tapped for scope mounting.

INTERARMS

ROSSI GALLERY PUMP-ACTION RIFLE

Tubular magazine, 22 Short, 22 Long or 22 LR, 23-inch barrel, weight about 5¾ lb. Simple takedown, bead post front sight, adjustable rear sight. Walnut stock with grooved forend, straight stock. Imported from Brazil.

MARLIN

MODEL 99 M1 AUTOLOADING CARBINE

9-shot tubular magazine, 22 LR, 18-inch barrel, 36¾ inches overall, weight about 5 lb. Ramp front and fully adjustable open rear sight. Walnut stock with pistol grip, composition butt plate with white spacer, sling swivels, gold-plated trigger, bolt hold-open latch.

GLENFIELD MODEL 60

Same action as M99, but with 18-shot tubular magazine, hardwood stock, walnut-finished. 22-inch barrel.

Harrington & Richardson Model 700 Auto Rifle

Interarms Rossi Gallery Pump-Action Rifle

Marlin Model 99 M1 Autoloading Carbine

Marlin Glenfield Model 60

MODEL 49 DL AUTOLOADING RIFLE

18-shot tubular magazine, 22 LR, 22-inch barrel, 40½ inches overall, weight about 5½ lb. Checkered walnut stock with Monte Carlo and capped pistol grip. Ramp front sight, open and fully adjustable rear sight. Grooved receiver with roll-on engraving, gold-plated trigger, bolt hold-open latch.

MOSSBERG

MODEL 353 AUTOLOADING RIFLE

7-shot clip, 22 LR, 18-inch barrel, 38 inches overall, weight about 5 lb. Walnut stock with checkered pistol grip and forend, black plastic fold-down forend with two positions, sling swivels and web strap. Ramp bead front sight and U-notch adjustable rear sight, receiver grooved for scope mounting.

MODEL PLINKSTER AUTOLOADING RIFLE

15-shot tubular magazine, 22 LR, 20-inch barrel, 40 inches overall, weight 6¼ lb. Molded plastic stock with thumbhole, no sights. Rifle comes with 4X scope, has bolt hold-open latch.

REMINGTON

NYLON 66MB AUTOLOADING RIFLE

14-shot tubular magazine, 22 LR, 19⅝-inch barrel, 38½ inches overall, 4 lb. Molded nylon stock with checkered pistol grip and forend. Blade ramp front sight, open and fully adjustable rear sight, receiver grooved for easy scope mounting, top tang safety. Also offered in black with chrome finish. Model 66GS is chambered for 22 Short round.

Marlin Model 49 DL Autoloading Rifle

Mossberg Model 353 Autoloading Rifle

Mossberg Model Plinkster Autoloading Rifle

Remington Nylon 66 MB Autoloading Rifle

MODEL 552A
AUTOLOADING RIFLE

Tubular magazine, chambered for Short, Long or LR, 23-inch barrel, 42-inch overall length, weight about 5¾ lb. Walnut stock with pistol grip, cross-bolt safety. Bead front and fully adjustable step rear sight. Carbine version also offered.

MODEL 572
FIELDMASTER PUMP-ACTION RIFLE

Tubular magazine, 22S, 22L or 22 LR, 24-inch barrel, 42-inch overall length, 5½ lb. Walnut stock with pistol grip and grooved forend, cross-bolt safety, gun can be converted to single shot. Bead front sight, open adjustable rear sight.

RUGER

MODEL 10/22
AUTOLOADING CARBINE

10-shot rotary magazine, 22 LR only, 18½-inch barrel, 37-inch overall length, weight about 5 lb. Uncheckered walnut stock with pistol grip and barrel band. Gold bead front and fully adjustable rear sight, cross-bolt safety. Receiver is grooved as well as tapped for choice of scope mounting systems, scope base adapter furnished with each rifle.

SAVAGE

STEVENS MODEL 80
AUTOLOADING RIFLE

15-shot tubular magazine, 22 LR, 20-inch barrel, 40-inch overall length, weight about 6 lb. Walnut stock with Monte Carlo, checkered pistol grip and forend. Blade front and open, fully adjustable rear sight. Receiver grooved for scope mounting.

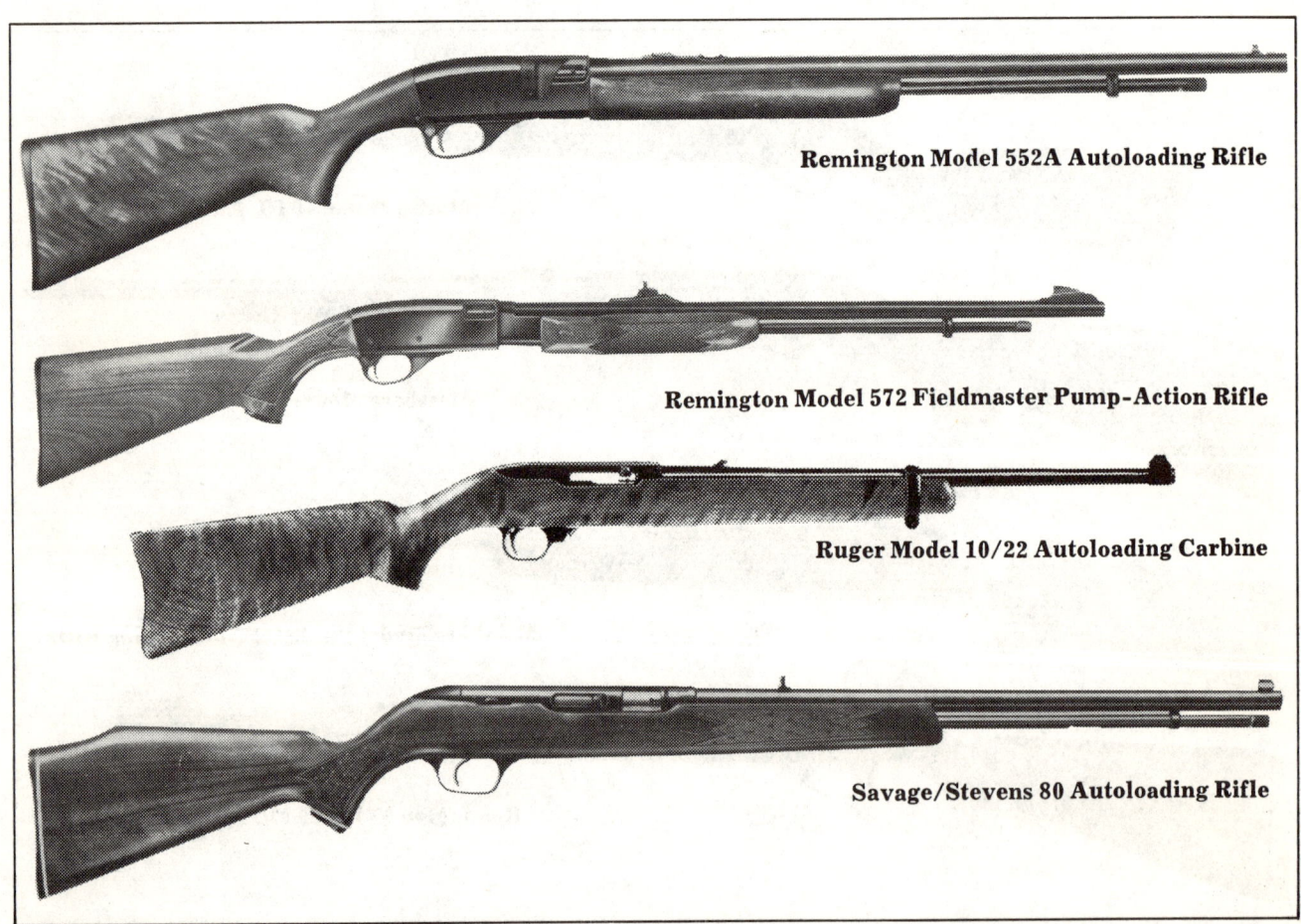

Remington Model 552A Autoloading Rifle

Remington Model 572 Fieldmaster Pump-Action Rifle

Ruger Model 10/22 Autoloading Carbine

Savage/Stevens 80 Autoloading Rifle

WEATHERBY	**MARK XXII AUTOLOADING RIFLE** Offered as 15-shot tubular magazine or 10-shot clip loader, 22 LR only, 24-inch barrel, 42¼-inch overall length, weight about 6 lb. Walnut stock with Monte Carlo and cheekpiece, checkered pistol grip and forend, sling swivels. Safety can be used to convert rifle to single shot. Gold bead ramp front sight, 3-leaf folding rear sight, receiver grooved for easy scope mounting. 5-shot clip available.		**MODEL 490 AUTOLOADING RIFLE** 5-shot clip, 22 LR only, 22-inch barrel, 42-inch overall length, weight about 6 lb. Walnut stock with checkered pistol grip and forend. Cross-bolt safety, hold-open latch, hooded ramp front and folding leaf rear sight, grooved receiver for scope mounting. 10-shot clip available.

LEVER ACTION

WINCHESTER	**MODEL 290 AUTOLOADING RIFLE** Tubular magazine for 17 22L or 15 LR cartridges, 20½-inch barrel, 39-inch overall length, weight about 5 lb. Two-piece hardwood stock walnut-finished, with checkered pistol grip and forend, black butt plate with white spacer, cross-bolt safety. Bead post front sight and open, fully adjustable rear sight. Receiver is grooved for scope mounting.	BROWNING	**MODEL BL-22 LEVER-ACTION RIFLE** Tubular magazine, 22 Short, 22 Long or 22 LR, 20-inch barrel, 36¾-inch overall length, weight about 5 lb. Walnut stock, uncheckered, straight grip. Bead post front and folding leaf rear sight, half-cock safety, receiver grooved for easy scope mounting, short lever movement. Offered in Grades I and II.

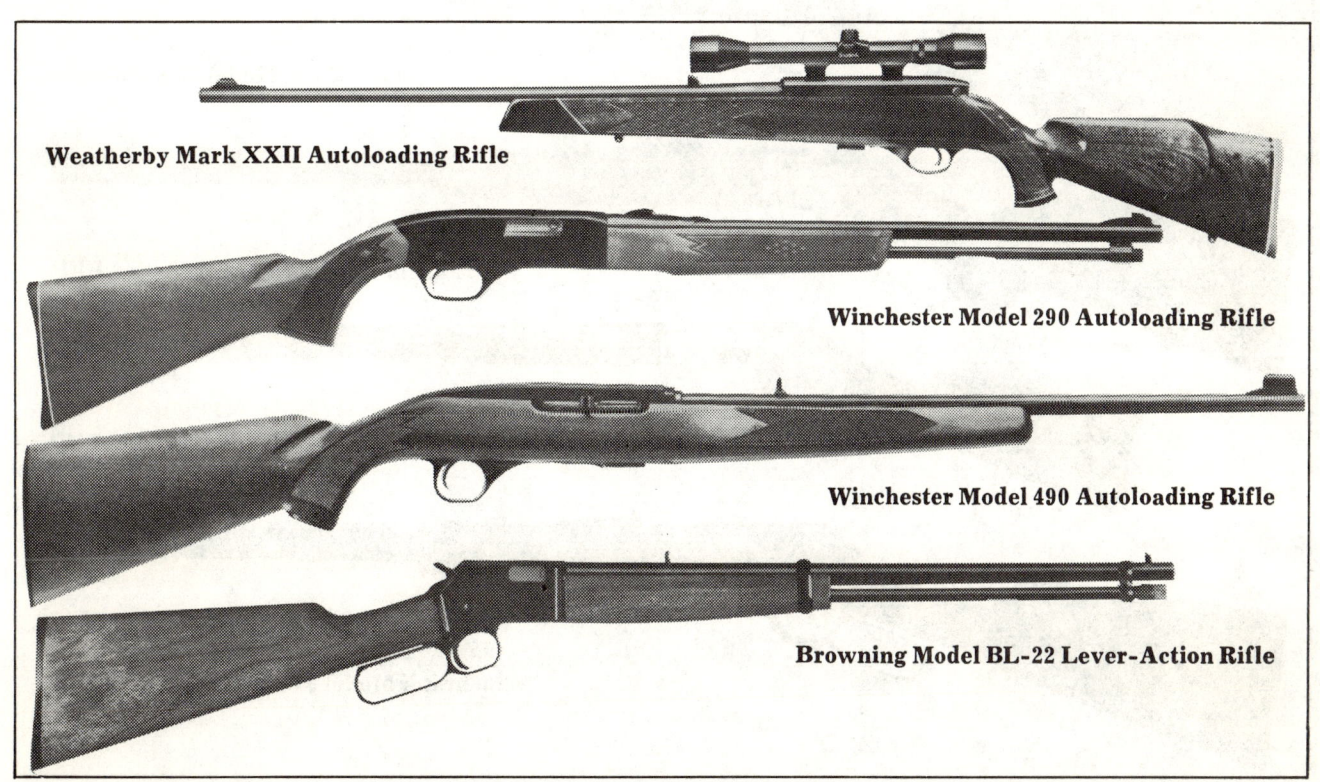

Weatherby Mark XXII Autoloading Rifle

Winchester Model 290 Autoloading Rifle

Winchester Model 490 Autoloading Rifle

Browning Model BL-22 Lever-Action Rifle

ITHACA	**MODEL 72 SADDLEGUN** 15-shot tubular magazine, 22 LR, 18½-inch barrel, weight about 5 lb. Straight grip walnut stock. Hooded front sight, open and fully adjustable rear sight. Half-cock safety, receiver grooved for scope mounting. Also offered in 22 Win Mag chambering.
MARLIN	**GOLDEN 39 LEVER-ACTION RIFLE** Tubular magazine, 22 Short, 22 L or LR, 24-inch barrel, 40-inch overall length, weight about 6½ lb. Takedown rifle, two-piece walnut stock with pistol grip, sling swivels, offset hammer spur, gold-plated trigger. Straight stock model with 20-inch barrel also available. Hooded bead ramp front sight, folding semi-buckhorn rear sight is fully adjustable. Scope mount supplied, action is drilled and tapped.
NAVY ARMS	**MODEL 66 LEVER-ACTION RIFLE** Tubular magazine, 22 LR only, 16½-inch barrel, copy of Winchester Model 1866 Yellowboy. Offered in three grades, selected wood, engraving, fixed front and folding rear sight.
WINCHESTER	**MODEL 9422 LEVER-ACTION RIFLE** Tubular magazine, 22 Short, 22 Long or 22 LR, 20½-inch barrel, 37⅛-inch overall length, weight about 6½ lb. Two-piece walnut stock, straight grip. Hooded ramp front sight, semi-buckhorn and fully adjustable rear sight. Side ejector, takedown action, receiver grooved for scope mounting, half-cock safety. Also offered in 22 Win Mag chambering.

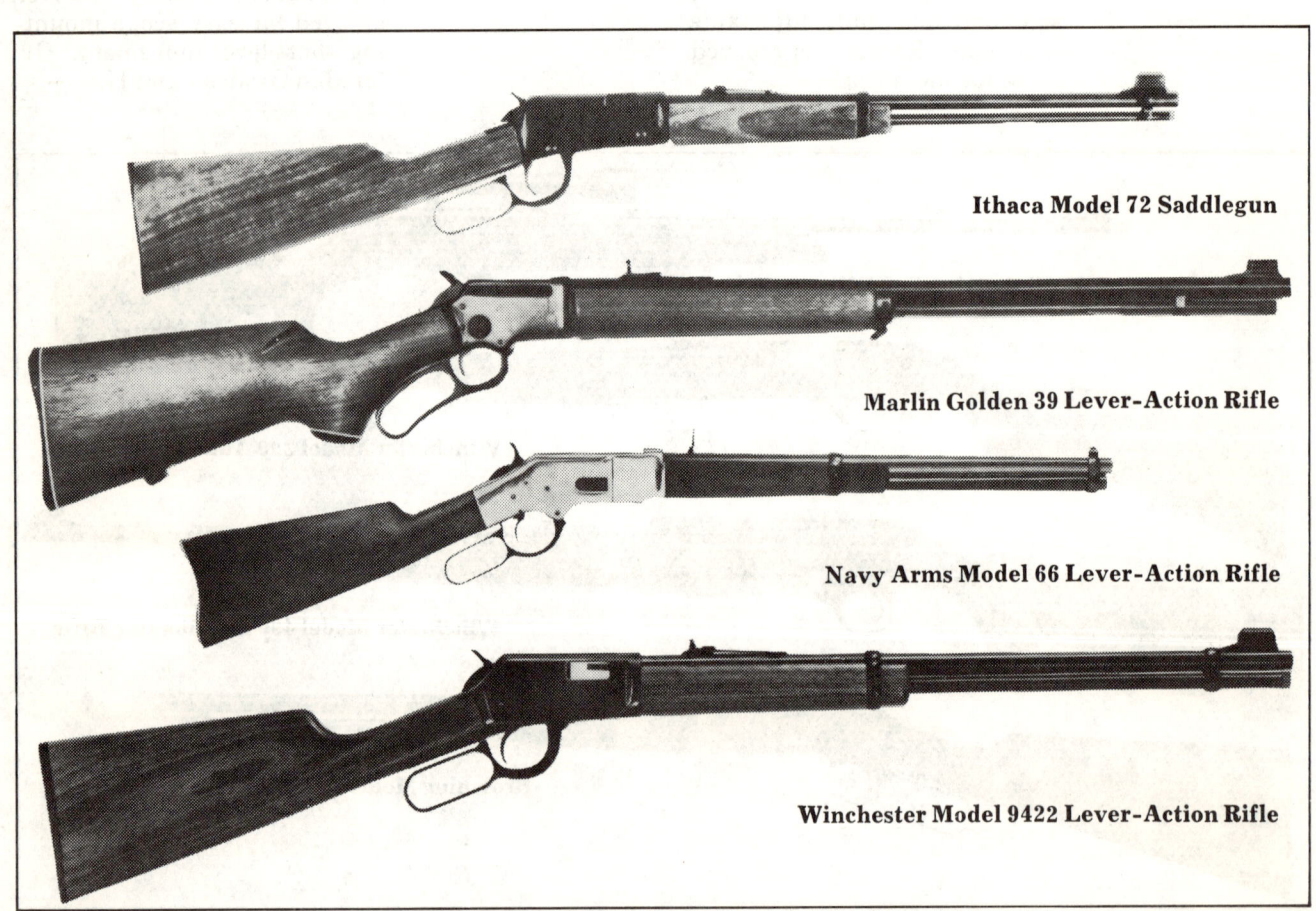

Ithaca Model 72 Saddlegun

Marlin Golden 39 Lever-Action Rifle

Navy Arms Model 66 Lever-Action Rifle

Winchester Model 9422 Lever-Action Rifle

BOLT ACTION

HARRINGTON & RICHARDSON

MODEL 865 PLAINSMAN RIFLE

5-shot clip, 22 Short, 22 L or 22 LR, 22-inch barrel, 39-inch overall length, weight about 5 lb. Monte Carlo and pistol grip, walnut-finished hardwood stock. Blade front, adjustable open rear sight, cocking indicator, sliding side safety, receiver grooved for easy scope mounting.

MARLIN

MODEL 780 BOLT-ACTION RIFLE

Rifle is offered as clip-fed and as tubular magazine model, chambered for 22 Short, 22 Long, 22 LR or 22 Winchester Magnum. 22-inch barrel, 41-inch overall length, weight about 5½ lb. Gold-plated trigger, hooded ramp front sight, adjustable open rear sight, receiver grooved for easy scope mounting. Walnut stock with pistol grip, white spacer and butt plate.

MOSSBERG

MODEL 340B BOLT-ACTION RIFLE

7-shot clip, 22 Short, 22 Long and 22 LR, clip adjusts to cartridge length. 24-inch barrel, 43½-inch overall length, weight about 6 lb. Walnut-finished hardwood stock with Monte Carlo, cheekpiece, sling swivels. Fully adjustable rear peep sight and hooded ramp front sight, receiver grooved for easy scope mounting.

MODEL 341 BOLT-ACTION RIFLE

Similar to Model 340B, except for walnut stock which has checkering on pistol grip and forend, butt plate with white line spacer, bead front and adjustable open rear sight. Clip adjusts for the three 22 rimfire rounds.

Harrington & Richardson Model 865 Plainsman Rifle

Marlin Model 780 Bolt-Action Rifle

Mossberg Model 340B Bolt-Action Rifle

Mossberg Model 341 Bolt-Action Rifle

A LOOK AT TODAY'S RIFLES

MODEL 640K CHUCKSTER

5-shot clip magazine, 22 Win Mag, 24-inch barrel, 44¾-inch overall length, weight about 6 lb. Walnut stock with butt plate and white spacer, checkered pistol grip and forend, Monte Carlo comb and cheekpiece. Receiver is grooved for scope mounting, is also drilled and tapped for receiver sight.

REMINGTON

MODEL 581 BOLT BOLT-ACTION RIFLE

5-shot clip, 22 Short, 22 Long or 22 LR, 24-inch barrel, 42⅜-inch overall length, weight about 4¾ lb. Walnut-finished stock with Monte Carlo and pistol grip, bead post front sight and open, fully adjustable rear sight. Receiver is grooved for scope mounting, sliding side safety. Also offered with tubular magazine and as left-hand model.

MODEL 541-S BOLT-ACTION RIFLE

5-shot clip, 22 Short, 22 Long or 22 LR, 24-inch barrel, 42⅝-inch overall length, weight about 5½ lb. Walnut stock with checkered pistol grip and forend, receiver and trigger guard scroll engraved. No sight, but drilled and tapped for scope mounting and receiver sight mounting. 10-shot clip available.

SAVAGE

SAVAGE/ANSCHUTZ MODEL 54 SPORTER

5-shot clip, 22 LR, 23-inch barrel, 42-inch overall length, weight about 6¾ lb. French walnut stock with Monte Carlo and rollover cheekpiece, checkered-pistol grip and forend, schnabel forend. Gold bead ramp front sight with hood, folding leaf rear sight. Receiver grooved for scope mounting, also drilled and tapped for scope blocks. Adjustable single stage trigger, wing safety.

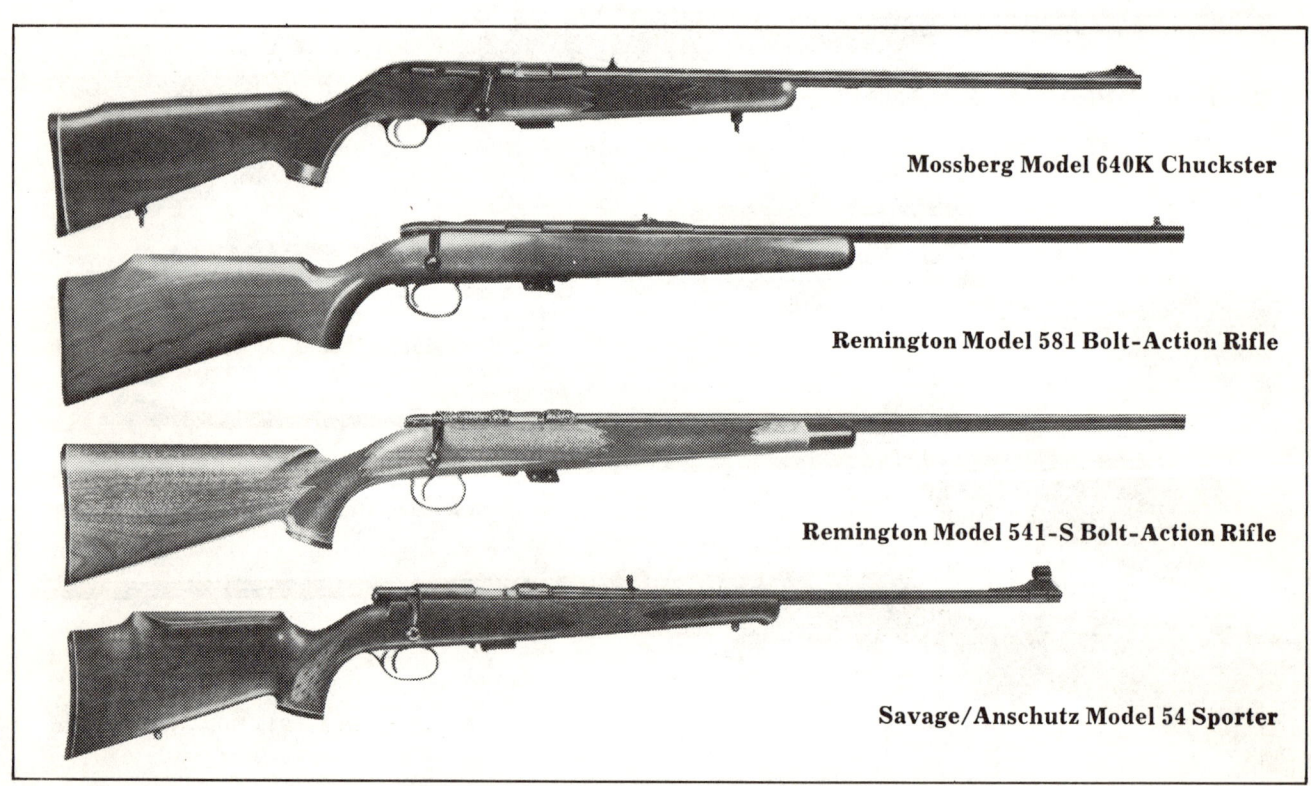

Mossberg Model 640K Chuckster

Remington Model 581 Bolt-Action Rifle

Remington Model 541-S Bolt-Action Rifle

Savage/Anschutz Model 54 Sporter

SAVAGE/ANSCHUTZ MODEL 164 BOLT-ACTION RIFLE

5-shot clip, 22 LR, 24-inch barrel, 40¾-inch overall length, weight about 6 lb. Walnut stock with Monte Carlo comb and cheekpiece, hand-checkered pistol grip and forend with schnabel tip. Gold bead on ramp front sight with hood, folding leaf rear sight. Fully adjustable single stage trigger, sliding side safety, receiver grooved for scope mounting. Also offered in Win Mag rimfire chambering. Same model with European Mannlicher-style stock, double set or single stage trigger, stock inlays and other special features, Model 1418 (22 LR) and Model 1518 (22 Mag).

SAVAGE MODEL 65-M BOLT-ACTION RIFLE

5-shot, 22 Win Mag, 20-inch free-floated barrel, 39-inch overall length, weight about 5 lb. Walnut stock with Monte Carlo comb, checkered pistol grip and forend. Gold bead front sight on ramp, open adjustable rear sight. Sliding side safety, receiver grooved for scope mounting.
Savage/Stevens Model 34 is same gun, but chambered for the 22 LR round and stock is walnut-finished hardwood.

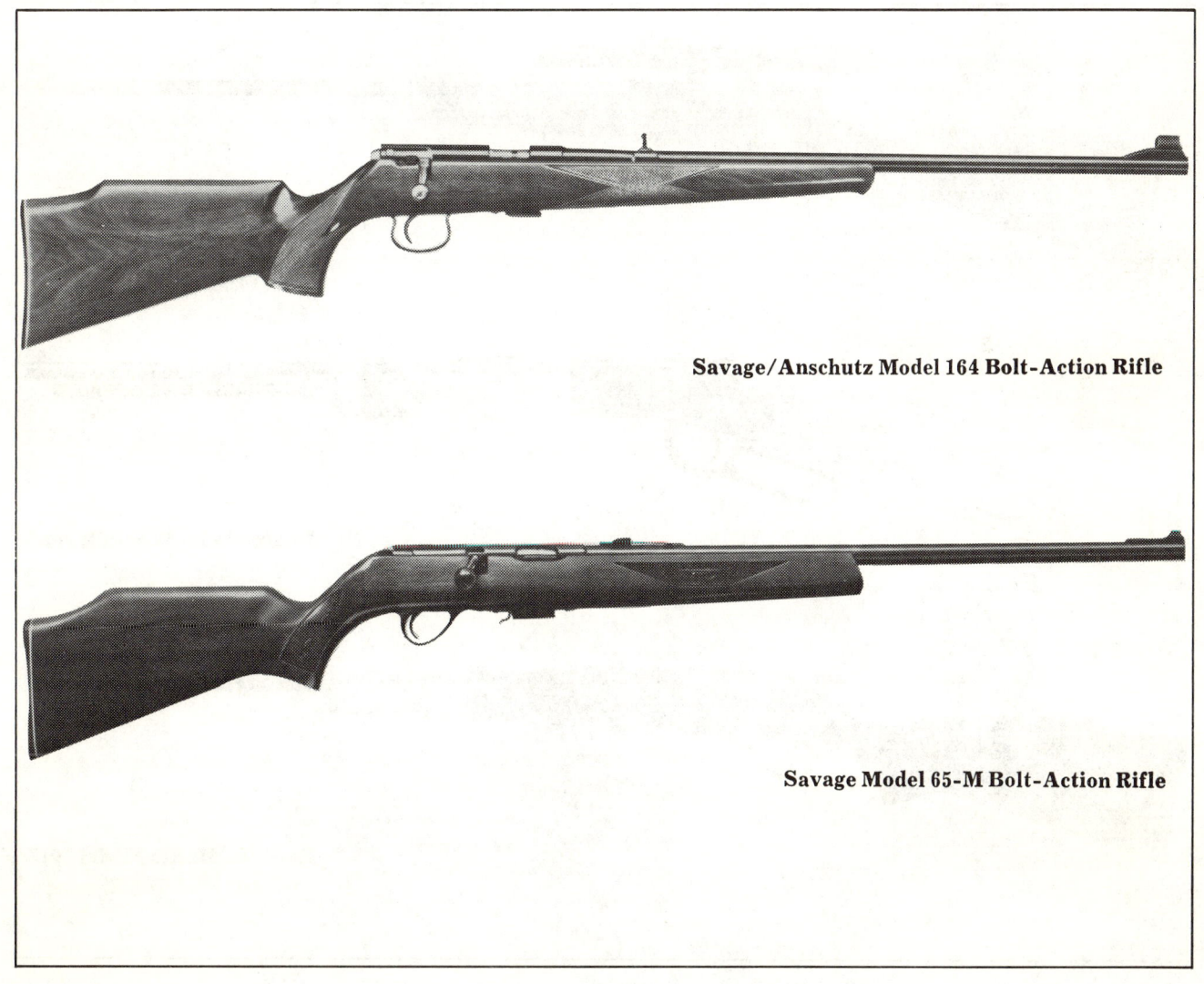

Savage/Anschutz Model 164 Bolt-Action Rifle

Savage Model 65-M Bolt-Action Rifle

SINGLE SHOT

HARRINGTON & RICHARDSON

MODEL 750 PIONEER

Handles 22 Short, Long and LR round, 22-inch barrel, 39-inch overall length, weight about 5 lb. Walnut-finished hardwood stock with Monte Carlo and pistol grip. Blade front sight and open adjustable rear sight, cocking indicator, sliding side safety. Receiver is grooved for easy scope mounting.

ITHACA

MODEL 49 SADDLEGUN

Handles 22 Short, Long and LR round, 18-inch barrel, 34½-inch overall length, weight about 5½ lb. Two-piece walnut stock, straight grip that is checkered, barrel band around forend. Bead on post front sight with open, adjustable rear sight. Rebounding hammer safety. Also offered in 22 Win Mag chambering.

MARLIN

MODEL 101

Handles 22 Short, Long and LR round, 22-inch barrel, 39-inch overall length, weight about 4¼ lb. Walnut Monte Carlo stock with pistol grip and white line spacer under black butt plate. Hooded ramp front sight, adjustable open rear sight. Manual cocking, gold-plated trigger, receiver grooved for scope mounting.

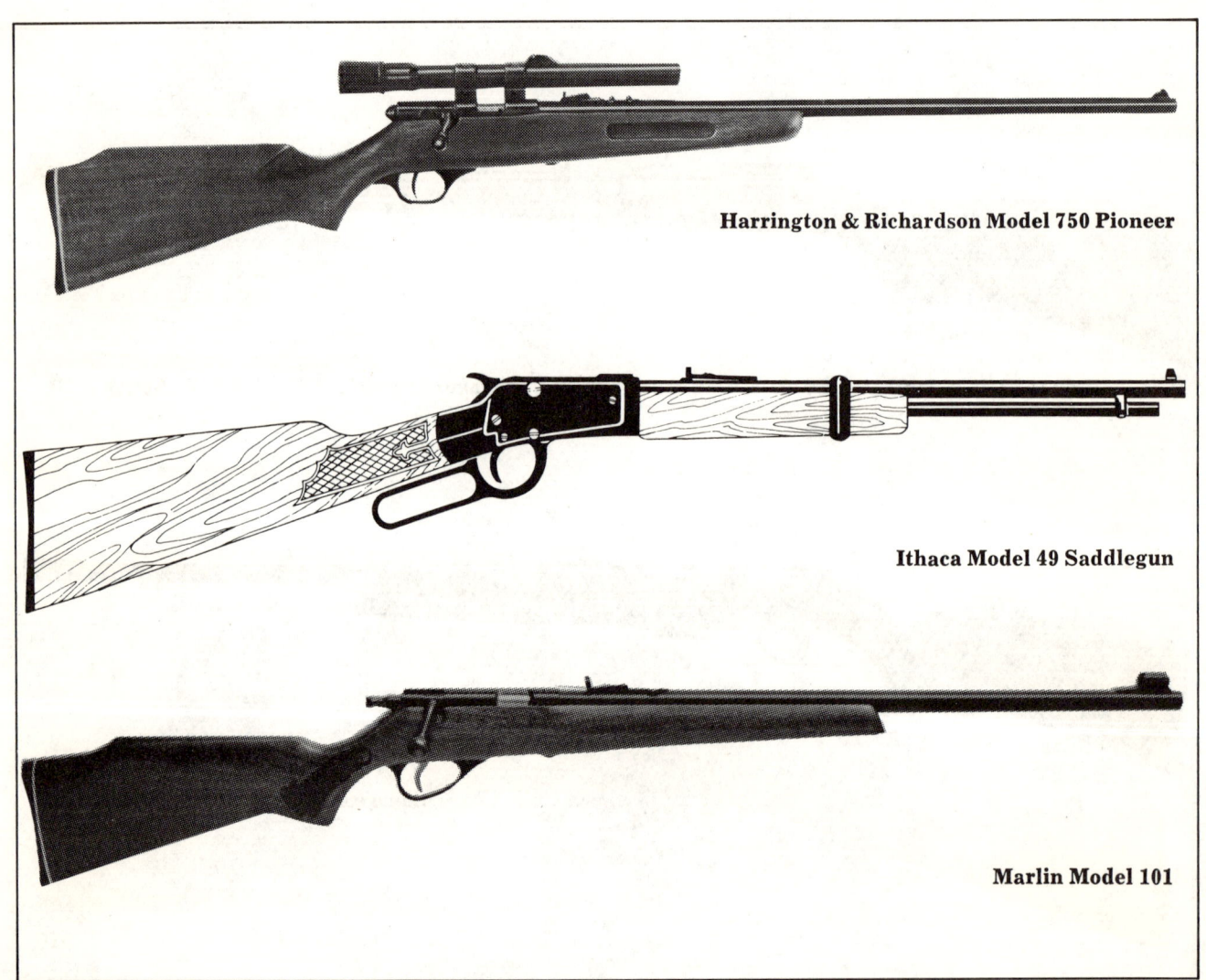

Harrington & Richardson Model 750 Pioneer

Ithaca Model 49 Saddlegun

Marlin Model 101

MOSSBERG

MODEL 321K
Handles 22 Short, Long and LR round, 24-inch barrel, 43½-inch overall length, weight about 6½ lb. Walnut-finished hardwood stock with cheekpiece and checkered pistol grip and forend. Ramp front sight and adjustable open rear sight. Automatic safety, hammerless bolt-action design.

REMINGTON

MODEL 580
Handles 22 Short, Long and LR round, 24-inch barrel, overall length 42⅜ inches, weight about 4¾ lb. Walnut-finished hardwood stock with Monte Carlo, pistol grip, black butt plate. Bead on post front sight, open adjustable rear sight. Simple takedown, sliding side safety, receiver grooved for scope mounting.

SAVAGE

SAVAGE/STEVENS MODEL 73
Handles 22 Short, Long and LR round, 20-inch barrel, overall length 38½ inches, weight about 4¾ lb. Walnut-finished hardwood stock with pistol grip. Automatic safety, action cocks on opening, key lock secures action. Bead on post front sight, adjustable open rear sight.

SAVAGE/STEVENS MODEL 89
Lever action 22 LR, 18½-inch barrel, 35-inch overall length, weight about 5 lb. Straight grip walnut-finished hardwood stock, blade front and open adjustable rear sight. Automatic ejector, hammer must be cocked manually.

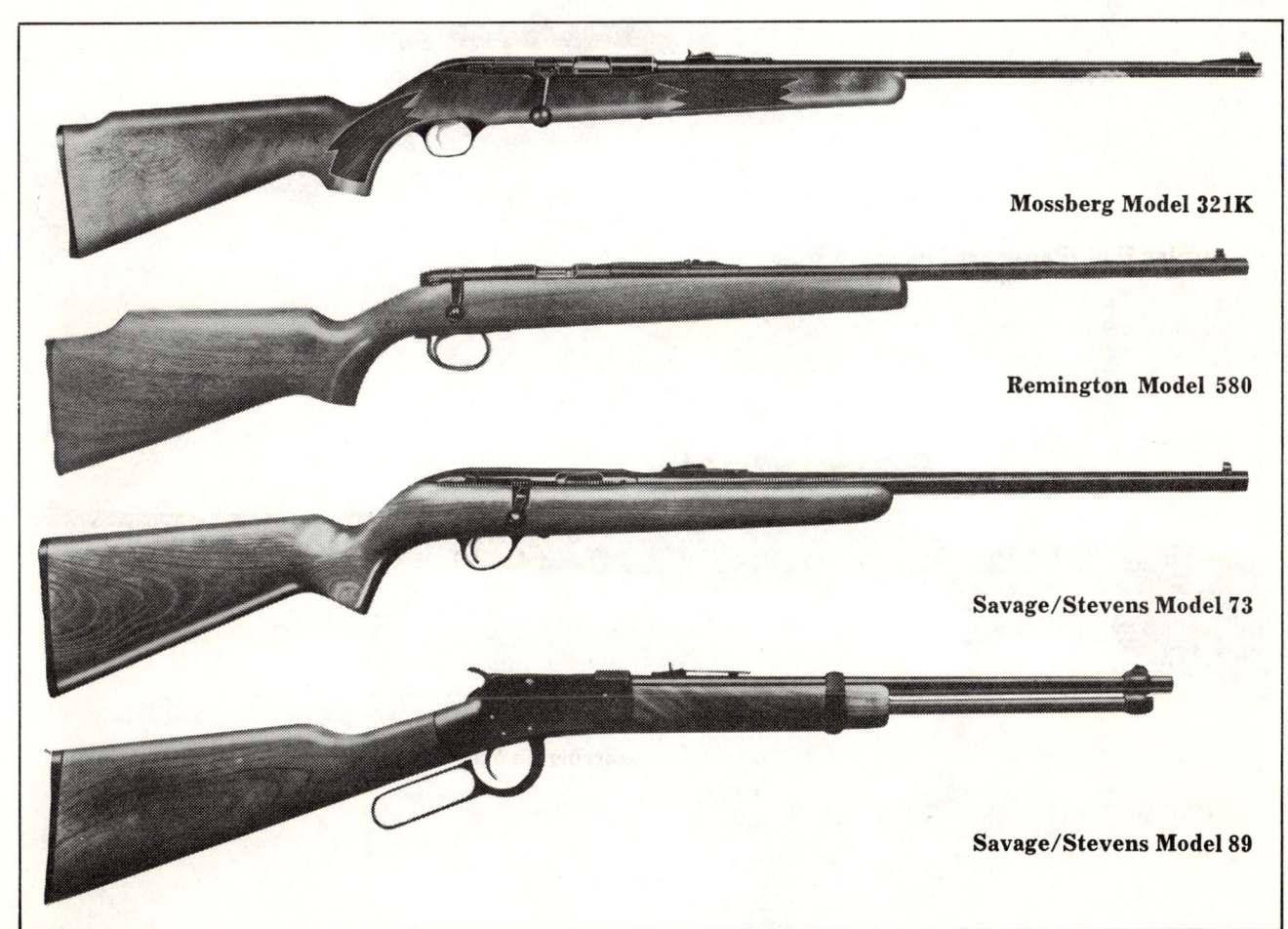

Mossberg Model 321K

Remington Model 580

Savage/Stevens Model 73

Savage/Stevens Model 89

CENTERFIRE RIFLES

SEMIAUTOMATIC & PUMP ACTION

BROWNING — HIGH-POWER SEMIAUTOMATIC RIFLE

243, 270, 30-06, 308, also 7mm Rem Mag and 300 Win Mag. Offered in Grades I and IV. 22-inch barrel on standard calibers, 24 inches on magnums, overall length 43½ inches and 45¼ inches, weight about 7⅜ lb. and 8½ lb. Detachable 4-round magazine, 3-round in magnums. Two-piece walnut stock with checkering on pistol grip and forend. Gold bead on hooded ramp front sight, adjustable folding leaf rear sight, tapped for scope mounts.

HARRINGTON & RICHARDSON — MODEL 360 ULTRA AUTOLOADER

308 Win only, 3-round magazine, 22-inch barrel, 43½-inch overall length, weight about 7½ lb. One-piece walnut stock with Monte Carlo, rollover cheekpiece, pistol grip. Gold bead on ramp front sight, fully adjustable open rear sight. Sliding safety is located in trigger guard, manually operated bolt stop, receiver tapped for scope mounting.

Browning High-Power Semiautomatic Rifle

Harrington & Richardson Model 360 Ultra Autoloader

REMINGTON

MODEL 742 WOODSMASTER

243, 6mm Rem, 280, 308 and 30-06, 4-shot detachable magazine, 22-inch barrel, 42-inch overall length, weight about 7½ lb. Two-piece walnut stock with checkered pistol grip and forend, cross-bolt safety. Gold bead on ramp front sight, open rear sight adjustable for windage. Tapped for scope mounts. Also offered in several fancier grades, and in plain version also as a carbine.

MODEL 760 GAMEMASTER PUMP ACTION

243, 6mm Rem, 270, 308 and 30-06, 4-shot detachable magazine, 22-inch barrel, overall length 42 inches, weight about 7½ lb. Walnut stock with checkered pistol grip and forend, cross-bolt safety, receiver is tapped for scope mounting. Gold bead on matted ramp, adjustable open rear sight. Also in carbine configuration and in fancy grades.

RUGER

MINI-14 CARBINE

223 Rem (5.56mm), 5-shot detachable box magazine, 10- and 20-round magazines available. Fixed piston gas-operated, 18½-inch barrel, overall length 36¾ inches, weight about 5¾ lb. One-piece walnut stock reinforced with steel, ramp front and fully adjustable rear sight.

44 SEMIAUTOMATIC CARBINE

44 Magnum with 4-shot tubular magazine, 18½-inch barrel, 36¾-inch overall length, weight

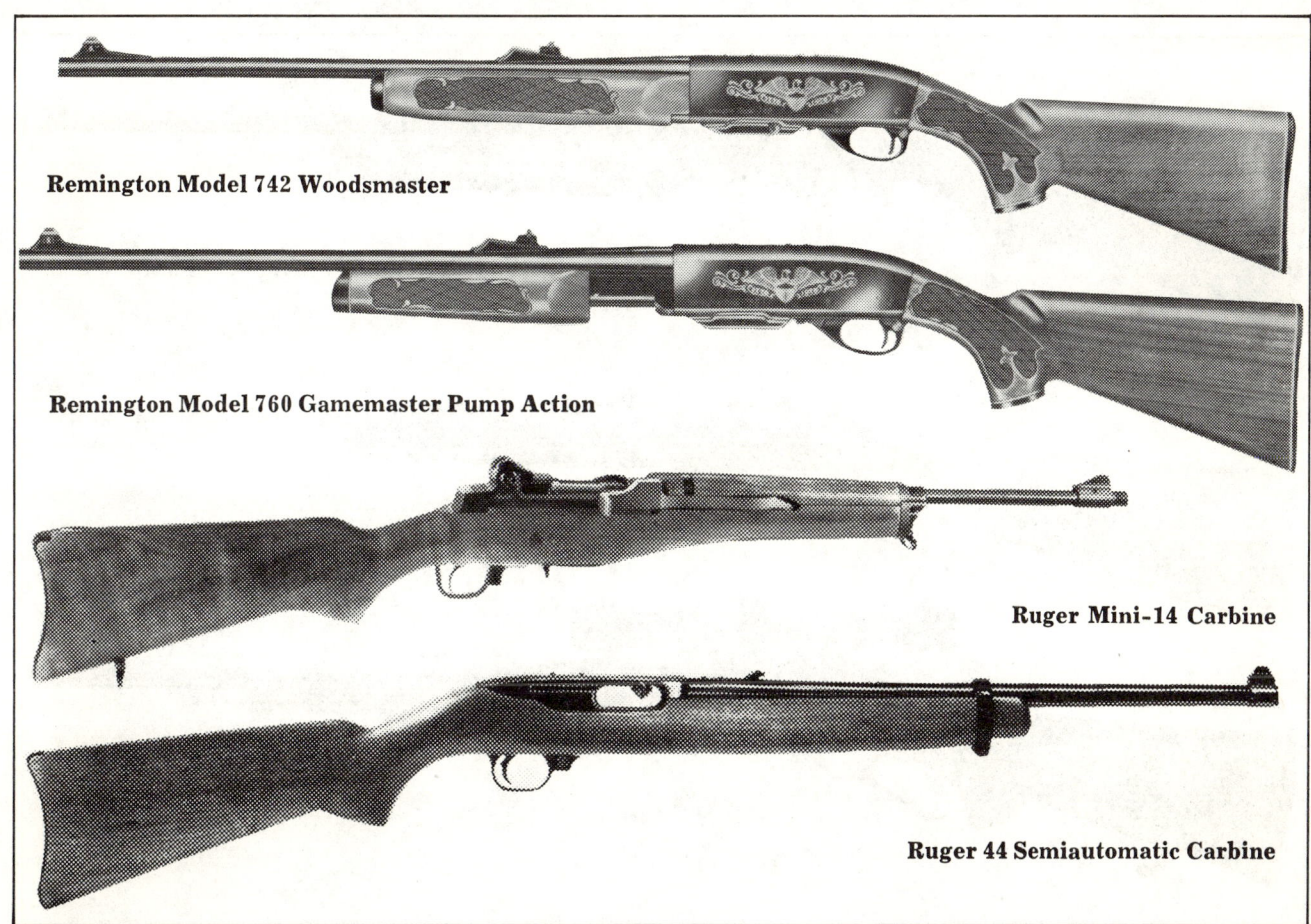

Remington Model 742 Woodsmaster

Remington Model 760 Gamemaster Pump Action

Ruger Mini-14 Carbine

Ruger 44 Semiautomatic Carbine

about 5¾ lb. One-piece walnut stock with pistol grip. Gold bead front and folding leaf rear sight, cross-bolt safety, receiver is tapped for scope mounting. Also offered in a deluxe edition.

SAVAGE — MODEL 170 PUMP ACTION
30-30 and 35 Rem, 3-shot magazine, 22-inch barrel, overall length 41½ inches, weight about 6¾ lb. Walnut stock with checkered pistol grip and black butt plate. Gold bead on ramp front sight, folding leaf-type rear sight. Hammerless, solid frame, top tang safety, tapped for scope mounts.

LEVER ACTION

BROWNING — MODEL BLR RIFLE
243, 308, 358 Win, 4-shot detachable magazine, 20-inch barrel, 39¾-inch overall length, weight about 7 lb. Two-piece walnut stock, straight grip and forend are checkered, stock is oil-finished. Half-cock hammer safety, recoil pad. Gold bead on hooded ramp front sight, adjustable square notch rear sight. Action tapped for scope mounting.

MARLIN — MODEL 444
444 Marlin, 4-shot tubular magazine, 22-inch barrel, overall length 40½ inches, weight about 7½ lb. Two-piece walnut stock, capped pistol grip, recoil pad with white line spacer. Hooded ramp front sight, semi-buckhorn folding and fully adjustable rear sight. Sling swivels with carrying strap, offset hammer spur, gold-plated trigger, half-cock safety. Action is tapped for scope mounts.

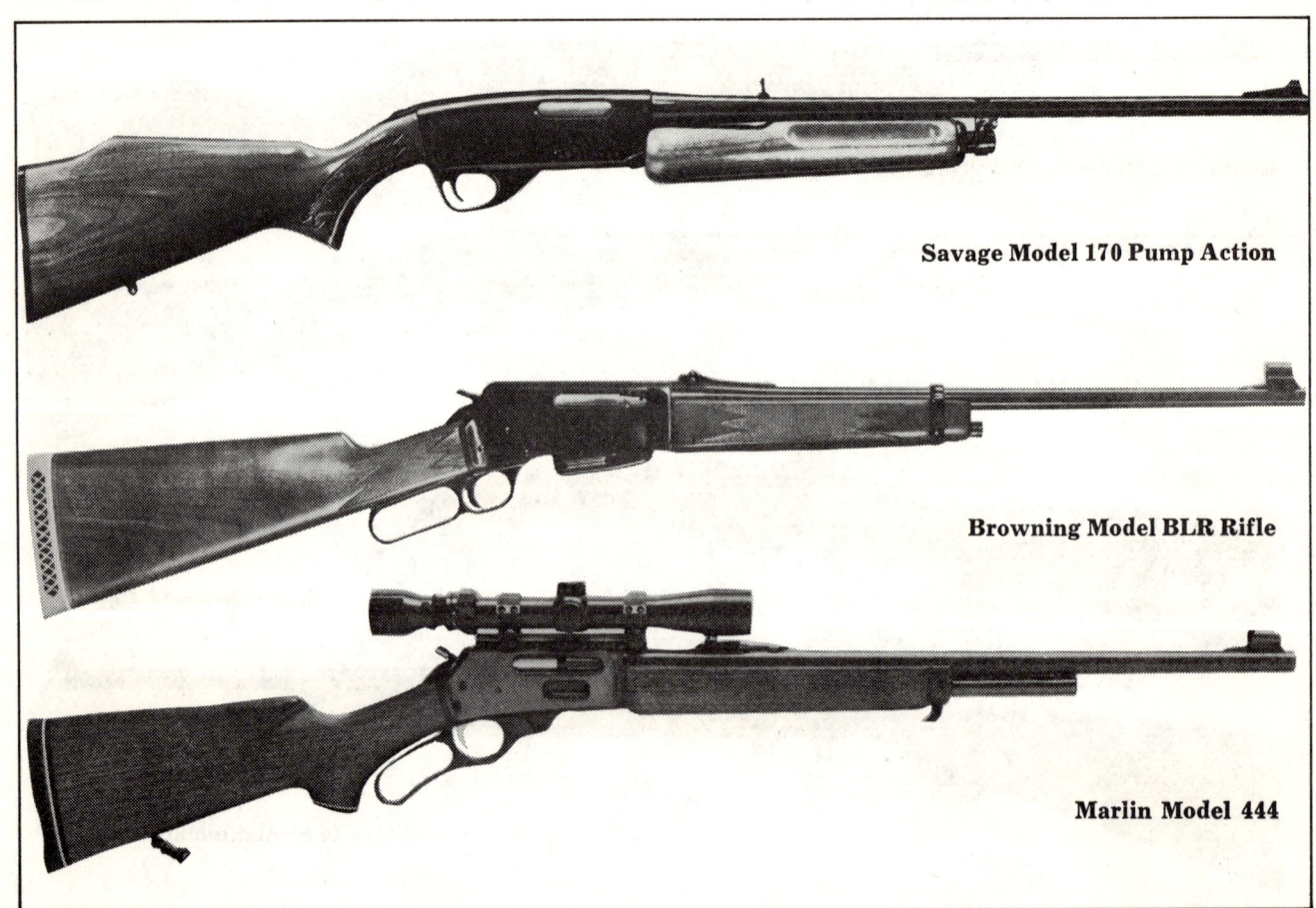

Savage Model 170 Pump Action

Browning Model BLR Rifle

Marlin Model 444

MODEL 336

30-30 or 35 Rem, 6-shot tubular magazine, 20-inch barrel, 38½-inch overall length, weight about 7 lb. Two-piece walnut stock, capped pistol grip, white line spacers. Hooded ramp front sight, fully adjustable semi-buckhorn holding rear sight. Non-glare finish on top of receiver, gold-plated trigger, offset hammer spur, receiver tapped for scope mounting. Three variations of the M336 are offered, including a straight stock model.

MODEL 1895

45-70, 4-round tubular magazine, 22-inch barrel, overall length 40½ inches, weight about 7 lb. Two-piece walnut stock, straight grip, white spacer under butt plate, offset hammer spur, tapped for scope or peep sight mounting. Bead front, fully adjustable semi-buckhorn rear sight.

MODEL 1894

44 Magnum, 10-shot tubular magazine, 20-inch barrel, over-37½ inches all length, weight about 6 lb. All other specifications same as for Model 1895. Gold-plated trigger is standard feature.

MOSSBERG

MODEL 472

30-30 or 35 Rem, 6-shot tubular magazine, 20-inch barrel, 38½-inch overall length, weight about 7½ lb. Two-piece walnut stock, fluted comb and pistol grip with white line spacer cap, spacer also under butt plate. Ramp front, open rear sight adjustable only for elevation. Hammer-block safety, tapped for scope blocks. Also offered with straight grip stock.

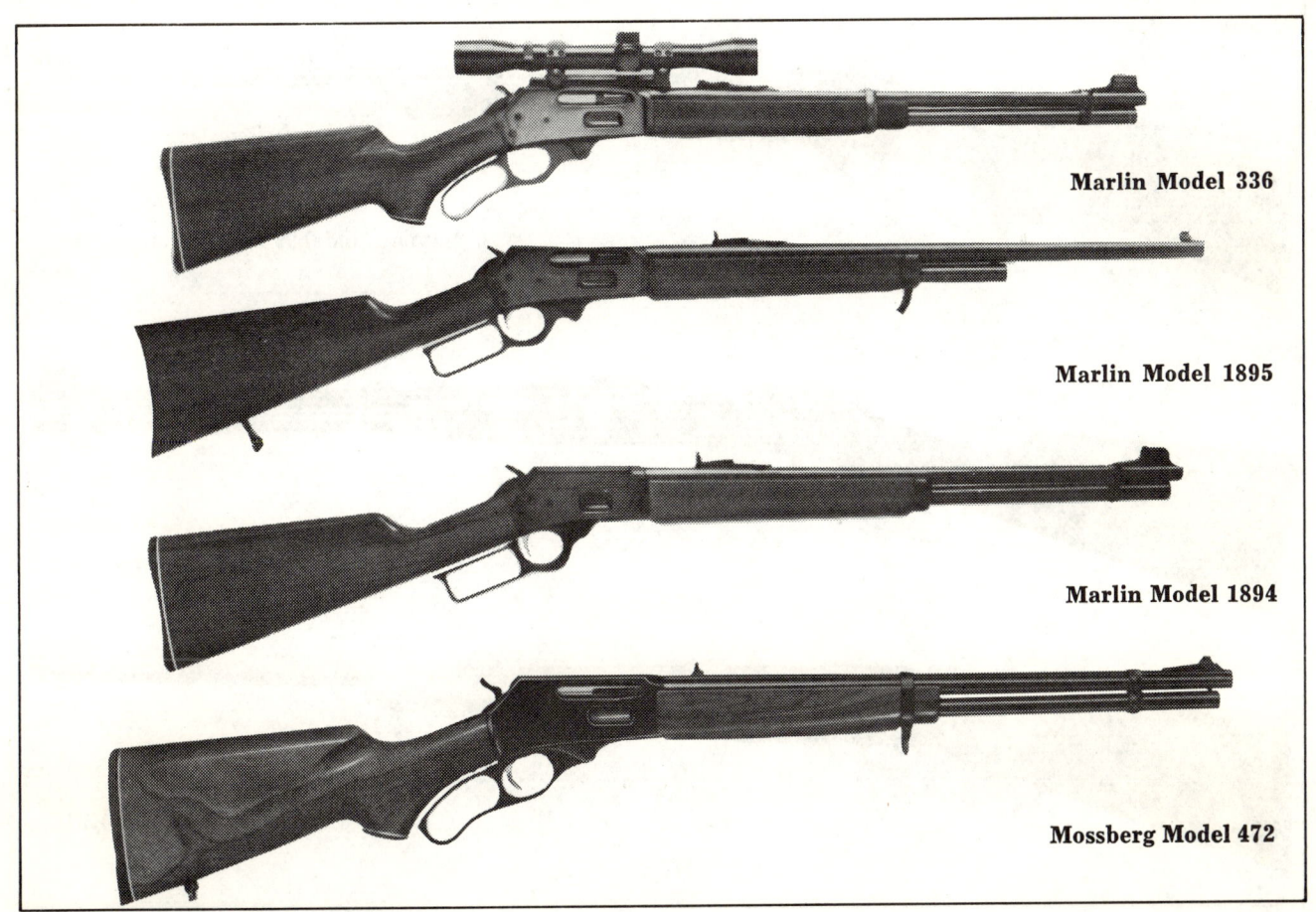

Marlin Model 336

Marlin Model 1895

Marlin Model 1894

Mossberg Model 472

SAVAGE — MODEL 99 LEVER–ACTION RIFLE

Five different models of the M99 are offered in a wide choice of calibers, stock styles and magazines. Walnut stock or walnut-finished stock. Average barrel length 20–22 inches, average overall length 39–42 inches, average weight 7 lb.

WINCHESTER — MODEL 94

30-30, 6-shot tubular magazine, 20-inch barrel, overall length $37\frac{3}{4}$ inches, weight about $6\frac{1}{2}$ lb. Two-piece straight grip walnut stock, top ejector, but can be scoped with special B-Square mount. Hooded bead on ramp front sight, open rear sight adjustable for elevation. Action is tapped for receiver sight, half-cock hammer safety.

BOLT ACTION

COLT — COLT SAUER RIFLE

Offered in a wide variety of American calibers, 24-inch barrel, overall length about 44 inches depending on caliber, weight about 8 lb., $10\frac{1}{2}$ lb. for 458 Win Mag. Walnut stock with Monte Carlo comb, checkered pistol grip and forend, white spacers, rubber recoil pad. Stock is hand checkered and well finished. Unique action, 3- or 4-shot magazine, depending on caliber. No sights except on 458 Win Mag rifle. Special scope mounts furnished for most scopes with each rifle.

Savage Model 99 Lever-Action Rifle

Winchester Model 94

Colt Sauer Rifle

RIFLE GUIDE

HARRINGTON & RICHARDSON

MODEL 300

30-06 only, 22-inch barrel, 42½-inch overall length, weight about 7¾ lb. Walnut stock with rollover cheekpiece and Monte Carlo comb, hand checkered pistol grip and forend. Gold bead on ramp front sight, open adjustable rear sight. Sliding side safety, sling swivels, recoil pad, receiver drilled and tapped for scope mounting. Hinged magazine floor plate.

INTERARMS

MODEL MARK X

Offered in four different models, wide selection of calibers, including magnums, hand-checkered walnut stock with sling swivels. Hooded ramp front sight, fully adjustable rear sight. Barrel lengths vary with models, average weight 7½ lb., except for the Alaskan model which weighs 8¼ lb. and is chambered for the 375 H&H and 458 Win Mag. Adjustable trigger. Most models are drilled and tapped for scope mounting.

ITHACA

ITHACA/BSA CF-2

7mm Rem Mag and 300 Win Mag, 3-shot magazine, 24-inch barrel, 44½-inch overall length, weight about 7¾ lb. Walnut stock with Monte Carlo rollover cheekpiece, skipline checkering on pistol grip and forend, contrasting wood tips, ventilated rubber recoil pad, sling swivels. Removable ramp front sight with hood, adjustable open rear sight. Receiver tapped for scope mounting, silent safety, trigger adjustable for pull from 3-5½ lb.

Harrington & Richardson Model 300

Interarms Model Mark X

Ithaca/BSA CF-2

ITHACA LSA-55

Offered in a wide choice of calibers, some with heavy or bull barrels, detachable 3-shot magazine, 23-inch barrel, overall length 41½ inches, weight with sporter barrel about 6½ lb. Adjustable trigger, top tang safety, drilled and tapped for scope mounting. Walnut stock with Monte Carlo, hand-checkered pistol grip and forend. Removable ramp front sight, adjustable rear sight. Also available in deluxe version, but only in smaller calibers.

KLEIN-GUENTHER
K-14 INSTA-FIRE RIFLE

Wide choice of calibers, including most of the magnum chamberings, with either 24-inch or 26-inch barrel, overall length about 43 inches, weight about 7⅛ lb. Choice of light, medium or dark European walnut stock, Monte Carlo comb, hand-checkered pistol grip and forend, cheekpiece, rosewood tips on forend and pistol grip. No sights, but available as optionals. Receiver drilled and tapped for scope mounting. Rubber recoil pad, hidden clip, trigger adjustable for pull, short bolt lift and very fast lock time.

MANNLICHER AND MANNLICHER-SCHOENAUER

These Austrian-made rifles are offered in nine styles, various stock design, and in U.S. as

Ithaca LSA-55

Kleinguenther K-14 Insta-Fire Rifle

Mannlicher and Mannlicher Schoenauer

well as some European calibers. Butterknife bolt handles and slick actions are typical, as are the hammered barrels. Stocks are walnut, hand-checkered, with pistol grips and spacers, with some rifles being equipped with recoil pads. Sights are furnished, actions are drilled and tapped for scope mounting. Mannlicher rotary magazine, sling swivels.

MOSSBERG   MODEL 800 SERIES

22-250, 243, 308, 30-06 and 7mm Rem Mag; also as varmint rifle in 22-250 and 243 with heavy 24-inch barrel without sights, but with scope bases. All others have sights, actions drilled and tapped for scope mounting. 22-inch barrel on all others, except magnum rifle which has 24-inch barrel. Walnut stock with pistol grip and Monte Carlo, hand checkered, depending on model either hinged floorplate or box magazine. Ramp front sight with gold bead and folding rear sight. Top tang safety.

NIKKO   GOLDEN EAGLE MODEL 7000

Wide choice of calibers, including magnums, 24-inch or 26-inch barrel, average overall length 43½ inches for standard calibers, weight about 7¾ lb. Walnut stock with Monte Carlo and pistol grip, checkered, rubber recoil pad. No sights, actions drilled and tapped for scope mounting. Top tang safety, removable clip magazine. Comes with luggage-type gun case, but no sling swivels.

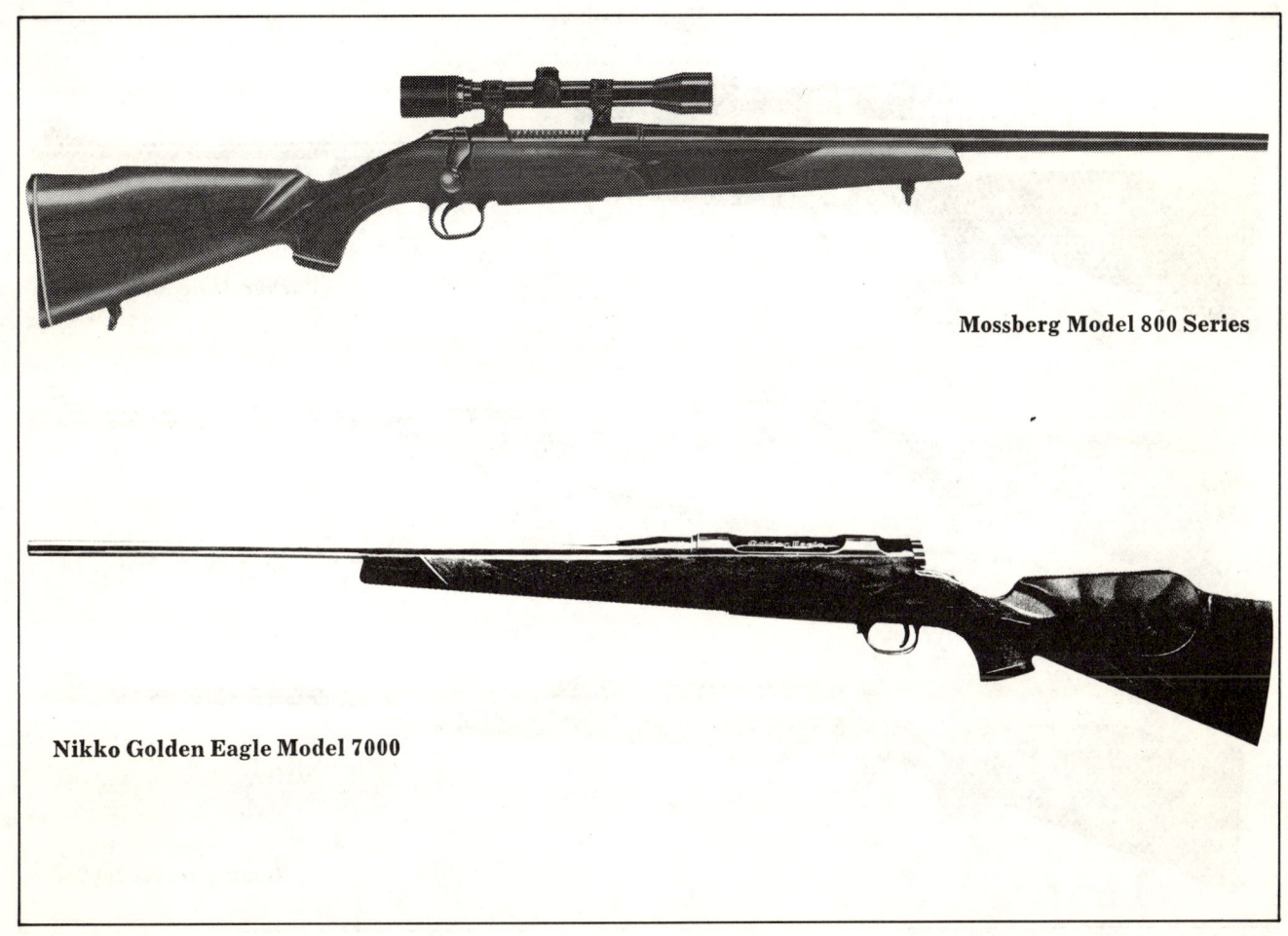

Mossberg Model 800 Series

Nikko Golden Eagle Model 7000

PARKER-HALE **MODEL 1200**
Offered in wide choice of calibers, including magnums. Made in Britain, imported by Jana. 24-inch barrel, overall length 45 inches, weight about 7¼ lb. Walnut stock with contrasting forend cap and pistol grip, checkered, Monte Carlo rollover, white line spacers, rubber recoil pad. Adjustable trigger, bead front and adjustable folding rear sight. Also offered as varmint rifle with heavy barrel, no sights.

REMINGTON **MODEL 700**
Wide choice of calibers, including magnums, left-hand version and varmint rifles also offered. Standard grade as well as deluxe versions with selected wood and eye-appealing features. 22-inch or 24-inch barrel, weight depends on barrel length and caliber. Ramp front sight with gold bead, step rear sight adjustable for windage. Walnut stock with Monte Carlo and pistol grip, type of checkering depends on grade. Side safety, receiver drilled and tapped for scope mounting.

MODEL 788
Wide choice of calibers, 22-inch or 24-inch barrel depending on caliber, detachable box magazine, ramp with blade front sight, fully adjustable rear sight, receiver drilled and tapped for scope mounting. Walnut-finished hardwood stock with Monte Carlo and pistol grip. Also in left-hand version.

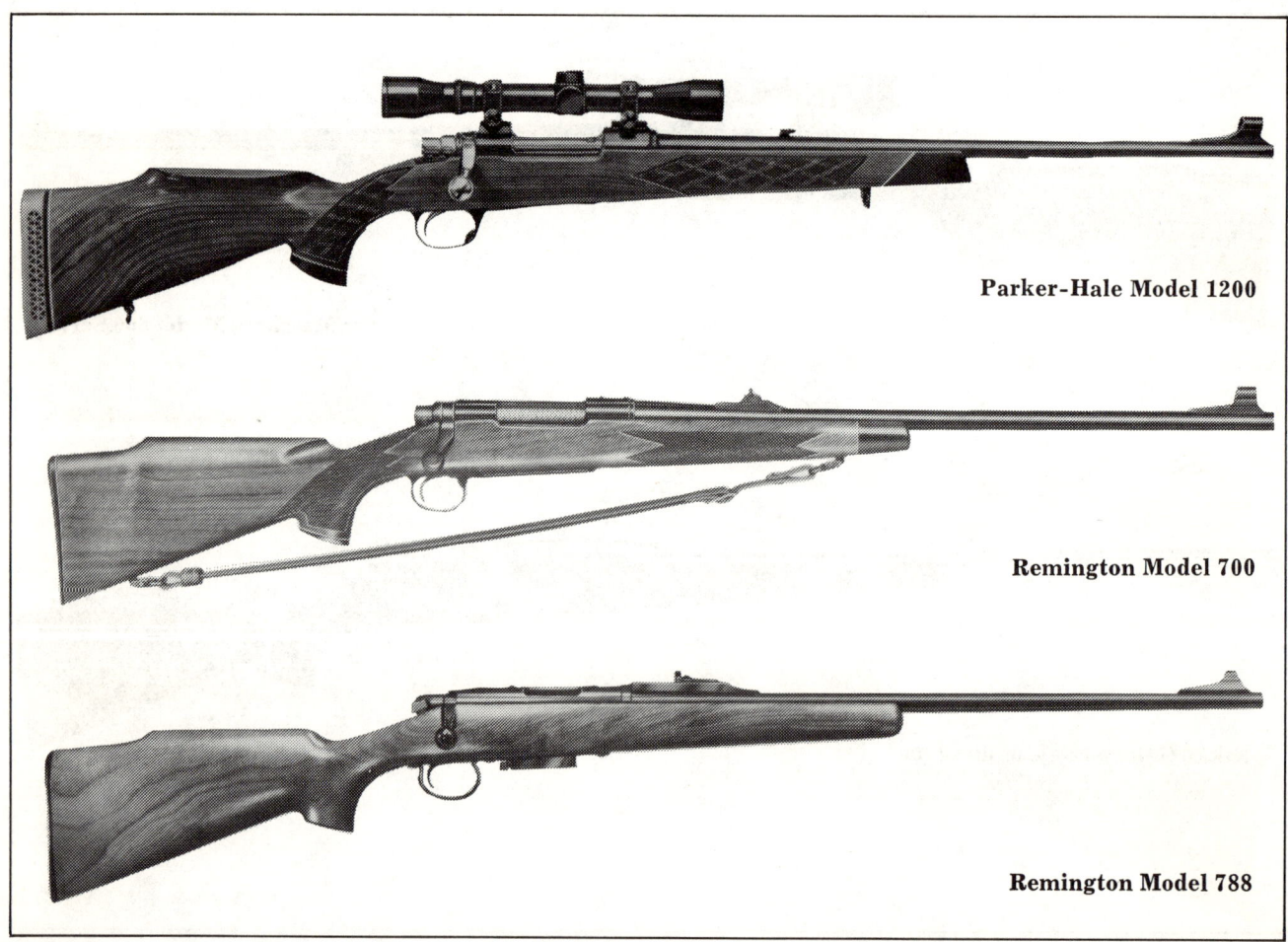

Parker-Hale Model 1200

Remington Model 700

Remington Model 788

RUGER
MODEL 77
Offered in many calibers, including magnum chamberings, also as varmint model with heavy barrel. Barrel length varies with caliber, as does weight and overall length. Walnut stock, pistol grip with cap, checkered forend and grip, rubber recoil pad on magnum rifles. No sights, action comes with integral scope mount, open sights optional, as is round magnum action suitable for standard scope mounts and rings.

SAKO
STANDARD
(FORMERLY MODEL 74)
Available in wide variety of calibers, three action lengths, as heavy barrel varmint version, deluxe sporter and as Mannlicher carbine in 30-06. Imported by Stoeger Industries from Finland. Walnut stock with Monte Carlo and pistol grip, hand checkered, rubber recoil pad and sling swivel studs. No sights, adjustable trigger, hinged floorplate, integral dovetail on action for scope mounting.

MODEL 78
Offered in 22LR and 22 Hornet, 22½-inch barrel, overall length about 48 inches, weight 6¾ lb. Walnut stock with Monte Carlo, hand-checkered forend and pistol grip, sling swivel studs, no sights, but rail-type scope bases are supplied. Adjustable trigger, detachable box magazine, 4 rounds in Hornet, 5 in rimfire version, low bolt lift.

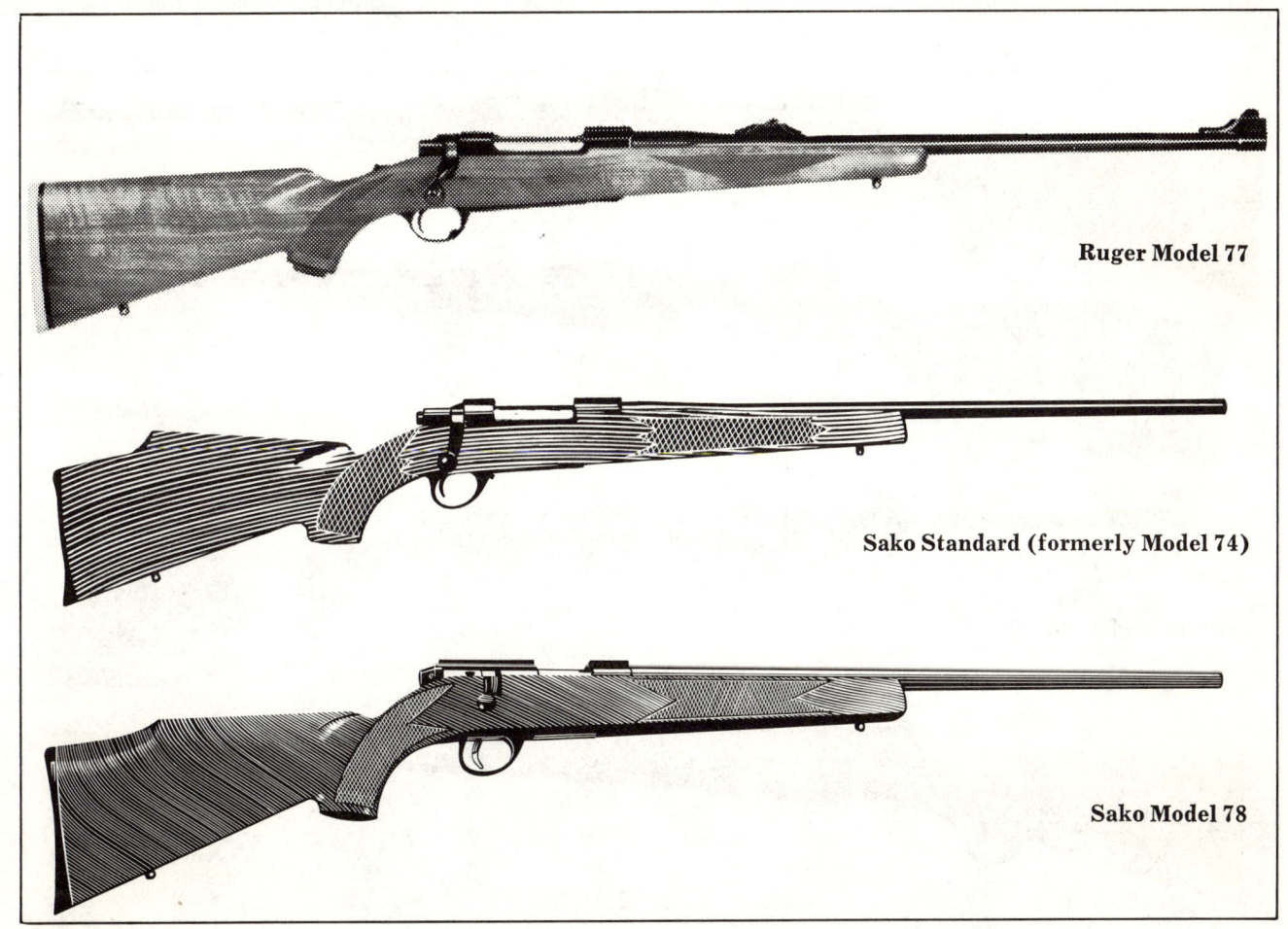

Ruger Model 77

Sako Standard (formerly Model 74)

Sako Model 78

SAVAGE

MODEL 110
Available in several models, a number of calibers, including 7mm Rem Mag, with two styles of magazines. 22-inch barrel, overall length 43 inches, weight about 6¾ lb. Some models also in left-hand version. Removable gold bead front ramp sight, adjustable step rear sight, drilled and tapped for scope mounting, top tang safety. Walnut-finished hardwood stock, Monte Carlo, impressed checkering on pistol grip and forend.

MODEL 111
Similar to M110, but with walnut stock which is hand checkered, wider choice of calibers, including 7x57, open rear sight which is fully adjustable. Standard calibers have 22-inch barrels, while magnums have 24-inch barrels.

MODEL 112-V
Varmint rifle with 26-inch barrel which is free-floated, single shot bolt action. Walnut stock with fluted comb, hand-checkered forend and pistol grip which has Wundhammer swell. White spacer with recoil pad, quick detachable swivels, no sights, action and barrel drilled and tapped for scope mounting.

MODEL 340
Detachable clip magazine holding 4 rounds in 22 Hornet, 222 and 223, 3 rounds in 30-30 caliber. 24-inch and 22-inch barrels respectively, weight about 6½ lb. Walnut stock with Monte Carlo, checkered forend and pistol grip, white line spacers. Ramp front sight with gold bead, folding leaf rear sight, receiver drilled and tapped for scope mounting.

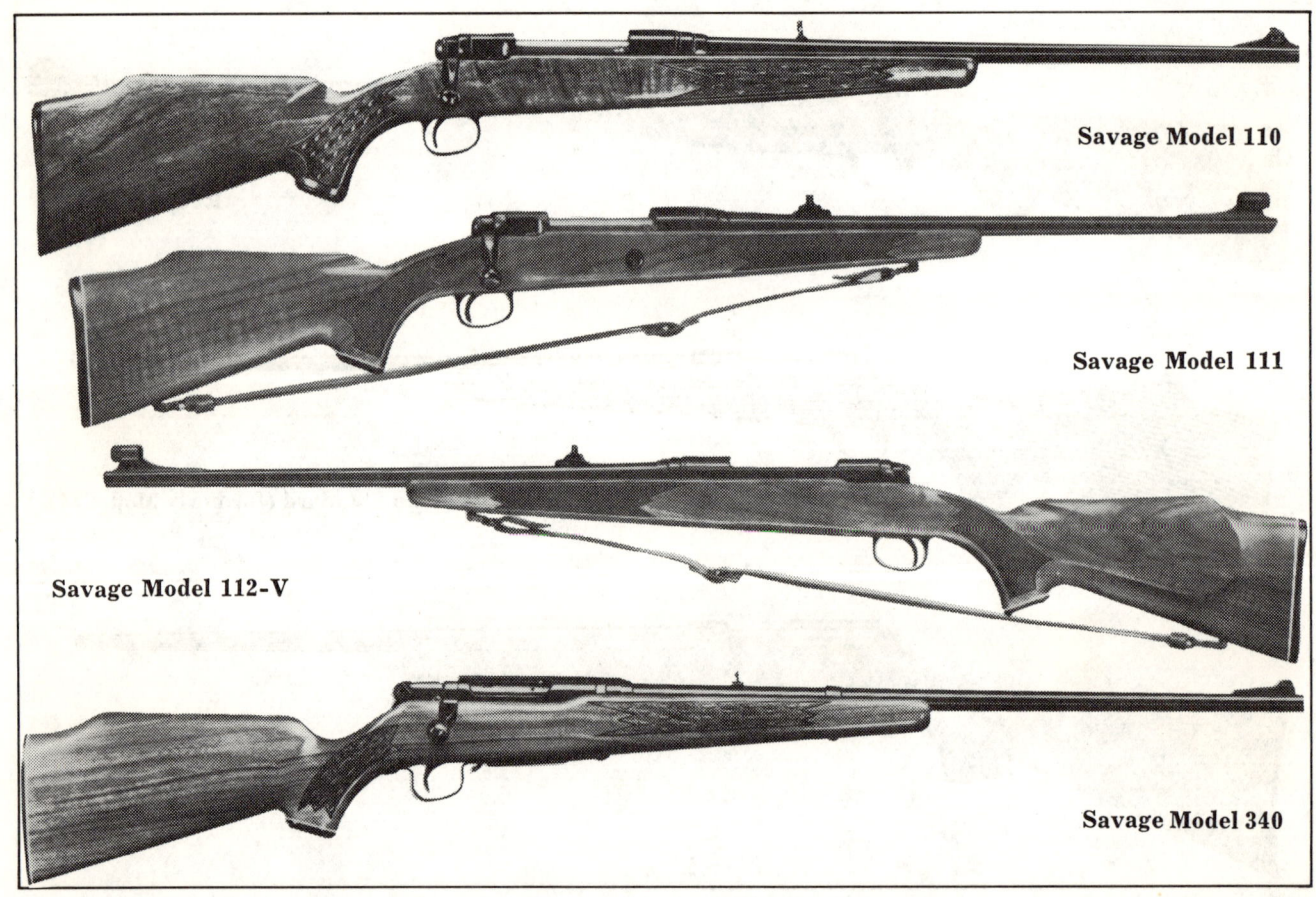

Savage Model 110

Savage Model 111

Savage Model 112-V

Savage Model 340

MODEL 1433-1533

Made in Germany by Anschutz, imported by Savage Arms. 22 Hornet and 222 Rem only. 19¾-inch barrel, 39¾-inch overall length, weight about 6½ lb. Mannlicher-style walnut stock with European cheekpiece, skipline checkering on pistol grip and forend. Ramp front sight with hood, folding leaf rear sight, sling swivels. Single stage trigger, double set trigger available.

WEATHERBY

VANGUARD

Wide choice of standard and magnum calibers, 24-inch barrel, 44½-inch overall length, weight about 8 lb. Walnut stock, hand-checkered pistol grip and forend, grip cap and forend cap, both with white spacers. Hinged floorplate, adjustable trigger, side safety. Sights are optional, action is drilled and tapped for scope mounting.

MARK V

Offered in all proprietary Weatherby calibers, as well as 25-06 and 30-06. Barrel length 24 inches or 26 inches, depending on caliber, weight also varies with caliber. Walnut stock with Monte Carlo and hand-checkered pistol grip and forend, rubber recoil pad, sights are optional, action is drilled and tapped for scope mounting. Adjustable trigger, cocking indicator, hinged floorplate, quick detachable sling swivels. Also in left-hand version.

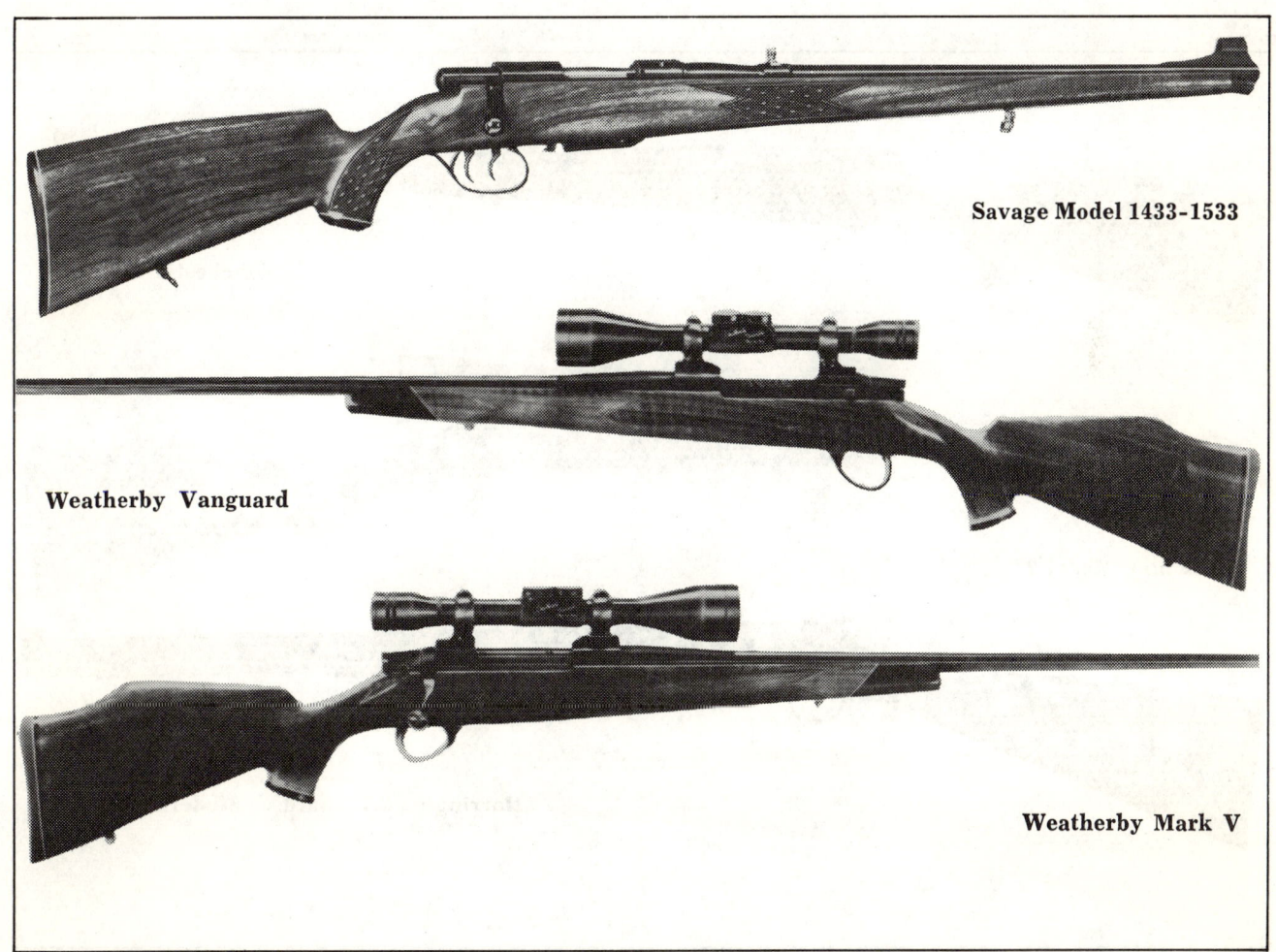

Savage Model 1433-1533

Weatherby Vanguard

Weatherby Mark V

WINCHESTER MODEL 70

Offered in a wide variety of standard and magnum calibers, including varmint, target and police configurations. Barrel length and style depend on model version and caliber, as does weight of rifle. Walnut stock with Monte Carlo comb, checkered pistol grip and forend, rubber recoil pad on magnum rifles. Hinged floorplate, sling swivels. Hooded bead ramp front sight is removable, open adjustable rear sight; no sights on varmint and target models, special rear sight on 458 Win Mag rifle.

SINGLE SHOT

BROWNING MODEL 78

45-70 with 24-inch heavy octagonal barrel, all other calibers with 26-inch tapered octagonal or heavy round barrel. 45-70 has straight grip walnut stock, others have checkered pistol grip and forend. Falling block action with exposed hammer, resembles Winchester Model 1885 High Wall, automatic ejector, adjustable trigger, half-cock safety.

HARRINGTON & RICHARDSON MODEL 155 SHIKARI

44 Mag and 45-70, magnum with 24-inch barrel, 45-70 with 28-inch barrel. Walnut-finished hardwood stock, blade front sight and adjustable rear sight. Color case-hardened frame, exposed hammer, brass cleaning rod with hardwood handle.

Winchester Model 70

Browning Model 78

Harrington & Richardson Model 155 Shikari

MODEL 158 TOPPER
22 Hornet and 30-30, 22-inch barrel, 37½-inch overall length, weight about 5¼ lb. Walnut-finished hardwood stock and forend, exposed hammer, side lever opening. Can be converted to 20 gauge with optional accessory kit.

TRAPDOOR SPRINGFIELD
Officer Model of 1873 and Cavalry Model replicas which are true to the last detail. Trapdoor action, 45-70 only, color case-hardened block and butt plate.

NAVY ARMS

ROLLING BLOCK RIFLE
Replica of Remington Rolling Block, in 45-70 and 444 Marlin. 26-inch barrel, in Buffalo Rifle style or Creedmore style. Walnut-finished hardwood stock.

RUGER

RUGER NUMBER ONE
Choice of calibers, including magnum chamberings, varying barrel lengths, depending on model. Two-piece walnut stock, checkered pistol grip and forend, hammerless falling block, auto ejector, top tang safety. Offered in several

Harrington & Richardson Model 158 Topper

Harrington & Richardson Trapdoor Springfield

Navy Arms Rolling Block Rifle

Ruger Number One

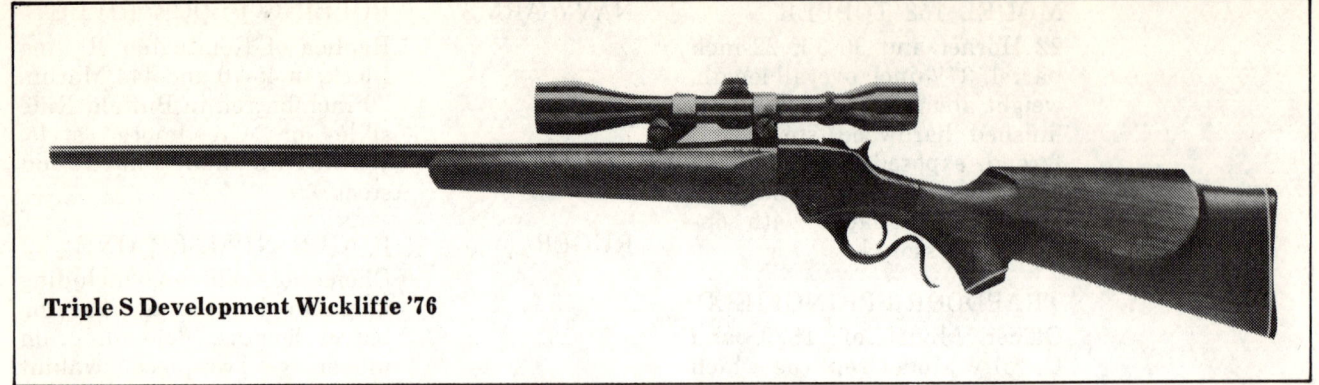

Triple S Development Wickliffe '76

TRIPLE-S DEVELOPMENT

WICKLIFFE '76
Falling block design in a number of calibers, heavy and light weight as well as sporter models are offered. Walnut stock, oil finish appearance, adjustable extractor and ejector, adjustable trigger. No sights, but scope mounts are installed on barrel with extension and 1-inch ring. Deluxe and commemorative models available, the latter only in a limited edition.

styles, such as light and medium sporter, varmint, with some models having sights, others without sights, scope rings come with rifle for integral mount.

Chapter Four
Playing the Numbers

Chapter Four
Playing the Numbers

The numbers used to describe the caliber of a rifle can tell the rifleman a lot of things, but caliber designations can also be confusing. Take the 45-70-500, which is the old Government round. Here, the first number indicates the bore diameter of .45 inch, the 70 refers to the powder charge of 70 grains, and the 500 represents the bullet weight. This cartridge is most often simply called the 45-70 and is best known for the rifle for which it was originally chambered, the Springfield Trapdoor.

What about some of the more modern numbers, like the 257? The first question that should and would be raised is: which 257 — the 257 Roberts or the 257 Weatherby? The Roberts round is based on the old German 7mm Mauser case, which is more precisely referred to as the 7x57, while the Weatherby case is a belted one that was designed by Roy Weatherby.

If a company name is hitched onto the caliber designation, the cartridge is referred to as a proprietary cartridge. Thus, there is the 264 Winchester Magnum, the 22-250 Remington and the Weatherby rounds. But the 257 Roberts, dreamed up by Ned Roberts and originally called the 25 Roberts, paradoxically is not a proprietary cartridge.

The 264 Winchester uses a .263-inch bullet, while the 250-3000 Savage, also known simply as the 250 Savage, uses a bullet with a .257-inch diameter. To make things more interesting, but also more confusing, the 22 Remington Jet cartridge calls for a bullet of .223-inch diameter, while all other 22-caliber rounds require a bullet of .224-inch diameter.

And what about the 30-06 Springfield? This is a 30-caliber cartridge, introduced in 1906, and again, the name of the rifle for which it was chambered was hitched onto the name. But the rifle was the 1903 Springfield, and the 30-06 cartridge, as we know it today, is a modification of the 30-03 round which is now a sought after collector's cartridge.

Because the inch system is gradually being phased out, shooters can expect to see more and more of the metric designations. Mention has

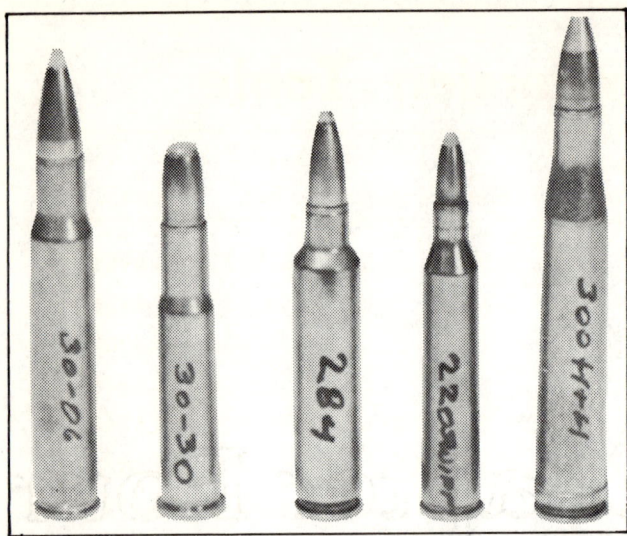

Case design is represented here from left: the 30-06 (rimless); the 30-30 (rimmed); the 284 (rebated); the 220 Swift (semi-rimmed); and the 300 H&H Magnum (belted) which is often used as the basis for powerful wildcat cartridges.

been made of the 7mm Mauser, which is also known as the 7x57. The first number indicates bullet diameter or sometimes the bore diameter in millimeters, while the second number describes the case length — here, 57mm or 2.244 inches. Germany was long a leader in the development of new rifles and cartridges; the exclusive use of the metric system to describe a cartridge goes back to days before World War I.

Like the British designers and North American cartridge designers, the Germans often hitched on special cartridge designations. The British gunmakers, developing loads and cartridges for double rifles, offered such descriptive numbers as the 500 No. 2 Express or the 500 Nitro Express for Black Powder. Winchester had the 38-90 Winchester Express, and the 351 Winchester SL (for Self-Loading) describes itself. The Von Hofe Super Express cartridges in their various configurations were once thought to be the hottest things in cartridges in Germany.

Belted cartridge cases have been around for a long time, as have rimmed cases like the 30-30 Winchester. The British rifle makers being rather precise, decided to give some cartridges extra designations that would better describe the cases. Consequently, we have the 375 Belted Nitro Express, now known as the 375 Holland & Holland, or simply H&H. There are two 333s around in Great Britain, one the 333 Flanged or Rimmed NE, this meaning Nitro Express, and the 33 Belted Rimless NE, which was produced for some time by BSA and was also known as the 330 BSA.

Caliber designations, then, indicate the inside diameter of the barrel, the measure being taken either from land to land, in which case the measurement is called the bore diameter, or from groove to groove, when it is called groove diameter. The illustration will make it easier to understand this matter of bore and groove diameter. However, there is no rational explanation why the Germans also call 8mm rounds 7.92 or 7.9.

WILDCATS

The 25 Roberts began as a wildcat cartridge — that is, no factory rifles were chambered for it, and no factory ammunition was available. The person who wanted one had to have the rifle made up by a gunsmith and then had to handload his own ammunition. Some of the better-known cartridges have been around for so long that a lot of shooters have forgotten that these rounds started out as wildcats. Gebby's 22-250 was originally called the Varminter, and there are at least eight different versions of the Varminter available. Some are based on the 250 Savage case, another on the 7x57, still another on the 257 Roberts case. For one such wildcat, the 250-22-4000, it was claimed that the necked-down 250 case with a .224-inch bullet could develop 4000 feet-per-second (fps) muzzle velocity. A few years ago, Remington Arms revived the old Gebby round, and now we have the 22-250 Remington, as well as the 25-06 which, of course, is nothing more than the necked-down '06 case with a .257-inch bullet.

What's the reason behind wildcat cartridges? Take that old warhorse, the 30-06 round, for instance. The shoulder angle of the '06 case is 17 degrees and 30 minutes, which means that the shoulder is fairly steep. P. O. Ackley increased the powder capacity of the case by altering the shoulder angle to 40 degrees. The degree of shoulder alteration for increased powder capacity varies from gunsmith to gunsmith, and

English-Metric Conversion Table

Inches Dec.	mm	Inches Dec.	mm	Inches Frac.	Dec.	mm	Inches Frac.	Dec.	mm
0.01	0.2540	0.51	12.9540	1/64	0.015625	0.3969	33/64	0.515625	13.0969
0.02	0.5080	0.52	13.2080	1/32	0.031250	0.7938	17/32	0.531250	13.4938
0.03	0.7620	0.53	13.4620	3/64	0.046875	1.1906	35/64	0.546875	13.8906
0.04	1.0160	0.54	13.7160	1/16	0.062500	1.5875	9/16	0.562500	14.2875
0.05	1.2700	0.55	13.9700						
0.06	1.5240	0.56	14.2240	5/64	0.078125	1.9844	37/64	0.578125	14.6844
0.07	1.7780	0.57	14.4780	3/32	0.093750	2.3812	19/32	0.593750	15.0812
0.08	2.0320	0.58	14.7320	7/64	0.109375	2.7781	39/64	0.609375	15.4781
0.09	2.2860	0.59	14.9860						
0.10	2.5400	0.60	15.2400	1/8	0.125000	3.1750	5/8	0.625000	15.8750
0.11	2.7940	0.61	15.4940						
0.12	3.0480	0.62	15.7480	9/64	0.140625	3.5719	41/64	0.640625	16.2719
0.13	3.3020	0.63	16.0020	5/32	0.156250	3.9688	21/32	0.656250	16.6688
0.14	3.5560	0.64	16.2560	11/64	0.171875	4.3656	43/64	0.671875	17.0656
0.15	3.8100	0.65	16.5100	3/16	0.187500	4.7625	11/16	0.687500	17.4625
0.16	4.0640	0.66	16.7640						
0.17	4.3180	0.67	17.0180	13/64	0.203125	5.1594	45/64	0.703125	17.8594
0.18	4.5720	0.68	17.2720	7/32	0.218750	5.5562	23/32	0.718750	18.2562
0.19	4.8260	0.69	17.5260	15/64	0.234375	5.9531	47/64	0.734375	18.6531
0.20	5.0800	0.70	17.7800						
0.21	5.3340	0.71	18.0340	1/4	0.250000	6.3500	3/4	0.750000	19.0500
0.22	5.5880	0.72	18.2880	17/64	0.265625	6.7469	49/64	0.765625	19.4469
0.23	5.8420	0.73	18.5420	9/32	0.281250	7.1438	25/32	0.781250	19.8437
0.24	6.0960	0.74	18.7960	19/64	0.296875	7.5406	51/64	0.796875	20.2406
0.25	6.3500	0.75	19.0500	5/16	0.312500	7.9375	13/16	0.812500	20.6375
0.26	6.6040	0.76	19.3040						
0.27	6.8580	0.77	19.5580	21/64	0.328125	8.3344	53/64	0.828125	21.0344
0.28	7.1120	0.78	19.8120	11/32	0.343750	8.7312	27/32	0.843750	21.4312
0.29	7.3660	0.79	20.0660	23/64	0.359375	9.1281	55/64	0.859375	21.8281
0.30	7.6200	0.80	20.3200						
0.31	7.8740	0.81	20.5740	3/8	0.375000	9.5250	7/8	0.875000	22.2250
0.32	8.1280	0.82	20.8280						
0.33	8.3820	0.83	21.0820	25/64	0.390625	9.9219	57/64	0.890625	22.6219
0.34	8.6360	0.84	21.3360	13/32	0.406250	10.3188	29/32	0.906250	23.0188
0.35	8.9000	0.85	21.5900	27/64	0.421875	10.7156	59/64	0.921875	23.4156
0.36	9.1440	0.86	21.8440	7/16	0.437500	11.1125	15/16	0.937500	23.8125
0.37	9.3980	0.87	22.0980						
0.38	9.6520	0.88	22.3520	29/64	0.453125	11.5094	61/64	0.953125	24.2094
0.39	9.9060	0.89	22.6060	15/32	0.468750	11.9062	31/32	0.968750	24.6062
0.40	10.1600	0.90	22.8600	31/64	0.484375	12.3031	63/64	0.984375	25.0031
0.41	10.4140	0.91	23.1140	1/2	0.500000	12.7000	1	1.000000	25.4000
0.42	10.6680	0.92	23.3680						
0.43	10.9220	0.93	23.6220						
0.44	11.1760	0.94	23.8760						
0.45	11.4300	0.95	24.1300						
0.46	11.6840	0.96	24.3840						
0.47	11.9380	0.97	24.6380						
0.48	12.1920	0.98	24.8920						
0.49	12.4460	0.99	25.1460						
0.50	12.7000	1.00	25.4000						

The metric system is quite simple once you learn a few of the metric landmarks. The 223 is the 5.56, the 6mm is the 243, while the 8mm is the same as the 323.

PLAYING THE NUMBERS

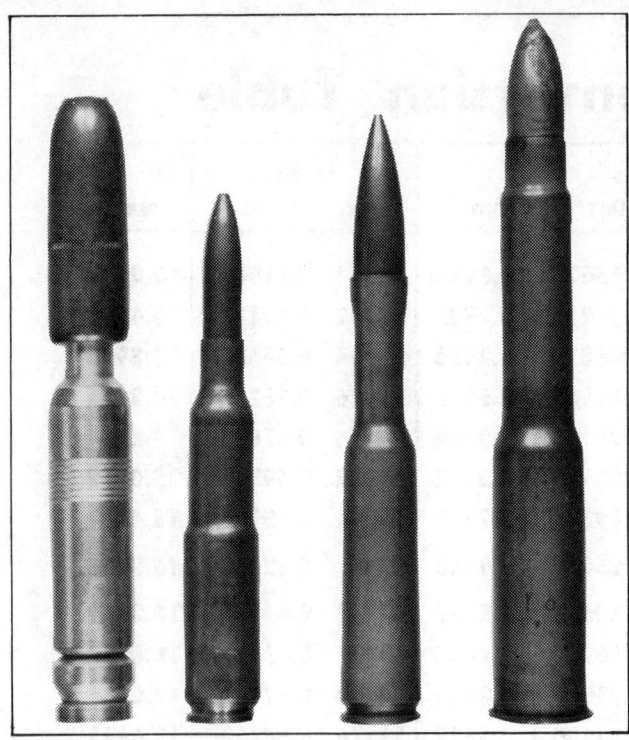

These impossible wildcats are the result of a couple of idle hours, some case forming dies, and the availability of a lathe for the way-out creation at left.

The carefully worked out design of a wildcat does not always guarantee that the new cartridge will do better than any of the existing numbers. The 7mm RCBS, based at first on the 9.3x64 case and then on the 300 Winchester case, fell far short of expectations.

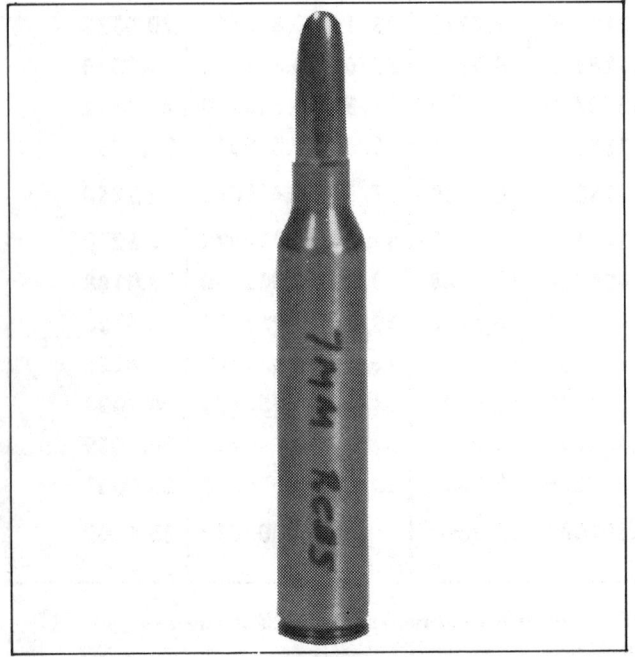

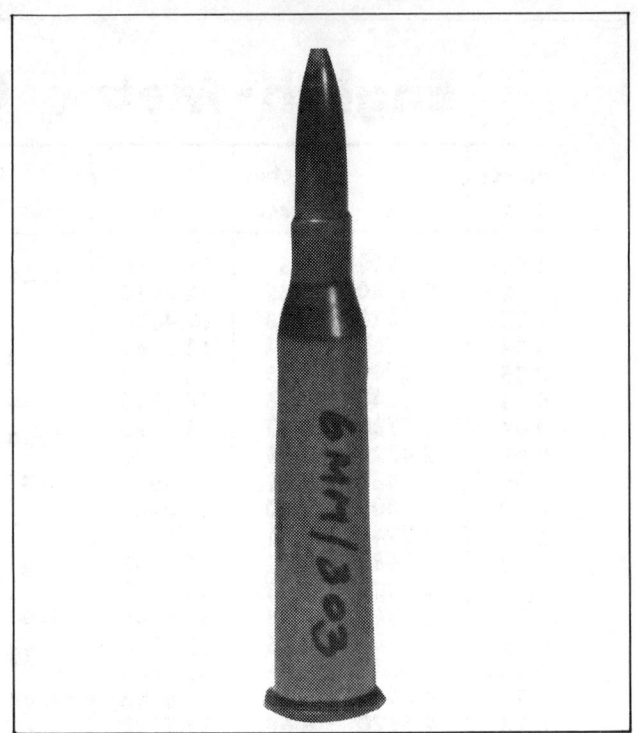

One of author's pet wildcat cartridges is the 6mm/303 British Improved. Very accurate out to 300 yards, cases for this round are made easily in contrast to some other wildcat designs.

there are at least six different versions of the 257 Roberts Improved, sometimes abbreviated to Imp. In the case of the 257 Roberts, it's a wildcat that's been wildcatted!

Converting one of your standard caliber rifles to an Improved caliber is not too difficult. The gunsmith will run an improved reamer into the chamber of the rifle, and in most instances, you then fire standard rounds in the improved chamber, with the brass coming out of the gun with the improved shoulder. Of course, such a cartridge is now a handloading proposition, so you'll have to get suitable loading dies, or have the old ones altered to conform to the new case configuration.

Some of the Improved wildcats are good, some mediocre, and others have proved to be useless. Stuffing more power into a case is no guarantee that the ultimate performance of the cartridge is going to be much better than the original performance level. As a dedicated wildcatter, I hate to admit it, but a lot of the wildcats one hears and reads about are busts.

Winchester High-Wall action with bull barrel were the basics for the 6mm/303 British Improved. Oregon myrtle stock blank had been seasoned for several years before being converted into this handsome stock. Scope is the old Balvar 24.

Some years ago, a friend and I dreamed up what we thought would be one heck of a wildcat. Using the 9.3x64 Brennecke case and necking it down to 7mm, we thought we would create an unbelted 7mm magnum. What we actually wound up with was a round that was not only costly because Brennecke brass is hard to get as well as expensive, but also, on the range and after chronographing the various loads, we had a round that was slower than the 7mm Remington Magnum and far less accurate.

On the other hand, I have a 6mm/303 British Improved that is an almost unbelievable tack-driver. Made on a Winchester High-Wall action with a heavy bull barrel, and stocked with a beautiful piece of Oregon myrtle, the performance of the rifle, as well as the rifle itself, creates a stir wherever I take the gun.

Obviously, not every wildcat cartridge will set the shooting world on its collective ear. However, there are just enough good ones around and just enough new ones are concocted with some regularity to make wildcatting an interesting aspect of rifle shooting. Sometimes, wildcats are purely accidental. When quantities of the Japanese Thai surplus rifle actions became available, the first question raised was, "What can I do with it?" The action does not lend itself readily to extensive internal alterations, but some genius discovered that the case head of the 30-06 round would fit the bolt perfectly, and as the result of some experimenting, an unrimmed version of the 444 Marlin was developed. The straightened-out '06 case delivers ballistics very similar to those obtained from the Marlin round, and that cartridge is a proven brush buster.

As with factory loads, a wildcatter will often add his name to his ballistic brainchild, or something that describes the cartridge. Thus,

PLAYING THE NUMBERS

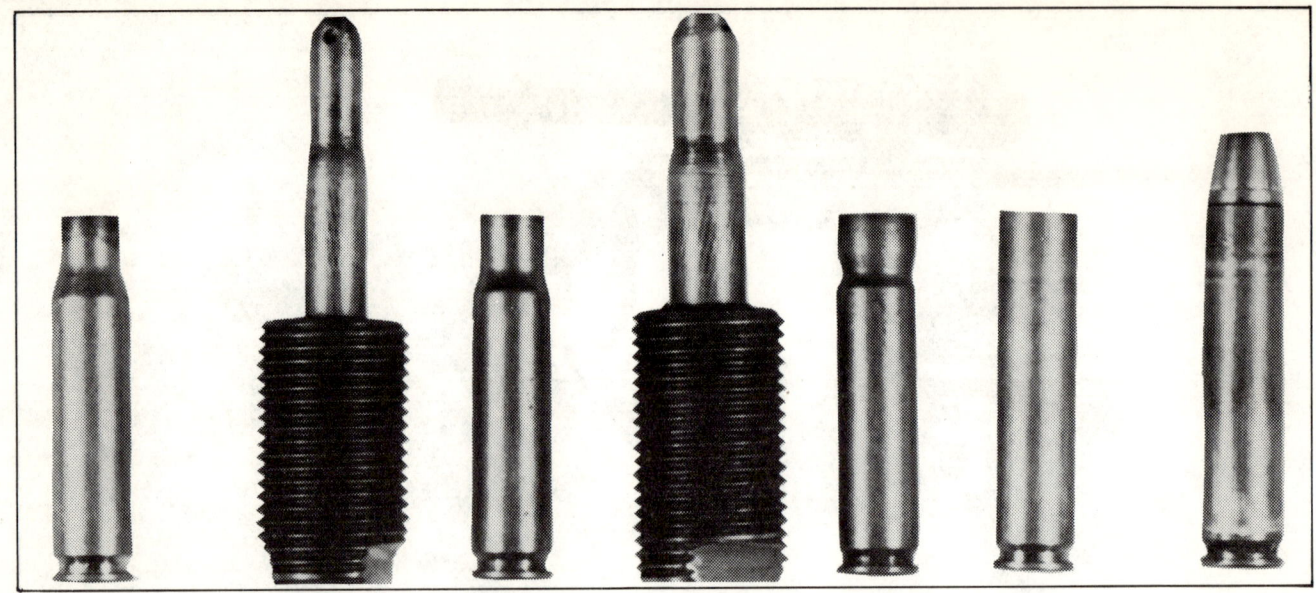

When the Japanese Thai actions were sold for about $20, the question that arose was: What can you do with it? Well, with a 44-caliber barrel you can make a rimless 444, the counterparts of the rimmed Marlin round. These are case forming steps, starting with the 30-06 case.

you have such handles as the 348-401 Longo Screwball, the late Warren Page's Super Pooper, the Arrow, Lightning and dozens of other more or less descriptive names. I prefer to use the designation I gave above for my pet 6mm, since it immediately conveys to the shooter an idea of what the case might look like.

Some of the more advanced wildcatters go overboard. In my wildcat cartridge collection I have a half dozen or more really wild wildcats. Some are based on rimmed cases that have had the rim lathed off and — believe it or not — an extractor groove added. In some, the shoulder has been blown out until it is almost totally flat; in others, the neck has been lengthened to permit more secure bullet seating.

RIFLE VERSATILITY

The search for greater versatility of a given rifle or caliber goes on and on. Some calibers lend themselves to greater versatility than others. The 30-06, for instance, does a reasonably fair job as varmint rifle when you use the 110-grain factory loads or when you load your own varmint ammo. The same rifle, with the 220-grain bullet, is a good big-game rifle and, in the hands of a good shot, has taken many large trophies, including the big bears. In contrast to that, most of the magnums have relatively limited versatility, such as the 44 Magnum round in rifles or carbines.

Almost every big-game hunter has been in the position of having a shot offered at a species for which he was, at the moment, sadly over-gunned. Moreover, the boom of a big bore rifle might scare his sought-after game clear out of the county, and so the hunter regretfully passes up the shot. For a time it was thought that rifles with interchangeable barrels, such as the Mauser Model 600, would be the answer — providing, of course, that you had the time and the tools to change barrels quickly. Unfortunately, extensive tests conducted on the M600 showed that the gun, although well designed and well made, simply was not spectacular as far as performance and accuracy were concerned.

German gun makers tackled the problem of rifle versatility many years ago and came up with some near-perfect solutions. Most suitable for bolt-action rifles, as well as some handguns, you can buy chamber inserts which allow you, for instance, to fire a 30 carbine round from a 300 Winchester Magnum rifle. This system of a chamber insert or auxiliary chamber was popu-

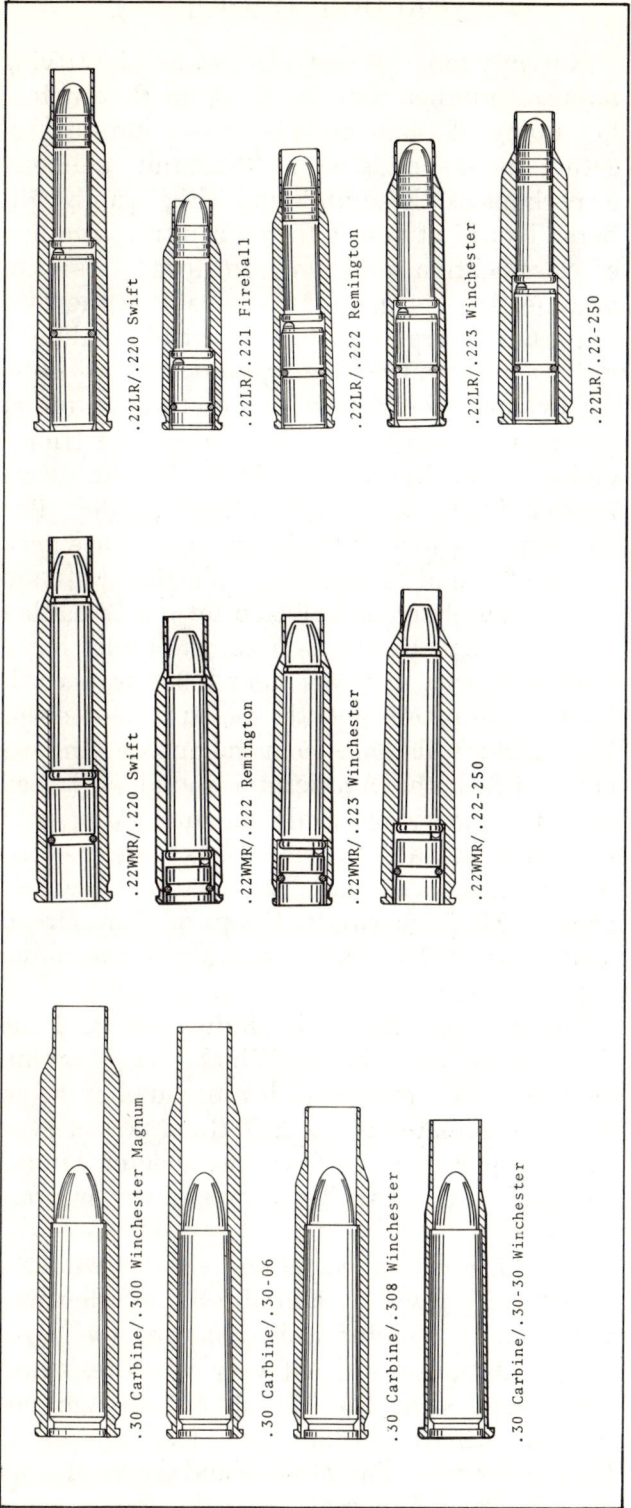

Barrel inserts allow the shooter to use either a rimfire or a smaller centerfire round. For instance, Sport Specialties offers five inserts for centerfire rifles which are used with 22LR inserts. Four such inserts are offered for the 22 Winchester RF Magnum round, while four are offered for the 30 carbine round.

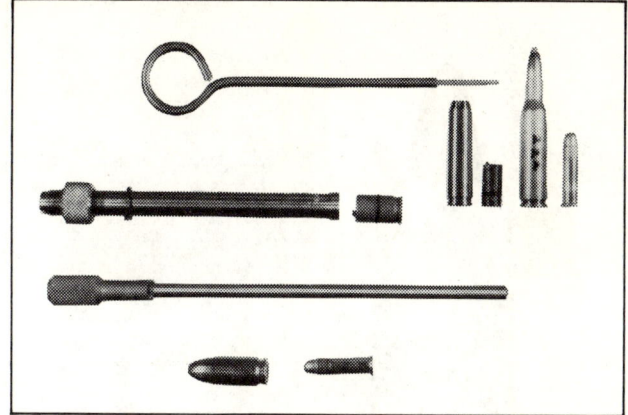

Barrel and chamber inserts probably had their origin in Germany where Walther has been the leader in making these inserts. Chamber inserts are used in rifles as shown in upper right, while barrel inserts are used in handguns, including semiautomatic pistols.

larized by Marble Arms many years ago, and these Marble chamber inserts are now rare collector's specimens.

The firing of a smaller caliber cartridge in a larger chamber and bore can be accomplished either by inserting a partial barrel with its own chamber into the gun, or by simply inserting a smaller chamber into the rifle's chamber and then utilizing the barrel of the rifle for the projectiles. The Walther chamber inserts, as well as those sold by Sports Specialties (P.O. Box 5337, Hacienda Heights, CA 91745), are highly functional accessories. However, they do not allow rapid or repeated firing of the smaller cartridge. In most of these, the chamber insert is removed from the rifle chamber by the extractor, and then the spent case must be pushed out of the auxiliary chamber. Once a fresh round is placed in the chamber insert, the insert itself must be chambered in the rifle, if a second shot is desired.

Barrel inserts for shotguns are based on a similar concept, and these often permit the owner of a double-barrel shotgun to use one or both barrels for firing rimfire rounds, most often the 22 Long Rifle cartridge. I have never seen a rifled shotgun insert that was chambered for anything but a rimfire cartridge, but this is reasonable because shotgun actions are not designed to withstand the much higher chamber pressures generated by rifle cartridges.

The Remington Accelerator round and a plastic sabot that falls away from the speeding bullet. Offered only in 30-06 at the present, the Accelerator round effectively converts an '06 into a 22-caliber centerfire rifle, although accuracy and effective range cannot be compared with that of the standard 222 Remington round or rifle.

CALIBER CHOICE

Not only have all cartridges some identifying name or number, such as the 6mm Remington, but many of them are also often lumped together under such labels as "Varmint" calibers, or perhaps as "Medium" and "Big" game calibers. This is, at best, a highly arbitrary method of classification, and you can always start an argument by stating, for instance, that the 243s or the 6mms are too potent as varmint calibers, but are just great for deer hunters.

Obviously, the 30-06 with the 110-grain bullet can easily double as a fair varmint cartridge, and when fed Remington's 30-06/224 Accelerator round, any '06 becomes a varmint rifle. The 55-grain .224-inch bullet is held in the case neck of the '06 round by means of a plastic sabot, and the powder charge is adjusted for the 22-caliber bullet. When the gun is fired, the bullet has a muzzle velocity of better than 4000 fps, according to Remington, and the plastic sabot drops away a short distance from the muzzle. In bolt-action rifles, the Accelerator round will feed from the magazine, while in autoloading and pump-action rifles, the round has to be inserted into the chamber manually. Accuracy averages about 2 MOA, or two inches maximum spread at 100 yards. Naturally, accuracy of the round depends also on the rifle and the rifleman.

Varmint Calibers: Excluding the 22 Long Rifle round and the 22 Winchester Magnum rimfire rounds, the choice is a broad one. From the 17 Remington to the 257 Roberts and even the various 6mms or 243s, the shooter can select a varmint cartridge from a rather impressive array.

The 17 Remington and the various wildcats in this caliber will do a creditable job downing varmints, if the wind is not blowing too hard. The light bullets are not very wind resistant, and handloading the 17 calibers, though not difficult, is more of a chore than loading some of the larger cases. The 218 Bee and the 22 Hornet are still around and will be with us for years to come. The 221 Remington Fireball in a rifle—but not commercially chambered—is a fair varmint number. The 222 Remington and the 222 Remington Magnum and the 223 (better known as the 5.56mm in military terminology)

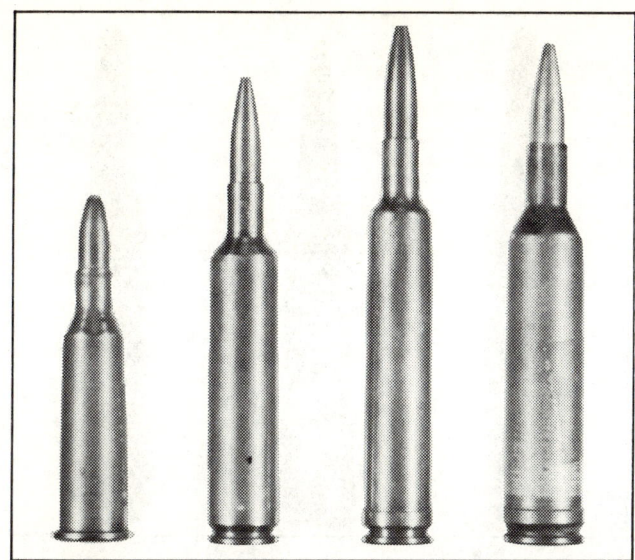
The search for a better 22 goes on and on. Four 22 caliber wildcats are shown here, from left: 22/Krag, 22/257 Roberts, a 22/240 Weatherby, and a 22/300 H&H which would be over bore capacity.

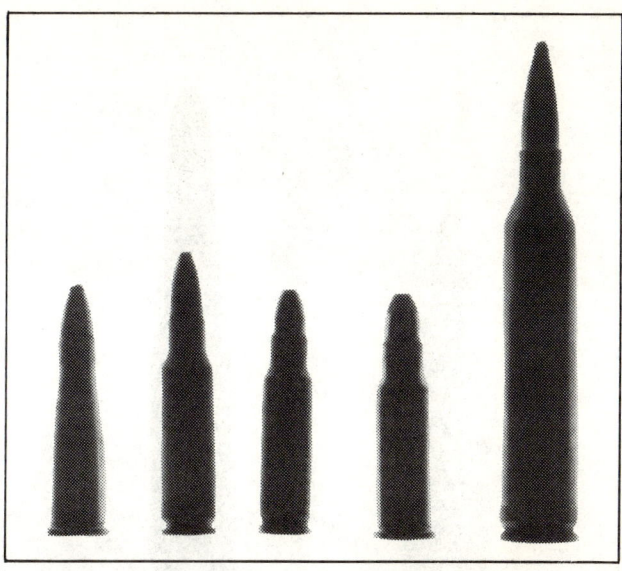
Factory rounds which have passed their peak of popularity. From left: the 22 Jet, the 221 Remington or Fireball, the 5.7mm Johnson, the 256 Winchester Magnum, and the 264 Winchester Magnum.

are good choices for the varmint hunter. All three cartridges have much to recommend them: easy reloading, ready availability of ammo and reloading components, as well as an excellent accuracy potential. The same goes for the 22-250 Remington.

The 224 Weatherby, dubbed the Varmintmaster, is just that. I have used this very flat-shooting cartridge on some long shots with complete satisfaction. The 6mms — and that includes the 243 Winchester, the 6mm Remington and the 240 Weatherby Magnum with its belted case — are good choices for the larger varmints, such as fox and coyote, at the longer ranges. These cartridges also do a fine job on deer of all kinds, providing you don't try using them in brushy country where the light bullets have little chance of punching through brush and vegetation.

In the 25 calibers, the 257 Roberts, the 250-3000 Savage, the 25-06 Remington and the 257 Weatherby are, with the light bullets, quite suitable for varmint hunting, and with heavier bullets are often thought of as ideal deer rounds.

The 270 Winchester with the 100-grain bullet, the 30-06 with the 100-grain bullet and the 308 Winchester, also known as the 7.62 NATO round, with the 100-grain bullet, are all adequate, providing your medium- or big-game rifle is properly sighted in for the light bullets.

Popping a rabbit with a rimfire round is perfectly acceptable, but once the range stretches out to 100 yards or longer and the intended target is a tough one, such as a fox, then a rimfire is not the ideal cartridge. Some of the cartridges are usually seen only in handgun configurations, such as the 22 Remington Jet, the 256 Winchester Magnum and the 22 K-Hornet. The Jet is a bit on the light side for the bigger animals, while the 256 and the K-Hornet have proved to be adequate in the hands of a rifleman equipped with a good, scoped rifle.

Medium-Game Calibers: In this class, I would consider whitetail and blacktail deer, mule deer, antelope, mountain goat and sheep. At the low end of the scale in rifles would be the 6mms, the 270, the 280 Remington and the 284 Winchester, the 308 Winchester, and the 30-06. The 25 caliber numbers would have to be considered as marginal, although I have shot deer and other game in this class with one of my favorite 257 Roberts rifles. For long range shots, the 7mm Remington Magnum and the 264 Winchester Magnum have proved to be effective.

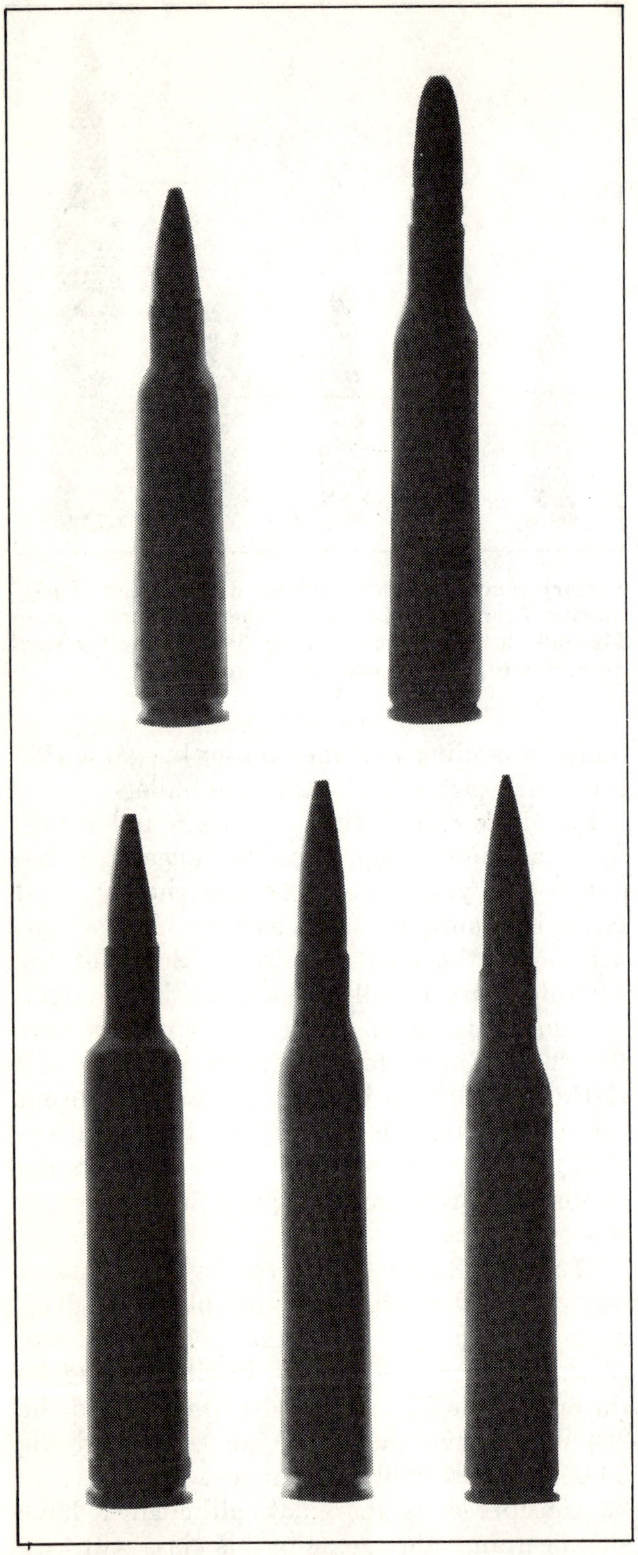

Shadowgraph of a family of 25-caliber factory rounds. In the usual order, the 250-3000 also sometimes called the 250 Savage, the 257 Roberts, the 257 Weatherby, the 25-06 which began life as a wildcat just like its smaller sisters, and the now obsolete 256 Newton.

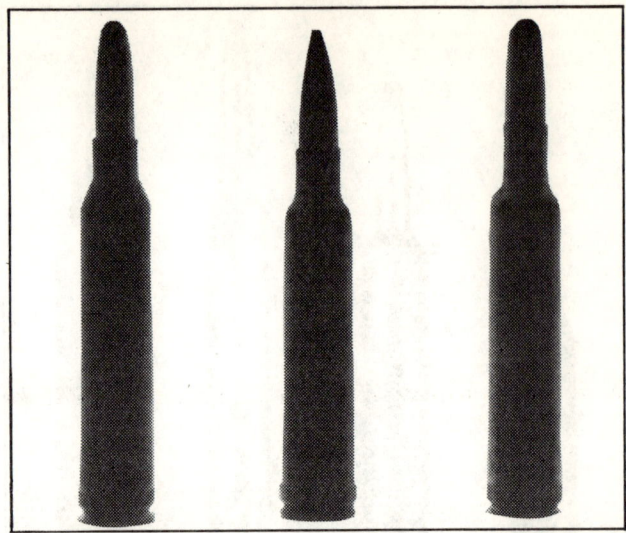

Sisters under the skin—the belted 7s, from left: the 7mm Remington Magnum, the 7x61 S&H, and the 7mm Weatherby Magnum. The shoulders vary considerably as shown in shadowgraph, but performances are quite similar.

In brush country, the picture changes dramatically. The 30-30 Winchester and the 35 Remington, the 444 Marlin and the 44 Magnum are good choices. With the heavier bullets, the 308 Winchester and the 30-06 will not let you down.

The 7x57 and the 6.5x55 Swedish Mauser, as well as the 6.5x54 Mannlicher-Schoenauer, are fine cartridges. The 7mm Mauser, made up into a light mountain rifle weighing no more than seven pounds, complete with scope and sling, is effective on medium as well as on large game with suitable bullets.

Big-Game Calibers: By North American standards, this group would include elk, moose and the big bears. On the other hand, many hunters would include elephants, tigers, lions, Cape buffalo and rhinos in this category. Therefore, it seems best to group these game animals together by the calibers used to hunt them, rather than by the size of the animals.

The '06 with the heavier bullets and the 308 Winchester will fill the bill at the lower end of the scale. So will the 7mm Remington Magnum, the 8mm Remington Magnum, the 338 Winchester and the 340 Weatherby Magnums. The venerable 300 H&H Magnum still has a number of followers, although it has been re-

Does the 340 Weatherby really kick?

PLAYING THE NUMBERS

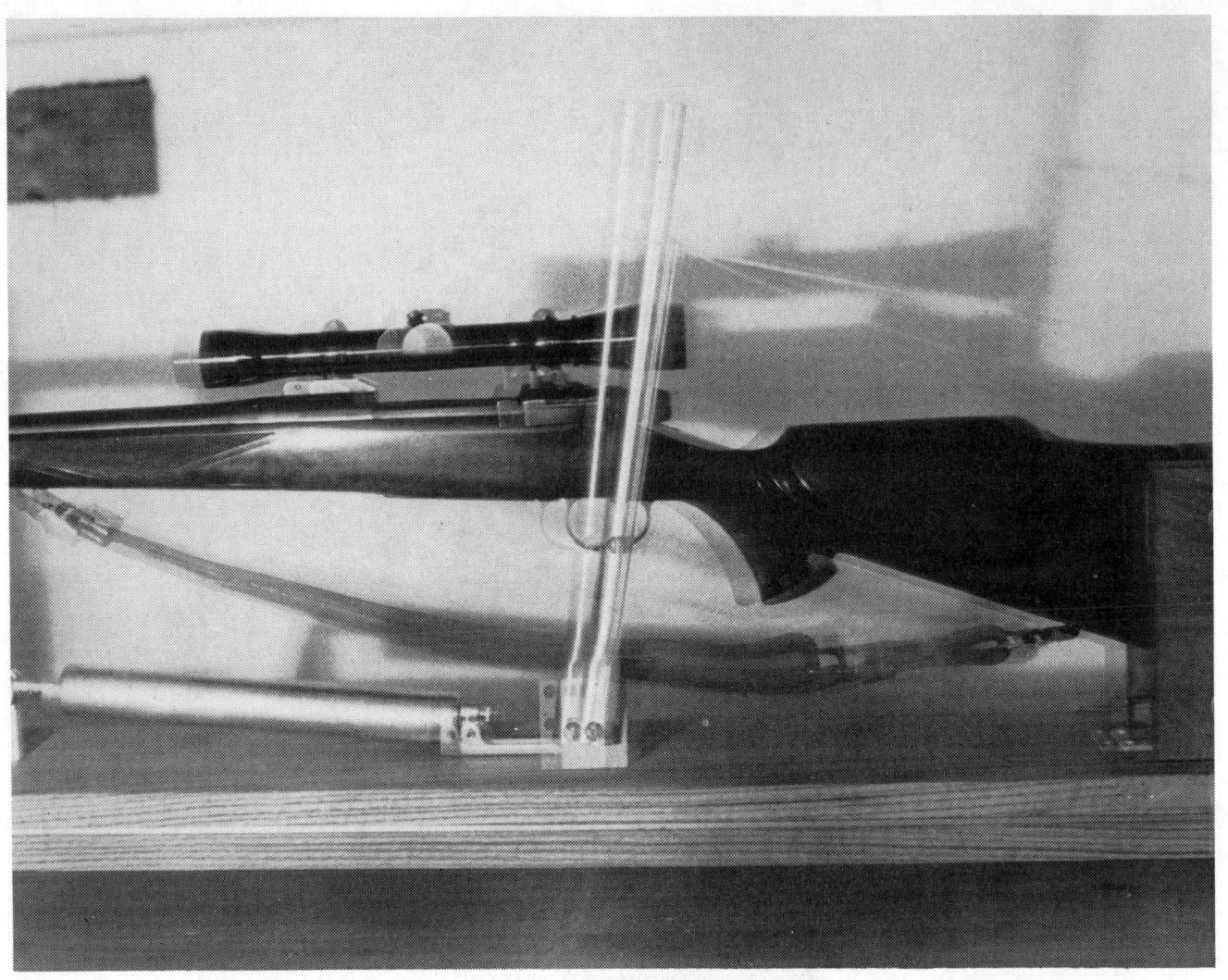

One of the better big-game wildcat cartridges is the 338-06, which is the '06 case opened up to .338 inch. Cartridge functions through a standard-length action, and rifle shown here is chambered for this wildcat. Recoil is much milder than that of the standard 338 Magnum or the 340 Weatherby which is quite similar to the 338.

placed to some extent by the 300 Winchester and the 300 Weatherby Magnums. The 308 Norma Magnum is in the same class as the other 30 caliber numbers, but has lost some of its popularity in recent years. Somewhere between the medium-game and the big-game class, especially in brushy country, are the 348 and the 358 Winchester rounds, both somewhat obsolete.

When it comes to the big bears and the big-game animals of Africa and India, you cannot be undergunned. If recoil and blast do not affect your shooting performance, the 375 H&H and even the 458 Winchester will do nicely.

Of course, the big Weatherby rounds have also stood the test of time.

Most of the British big-game cartridges were designed for double rifles, and quite a few of these are black powder cartridges. Ammunition for all the British big-game calibers is hard to find, and should you fall heir to a double rifle, you may have to resort to handloading. The black powder rifles, in particular, can often be found relatively inexpensively—note that I said "relatively." All of these double rifles are regulated for a given bullet weight and a specific powder charge. Regulating, in this instance, means that both barrels will shoot very close to

Grizzly squared 8½ feet, fell to one 150-grain 30-caliber bullet fired from a wildcatted 300 H&H rifle. Although a bit small for this type of game, proper bullet placement did the trick for author.

PLAYING THE NUMBERS

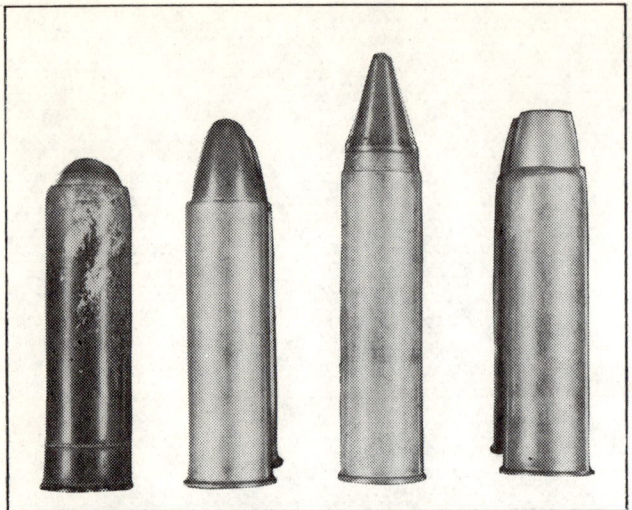

British gun makers for years produced shotguns which had the last several inches of the barrel rifled. The Explora and the Paradox were often used in India on the big Bengal tigers at very close ranges. At far left, a brass shotshell loaded with an Explora slug, two original Paradox rounds, and a handloaded copy of the Paradox. Cast very hard, the load grouped within two inches at 50 yards which is just about maximum range for the Paradox gun and load.

point of aim with the correct ammunition for that particular rifle. Of course, this becomes very important when a rhino is charging you at 60 miles per hour.

Worth noting here is the British Paradox. Designed for hunting Bengal tigers in high brush from atop an elephant, the Paradox guns are smoothbored except for the last few inches of the barrel near the muzzle. The ammunition comes in 8, 10 and 12 bore, and there are at least two types of projectiles that look more like a slug, but behave more like a bullet, because of the rifling.

More than one airborne Bengal tiger has dropped dead when hit by one or two of these 750-grain slugs. As a result of the shallow and rather broad rifling, the projectiles from these guns are accurate at 100 and 150 yards. The Explora is the name Westley Richards gave to their version of this round. It is said to have a muzzle velocity of about 1300 fps. A word of caution might be in order — if someone should ever ask you to fire either a Paradox or an Explora, be sure it's a 12-bore gun. The 8-and 10-bore guns, although usually quite heavy, are sure to induce a badly bruised shoulder, as I found out some years ago when I was asked to develop special handloads for an 8-bore Paradox.

It is better and a lot safer to be somewhat overgunned when hunting grizzlies and other big game that have a reputation of being short tempered. Some Alaskan guides use shortened 375 H&H rifles for backup in thick brush, and though the blast and kick are on the fearsome side, you won't really notice it when a big Kodiak bear comes straight at you.

By the same token, nobody would consider the 7mm Remington Magnum as the ideal varmint rifle, especially when loaded with a 175-grain bullet. But on a remote hunting trip in the Yukon Territory with no meat in camp, I used just that combination to collect some whistling marmots for the stew pot. Obviously then, caliber-game recommendations are very general guidelines at best.

Chapter Five
Rifle Ballistics

Chapter Five
Rifle Ballistics

Ballistics — the term comes from the Latin *ballista,* the military engine the old Romans used to hurl large missiles at the enemy — is a fascinating but somewhat complicated subject. By definition, ballistics is the science of a projectile in motion, but it is necessary to differentiate between internal and external ballistics.

Internal ballistics, despite highly sophisticated technology, is still not wholly understood, since it concerns phenomena which take place inside the cartridge case as the powder burns. Up to now, we have not found a way of looking inside the case at that precise moment. After the bullet has been forced out of the case mouth by the mounting gas pressure created by the burning powder, it engages the rifling; while the bullet is moving the length of the barrel and before it exits from the muzzle (this time span being known as barrel time), it is all part and parcel of internal or interior ballistics.

Once the bullet leaves the muzzle, gravitational pull begins to exert its force on the bullet, as do atmospheric conditions such as wind and rain. When the bullet finally either hits the intended target or has lost all its velocity, we refer to terminal ballistics. However, terminal ballistics has also come to mean the ballistics of a projectile at the target, and here we are usually concerned with the velocity and bullet energy, or knock-down power. The deer hunter taking a shot at a whitetail 75 yards away is not interested in the terminal ballistics of the bullet at 2000 or maybe 5000 yards. He wants to know whether his load will do the job at 75 yards, and that is the terminal ballistics we are most concerned with.

Internal ballistics includes not only the burning rate of the propellant powder as well as the amount of powder, but also the temperature of ignition, the shape of the powder charge and the powder particles and the number of burning surfaces each granule has, plus the moisture content of the powder. The location of the powder charge in the cartridge case, near the primer or perhaps concentrated near the base of the bullet, affects the rate of the burning and the formation of the gases created by the burning powder. Bullet pull, or the force

The ancient Greeks used the ballista and catapult with telling results (from W.W. Greener).

needed to push the bullet from the case mouth, also affects the eventual flight of the bullet. The degree of brisance, a fancy word for the explosive power contained in the priming mix, affects internal as well as external ballistics.

The degree of hardness of the primer cup metal, as well as that of the cartridge case, plays a role in internal ballistics. There is even some evidence that the handloader who cleans the primer pockets of cartridge cases will get results somewhat different than the fellow who fails to clean primer pockets on his brass.

Just how carefully the chamber of the rifle was cut, the amount of free-bore, if any, the distance the bullet has to move from case mouth until it meets the first land, the degree of wear on the leading edges of the land, rust and corrosion, and even barrel temperature and barrel time affect the bullet's flight.

The shape of the bullet is another important ballistic consideration. The flat-nosed bullet of the 44 Magnum round encounters more air resistance than the spitzer bullet, and jacket thickness and bullet core hardness dictate how easily the bullet will accept the rifling. As we have already seen, bullet spin is the key to accuracy at almost any range.

Some aspects of internal ballistics have a profound effect on the ultimate performance of the bullet, and the shooter can, to some ex-

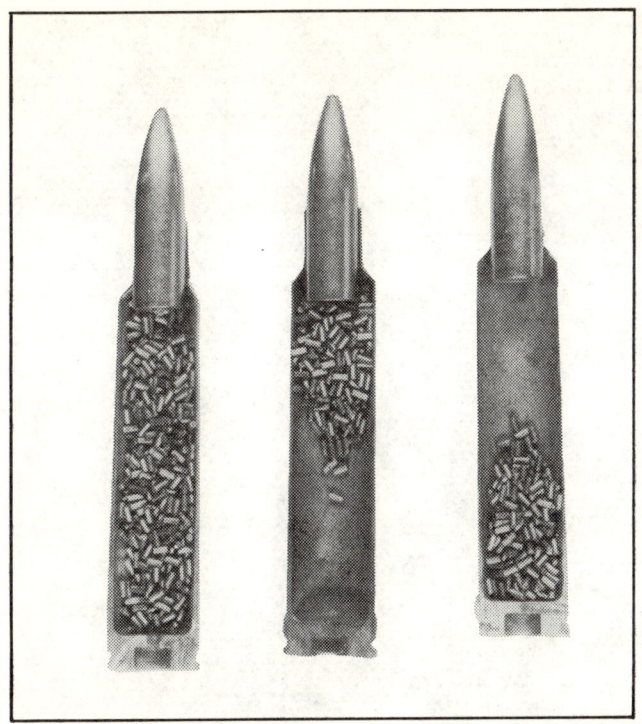

Location of the powder charge is important for even ignition of powder as shown in left case. Concentration of powder, either near bullet base or near primer, can produce unexpected fireworks and is thought to be responsible for some rifle blow-ups, especially when reduced charges of a slow-burning powder are used.

tent, control those. For instance, target rifles have heavier and stiffer barrels than do lightweight hunting rifles. Shoot a light hunting rifle as fast as you can and you will heat up the barrel to a point where you cannot touch it. The heavier and stiffer target barrel not only will have less barrel whip than that of the light sporter barrel, but it will also dissipate heat better. On a hot summer day on the range, when barrel temperature is high, such barrel heating will widen the groups you usually get with this rifle and the same ammo. Heat and cold can affect the performance of your rifle as well as the ammo you use. The conditions under which you store ammunition, temperature and humidity will also affect the performance of the cartridge.

Dozens of variable factors literally affect internal ballistics. The easy availability of chronographs has served to open the eyes of a lot of shooters and reloaders. It's nice to know how fast a particular bullet goes with a certain load, but some shooters are overly concerned with velocities. Even with a benchrest rifle and the most carefully assembled handloads, and shooting in an indoor range where temperature and humidity can be controlled, velocity variations from shot to shot can run as high as 100–150 fps. Although bullet energy at any given point of its travel is a mathematical function of bullet velocity at that point and bullet weight, too much stress is being placed on velocity and too little on accuracy per se.

Benchrest shooters, who are constantly striving to put five bullets into the smallest hole possible, learned long ago that hot loads are not necessarily the most accurate ones. Moreover, hot loads burn out a barrel a lot faster than slower loads. Once the erosion caused by hot gases starts on the rifling, accuracy diminishes as does the ballistic performance of the bullet.

Most of us who have chronographs are hampered by not having unlimited range facilities. Since muzzle blast can affect the start screen of a chronograph, this screen is usually set at a measured distance from the muzzle. For example: the start screen is set at 10 feet from the muzzle, and the distance between the start and stop screens is 10 feet, so the velocity is not true muzzle velocity, but that of the bullet 15 feet from the muzzle. If:

d = distance from muzzle to start screen, and
S = distance between screens,

then

$$D = d + \tfrac{1}{2}S.$$

So, if $d = 10$ ft. and $S = 10$ ft., then $D = 15$ ft.

Knowing the velocity of the bullet, as measured by the chronograph at 15 feet, it is easy to calculate the true MV. Since air density affects velocity, we incorporate the air density factor, using the Army Ordnance figure of 0.64 fps. If:

IV = instrumental velocity, and
C = air density factor Rho, or 0.64 fps,

then

$$MV = D \times C + IV.$$

View from target area through Avtron photoelectric screens toward shooting bench. Author's indoor range has heat, can be cooled in summer and is fully soundproof.

So, if IV = 2700 fps, MV = 15 × 0.64 + 2700 or 2709.6 fps.

Chronograph data does not always specify whether the MV listed is corrected for true MV or is uncorrected data and, of course, if you take a shot at a buck at 183 yards, that extra velocity of 9.6 fps in the above example won't make much of a difference. However, it is important when comparing the performance of one caliber with another.

Any such comparison is valid only when you compare identical bullet weights and use either factory tables or data derived from a reliable chronograph. Nearly all of the published velocities for rifle calibers are taken with special 26-inch length heavy pressure barrels. Most of the data are corrected for true MV, but in some instances, the figures you see in these tables are rounded-off. In other words, the corrected MV might be 2287 fps, while the published figure will show that the bullet moves along at 2280, 2285, 2290 or even at 2300 fps.

Comparing muzzle velocities of identical bullet weight and calibers where case capacity is similar or nearly so is one means of drawing valid conclusions about the performance of a

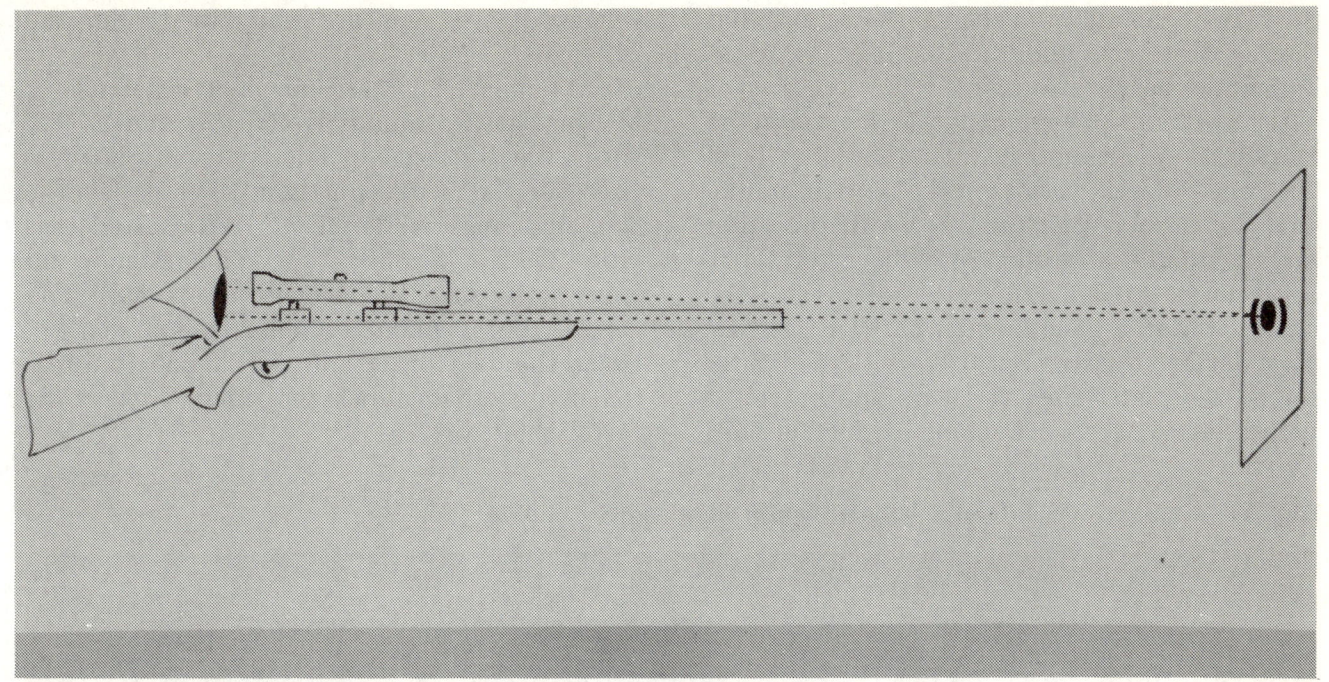

Bore-sighting of rifle is possible only if bolt can be removed. Pre-sighting rifle will save much time and ammo. Align bore of rifle with target by looking through the barrel. Now, without moving the rifle from its rest, adjust the crosshairs of scope so that they too are on the target—and presto, you have bore-sighted your rifle.

cartridge, and such comparisons are usually made for purposes of doping out how flat a cartridge might shoot or how effective it might be in the game fields. There is a fallacy, however, since the comparison is made at muzzle velocity, and neither trajectory nor knockdown punch is of much interest at the muzzle, ballistic performance comparisons should be made at 200 or even 300 yards. These would indicate the bullet's performance at striking velocity, which I define as the velocity of a projectile at the point of impact. Strictly speaking, terminal velocity in small arms ballistics is the constant speed of a projectile after air drag and gravitational pull have reached the point where the two forces cancel each other's effect on the projectile. However, in popular usage, the term is used interchangeably with striking velocity.

Thanks to higher mathematics and computers, a great many of the long-range velocities one finds in the ballistics tables are calculated, rather than representing data actually measured by chronograph. The following tabulation demonstrates this.

22 CENTERFIRE RIFLE CARTRIDGES FACTORY BALLISTICS

Caliber	Bullet/gr.	MV	V_{100}	V_{200}	V_{300}
22 Hornet	46	2690	2030	1510	1150
220 Swift	48	4110	3490	2930	2440
222 Rem.	50	3200	2660	2170	1750
222 Rem. Mag.	55	3300	2800	2340	1930
223 Rem.	55	3300	2800	2340	1930
224 Wby.	55	3650	3150	2685	2270
225 Win.	55	3650	3140	2680	2270
22-250 Rem.	55	3760	3230	2745	2305

Many interesting bits of information can be gleaned from such a compilation of published ballistics data. Although there is a difference in bullet weight, the difference of nine grains between the lightest and heaviest bullets is so slight that the table is still of value when you begin to look at the velocity data. Note, for instance, that the 222 Remington Magnum and the 223 Remington deliver identical ballistics, a fact which is not surprising since the 223 case is the twin of the magnum round. Note, too, that the 224 Weatherby and the short-lived 225 Winchester are nearly identical.

Let's assume for a moment that you are in the market for a varmint rifle. You have two good used ones offered, both scoped and with ammo. One is chambered for the 220 Swift, the other for the equally obsolete 225 Winchester. The Swift ammo carries a 48-grain bullet; the Winchester round a 55-grain bullet. You have almost decided that you could live with the lighter bullet, especially since it leaves the barrel at better than 4100 fps. Looking at the 300-yard velocity figures, you are ready to opt for the 220 Swift.

But hang on for a second. The difference in MV for the two rounds is 460 fps, and at 300 yards, the difference in velocity is only 170 fps. However, the Swift round loses 1670 fps over the 300-yard range, while the 225 Winchester loses only 1380 fps. Suddenly the Winchester round looks better since the velocity loss is less. You can, of course, make a similar comparison between the 22 Hornet and the 22-250 Remington, or any other calibers for which you have the factory ballistics.

This sketch explains the difference between line of sight and line of bore.

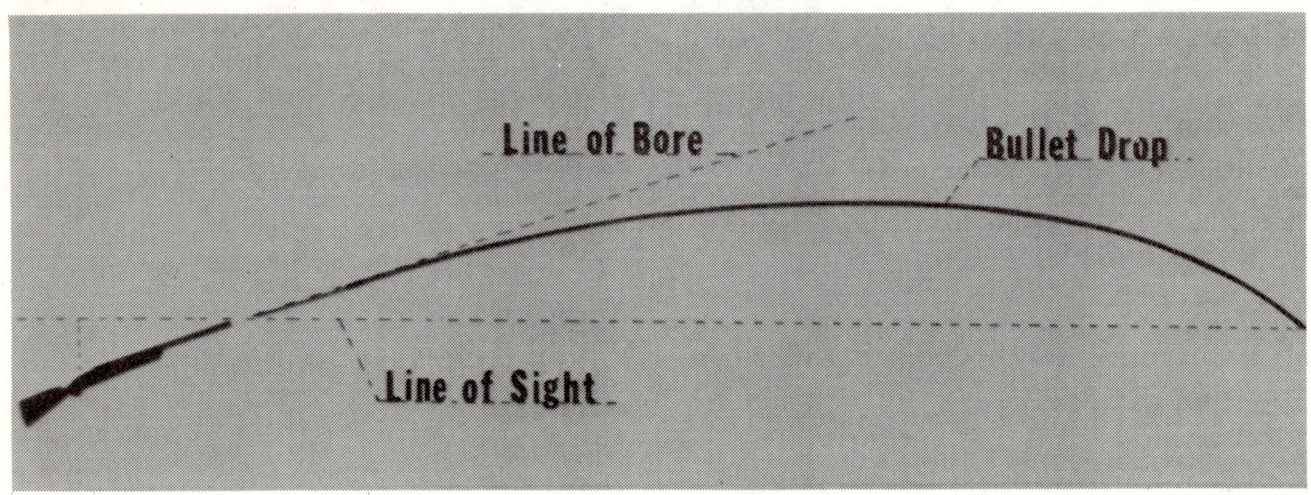

Once sighted-in, line of bore and line of sight will coincide with each other at target at given distance. The MRT is the mid-range trajectory, or exactly half the distance between muzzle and target as outlined in this sketch.

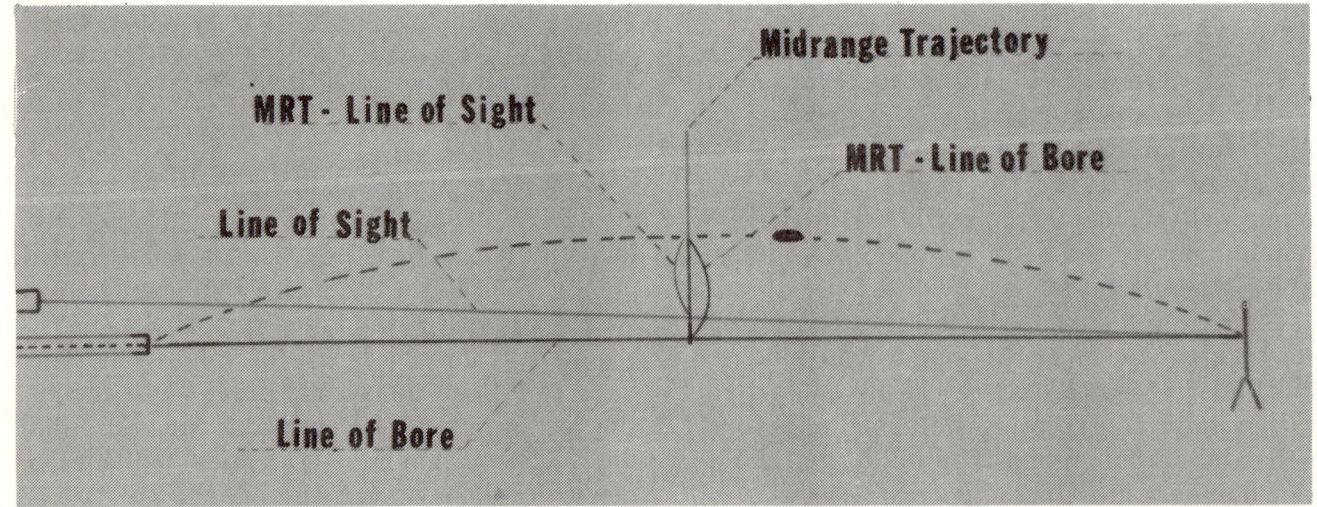

Velocity and bullet design go hand in hand with trajectory. Before getting into midrange trajectory, line of bore and line of sight, let's return to the ballistics tables for a minute. A good comparison would be the 150-grain bullet, factory loaded, in the 270 Winchester and the 30-06. Sighted-in to print dead-on at 100 yards, the bullet from the 270 will be 3.5 inches low at 200 yards, 13 inches low at 300 yards, and by the time it reaches the 400-yard marker, the bullet will print 30 inches low. According to the factory, the bullet has an MV of 2900 fps.

The 150-grain bullet from the 30-caliber rifle, also sighted to print dead-on at 100 yards, will be 3.6, 13.5 and 32 inches low at 200, 300 and 400 yards respectively, and the MV listed is 2970 fps. Wouldn't you say that those two rounds are pretty evenly matched? But now, compare the velocities and energy data of the two.

Caliber	V_{100}/E_{100} fps/ft-lb	V_{200}/E_{200} fps/ft-lb	V_{300}/E_{300} fps/ft-lb
270	2620/2290	2380/1890	2160/1550
30-06	2620/2280	2300/1760	2010/1340

As can be seen, the 150-grain bullet from the 270 has, at 300 yards, 210 ft/lb more energy than the bullet from the '06. Suddenly the 150-grain bullet from the 270 begins to look a lot better than it did.

An important aspect of external ballistics is the trajectory of a bullet. It makes little difference whether you punch holes into paper, shoot woodchucks or hunt big game, a properly doped trajectory is important to you. One of the least understood terms is midrange trajectory, or MRT. By definition, MRT is the height of the bullet's trajectory, in inches, either above the line of bore or the line of sight, at a point halfway between the muzzle and whatever distance is stated.

Line of bore and line of sight may be somewhat difficult to visualize. Line of bore is simply the straight line extension of the bore, or if you prefer, the hole in the barrel. Think of it as an endless non-flexing cleaning rod pushed down the barrel. Even more easy — pull the bolt out of your rifle, set the gun on a sandbag rest on the shooting bench, then sight through the bore at a distant target ... does this sound like bore sighting? Well, that is exactly what you are doing!

Line of sight is almost as easy. Let's say that your rifle has the conventional factory sights, and that you still have the rifle on the sandbag rest, pointing at the target. Now sight through the sights at the target, and the line formed between your eye, the rear and the front sight, and the target is the line of sight. If you have a scope on the rifle, the line of sight is that line formed by your eye, the point where the crosshairs meet and the target. Since all sights

This diagram shows how angle of elevation and line of sight are in relationship with each other.

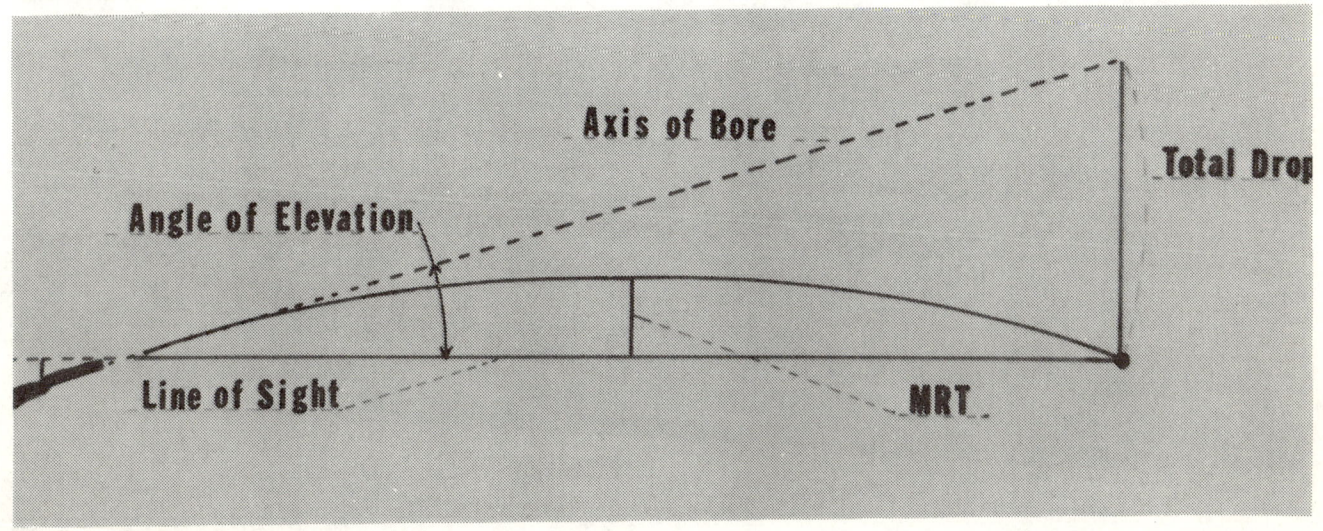

are mounted above the barrel, and sometimes are much higher than the line of bore, the trajectory of the bullet will seem to be flattened, and the midrange trajectory for a scoped rifle will be less than the line of bore. This means that the line of sight is higher than the line of bore, and this extra height must be taken into consideration.

Most iron sights are mounted about 0.8 inch above the line of bore; and most scope mounts place the line of sight 1.5 inches above the line of bore when the scope has a one-inch diameter tube and standard U.S. bases are used for mounting the scope.

Assume that the MRT for a given bullet is two inches, based on the line of bore, and that this is the trajectory for a 200-yard shot. In effect then, the bullet will print about two inches high somewhere around 100 yards. Now add iron sights, and since we are now considering line of sight, you must add the height of the sight which is, 0.8 inch. Since we are halfway to the target, take only half that 0.8 inch, or 0.4 inch from the two-inch MRT; this gives a corrected MRT of 1.6 inches. If a scope was used — and here we consider the added height as 1.5 inches — then half of that, or 0.75 inch, is subtracted from the 2.0 MRT, with the corrected MRT for scope being 1.25 inches.

Most of the ballistics tables do not indicate whether the listed MRT is based on line of sight or line of bore; if line of sight is listed, it may not indicate whether this is based on iron sights or a scope. In recent years, some of the newer ballistics tables have included detailed information, but you can still dope out your trajectory by assuming that the table specifies only line of bore. In some calibers you will introduce a

Measuring from exact center of bore to center of scope. This will explain the magic number of 1.5 inches.

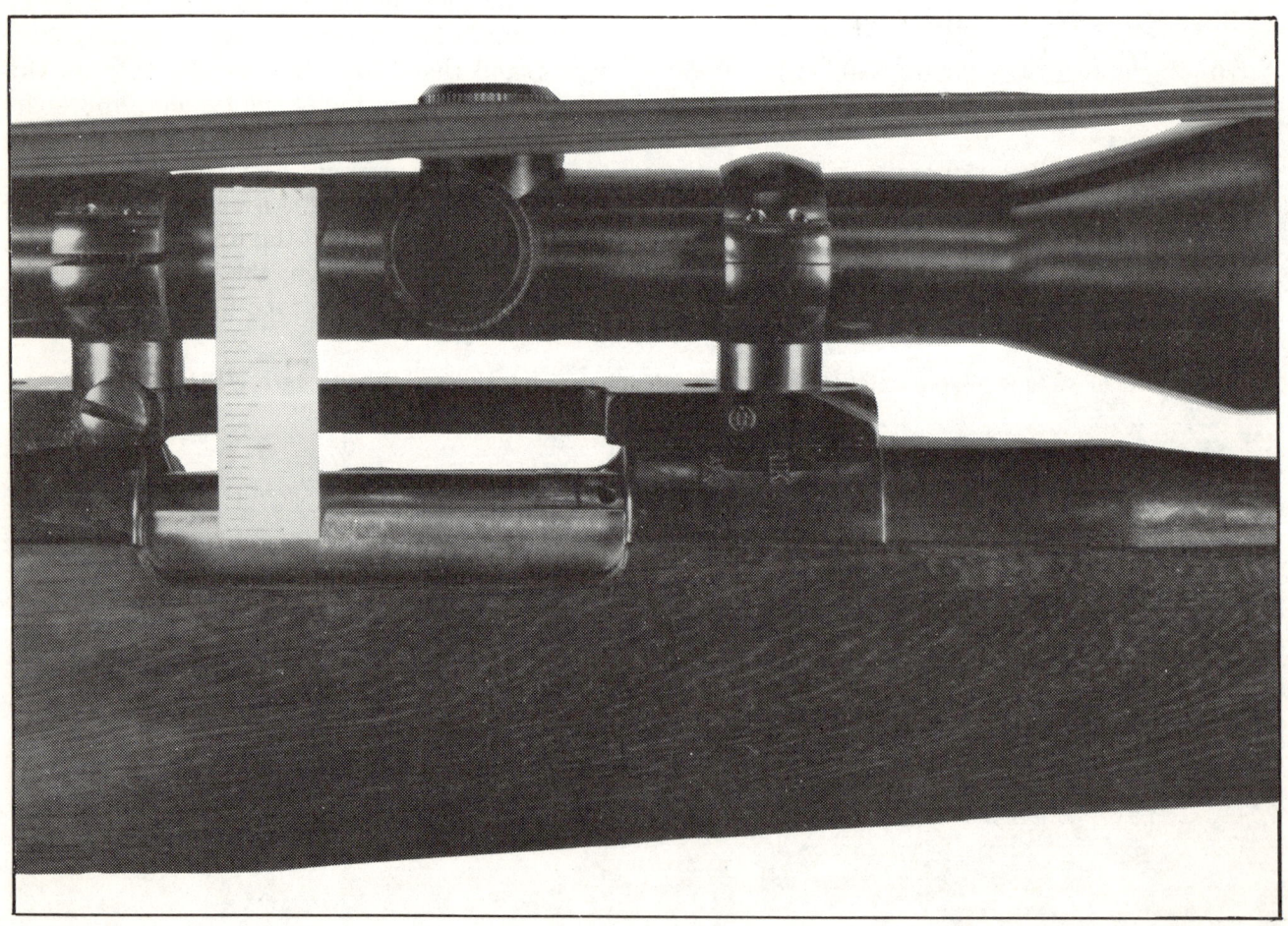

small error, but most of the mathematical niceties can be ignored. If you are sighting-in a 30-30, for example, to print dead-on at 100 yards, the MRT is 0.8 inch. Since you are not using the line of bore but an iron sight, the actual MRT would be 0.4 inch, an adjustment that cannot even be made with the factory sight; therefore it is of little or no consequence.

Sighting-in by the Rule of Three is an almost totally foolproof way of getting the job done, but no matter how you sight-in a rifle, there is only one way of being absolutely certain of the accuracy of your efforts — test firing for group size and group location at the various distances.

The velocity, energy and the MRT of each factory load differs, especially in view of the various bullet weights offered in factory ammo. If you routinely use the 180-grain load in your '06 and then decided to try the Remington Accelerator round, you must re-sight your rifle. If you want to avoid repeated long trips to the range, make a day of it, either making notes in your range book or saving the various targets for later study and reference.

You know that the 180-grain load shoots three inches high at 100 yards. Fire three shots and mark the group as to distance and bullet weight. Using the same hold on the same target, fire three rounds of the Remington Accelerator ammo. This group might be two inches low at 100 yards, with the point of aim being identical for both rounds, right in the center of the bullseye of the target. Firing three more shots with yet another load, for instance the 150-grain bullet load, these rounds, with the same hold, will probably print in yet another location, perhaps somewhere between the 180-grain load and the Accelerator rounds. Short of re-sighting the rifle each time you change your load, write down the scope or sight settings, or at least remember where each of the loads prints at 100 and perhaps 200 yards. You might even want to tape a reminder somewhere on the stock of your rifle.

Understanding the trajectory and learning how to sight-in a rifle are basics of good marksmanship. But there are some shooting conditions where only luck and some guesswork can help. The wind whistling around a mountain plateau in unpredictable gusts means that you should take into account the wind factor. A light varmint bullet will be affected more by wind than a 500-grain slug from a 458 Winchester Magnum. Although there are some pretty fancy empirical formulas for doping wind, I've found that a good guess is a lot faster and just as reliable as a lot of fancy math.

Another atmospheric condition that you have to learn to cope with in some parts of the country is mirage. You have seen it in the summer while driving along a hot blacktop road, and only experience will help you to become reasonably proficient in figuring out this phenomenon.

If you sight-in at sea level and then shoot the rifle in the Colorado mountains, you will find that the rifle does not print to the same point of aim as it did because of the change in air density and resistance. The more knowledgeable guides will caution their clients about this and will arrange to find a place where the gun can be re-sighted. So don't forget to take an extra box of ammo along on such a trip.

From the practical standpoint of the hunter and shooter, neither internal nor external ballistics are very complex. However, there are areas where some confusion exists, and it might be well to explore these. You must have chamber pressure to dislocate the bullet from the case mouth and force it into the rifling of the barrel. When normal levels of operating pressure are exceeded, either as a result of careless handloading or perhaps to a barrel obstruction or excessive headspace, the higher-than-normal pressures can wreck rifles and injure the shooter and possibly even bystanders. If you believe that you are getting excessive pressures when shooting factory ammo in a gun that never gave trouble before, let a competent gunsmith check your gun. Pressure levels for all calibers have been established by the Sporting Arms and Ammunition Manufacturers Institute (SAAMI), and these pressures are given in pounds-per-square-inch.

In this method of measuring pressures, it is generally accepted that chamber pressures running higher than 55,000 psi are either excessive or verging on it. This method of determining pressure calls for a crusher gage where a

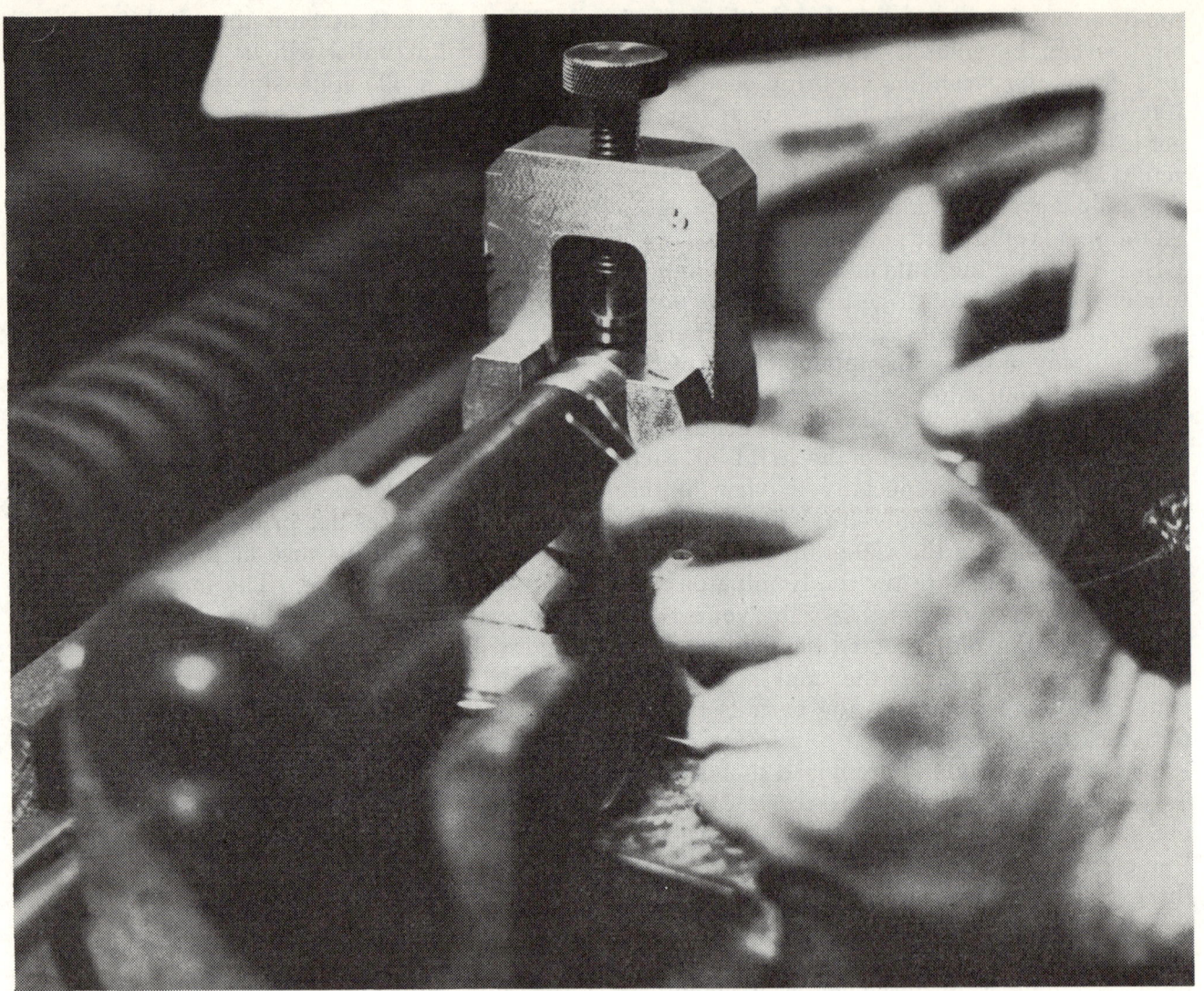

To determine chamber pressure, a pressure gun or receiver is used. Here, the gas check has been seated and the crusher is in its place. The piston of the crusher gage system is about to be seated. Compression of crusher indicates the amount of pressure in chamber.

copper piston is crushed or reduced in length, as a result of the pressure exerted on it. With the help of a tarage table, the shortened crusher can be used to determine the pressure exerted on it. Strain gages and piezo-electric crystals have been used as yet another means of determining chamber pressure, and still further advances in technology have led to the use of LUP and CUP, where LUP stands for Lead Units of Pressure and CUP for Copper Units of Pressure. The former is used for shotguns, the latter for rifle and handgun pressure determinations.

Because of these changes in measuring chamber pressure, still another term in pressure terminology has appeared. This term, referred to as either absolute chamber pressure or PSIA (Pounds-per-Square-Inch-Absolute), is a relative one, indicating essentially that another method of measuring pressure was used rather than the crusher system. Absolute pressures invariably indicate a higher level of pressure than the crusher gage does. Thus, a crusher gage reading of 55,000 psi might show up as 70,000 or more psi in the form of absolute pressure.

The high pressures in the cartridge case last only an incredibly short time. Research in past years has shown that the slowest reaction is less than a nanosecond, which is a billionth of a second (1/1,000,000,000 or 10^{-9}). High-speed photography with exposures of over 6000 frames per second, and with an exposure time of a picosecond or less (1/1,000,000,000,000 or 10^{-12}), have shown that there is considerable gas leakage between bullet walls and barrel walls before the bullet is engaged by the rifling. This free-travel distance varies with each chamber and barrel, and is, of course, also influenced or affected by free-boring. Consequently, small amounts of gas actually bypass the bullet and precede it down the barrel and out the muzzle.

Because pressure equipment is costly and therefore out of the reach of most shooters and handloaders, we will have to live with the knowledge that, long before a gun blows up due to excessive pressure, there are a number of warning signs which indicate that the pressure is higher than it should be. Shiny areas on the cartridge case head show where the case was forcefully shoved back against the bolt face — that is one manifestation of pressure. Stiff bolt lift, where the lift was normal and easy before, is another certain sign of excessive pressure. If the primer is pushed out of the primer pocket, or there are signs that the brass has melted in the chamber, you know that there is higher-than-normal pressure.

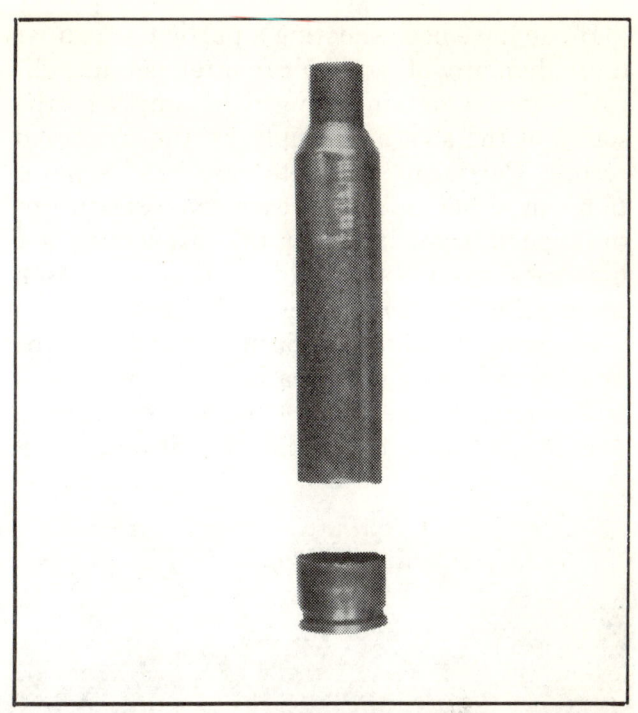

Case with incipient rupture was reloaded with standard powder charge "just one more time." Pressure was not excessive, but there was gas escape through the action when body and base of case separated.

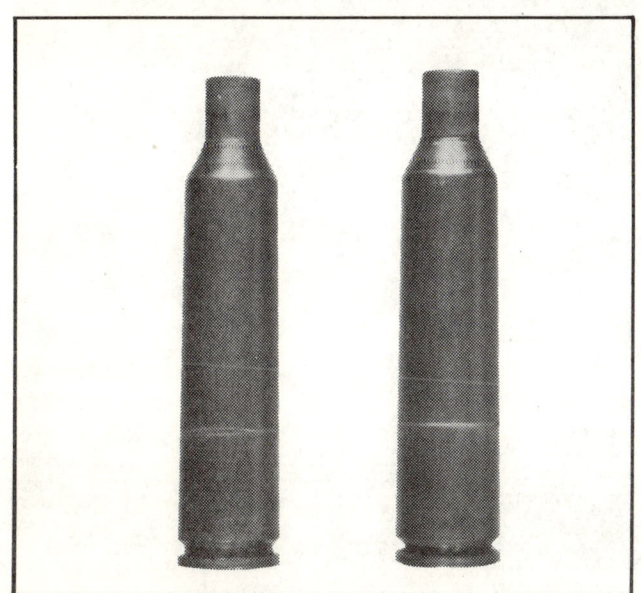

Incipient case ruptures near the base of the cartridge case. Some ruptures are not as readily seen, hence inspection of brass prior to reloading is essential.

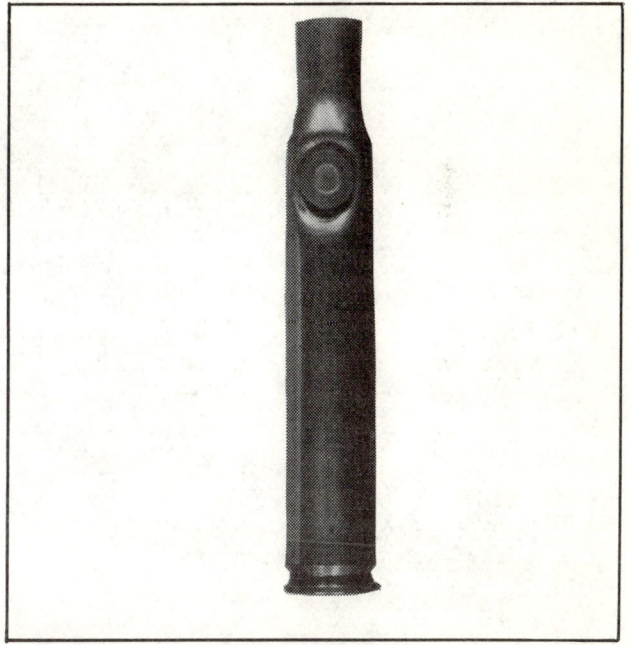

Disc, affixed to specially prepared case, is used to determine pressure inside the case. This system, developed by John Nosler of bullet fame, does not give the exact readings the pressure gun is capable of giving, but readings of pressure-sensitive disc are more than adequate for most uses.

RIFLE BALLISTICS

If you have been shooting a particular caliber more than any other, you can often get an indication that something is not right simply by the sound of the shot or possibly by the increased recoil. Partial or complete case head separation can either be due to excessive pressure or to fatigued brass, but when the case lets go, gas blowback is almost certain — one more reason for wearing shooting glasses at all times.

Stopping power has been defined as the amount of kinetic energy a bullet is capable of transferring to the target. Bullet, or kinetic, energy is a function of bullet weight and bullet speed at the point at which kinetic energy is to be determined. Since velocity decreases along the bullet's path while bullet weight remains constant, the energy or stopping power decreases as the range increases. To determine kinetic bullet energy, this formula is used:

$$E = \frac{WV^2}{450,240}$$

where
V = velocity in fps,
W = weight of bullet in grains, and
E = energy in ft/lb

Just how strong are some actions? This rifle was blown up on purpose by obstructing bore with patches, oversized bullets and molten lead; powder charge in factory cartridge was replaced by pistol powder. Estimated pressure was about 70,000 psi.

Target mirage becomes especially bothersome with high power scopes. These benchrest shooters are trying to dope wind and mirage, where wind is the "easier" one to resolve.

This energy is variously known as terminal bullet energy, stopping power, kinetic energy, target energy, and even as knock-down power or punch. Much has been written about the Hatcher formula, which was designed for determining the relative stopping power of handgun bullets, and the formula developed by John Taylor, the white hunter in Africa who was also known as Pondoro. The latter developed a system of calculating stopping power for the various cartridges so that all of them could be neatly pigeonholed and classified as to their abilities in the game fields.

The kinetic energy transferred to the target results in tissue shock, and here we find that bullet design as well as the internal and external construction of the bullet plays an important role. Bullet makers and ammunition manufacturers spend vast amounts of money on bullet testing and research. A bullet that does not expand, such as the fully jacketed military spitzer bullet, causes relatively little tissue damage. The classic mushrooming of a bullet, in which the forward portion expands geometrically and the base holds together to act as pushing force, causes a great deal of tissue damage.

Another type of tissue damage is often caused by hydrostatic shock. On the other end of the bullet design scale are the heavy, round or flat-nosed slugs that do not expand or mushroom in any way. These punch through heavy hide, breaking the most massive bones and producing a great deal of tissue damage and shock. Such bullets are used primarily in the large-caliber rifles, from 375 H&H on up, and are a must for the heavy and dangerous game found in Africa.

Handgun bullets differ from rifle bullets in shape and internal design, and therefore the Hatcher formula cannot be compared to the one developed by Taylor. It should be understood that any formula depends not only on a high degree of mathematical probability, but also on ideal laboratory testing conditions.

Gelatin blocks have been long used as a test medium to determine how well a bullet expands. A wood byproduct that becomes pulpy when moistened has been used and so has a rather messy mixture of wax and heavy oil that is cast into blocks. Oiled hardwood sawdust,

Excellent bullet expansion is shown by the 250-grain .338-inch Bitterroot bullet. Expanded bullet retained better than 90 percent of its original weight.

polyurethane foam scraps, and wet telephone books and Sears catalogs have been tried. Every so often someone rediscovers fine sand, dry or moist, as an expansion test medium.

Hollow-point handgun bullets in sand, for instance, never expand, but will do so beautifully in the wax-oil mixture blocks. In moist sand, the bullet cavity fills with tightly packed sand, but the external pressure of the sand is equal to the forward push or force exerted by the ogive portion of the bullet so that one force cancels the other and there is no expansion.

The major problem with all of the expansion media is that they only re-create or simulate soft tissue. The skeletal structure cannot be duplicated in such media, and since it is almost impossible to shoot a chuck or a deer without hitting bone, predictions as to anticipated bullet behavior become highly educated guesses. Ultimate bullet performance does not depend solely on bullet weight and velocity, bullet shape, internal bullet design and structure, jacket uniformity and thickness, hardness of

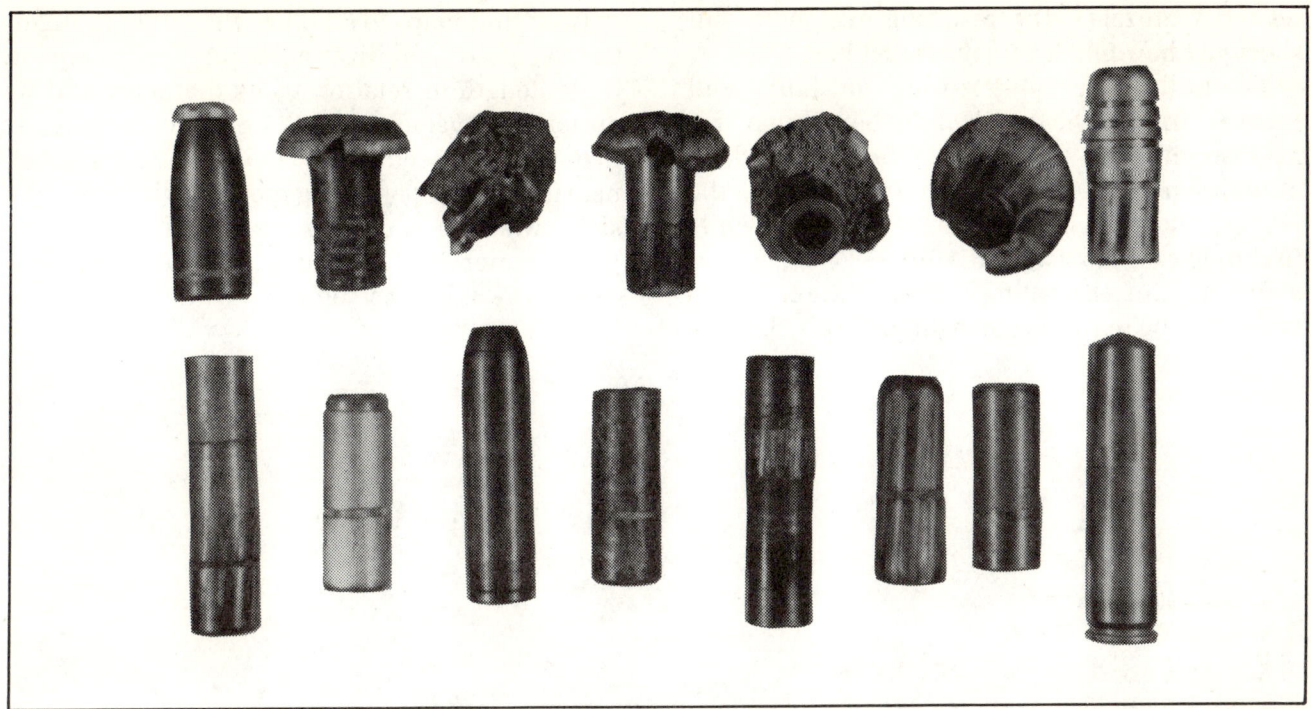

The late John Buhmiller was not only a barrel maker, but also a first-class wildcatter, specializing in big bore numbers. These bullets, most of them machined and some showing that jackets originally were cartridge cases, were used in Africa where Buhmiller was a licensed hunter controlling elephant and buffalo herds.

bullet core, condition of the rifling of the barrel, or shot placement.

Of course, these elements are important, but a great many carefully observed game shots and kills lead me to the conclusion that each animal will respond differently to bullet impact. Age, physical condition, sex, whether rested or running, and previous hunter experience are just a few of the more predictable game-kill variables that must be anticipated.

As it leaves the barrel, the bullet not only spins, which gives it gyrational stability, but it also has some yaw or wobble. Although yaw is most often considered as normal and degree of yaw is dependent on bullet configuration and velocity, wobble or wabble is caused by either a defective bullet or a faulty bullet design. If, for example, the bullet jacket is not of even thickness all around the ogive, wobble will result. Yaw is thought to be a contributory factor in creating tissue damage since the diameter of the entrance hole is larger than the caliber of the bullet. That a bullet has yaw can easily be seen when a paper or cardboard target is placed

Bullet expansion is best tested in lab by firing into blocks of a mixture of lubrication grease and wax. Blocks are recast every so often; bullets are recovered expanded if they tend to expand.

RIFLE BALLISTICS

near the muzzle — the resulting oval hole will show just how much yaw the bullet has.

The bullet gets its spin from the lands and grooves running the length of the barrel in a spiral fashion. This twist may be fast, like 1:8, or slow, as in 1:24. In the fast twist barrel, the rifling makes one full turn in eight inches, while in the slow twist barrel, it requires 24 inches for a full turn of the rifling. The rotation of the twist may be to the left or right, and it is the rate of twist that helps to stabilize the bullet in flight, the degree of stabilization being dependent on bullet length in relation to its diameter and its anticipated velocity. A long bullet moving at high velocity needs a fast twist, while a shorter, heavier projectile moving more slowly requires a slow twist for complete stabilization. Rifling pitch is merely the angle of the rifling in relation to the axis of the bore.

Chapter Six
Handloading

Chapter Six
Handloading

The next time you go to a rifle range look at some of the shooters. The fellow who gets his shooting over with as fast as possible, leaves his empty brass on the bench or ground, has in all likelihood also fired some pretty poor groups. But the fellow who times his shots, saves his brass with care, even wipes it off on the seat of his pants is a handloader and probably shoots some nice tidy groups that a lot of other shooters would be envious of.

The cartridge case represents between 20-35 percent of the cost of the round. By resizing the case to its original dimensions, knocking out the spent primer and seating a new one, adding a charge of fresh powder and then seating a bullet, the handloader drastically cuts his shooting costs. The handloader or reloader can also make ammo that he cannot buy at any gun shop. By casting his own bullets or swaging them, he further reduces his ammunition expenditures. He can also produce special loads and loads for rifles for which ammo is no longer produced — or he may be a wildcatter. Wildcat cartridges are those special creations which hopefully give somewhat better ballistics than their factory counterparts; such specially chambered rifles, of course, call for handloaded ammo.

If you have only one centerfire rifle, and shoot more than three or four boxes of ammo in the course of a year, handloading the brass is feasible without a great outlay of money for tools or equipment. The Lee Loader, though slower to handle than a bench reloading press, makes perfectly good ammo if you follow the instructions that come with it. Lyman's Tong Tool falls into this class, as does Bill English's Pak-Tool, although the latter is a bit more complicated and sophisticated. Benchrest shooters use the same cartridge cases over and over, reloading their cases right at the range, and most of them use custom dies which have been made so that brass will not be resized more than necessary.

If you have the space, you can take your choice of a variety of bench-mounted loading presses or tools: from a simple C press or an

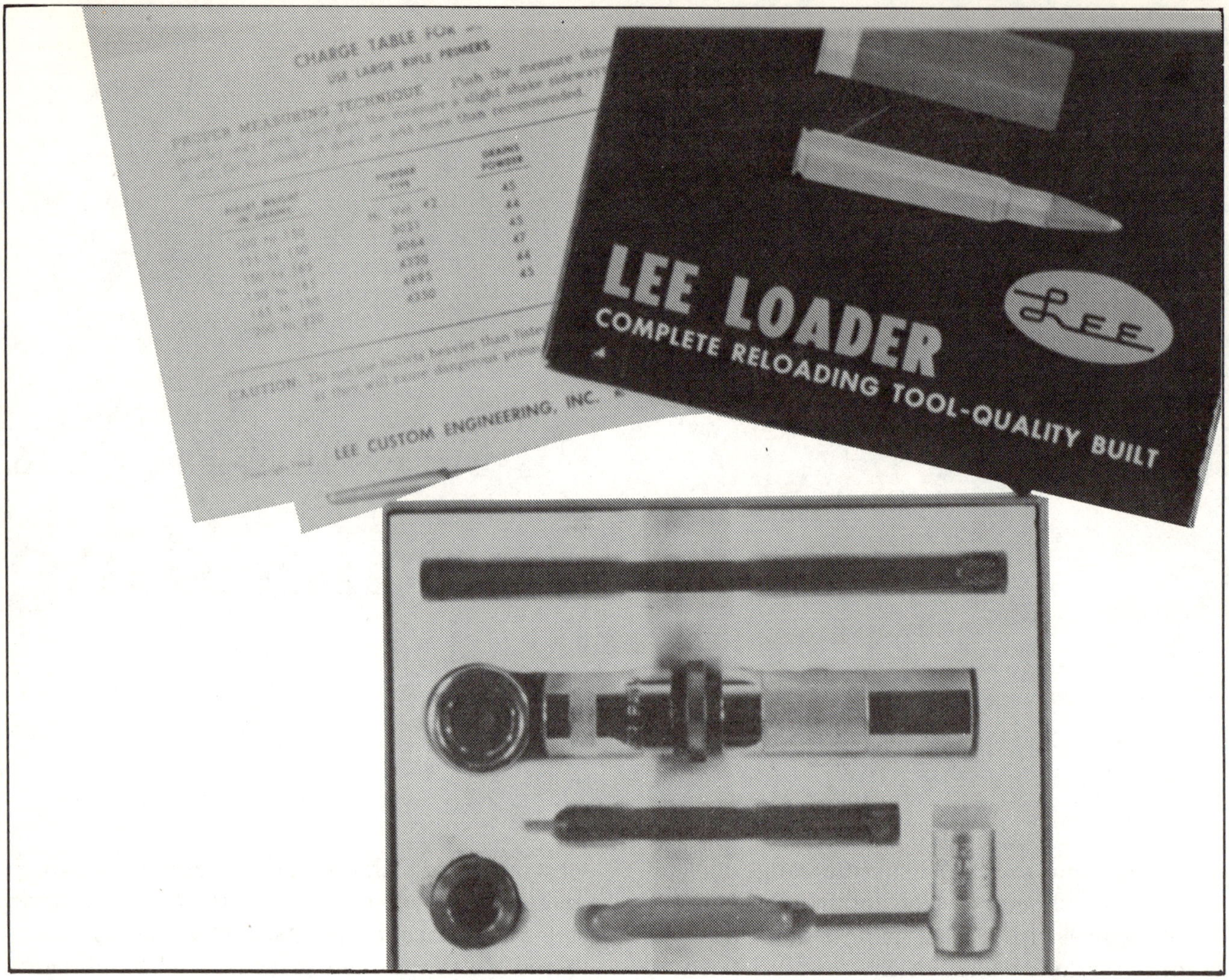

Simple to use, inexpensive and highly portable, the Lee Loader is a good choice if not much ammo is to be loaded and when budget and space are limited.

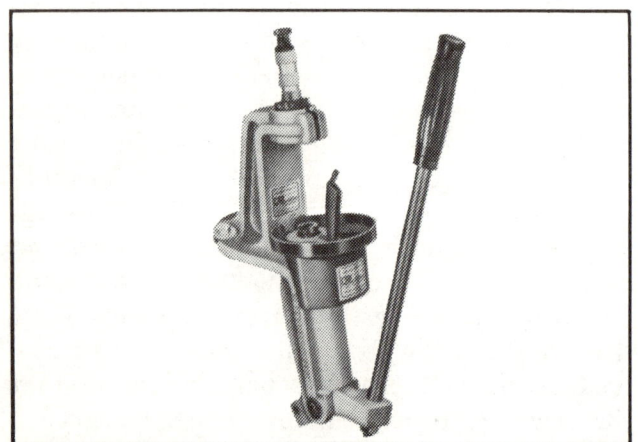

The C press is suitable for all of the usual reloading operations, but the lighter models tend to develop a springiness.

O frame press to an H press. There are even turret tools available which enable you to leave several fully adjusted dies in the press. In addition to the press and dies, and a shellholder for the specific caliber you want to reload for, you should have a simple powder scale, a case trimmer and vernier calipers, as well as a case mouth chamfering tool. Later on, you may want to add a separate priming tool, bullet casting equipment or perhaps even bullet swaging equipment. If the latter sounds intriguing, buy a heavy-duty O frame press, since you will need it for swaging operations.

Depending on the caliber, you'll need either small or large rifle primers; again, depending on caliber and powder choice, you may want to

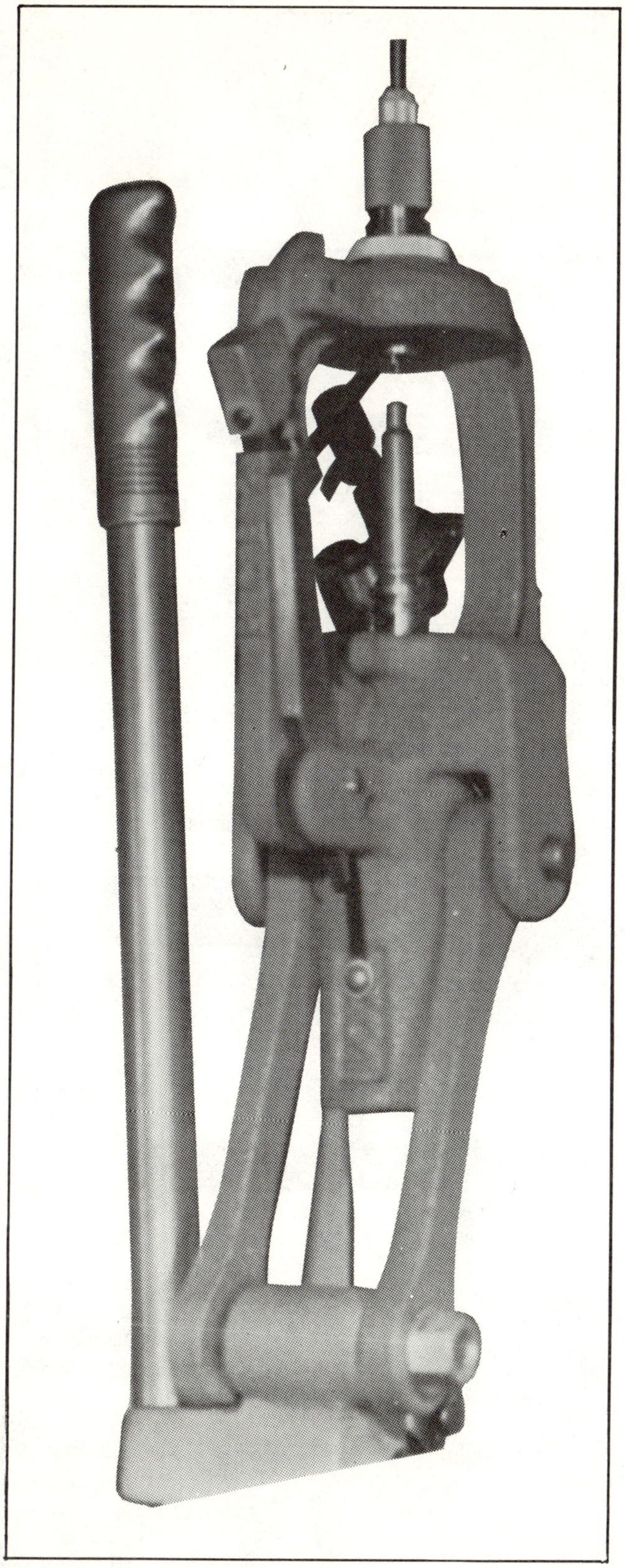

The H type press has lost some of its former popularity. It can be used for all loading operations, but not for case forming or bullet making.

The turret press permits the user to leave all loading dies set up in press and is most often used for loading quantities of handgun ammo. Not suitable for case forming or bullet swaging.

The O press is essentially a beefed up C type press. It is suitable not only for all loading steps, but also for case forming and bullet swaging.

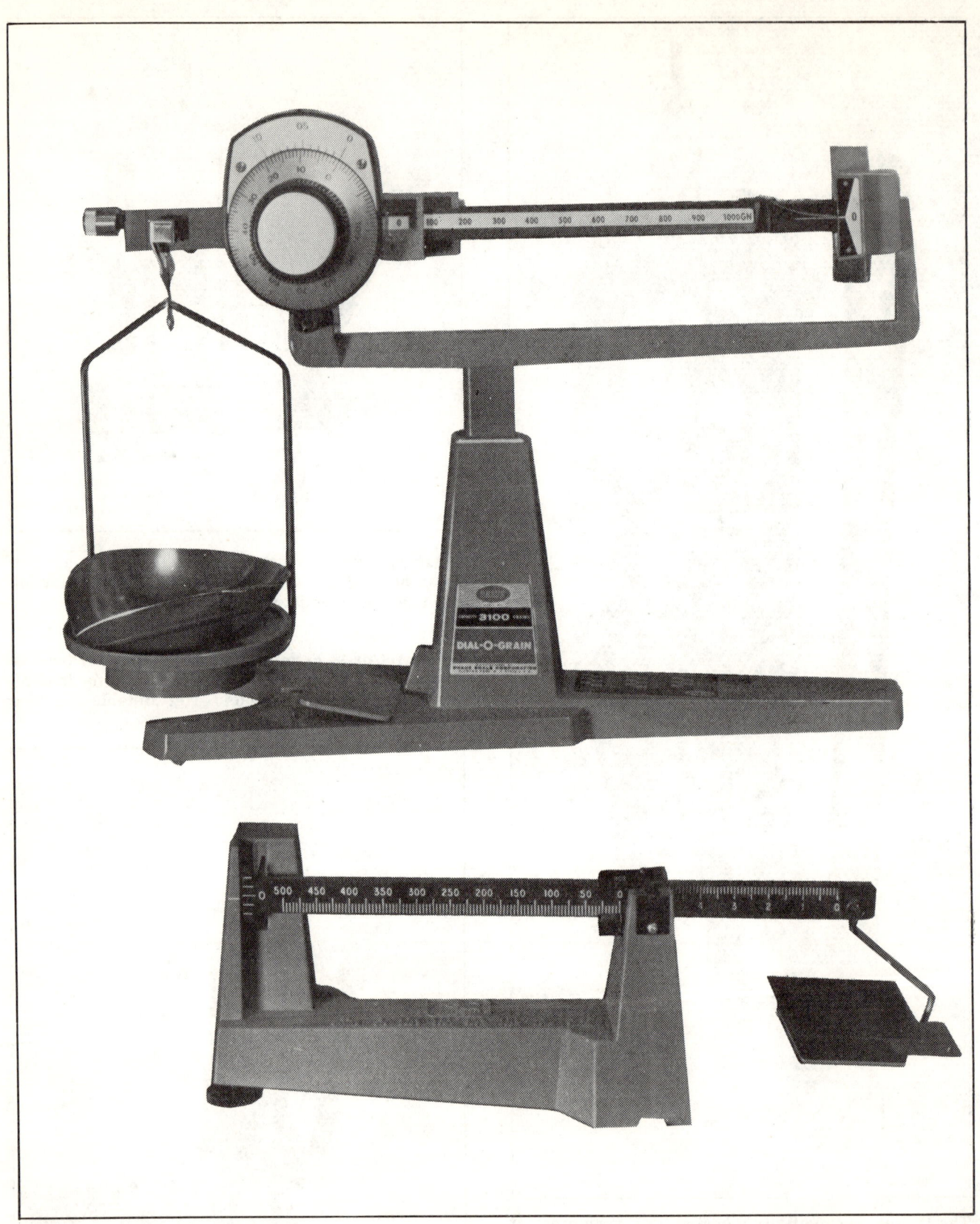

A simple powder scale is essential for reloading. The one on top is more than adequate for most handloaders, while the one on bottom, the Ohaus Dial-O-Grain, is for the advanced loader.

use magnum primers which are offered in both sizes. You will also need a can or two of powder and bullets of suitable caliber and weight. Before buying powder, bullets or primers, study one of the available loading tables. Among the better sources of information for handloaders is my *Reloaders Guide* published by Stoeger Publishing Company and available from most gun stores, sporting goods stores and bookstores.

Determine in the caliber listing which bullet weight you want to use, ascertain what are the primer specifications and also which bullet/powder combinations may give you the best performance. When you have your components and your loading press is set up, you are almost ready to start reloading. A loading block, though not essential, is a very handy item to have, and you can either buy one of plastic or make your own wooden block. A few labels to mark the boxes of reloaded ammo and a place to store all your reloading gear will be needed. If you don't have a workbench you can mount the loading press on a board, and using a couple of fair-sized C-clamps, simply clamp the board with the press to the kitchen table. I have seen loading components and accessories stored in shoe boxes, in GI ammo boxes, and even in an old suitcase. If there are children in the house, lock your loading stuff away so that inquisitive young fingers cannot get into trouble.

Before you start worrying about quantities of smokeless powder being stored in the house, a can of gasoline for the lawn mower is a lot more dangerous than two or more cans of propellant powder. Powder gives off gases when it burns, but the burning gases and gas pressure thus generated only become critical when the burning powder is confined, as in a cartridge case, and when that case is contained in the chamber of a rifle.

When the powder burns and the gases begin to exert pressure, the brass cartridge case stretches and fills the chamber of the rifle completely. In lever-action, autoloading and pump-action rifles, the brass usually stretches more in length than in bolt-action rifles, and each case must be measured and perhaps trimmed to its original and specific length before it is resized.

After a case has been trimmed in the case trimmer, sharp edges of the case mouth must be chamfered inside and out. As long as you load for only one rifle in a given caliber, cases from bolt-action rifles can be neck sized only. Neck sizing tightens up the neck and case mouth, which have stretched during firing, so that the new bullet can be held in the case mouth and so it won't be pushed back into the case body while the round rests in the magazine and the gun is being fired. All other cases should be resized to their full length.

For handloaders, Lyman and RCBS offer starter kits that contain all of the needed tools, dies and accessories. Most of the tools come

Brass stretched when fired, and case length must be checked before reloading. Checking is done with pre-set vernier caliper; trimming is quickly accomplished by means of a lathe-like case trimmer as shown here.

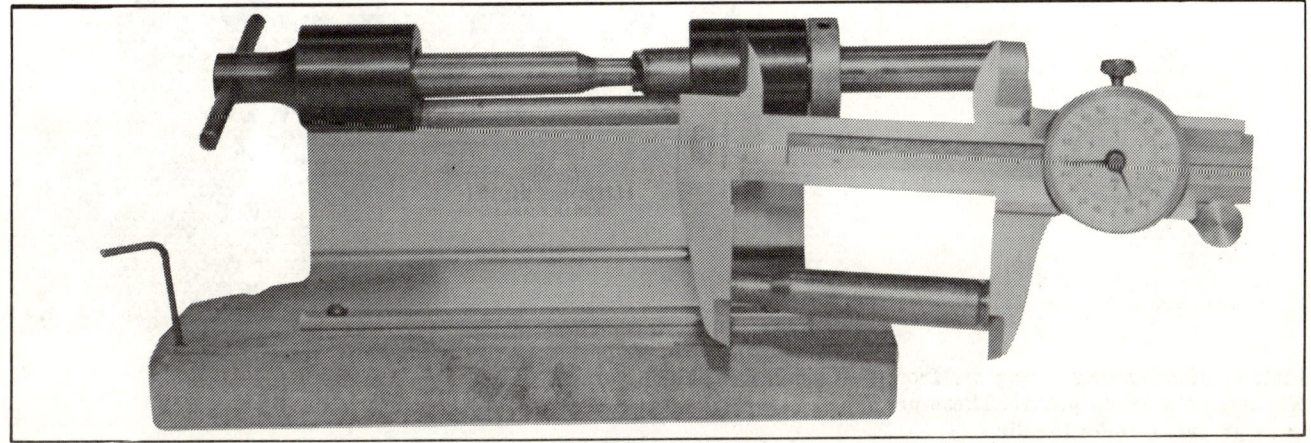

Instead of adjusting sizing die from full length resizing to neck sizing, or vice versa, use the Neckers sold by B-Square. These precision washers fit under die lock ring, adjust sizing by their mere presence under the die.

with comprehensive instructions, but should these be missing, here is how to set your loading dies, plus some tips.

Let's assume that you have a 243 Winchester and use the 100-grain bullet loads. Begin by taking a live round from a box of factory ammo. From now on, this will be one of your master rounds, and will help you to adjust your bullet seating die for reloading 100-grain bullets. Later on, you can use this live master round as the first step in adjusting the bullet seating die if you want to load some 75-grain hollow-point Speer bullets. The shorter 75-grain bullet will require that you move the bullet-seating stem down a bit. After you loosen the lock nut on the seating stem of your die, turn the stem down a turn or two at most. Run an empty but full-length sized case into the die, with the 75-grain bullet seated lightly in the case mouth. Next bring the tool handle all the way down, and your bullet will be seated. Now take that dummy round, place it into the magazine of your rifle, and determine whether the dummy will chamber and then extract. Check to see if the first lands of the rifling left any marks on the bullet. If so, you may have to move the bullet seating stem down another half turn or so, until the dummy round functions smoothly through the action. Save this dummy and mark on it with a felt pen the bullet weight and make of bullet.

From this point on, follow the same procedure for another dummy round whenever you add a new bullet weight for that rifle. Then, when you have to adjust the bullet-seating die for a particular bullet, you simply insert that dummy round into the shellholder of the tool and move the ram all the way up. Next, screw the die body into the top of the press and when this is seated properly, you screw the bullet-seating stem down in the die until you feel it make contact with the bullet of the dummy round.

The sizing die adjustment is just as easy, but the seating die was described first since it teaches you to "feel" the stem making contact. If you are full-length sizing cases, simply thread the sizing die into the top of the press, insert the suitable shellholder into the ram of the press and move the handle of the press down, or the ram up. When the bottom of the die makes contact with the shellholder, turn the die out about a quarter turn, then lock it in place with the lock ring. The decapping pin should protrude just enough from the die body to push the spent primer out of the primer pocket of the case in the die.

The B-Square Co. (P.O. Box 11281, Fort Worth, Texas 76110) manufactures special neck-sizing rings, which I recommend. Instead of adjusting the die for a handful of cases that you want to neck size only and then readjusting the die for full-length resizing, simply remove the die from the press, slip one of the special washers over the die body and reseat the die in the press. Complete instructions come with these neck-sizing rings, and they will save a lot of adjusting and readjusting.

Let's assume that you have a batch of once-fired 243 cases to load. You have adjusted your sizing die for full-length resizing, the primers are all set and you are ready to size and decap that box of brass. If you bought a complete reloader's starter kit, some case lube will be included. Cases have to be lubed very lightly so that the case won't stick in the die. Remember that every time you resize a case, you are, in effect, working the relatively soft brass; consequently a very light coat of lube over the case mouth and around the neck is essential. A little lube will also be transferred to the case body. In some kits, a large un-inked stamp pad is included, and once this is loaded with lube, you simply roll the cases across it lightly. You can get along with some Crisco from the kitchen if you don't have any store-bought lube.

Insert the case into the shellholder, move the ram up until it has completed its upward travel and stops. Now simply operate the handle of the press in the opposite direction, and there is your resized case. If the decapping pin was adjusted properly, the spent primer has also been knocked out of the primer pocket. By placing a wastebasket, an old cardboard box or an empty coffee can directly beneath the ram of the press, all the spent primers will fall right into that container instead of rolling all over the floor.

The primer pocket is partly filled with a hard, black residue. There are special primer-pocket cleaning tools, but a small-bladed screw driver from your tool box will do. Run the blade

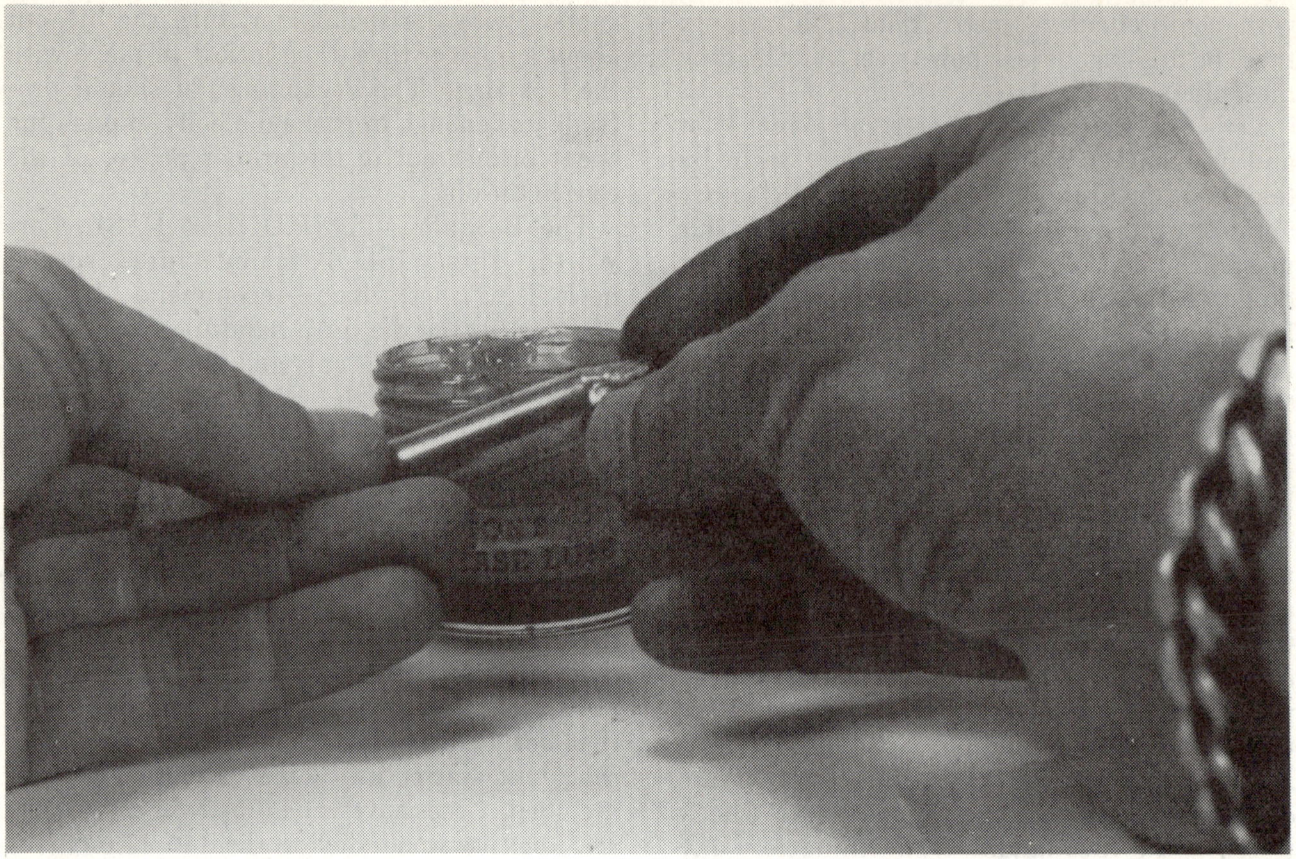

Pick up a very small amount of lube on your finger tip, wipe around neck and across case mouth. One such dab of lube should lube three to four cases adequately. Forgetting to lube case can mean a case stuck in the die—then the stuck case remover is worth its weight in gold.

Rolling a bunch of cases across lube pad is another simple way of lubing cases, but be sure to lube case mouths also.

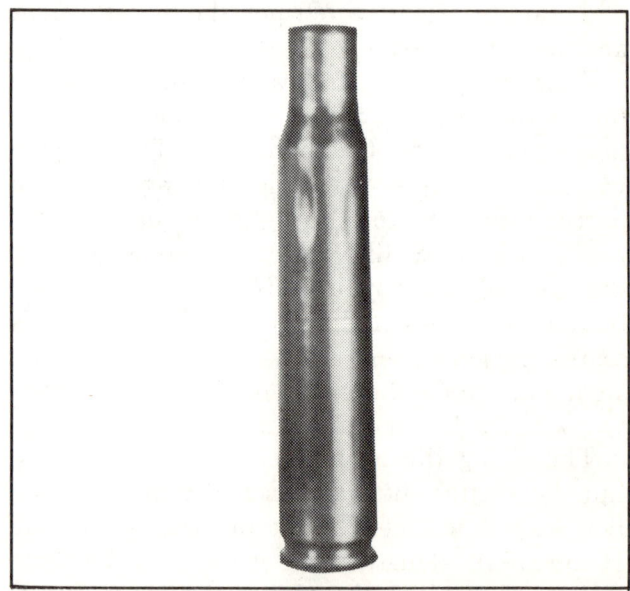

Too much lube invariably will result in an oil dent. Small dents will be smoothed out at the next firing, but seriously dented cases should be discarded.

Priming sorted, trimmed and chamfered case can be done either on the loading press or on a special tool. Shown here is primer seating on the C-H priming tool.

around in the primer pocket once lightly to loosen all the black deposits; then tap the head of the case on the bench or table once or twice. Hopefully, this will loosen the rest of the residue. Now is a good time to wipe the case clean of any adhering lube.

All bench presses come with a priming arm, and you should make certain that you have the right size — there is one for small primers and another for large ones. The 243, to continue the example, takes a large rifle primer and the primer will fit not too snugly into the spring-loaded cup on the primer arm. Spill a few of the primers from the box into a small dish next to the press, make sure your fingers are free of all grease and pick up a primer, placing it open side up into the primer cup of the priming arm. Replace the case in the shellholder, move the case up until the primer arm can be pushed into the machined slot of the ram where it will bottom against the opposite side of the ram. Now move the handle of the press so that the ram is being lowered — you will feel the primer being seated in the primer pocket. When this happens, move the ram up a bit, release the spring-loaded primer arm, letting it snap forward; then bring the now-primed case down and remove it from the shellholder. The primer should be seated just a hair below the edge of the primer pocket.

There will be times when the primer has not been fully seated and the protruding primer, sticking out of the primer pocket, won't allow you to remove the case from the shellholder. Simply reseat the case in the shellholder, move the ram up, insert the primer arm as before — but this time exert a bit more pressure on the handle of the press, and the primer will seat in the pocket.

The only thing you have to watch out for is that the primer is placed open end up in the primer cup of the priming arm. If a primer is seated incorrectly in the primer pocket, it will have to be removed. Clear the bench of all primers and powder, and keep your hands clear of the bottom and top of the ram. Insert the mis-primed case in the shellholder, then gently raise the ram until the decapping pin in the sizing die pushes the primer out. Don't try to save this primer; junk it. Remember that the mix in primers is explosive, so dispose of it where there is no chance that it will be exposed to flame, as in an incinerator or fireplace.

Now that your 243 cases are resized and primed, you may decide to load 75-grain bullets in those cases. The Speer manual, as just one example, lists a number of powders suitable for those bullets, and you can pick any powder listed in this or other loading manuals from recognized sources and be sure that you are on safe ground with the powder selection you make. The Speer manual lists IMR 4350 as one of the suitable powders. You'll probably find that the median load listed for the 75-grain bullet — that is, 45.0 grains of IMR 4350 — is about as good a load as you are going to get, at least when compared with factory ammo.

However, you can get better results from your handloads if you do some load development. The low load is listed as 43.0 grains, the median load as 45.0 grains, and the maximum is listed as 47.0 grains of IMR 4350. Take a few envelopes and mark them: 1) 43.0/4350, 2) 43.5/

Wooden loading blocks can be made by anyone who is handy and can use a drill, while plastic loading trays must be bought. Always load enough cases to make a full box of ammo.

4350, 3) 44.0/4350, and so on, in 0.5 grain increments until you get to 46.0 or 46.5 grains.

Set your powder scale for the lowest load listed, and with the help of a coffee spoon dribble the correct amount of powder into the scale pan. When the beam swing has stopped and the pointer on the scale beam shows that the powder weight is right on the button, use the plastic powder funnel from your reloader's kit and pour the powder into one of the primed cases. Charge three cases with this low load, seat the bullets, and stick those loads into the first envelope. Do the same with all of the loads, then take your 243 to the range and see how each of the first handloads performs as far as grouping is concerned.

For such load development, I use large paper targets turned with the blank side toward me, and make a number of aiming points on each one. Then I shoot the various loads, marking the groups as to the loads used. This gives me an immediate look at the accuracy potential of each load. The load that is the most accurate is the one I stick with. Later, when I want to try a bullet of another manufacturer or weight, I work up a load for that, following the same steps.

Now that you have reloaded all of the brass, you may stick the reloads back into the factory box, but six months from now, when the varmint season is about to start, you probably wouldn't remember which load you used. A load label, even a simple one, will do. It should show bullet make and weight, size and make of primer, amount and identification of powder used, as well as the number of times the cases have been reloaded. I load for some 61 calibers and make no attempt to remember each and every load, so I also have a card file in which I enter all the needed data.

From experience, I know that 243 brass, fired in a bolt-action rifle, does not stretch much, if at all. Now let's assume that the batch of brass now on your bench has been fired and loaded several times. Before you start resizing and decapping, look in your loading manual for the specified case length — it is 2.045 inches or 51.94 mm. Set your vernier calipers for that measurement, then see if all cases pass through the jaws of the calipers. They should just barely

With case in shellholder which is set into the ram of the loading press, and with the bullet seating die screwed into the top of the press and adjusted for correct bullet seating depth, seating bullets becomes a simple operation. Here bullet is seated on case mouth and is fully seated when stroke of ram is completed.

pass through without tipping the case. If several of them don't pass, they need to be trimmed back to the specified length.

The case trimmer works very much like a miniature lathe. Again, putting a master or dummy case aside for future reference makes trimmer setting a lot easier. After trimming all of the cases that need it, all cases should get a touch of the case mouth chamfering tool, and just a light rotation inside and outside the case neck will do nicely.

Even once-fired cases that have been resized and primed now should also be given a touch of the chamfering tool. Some reloaders skip this step when loading jacketed bullets and only chamfer the case mouth of those cases that had to be trimmed; others only chamfer when loading cast lead bullets. With lead bullets, it is essential to prevent shaving lead; with jacketed

The loading components are cases, primer, powder and bullets.

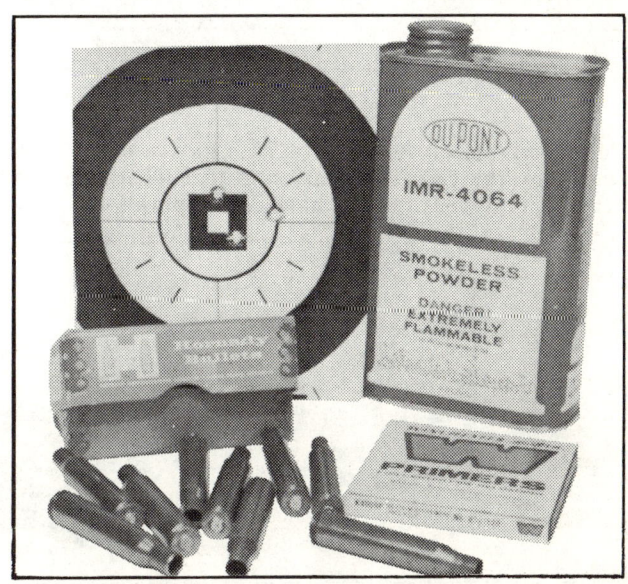

HANDLOADING

Each box of reloads should be labeled. Shown here is a homemade label with all of the essential information. In case of wildcats or where chamber is not standard size, be sure to indicate for which rifle load is suitable.

Additional data, such as other loads or perhaps case forming instructions are listed on a special file card.

bullets, I also prefer just a touch of the chamfering tool to remove any and all accidental burrs from the case mouth.

Once you begin to reload, you will find yourself shooting more, and this in turn means that you will begin to reload more. Sooner or later, you will probably add another rifle or two to your collection.

If you start to load cast bullets, you'll have to crimp the case mouth so that the bullet stays put. The case neck tension of a resized case is adequate to hold jacketed bullets, and I prefer not to crimp jacketed bullets in place, except on heavy recoil rifles, such as the 375 H&H and the 458 Winchester Magnum. You will note that some bullets have a cannelure or crimping groove; if you feel that you must crimp, that is where the case mouth must be crimped onto the bullet. However, there are lots of bullets which don't have a cannelure, and these should not be crimped at all. Cold crimping works the brass needlessly and shortens case life.

Weighing each and every charge on your powder scale is the most accurate way of getting your powder charges ready for dumping into the waiting cases, but it is also the slowest way of getting the job done. Sooner or later, you will want to speed up your reloading operation, and then a powder measure is a good investment. They come in various sizes, shapes and colors, and all of them are good. The simplest one is the measure made by Belding and Mull; the others, operating with an adjustable drum system, are quite alike in design, method of setting and operation.

Before bullets are seated, the case mouth of each case should be chamfered inside and out, as shown by the case on chamfering tool where case mouth has shiny surface. Just a little bit of brass is removed during chamfering operation.

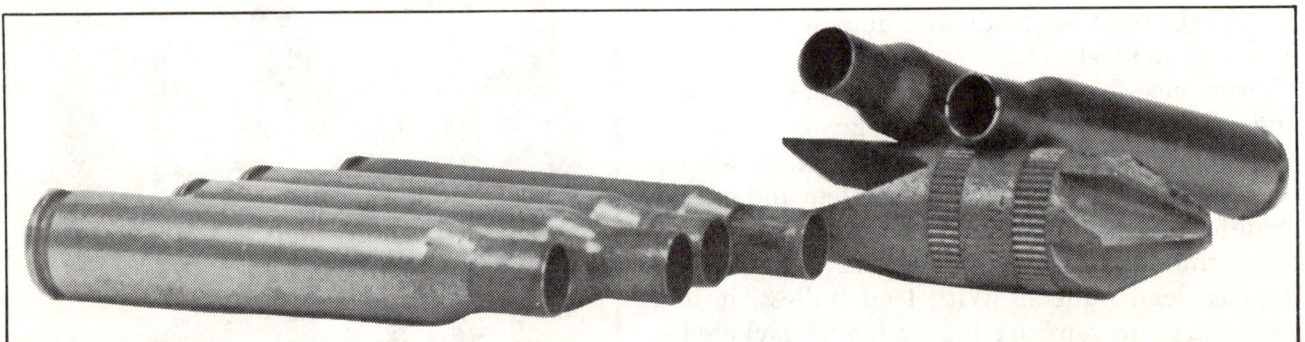

RIFLE GUIDE

 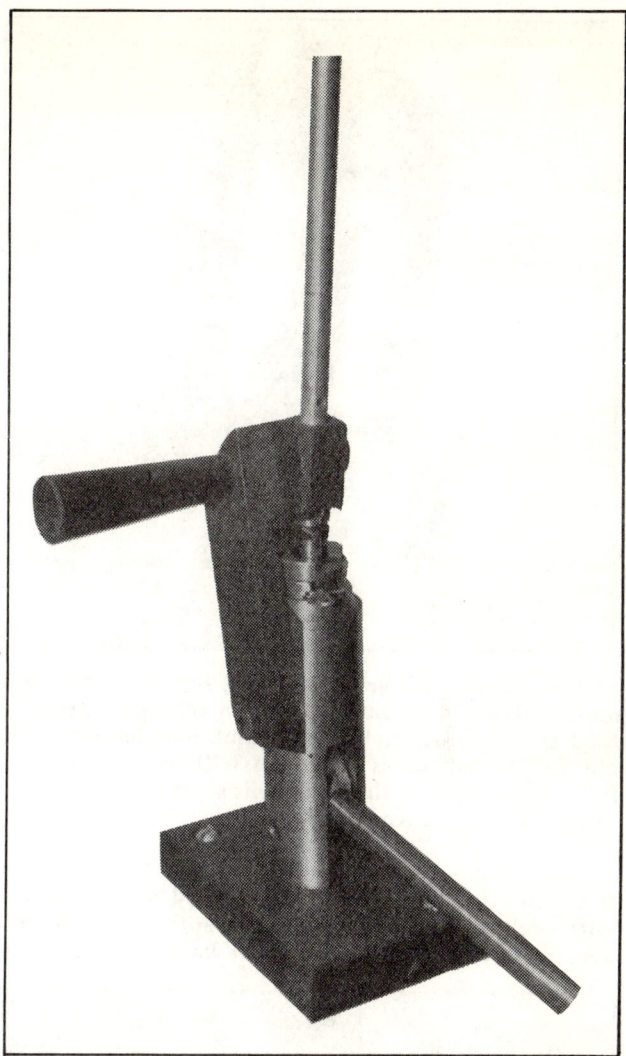

A powder measure will simplify your loading operations. Shown here is the Belding & Mull powder measure, which is highly accurate and very compact. Tube is measuring tube which must be used with this tool.

C-H primer seating tool. Shellholder is the same as used in loading press. Primer feed tube drops one primer at a time into primer seating cup. Operation is quick and you can learn to "feel" primer being seated.

If large amounts of brass have accumulated for reloading, and such a heap of dirty brass tends to scare you away from your loading bench, there is a simple way of tackling the job. If all cases are of the same caliber and from the same rifle, begin by resizing and decapping the brass one night. The next night clean the lube off them, and seat fresh primers. I prefer to prime my cases after primer pocket cleaning and case inspection, and therefore have been using a separate priming tool. The one shown is made by RCBS, and has an automatic primer feed that saves me the trouble of picking up each primer by hand.

Cases that have been fired repeatedly must be inspected before they are resized, and here is what to look for: fine dark lines or actual cracks or fine fissures in the brass a short distance above the case head, fissures running from the case mouth to the shoulder, damaged cases with large body dents. All such cases should be discarded. Reloading them would be a wast of time, effort and components. If one of these cases should let go, you could very possibly ruin a rifle or get hurt.

Brass that has been worked repeatedly can be given a new lease on life by annealing it. By heating and then cooling the neck and shoulder

Primer seating can be done on the loading press, and most of them have provisions for an automatic primer-feed system that saves much time and bother. This old RCBS A-2 press is shown with primer arm in forward position so that primer is seated in case when ram is brought down.

portion of the case, the crystalline structure of the brass is heat-treated and made more ductile. After annealing, the cartridge case can be reloaded and fired as often as a brand new one. The simplest way to anneal cartridge cases is also the best. Get a fairly shallow pan and put some cold tap water in it. Then stand the decapped and resized cases in the water so that the water reaches about halfway up the case bodies. Use either an electric heat torch, which is essentially a powerful hair dryer, or a propane torch. Heat each case neck and shoulder until it turns color, then, with a nail or pencil, tip the heated case over into the water, quenching it. Be careful not to let the flame play much below the shoulder of the case, and never heat the base or head of the case. This portion of the cartridge case must retain its hardness.

If you have a lot of cases to anneal — and I usually save this job until I have enough cases to make it worthwhile — the water in the pan will get quite hot, so change it often. For years, some writers have proposed annealing in hot

Brass that has been worked or resized often might need annealing. Stand cases in shallow pan with some water, heat each case mouth and neck until it changes color, then tip case into water and go on to the next case. Cases have been decapped, must be dried before next loading step.

132

RIFLE GUIDE

Wildcat cases can be de-rimmed, de-belted, or even a new extractor groove can be cut into a cartridge case with the help of a lathe.

molten lead, where the case is first dipped in oil and then into hot lead. However, you will not only have the job of cleaning up the oily cases but, according to metallurgists, you probably will also get an annealing job that is uneven, thus defeating the whole purpose of the work.

Some wildcat cases can be made by firing a standard case in an improved chamber. Other wildcats call for lengthening the neck, derimming a rimmed case, adding an extractor groove, and there is even a die that will swage a belt into a 357 Magnum case. Cases can be shortened or brass from another case can be added to an existing case, thereby lengthening the whole case by as much as 1.5 inches. There is no end to wildcatting, and all this is very much a part of handloading.

There are probably at least six if not more versions of the original 17-caliber wildcat. The most frequently used case is the 222 Remington case, this being closely followed in popularity by the 223 and the 222 Remington Magnum cases. The 218 Bee as well as the Hornet brass has been used successfully, and I have a dummy round that is based on a cut-off 30 M1 Carbine case.

Sometimes, one manufacturer knows that the introduction of a cartridge is imminent and will market rifles for which ammo is not yet commercially available. On the other hand, a big stainless steel selfloading pistol — the Auto Mag — is offered in three calibers, and if you are not a handloader, you'll have to have your ammo custom loaded. The case for the 44 Auto Mag is based on a chopped-off 308 Winchester case, and before you can make brass for either the 41 or the 357 Auto Mag calibers, you have to make 44 Auto Mag cases. Incidentally, the 41 Magnum was dreamed up by Lee Jurras, and is best known as the 41 Jurras Magnum.

Better or at least improved ballistics is the aim of the wildcatter. In dreaming up a wildcat, it helps to understand the questions of case capacity, overbore capacity, and a few other considerations. But long before they come into play, the wildcatter should ascertain the availability of brass for his new brainchild; if an off-beat caliber is contemplated, he should discover whether suitable bullets are available.

A wildcat that requires hours and hours of work to make up a handful of cases may be a labor of love for the inventor, but becomes a real headache for the unsuspecting rifleman who acquires a rifle chambered for the 22/458 Super Deluxe Dislocator wildcat.

Handloading also has the advantage that you can make up all sorts of special loads, from small-game and varmint loads for your '06 to special turkey loads — all for the same gun. These reduced charges, many of them using pistol powders, were at one time factory produced, but now only the handloader can have them. Reduced charges have several advantages, foremost among them being that those charges have greatly reduced recoil and muzzle blast — important considerations for backyard plinking and for teaching other members of the family to shoot.

Some of the best loads of this type that I have used are based on cast bullets, and that means that your bullet costs are greatly reduced. Lyman's *Cast Bullet Handbook* is a good source of data for loads of this type. Under no circumstances should you ever attempt to create reduced charges by pulling the bullets from any load, factory or handload, dumping some powder out and then reseating the bullet. A reduced charge of a slow-burning powder, especially when the charge is not located properly in the case at the moment the firing pin hits the primer, can make a virtual bomb of that cartridge.

Ballistic performance and accuracy of a bullet can be spoiled when the bullet nose becomes deformed and battered. Load your hunting rifle, fire one shot and get your buck. The rest of the ammo from the magazine goes back into the box, and next year, that same ammo is once more stuffed in the magazine. Do this several times, and because of recoil, the bullet nose or point will be so battered that the bullet will not fly true, and it may not even hit anywhere near the anticipated point of impact. I salvaged some of these battered bullet rounds and fired them into an expansion media. A few bullets mushroomed perfectly but never penetrated, others came completely apart.

If bullet nose battering occurs with some of

One end of author's loading room which is commonly called the "Playpen" or the "Lollipop Shop" by visitors.

your handloaded ammo, you can pull the bullets with a bullet puller and simply replace the battered bullet with a new one of the same make and weight. If the misshapen bullets are from factory loads, either pull those bullets, dump the powder and use the primed cases for reloading, or replace the factory bullets with ones of identical weight. However, be forewarned that you may find accuracy is off with these rounds, and such ammo should then be used only for practice. Never attempt to salvage powder from factory or military rounds — such powders are best destroyed.

One more piece of advice: When making up hunting ammo, even if you have not changed the setting of your dies, and the rounds you have loaded previously functioned perfectly through your rifle, verify their feeding from magazine to chamber as well as their extraction. If you can remove the firing pin from the bolt, do so before you run the handloads through the action of your gun. If firing pin removal is difficult or beyond your capabilities, do that testing on the range with the gun pointed toward the target butts, and with your finger away from the trigger. Start with the filled magazine and an empty chamber, operate the action and chamber a round, then eject it, making sure to catch the round on the bench. Continue this process for each round of ammo that you plan on taking along on the hunting trip.

Chapter Seven
This Thing Called Accuracy

Chapter Seven
This Thing Called Accuracy

Accuracy in relation to guns with rifled barrels has been defined as the ability of such a gun to place or cluster a number of projectiles into a small group at a specific distance. Accuracy decreases as the range or as the angle of trajectory increases, and it is also governed by many other factors. In rifles, especially centerfire rifles, accuracy depends on the caliber, the bullet, the powder charge and the primer and also on the care with which the barrel was made. Accuracy also depends on whether or not the barrel steel was prestressed, and on the barrel bedding and the care with which the action was first inletted and then bedded in the stock. Accuracy is dependent, too, on the sights used, on the wind and the distance and, obviously, on the shooter. Worn rifling, or damaged rifling as a result of the careless use of a cleaning rod or an accident will also affect accuracy.

Accuracy is usually discussed in terms of minute-of-angle, or MOA. Roughly, one MOA means that a given rifle with a specific load fired a predetermined number of shots at 100 yards into a group measuring one inch, this measurement being taken from extreme to extreme. To measure a group, locate the two bullet holes which are farthest apart and determine the center of each hole: The distance between those centers is the group size. If there is a flyer or a called shot where the shooter knew that he had pulled the shot the moment he touched the round off, it is permissible to exclude that shot from the group size measurement — except, of course, on match targets.

Two MOA means that the group measured two inches at 100 yards. A rifle grouping MOA at 100 yards should theoretically group ½ MOA at 50 yards, two inches at 200 yards and three inches at 300 yards. While some guns will do just about that, most of them won't be quite as predictable.

There are a few points that must be remembered in considering the accuracy capability of a rifle. When Remington introduced its belted 350 Magnum, my test gun with factory ammunition consistently delivered groups that did

To measure a group, take the two most-distant bullet hole centers and measure the distance between them. As indicated on this target, this group measures .41 inch, a low score fired with a 222 Remington benchrest rifle at 100 yards.

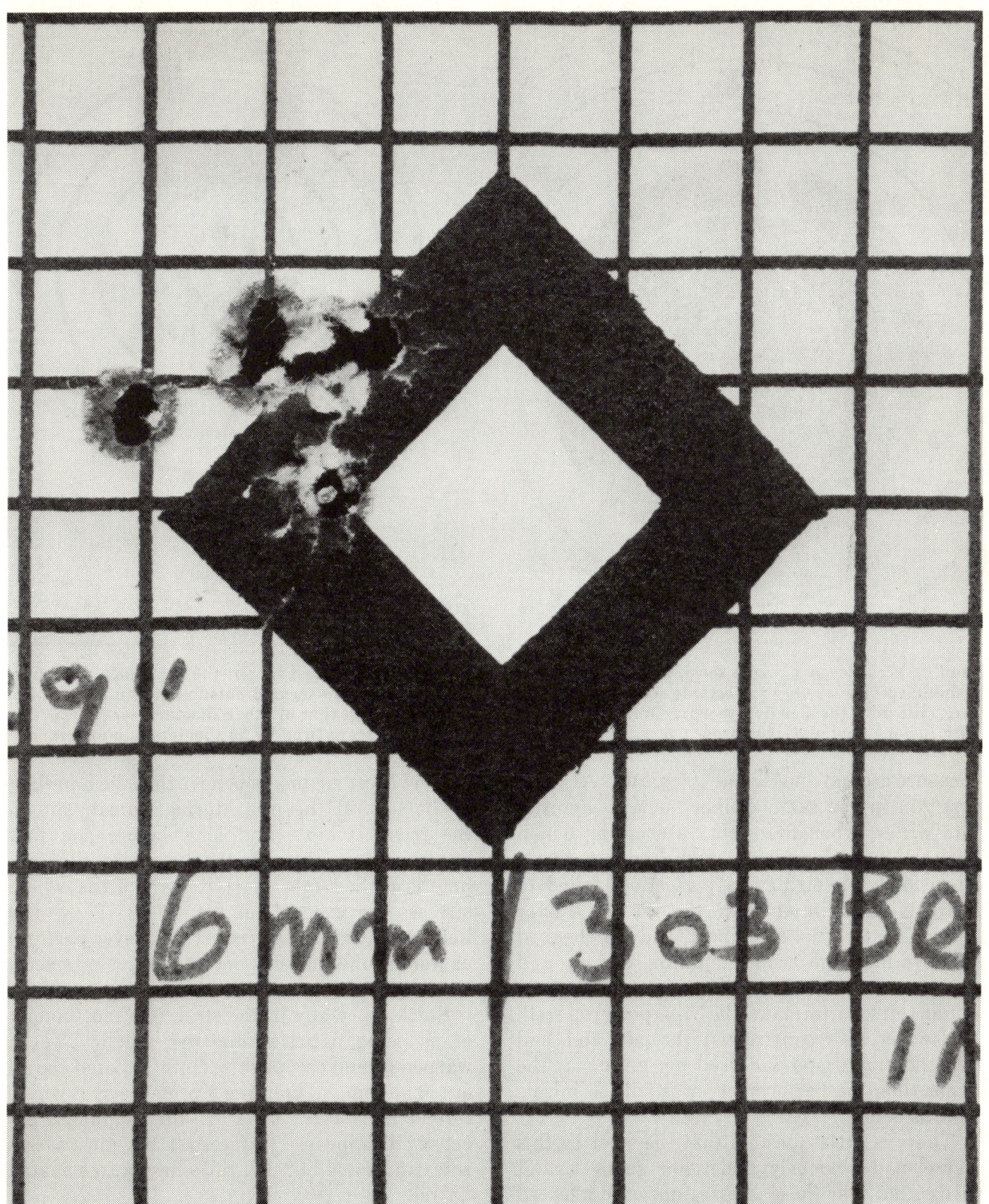

A practice target, somewhat similar to the regulation benchrest target. A five-shot group fired from a heavy barrel wildcat rifle measured .29 inch. Cartridge is one of author's pet wildcats, the 6mm/303 British Improved.

THIS THING CALLED ACCURACY

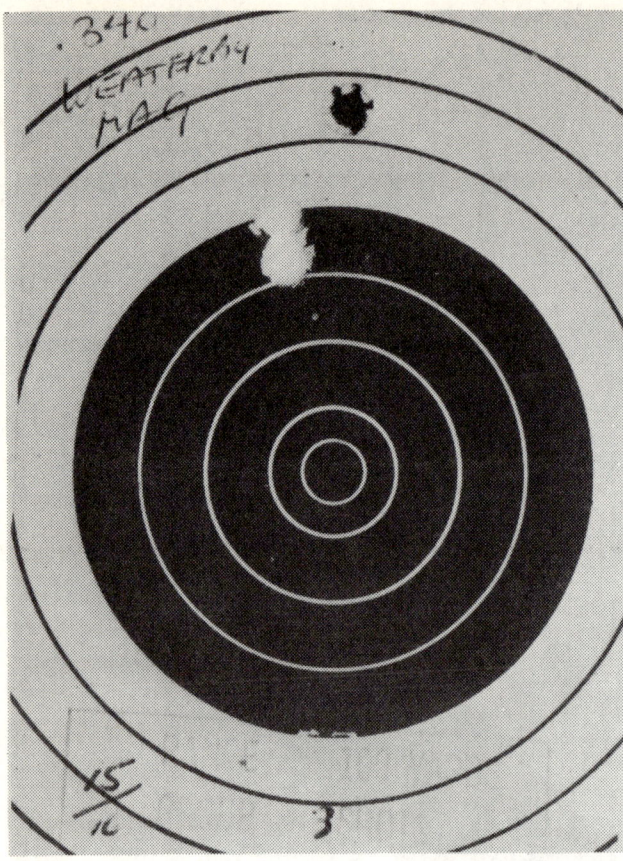

Hunting accuracy is a vague term, but this 1.25-inch 3-shot target shows very respectable accuracy for a big bore rifle like the 340 Weatherby. Group was fired with factory ammo at 100 yards.

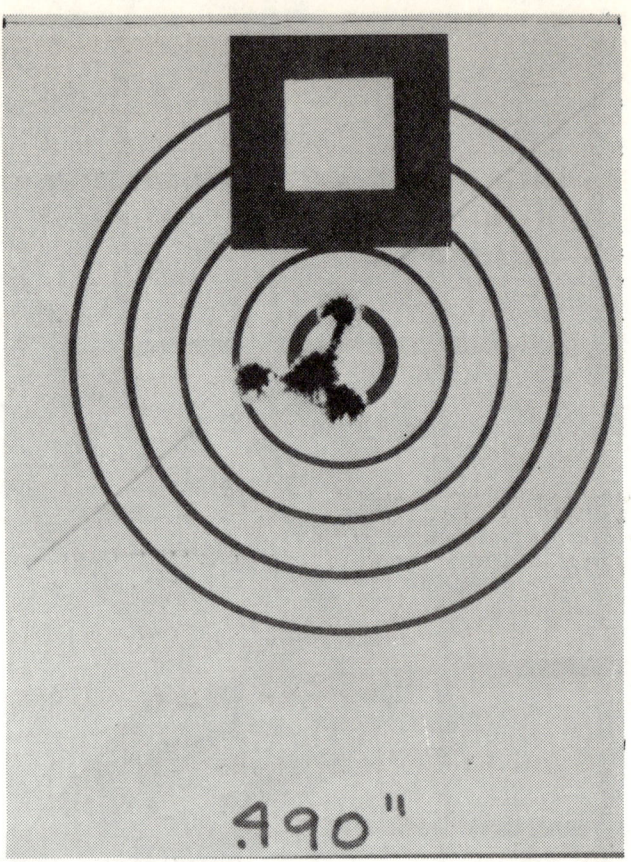

Regulation benchrest target—the first one author fired years ago. Group seemed outstanding until score was compared with that of other shooters—target was second lowest score fired by 50 shooters in a match.

measure around one inch at 100 yards. Another test gun in the same caliber, sent to another gun writer, when fired from a shooting bench with the usual forend rest and sandbag, plus a precision scope sighted to perfection, failed to place five shots into a target the size of a dinner plate. We tore the rifle apart, and we checked the bedding, the scope mounting screws and bases, and the ammo. We did everything we could think of to make the rifle perform well, and when we reconstructed the gun and had switched my scope and used my ammo in the other rifle, the performance was still as miserable as before.

There is little question that the steel in this barrel had obviously undergone some sort of stress, and that these stresses not only affected the molecular structure of the steel, but also the performance of the barrel after the piece of round steel stock had been converted into a barrel. Most engineers believe that the handling of the steel at the mill, during transit, and in the barrel plant—and long before the first broach is run through the barrel or the first hole is drilled into the rod—are areas where stresses are exerted on the steel. They also believe that a stressed barrel will never perform as well as one that has not been stressed excessively.

Steel, especially barrel steel, is often thought of as being extra strong and tough. Yet a warped forend can push a slimly tapered barrel out of alignment, creating a pressure spot where forend and steel meet. If this happens, accuracy disappears. To forestall this, most target rifles and some hunting rifles have a free-floated barrel.

A free-floated barrel does not make contact with the wood of the forend, and the bedding of the action and barrel shank must be perfect.

Target rifles have heavy, or bull, barrels which are not tapered and are thicker and heavier than the normal sporting barrel. The stiffer barrel not only delivers better accuracy, but also helps to dissipate the heat from the barrel, thereby reducing the optical phenomenon known as mirage.

While on the subject of barrel and action bedding, I feel that a word in defense of glass-bedding is indicated. Glassbedding is often used in lieu of good inletting and careful workmanship, and the stock maker who glassbeds every rifle that leaves his shop will soon get the reputation he probably deserves.

On the other hand, I have rescued a number of rifles which had gone sour, or which would have required completely new stocks, by glass-bedding them or by having the job done when I was too busy to do it myself. The area where the action and the recoil lug are bedded in the wood is critical, and here glassbedding not only makes sense, but will also help with those caliber rifles that develop a hefty recoil.

Accuracy, then, is more than just a definition. When the varmint hunter talks about accuracy, he is probably talking about a rifle that delivers MOA, or one-inch groups, at 100 yards. The target shooter and the benchrest competitor talk about accuracy in decimals of an inch, with some of the record groups that have been fired being so small that they are almost incredible. A 222 Remington uses a .224-inch bullet, and five such bullets in a 100-yard benchrest target may measure between .224 and .227 inch. If the group you have shot is any bigger than that, you might as well pack up your shooting gear and go home. Accuracy that is measured in MOAs simply is not good enough for the benchrest shooter or for most of the other shooters who compete in rifle matches.

Often some reader tosses me a curve ball question: "I just bought XYZ rifle in 30-06, and am wondering how accurate it should be." Accuracy depends on a lot of things; moreover, some calibers, like the 222 Remington and the 257 Roberts, are inherently more accurate than most 458 Winchester Magnum rifles, although I have one that belies this statement. Some hunters and some gun writers refer to something they call "hunting accuracy." Since the term is not readily defined, and the user of it usually sidesteps questions as to what he might consider hunting accuracy, let's take a brief look at this term.

The deer hunter seeking his winter venison in brushy country can be content if his rifle groups between one and two inches at, let's say, 75 yards. Compare this with the sheep hunter who may be hunting his trophy ram at an elevation of 8000 or more feet, at 200 or even 300 yards. Obviously, the accuracy requirements for those two rifles can hardly be compared. The moose and elk hunters, the grizzly hunter, and others who stalk big-game animals require a heavier caliber rifle, and the heavier the bullet, the more parabolic the trajectory. Consequently, the 458 Winchester Magnum is seldom considered a tackdriving caliber. Although the 338 Winchester, the 340 Weatherby and other calibers in this class are flatter-shooting than the 458, they simply generate too much recoil for most shooters, and prolonged shooting sessions can lead to flinching, a condition not very conducive to accurate shooting. The shooting position at the bench is a far cry from the pretzel-like position the sheep hunter flops into when a ram comes stalking around a

Free-floating barrel means that wood exerts no pressure on barrel, and this in turn means that slightly better accuracy can be obtained in most cases.

rock outcropping, or the offhand snapshot of the deer hunter.

In the past 20 or more years, I have tested hundreds of rifles, have hunted and collected big-game heads, shot varmints and competed in rifle matches, from small bore four position matches to benchrest matches. Most of us who write about guns shoot enough in one year to keep five other hunters and shooters in ammo for a couple of years. This means that we have either learned how to shoot from a bench through practice, or else got our target shooting experience through the military, or from competing in matches.

It becomes obvious that such experience counts when you think of targeting-in and then firing for groups with a 375 H&H rifle. Let's assume two different loadings, with 100 rounds of each — now there's a fair bit of recoil to absorb. Such an afternoon at the range is, of course, no longer fun but hard work, but it must be done, for tomorrow it might rain or snow. I have learned over the years to concentrate completely on the sight picture and the trigger squeeze while disregarding everything else around me. I have even learned to ignore recoil almost completely. This does not mean that I don't get a sore shoulder, but I usually don't discover it until later.

If a lot of bench testing of rifles is called for, the use of a sissy bag is recommended. A 25-pound bag of No. 6 or No. $7\frac{1}{2}$ shot is placed between the butt of the rifle and the shooter's shoulder. With the forend of the rifle resting on a solid rest, such as a sandbag and a pedestal or forend rest, it may mean that you have to stretch a bit to reach the trigger. But since you should not fire faster than one shot per minute to avoid barrel heating, you should have plenty of time between shots to examine the fired case, chamber a fresh round, resettle yourself behind the butt of the gun and regain the sight picture.

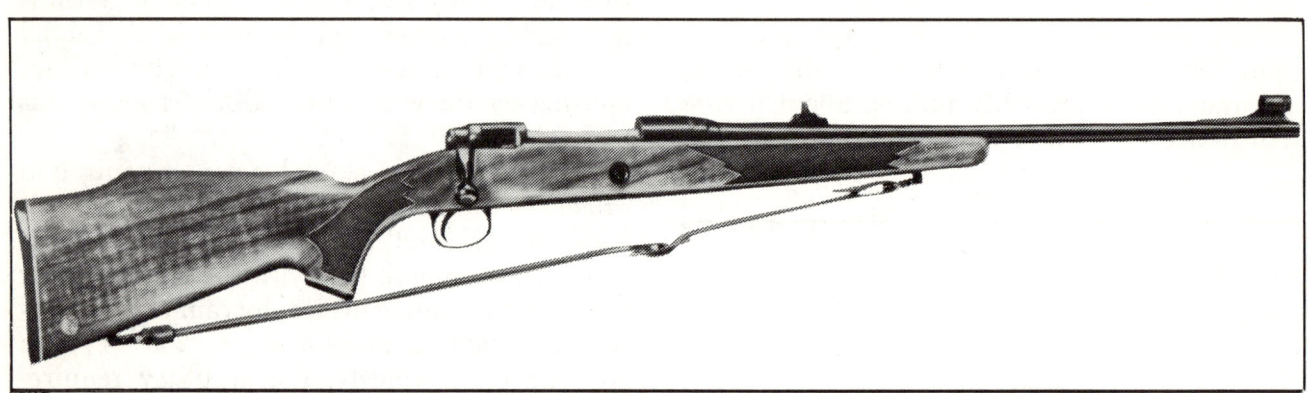

Modern sporting rifle, the Savage Model 111 as it comes from the factory. Compare this configuration with that of the rifle shown in next photograph.

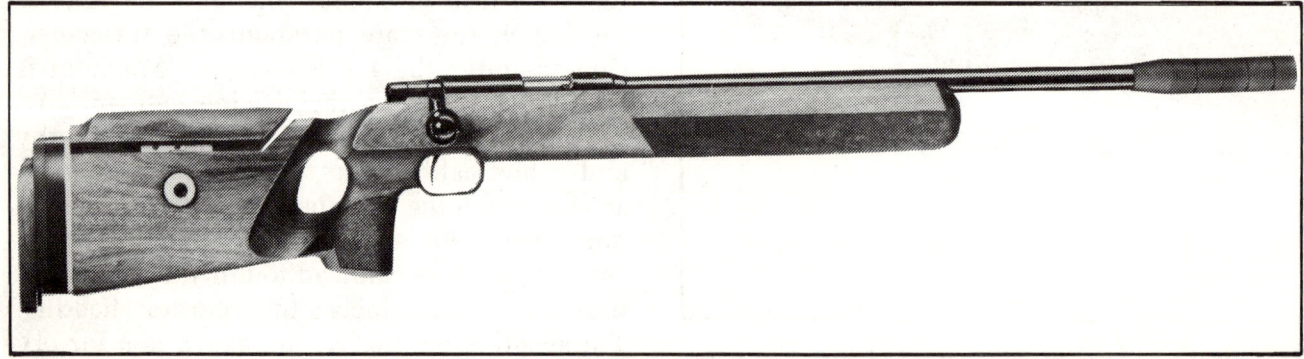

This rifle was especially designed for the Running Boar target match—the Anschutz Model 1408-ED, sold by Savage.

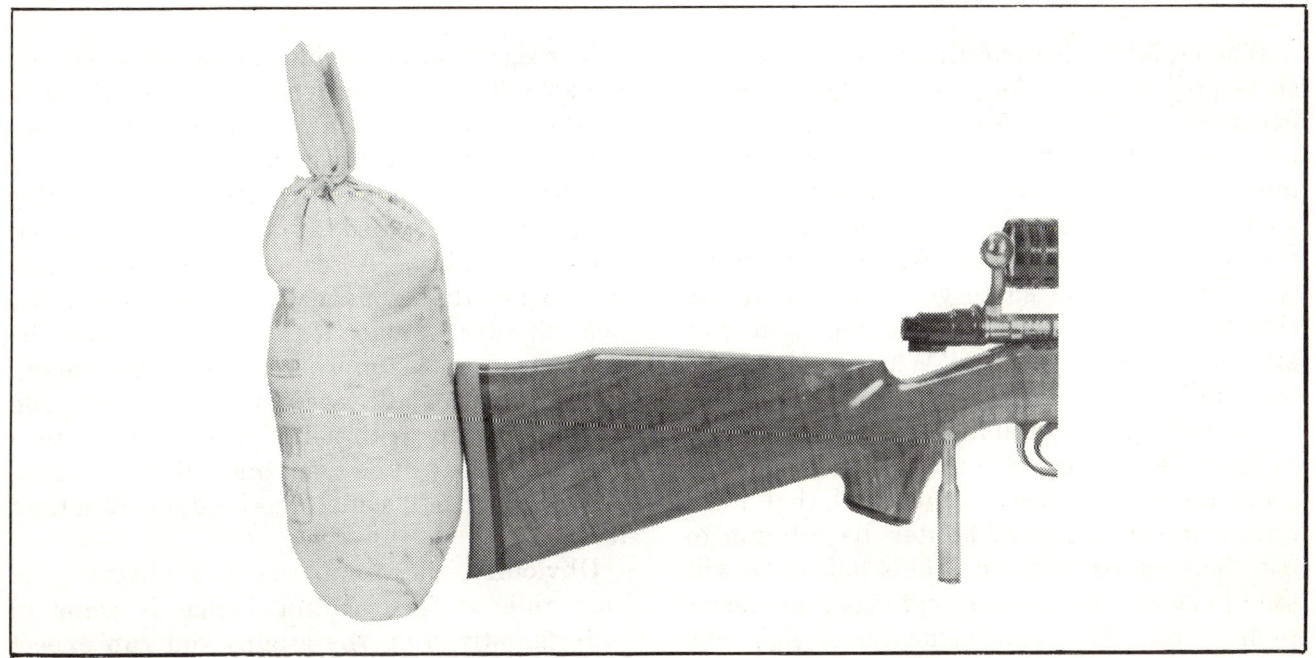

Obviously, this rifle does develop recoil, but shooter was not really aware of being kicked. Concentration on sight picture and uniform trigger pull does much to overcome the fear or anticipation of recoil.

If anticipated recoil is bad and shooter is overly sensitive to it, stick a bag of shot between shoulder and butt of rifle stock. Shot will absorb much of the recoil.

THIS THING CALLED ACCURACY

The Wailing Wall is where you meet the other shooters, compare notes, and blame yourself for lousy scores. Griping does not help—the targets are measured and group sizes recorded for the record book.

When talking about accuracy, the number of shots fired to form the group being discussed becomes important. Military tests called for ten shots, but this was cut back to five shots for most sporting rifle testing. From the point of view of evaluating a rifle's accuracy potential, the five- ten-shot target will tell you more, providing that you space your shots, and the rifle barrel does not overheat, and you can absorb recoil like a sponge. When you consider that most hunters seldom get off more than one or two shots per game animal downed, the value of the five-shot group becomes questionable. Since no buck or bear stands still that long, quite a few shooters and hunters have begun to use the three-shot group. This naturally will tend to shrink group sizes, and it is a lot easier to fire a tidy MOA three-shot target than one that contains ten shots within the one-inch group.

The sights on most rifles are great when you have 20-20 vision and when you are willing to limit the range at which you are shooting. Since you can't always do the latter and few of us have 20-20 vision for our entire lifespan, a sighting system must be added to give that rifle extended range capability. A scope is the answer, and how to pick the right one will be discussed in the next chapter. Suffice it to say, the greater the magnification, the more you see of the target. Therefore, it would seem easier to get good bragging groups with a 10X scope than with a 4X scope. As will be seen, magnification helps, but too much of it sometimes hinders more than it helps.

Obviously, the group size you obtain from your rifle at the shooting bench is going to differ greatly from the groups you can expect from your hunting rifle while kneeling, sitting or shooting offhand. In field shooting, you

In Alaskan sheep camp, benchrest accuracy becomes a memory, and altitude, wind, mirage, and shooting up or downhill must be kept in mind, plus the fact that the target is often a moving one.

must use any support that you can find — a tree or fence post, or a variation of the sitting or kneeling position. Even the prone position or some variation of it can be used, providing the recoil won't shove you over the rocky ledge you may be perched on.

The stock of the commercial hunting rifle is designed for that mythical human being — the average person. Cheekpiece and Monte Carlo stocks are now in vogue, and both of these stock features increase accuracy by absorbing some of the recoil and by consistently positioning the shooter's face in the same place on the stock. They also add the eye-appeal and cosmetic touch that so many shooters feel is important. On the other hand, a couple of million sporting and military rifle stocks without these features are in use, and their owners are just as happy as those whose rifles have both features.

Although some stock features are important, such as the pistol grip which enables you to pull the stock in closer to your shoulder, other features are less critical. For instance, the shooter now owning a 300 H&H rifle with a Monte Carlo stock complete with cheekpiece and pistol grip may find it difficult to get used to the stock of a Model 94 Winchester which lacks these features. However, a little practice will make it possible for anyone to accomplish such a switch. The important point about factory stocks is that they are designed for all shooting positions in contrast to match or target rifles, which have stocks designed for specific shooting positions, such as offhand, prone, benchrest, etc.

Should a factory stock be too short, the addition of spacers and even a recoil pad will work wonders, while a too-long stock can be cut off so that it will fit the shooter. Most stocks of rifles

THIS THING CALLED ACCURACY

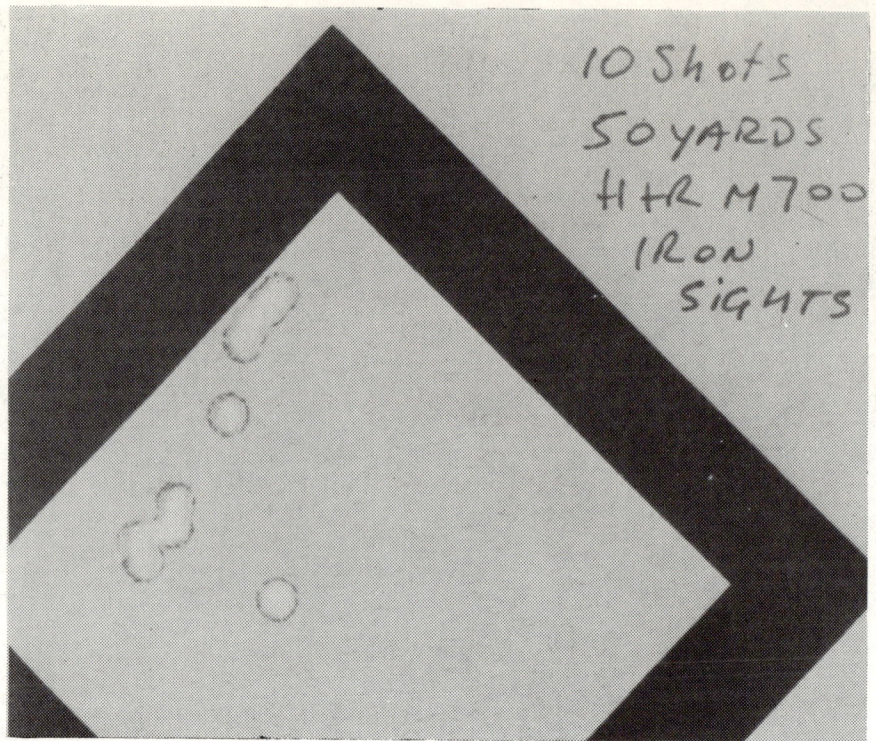

How many shots should be fired for a group? Two of the bullet hole clusters would indicate good potential accuracy, and obviously, shooter did not maintain a good sight picture while firing this ten-shot string.

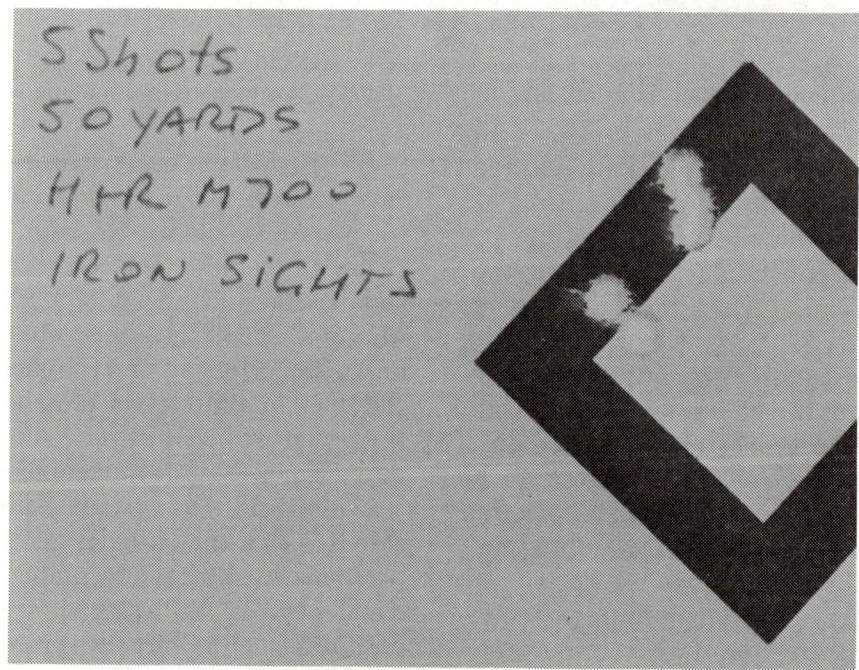

This five-shot group measures just a shade over one inch, with three bullet holes making a tidy group. This target, and the one before and the one following were fired with **H&R Model 700** at 50 yards from benchrest, but with iron sights. Rifle is chambered for the Winchester 22 rimfire magnum round.

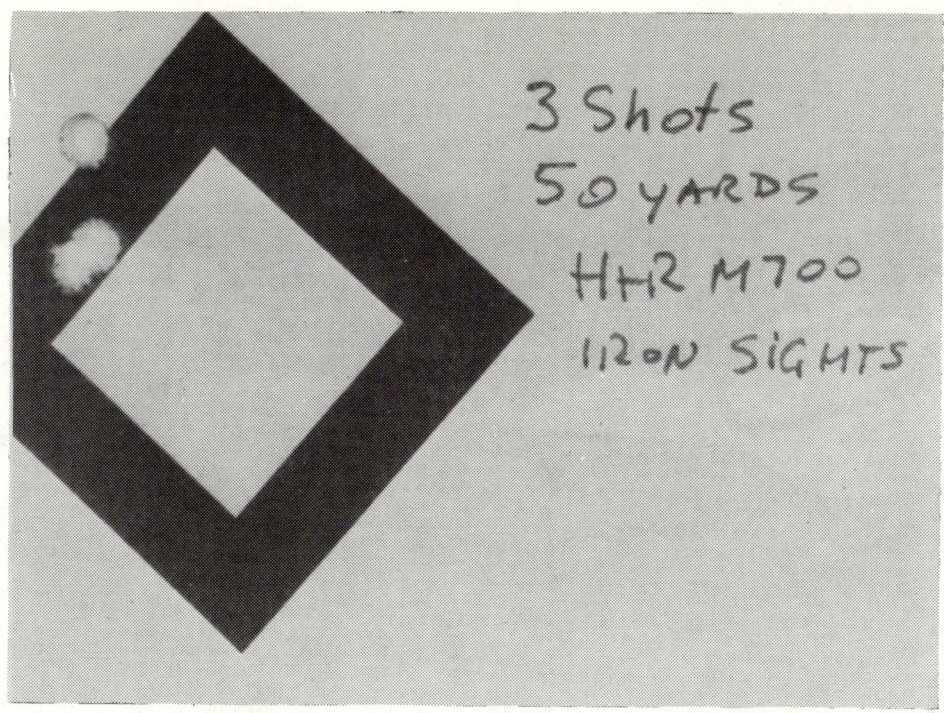

Just under ½MOA, this group, also fired with the H&R M700, shows good accuracy, especially since shooting was done with iron sights.

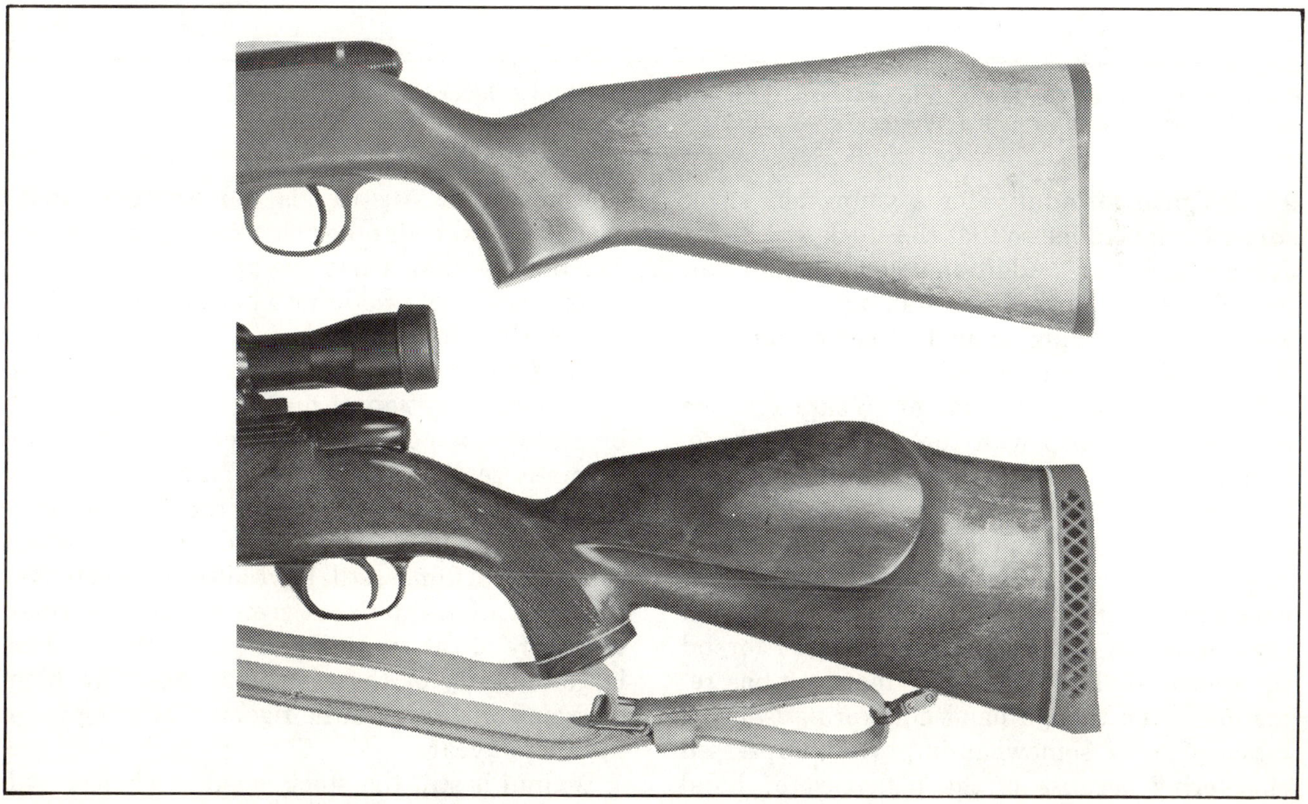

Lower rifle stock has cheekpiece, rubber recoil pad, contrasting wood pistol-grip cap and skip line checkering. Stock of rifle above has a Monte Carlo buttstock, hard-rubber butt plate.

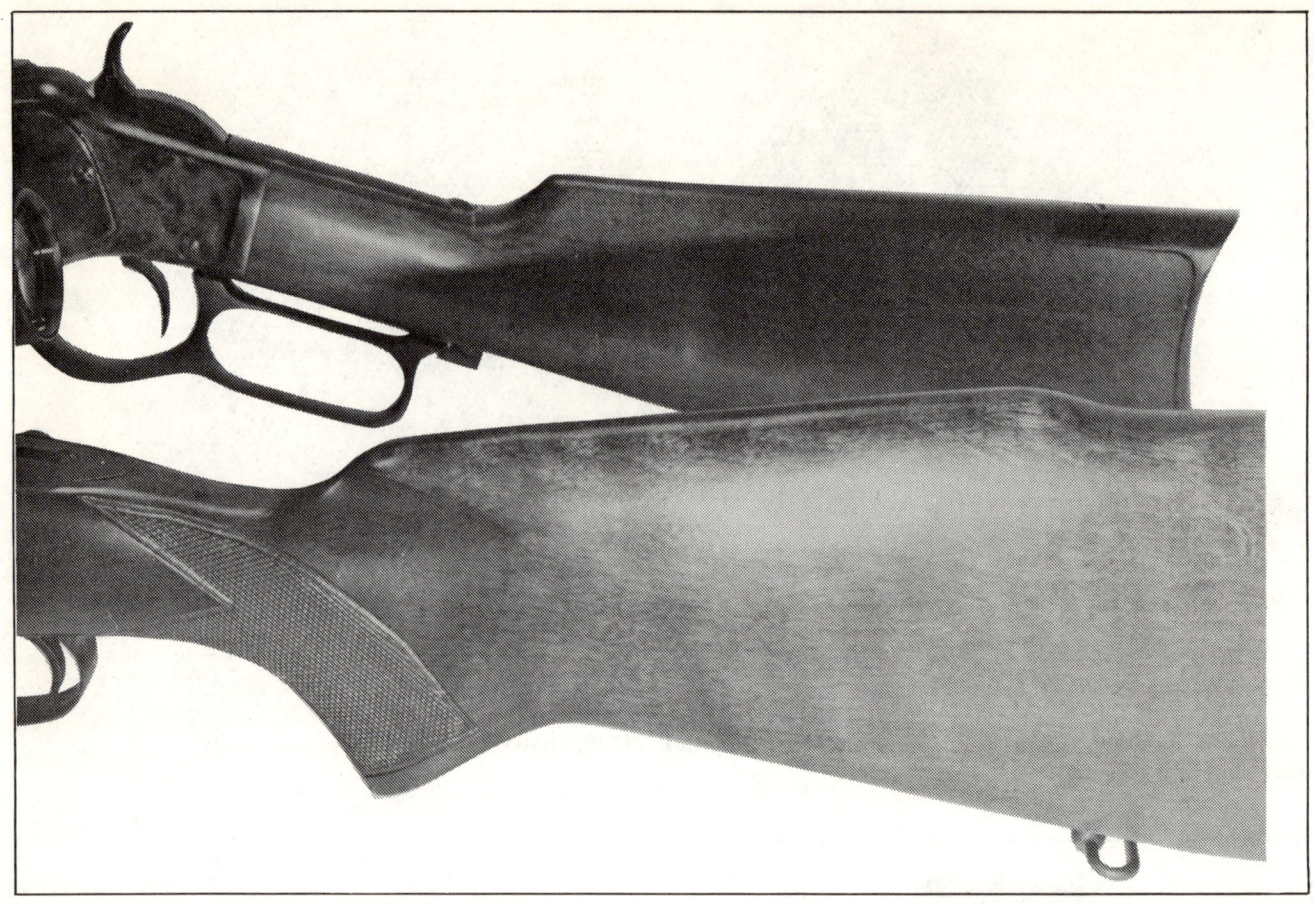

Pistol-grip stock on the lower rifle contrasts with straight stock of a lever-action rifle. Straight stock is sometimes also called Western-style stock.

are designed for adults; for a youngster, stock surgery can be done so that the stock will fit for at least one year. Additional stock length can be achieved later by reinstalling the cut-off wood or by adding enough spacers and an extra-thick rubber recoil pad.

Stock extremes come and go. Years ago, the extreme pistol grip with the swept-back base, forends which were anything but half-round, and excessive Monte Carlo stocks with contrasting wood spacers (or even inlays) were in vogue. Then came thumbhole stocks, forends which looked like unfinished hunks of 2x4, and even extremes of the German Schnabel forend tip appeared. But the classic rifle stock has remained, even though hand checkering is being replaced by a somewhat improved impressed checkering because of the high cost of hand labor. Skip line checkering, primarily found on rifles imported from Europe, notably from Germany and Austria, is handsome if well-executed. Like all other checkering, it must be well done so that it has eye-appeal, in addition to its function of providing a better gripping surface on the gun.

The finish on a stock is important insofar as it prevents absorption of moisture into the wood by sealing the pores of the wood, as well as for cosmetic reasons. The traditional oil finish on rifle stocks has gone the way of the five-cent cup of coffee. Again, a few imported high-class guns, especially drillings, still have oil-finished stocks, but most of the finishes seen on factory rifles today are of the synthetic or plastic type. The large majority of these stock finishes are high gloss and will survive the rigors of hunting for a number of years.

Walnut is still the stock wood of choice, and if you see the words "walnut finish" in a catalog, it means that the stock is made from some other

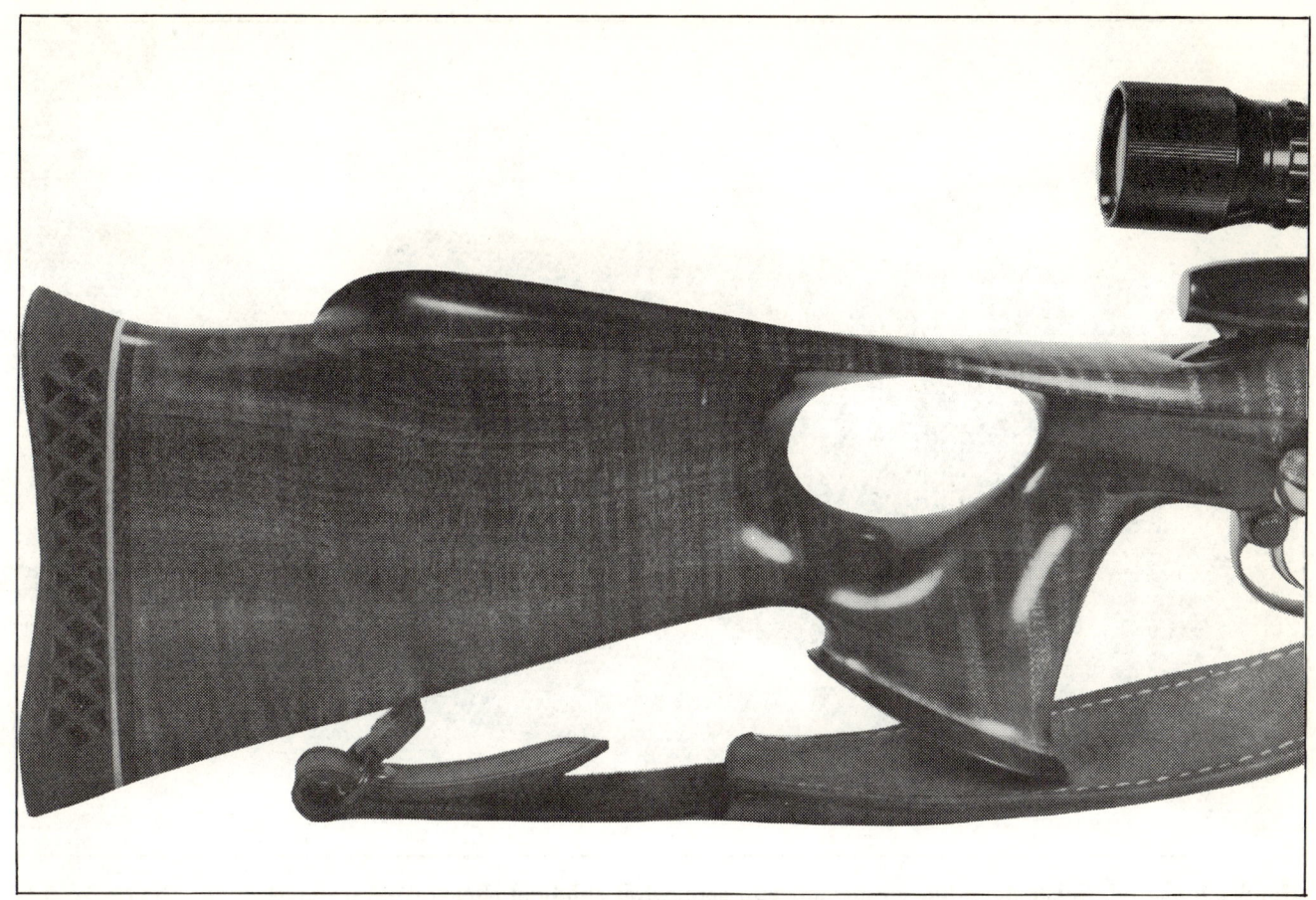

Extreme of stock design is shown by this far-out stock. Oversized pistol grip, curved rubber recoil pad and thumbhole stock plus streamlined cheekpiece on other side of buttstock.

hardwood that has been stained to resemble walnut. Many of these stocks are every bit as good as the walnut stocks, but cost less to manufacture and are therefore seen on rifles which are lower in price. Plastic stocks, although completely weather-resistant, have never caught on with the shooting public, the Remington rimfire rifles being an exception. Even here, buyer resistance has been considerable until the shooter tried the accurate and smoothly performing rifle. Plastic stocks can take a fantastic amount of abuse and beating without even showing a scratch.

The matter of trigger pull, and the amount of trigger pull that is right for a hunting rifle is often barely considered. The two-stage military trigger pull found on the military rifles of most countries is designed as a "give pause" and safety feature. For the hunter and the target shooter, such a trigger pull, when using a military rifle in either "as is" condition or when customized and sporterized, should either be corrected or the trigger should be replaced with a suitable commercial model. The amount of trigger pull required to "break" the trigger, and the various trigger motions are often stressed as being vitally important. A smooth trigger pull is important, but whether the trigger breaks at four or six pounds, and how much trigger travel there is, is only of real importance to the match shooter and to a few others who like to tinker with their rifles. For instance, all of my personal hunting rifles are tuned so that they all have an identical trigger pull. It must be remembered that the measured trigger pull varies somewhat, and that checking the trigger pull is a matter of averaging ten such measurements.

While extra-light triggers are great for the match shooter, an excessively light pull on a hunting rifle is not only useless but can also be

THIS THING CALLED ACCURACY

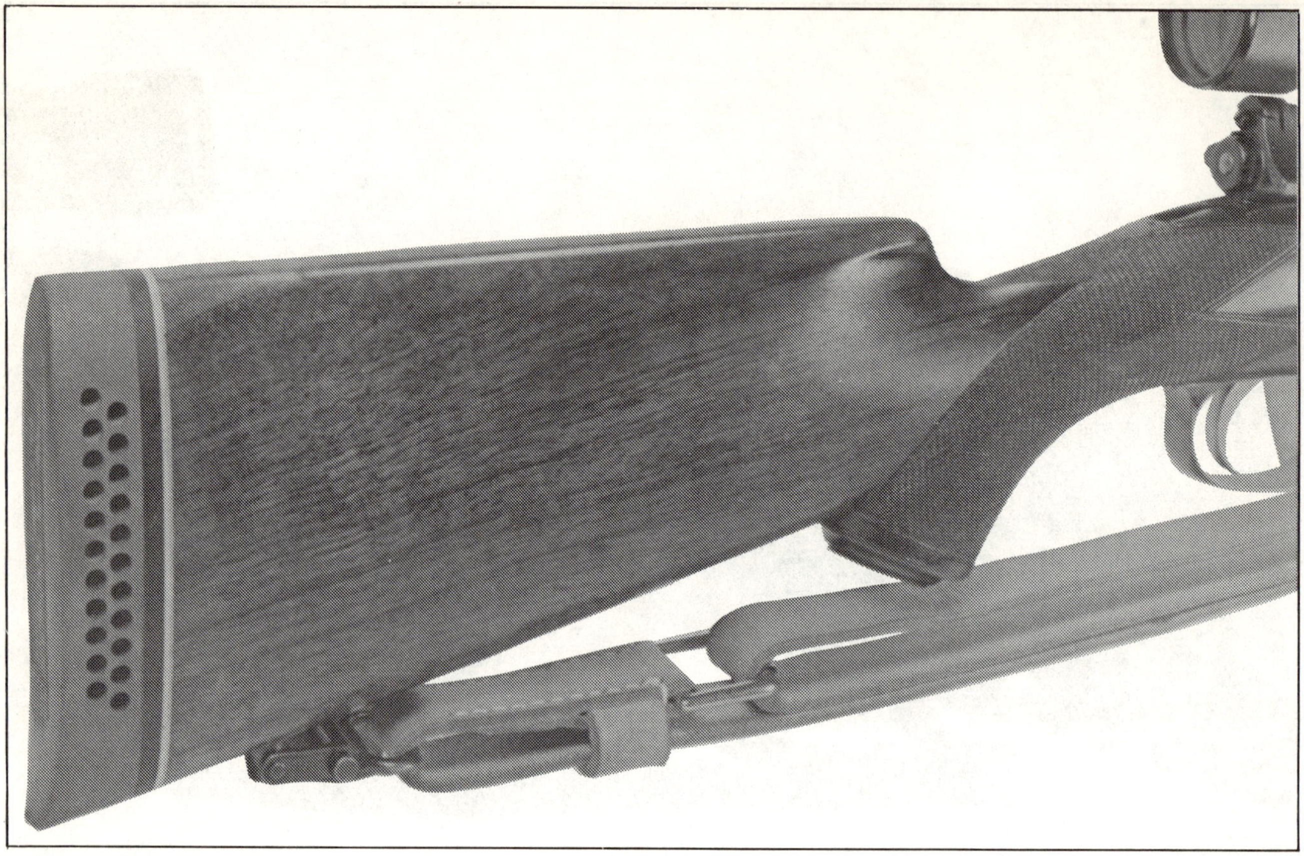

Hand-rubbed oil-finish stock has an elegant and somewhat subdued sheen.

downright dangerous, since such light triggers can be jarred loose by even a light impact of buttstock on a rock, or when the stock makes contact with some other hard object. Some rifles come with an adjustable trigger, and these can be tuned by anyone who can handle a screwdriver. If tuned to the point where the pull is too light, the gun may fire when the bolt is closed. In commercial triggers, the trigger slack take-up is incorporated in the trigger let-off. The long first pull of the military trigger accomplishes the same thing. For a hunting rifle, the trigger pull should not be less than four pounds and should not exceed six pounds. If the trigger pull is too hard, the force exerted on the trigger will affect your sight picture adversely.

Set triggers, where the trigger is moved forward or set, so that the rearward trigger pull is extra light are again reserved for target rifles and a few varmint rifles. Such a trigger must be installed by a gunsmith, and trigger pull is often given in ounces rather than pounds. Double

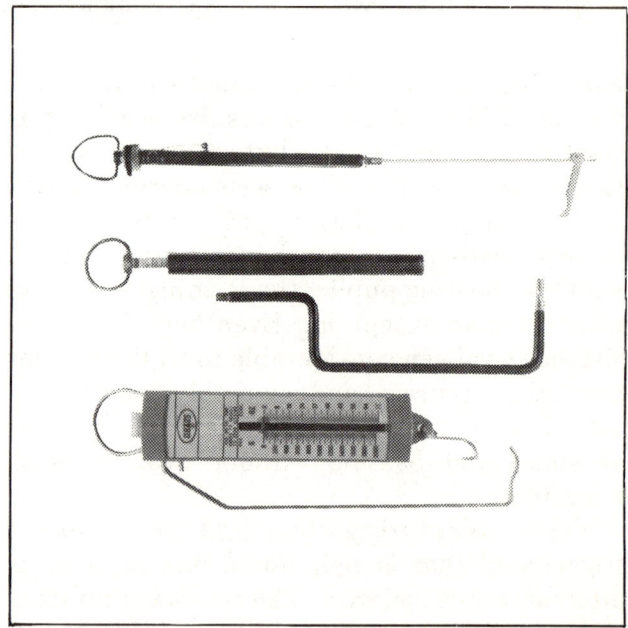

Three of the most widely used trigger-pull scales. The trigger pull on match rifles is measured by means of weights since the spring-loaded scales do not have the degree of accuracy required by match rules.

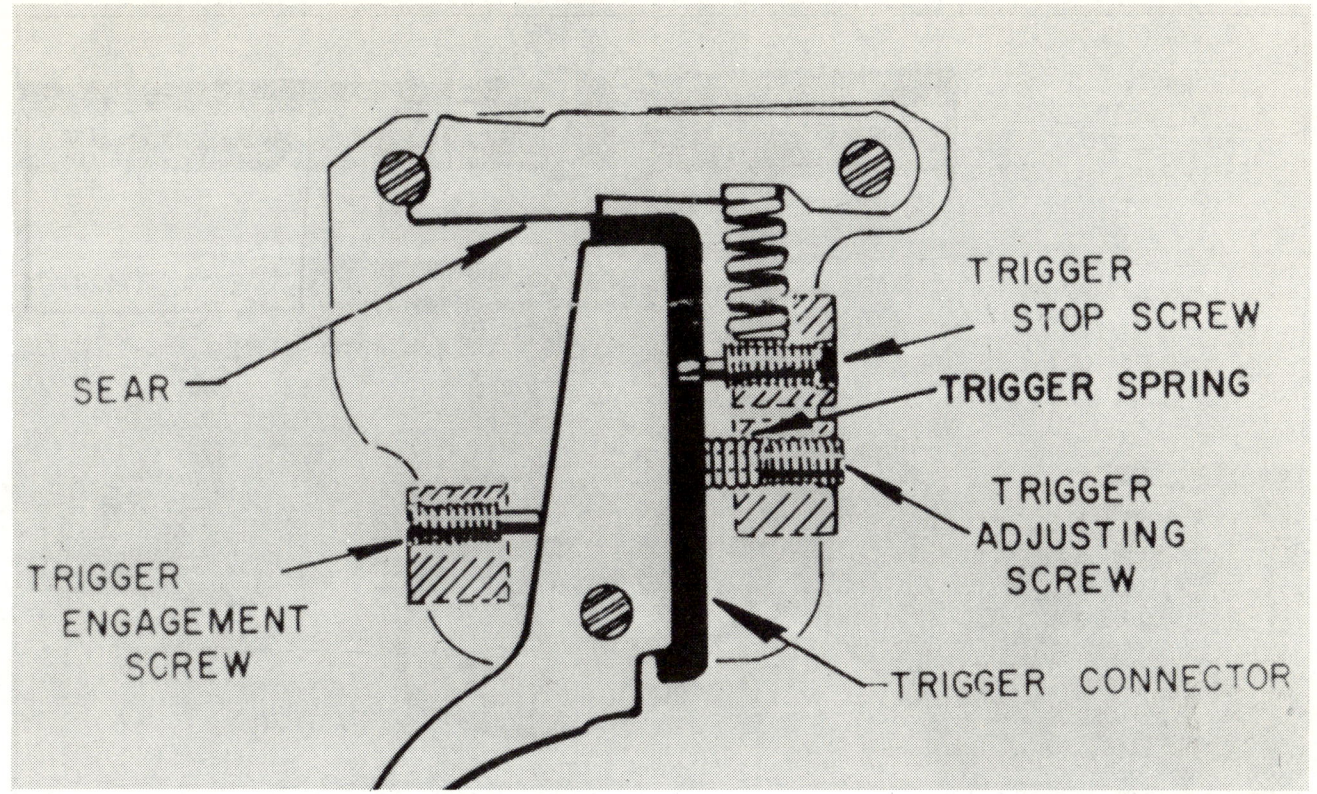

This diagram shows how the trigger of a Remington Model 700 is adjusted. Sketch is reproduced from product folder that comes with each rifle.

triggers, where one trigger sets the engagement of the other trigger, are found mostly on German guns; this trigger system, although excellent, has not been widely accepted.

The use of a sling is mandatory in some types of rifle matches, while the benchrest shooter does without sling. For the hunter, a sling is not just a mere convenience, but a necessity as far as I am concerned. These days, when I buy a hunting rifle that does not have sling swivels, I install them even before I mount a scope on the rifle. A carrying strap or sling not only helps to reduce arm fatigue, but also frees the hunter's hands for pushing aside brush or for climbing if stalking goats or sheep. With a little practice, it is amazing how fast you can learn to swing a rifle from the carrying position into the shooting position. Slipping into a hasty sling (that is, a sling arrangement where the sling and the shooter's arm form a supporting triangle for the gun) is a simple matter to master.

The old military sling with its keepers is almost a forgotten item these days, and carrying straps, with a wider and often padded area where the strap fits over the shoulder, can be used as a hasty sling, but not too successfully. After trying a number of sling designs I settled on the Brownell Latigo sling years ago. The Latigo sling is by far the easiest one to install and to handle afield and at home. Conversion from carrying sling to shooting sling is so fast that you can alter the sling while the gun moves from the carrying position to the shooting position. Sling swivels and bases for them are made for all makes of rifles, and those available through Uncle Mike's are not only good, but are found in nearly every gun shop, thanks to their popularity. Special drills for installing swivels are also offered by Uncle Mike's, and all you need to install your own set of swivels is a ruler, an electric drill, and the special drill bit.

Since the thickness of the receiver and its configuration varies greatly from one rifle to another, it is essential that you buy the scope bases designed for the action of your rifle. You have the choice of one- or two-piece bases when

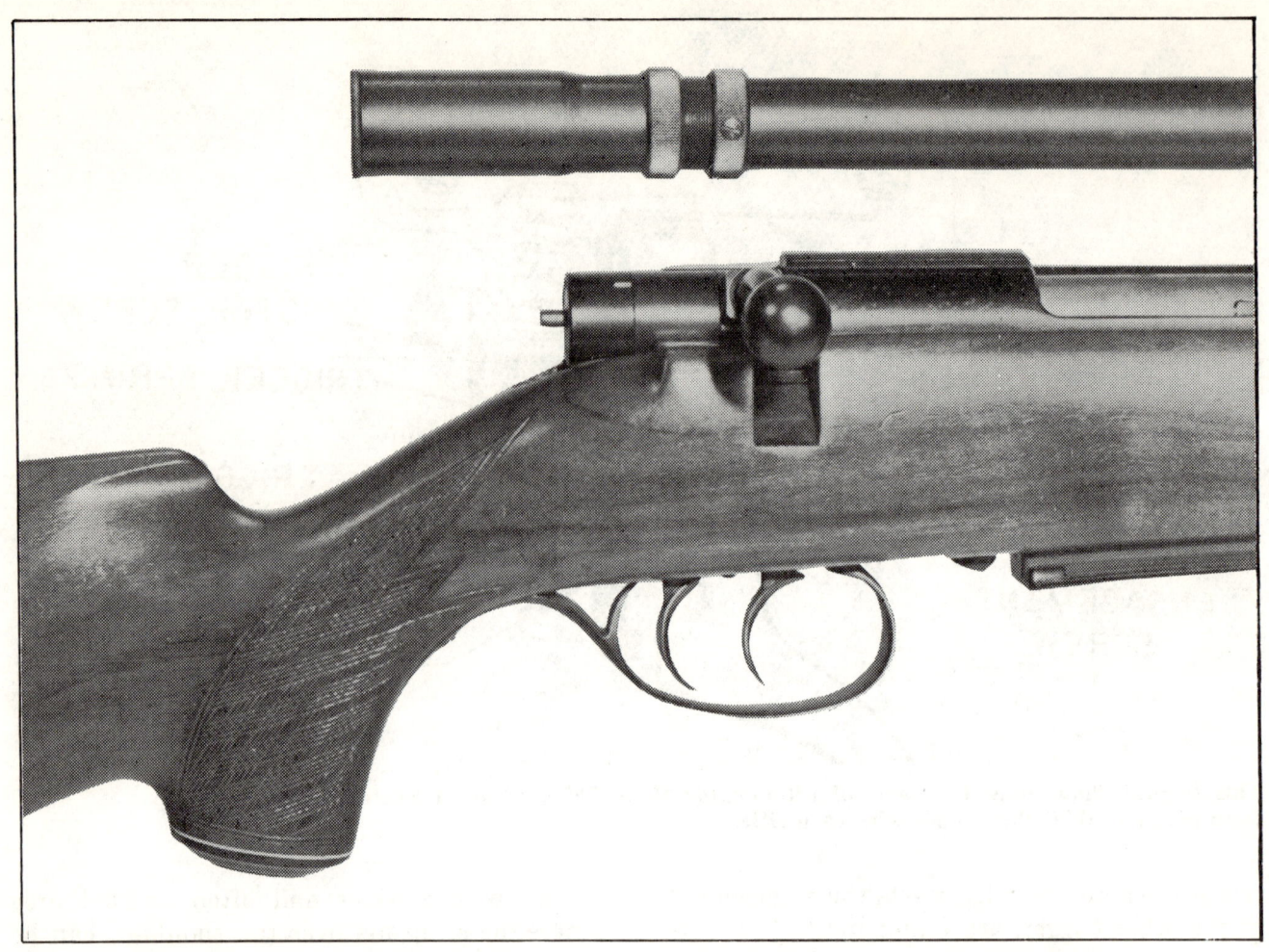

Double triggers, also known as set triggers, are seen mostly on European rifles. When pulled to rear, the rear trigger sets the front trigger which then becomes a hair trigger. If rear trigger is not set prior to firing, front trigger will have a heavier pull.

selecting scope bases, and although it is sometimes possible to use the bases of one manufacturer and the rings from another maker, it is far better to stick to rings and bases of one make. Ruger's Mini-14, the M94 and other such rifles require special mounts. The B-Square Co. of Fort Worth is the primary source for mounts and rings, as well as for mounts and rings for a number of other models. Weaver, Redfield, Leupold and many others offer scope mounting systems and scopes for nearly every purpose.

The target shooter will almost certainly want to use a sun shade or shield over his scope, while the big-game hunter who goes afield without scope covers almost certainly handicaps himself. Snow, rain and dust will obscure the sight picture so quickly that an offered shot will often be missed because the target was not clearly defined. Snap-off scope covers, such as those produced by Durfee & Deming under the name Ka-Ram-Ba, are an essential part of all of my hunting rifles. One snap of a fingernail against the rear scope cover and both of the covers pop off, being retained on the scope tube by a strong rubber band.

So far as weight, caliber, sights and stocks are concerned, target rifles will vary with the type of target shooting. The offhand ISU rifle differs from the four-position rimfire in stock design and weight, while the use of peep sights or target scope is dictated by the rules of the event being fired. Benchrest rifles are classified by weight — that means the complete rifle with scope and sun shield is weighed — while the

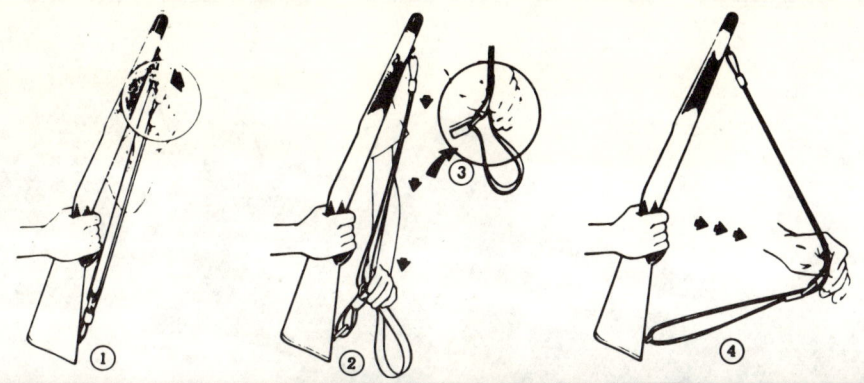

TO OPERATE THE LATIGO SLING
1. Grasp the two outside straps of the *Latigo Sling* immediately below the keeper, see Fig 1.
2. Pull downward as far as you can for FULL extension of sling. If this is too far for maximum sling comfort, pull downward only as far as needed to get your best length. A few trys will establish correct length.
3. Change the position of your hold on the sling, as shown in Fig 3, to include both main straps.
4. Quickly snap both straps outwards as shown in Fig 4. You are now ready to shoot!

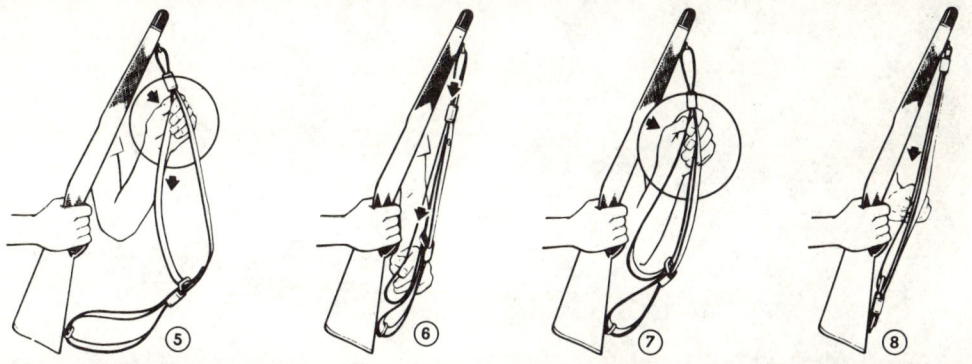

TO RETURN THE LATIGO SLING TO THE TIGHT OR PARADE POSITION
1. Grasp the inside strap of the sling just below the keeper at the top swivel, as shown in Fig 5.
2. Pull downwards as far as you can, see Fig 6. If sling is fully extended, pull down again, see Fig 7 & 8.

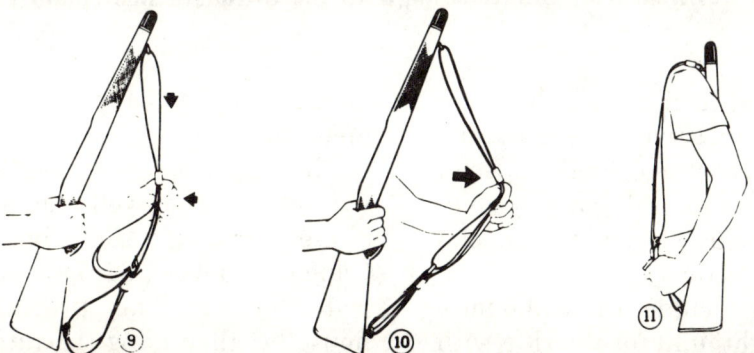

TO USE YOUR LATIGO SLING AS A CARRYING STRAP
1. Pull sling approximately half-way down as shown in Fig 1 and Fig 9.
2. If sling is not comfortable for carrying, as in Fig 11, it may be extended to length desired.

The Brownell Latigo sling is the most easily adjusted sling on the market. Changing sling from extended—that is carrying or hasty sling position to parade position—takes only a second.

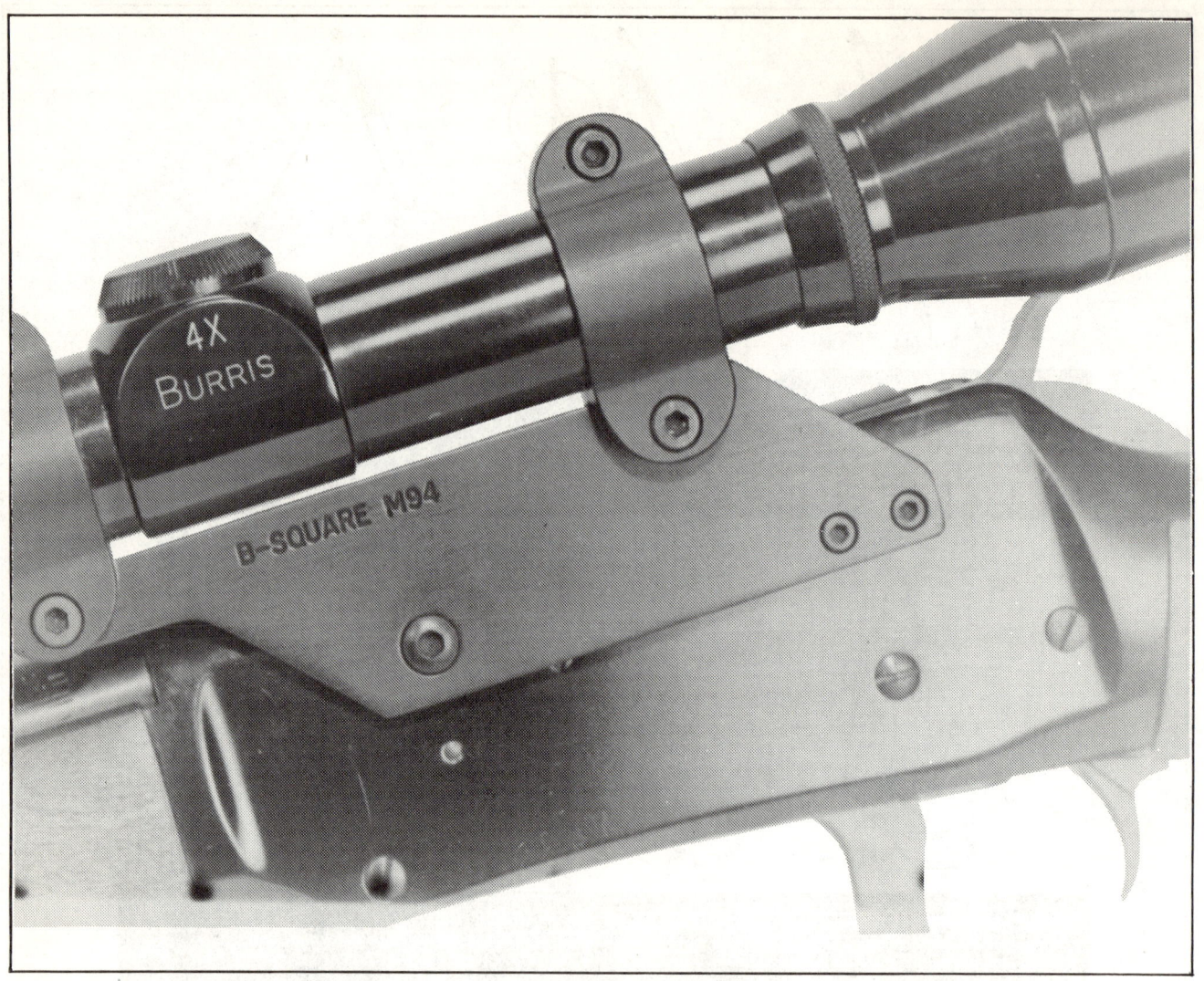

The Winchester Model 94 was a difficult rifle to scope until the B-Square side mount became available.

caliber is not considered in most matches. In contrast to other competitive riflemen, the benchrest shooter does not use a sling or special shooting jacket, but rests his rifle on two sandbags, the forward one being placed on a special and fully adjustable pedestal.

Other rifle matches include the silhouette matches where the weight limit for the rifle with scope and sling is 10 pounds, 2 ounces, and 1000-yard benchrest shooting calls for still other rifle rigs and calibers. Most of the bench guns for the regulation 100- and 200-yard matches are in the smaller calibers such as the 222 Remington, the 6mm International or 6x47; the silhouette matches call for a rifle caliber that can knock over the heavy metal targets at the 500-meter mark.

The target sports have developed their own variants of the well-regulated target events. Some years ago, some benchrest shooters on Cape Cod developed their own style of Chinese water torture. They printed targets of a large housefly, then hung the targets across an inlet or creek so the shooter had to sight and fire over water at 100 or 200 yards. Targets were scored by the number of flies "killed," and that meant that each shot had to be dead-on on a printed fly which was about half the size of a dime or perhaps even smaller. It would be nice if I could say that I competed with honors, but the records are there, and all I want to say about this match is that it was a very humbling experience.

Most of the centerfire rifle competitive events are fired with factory ammunition, but benchrest shooters load their own. Many of these benchrest cartridges are wildcats, some being merely improved factory rounds, others being designed by the competitor. Many of these shooters do their own rifle work, including chambering, making their own reamers and loading dies.

The stiff and quite heavy leather coat, worn for ISU matches, becomes impossibly hot during the summer months when most of these events are fired, and it is a far cry from the traditional small-bore jacket. Participation in the various position centerfire events, as well as rimfire events, favors boots which give solid ankle support, and the issue paratrooper boot is by far the best. Pants that allow unrestricted movement are important for maximum comfort; the padded undershirt, once readily available, seems to have disappeared from the shooting scene along with other cotton products. A heavily padded glove or mitten for the hand that is solidly jammed against the forend swivel, special slings, ear protection and shooting glasses with blinders round out the clothing for the paper puncher.

Many of the bolt-action match rifles are single shots since the absence of a magazine and magazine well reduces the area of possible stock weakness, and the extra stiffness imparted to

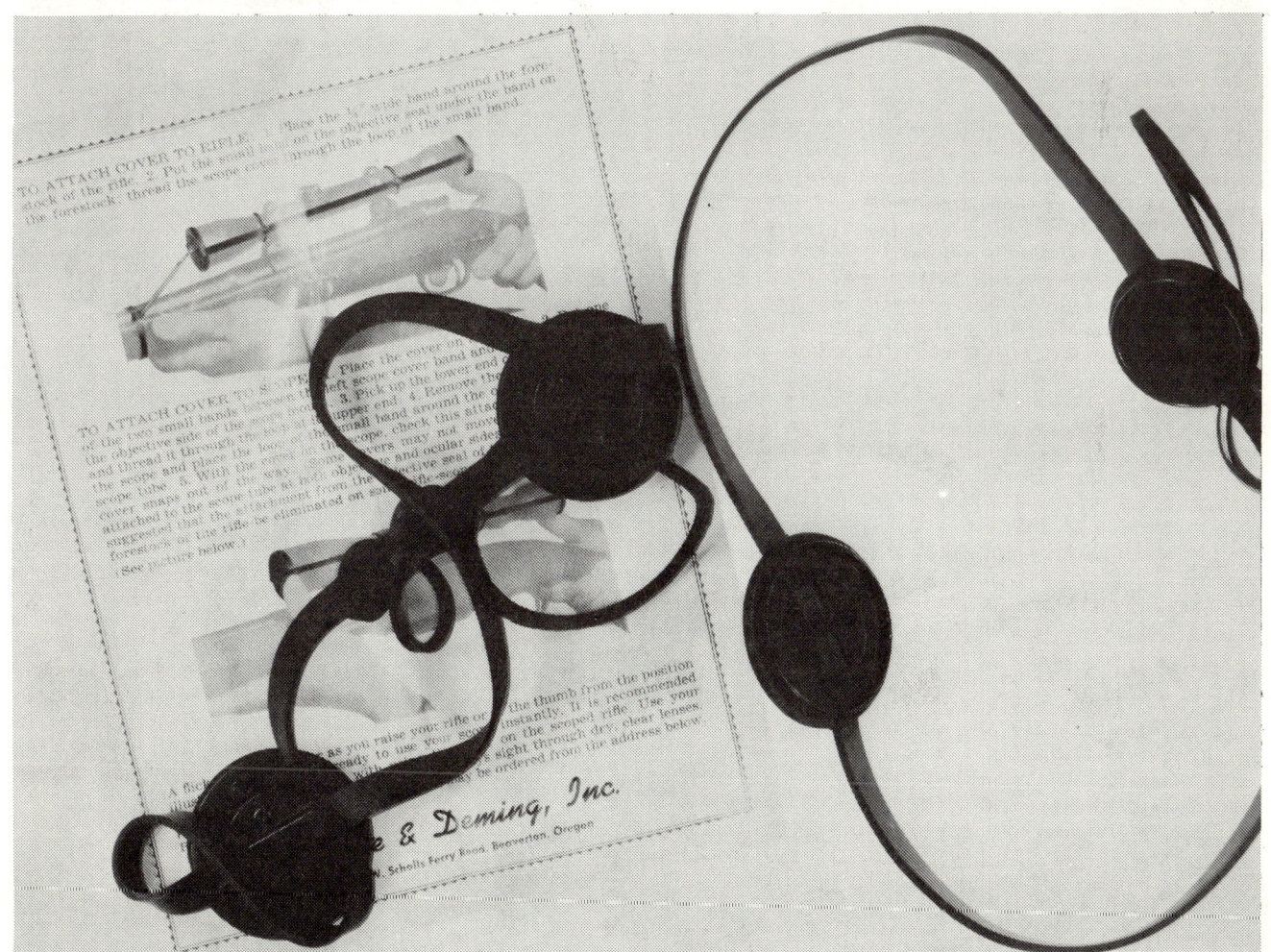

Scope covers that come off fast without getting lost are essential on big-game hunting rifles. The ones at left are made by Durfee and Deming, and are sometimes hard to find in stores. The ones at right are the well-known Storm Queen covers.

The late John Dewey was a top-notch custom gunsmith and benchrest shooter. Here he reloads ammo during a benchrest match. Note the Belding & Mull powder measure and other reloading gear on portable table that serves as loading bench during matches.

the action and stock by omitting the magazine also means a greater accuracy potential. Because of its design, the bolt-action rifle is inherently somewhat more accurate than any rifle design that employs a two-piece stock. The Unlimited Class rifle of the benchrest competitor is more like a shooting machine than a rifle since the weight is unlimited, and when the mechanical monster is examined, it really is more of a machine rest with a barrel and action than a rifle in the conventional sense of the word.

Despite the fact that the laminated wood stock makes a lot of sense from the point of humidity absorption and warpage, it has not become overly popular with hunters. However, laminated stocks are offered by makers of target rifles. Stock makers, especially the larger ones like Reinhart Fajen, feature laminated stocks. Fajen offers laminated blanks or will stock a rifle with laminated wood, the type of lamination depending on the type of stock wanted. Maple and cherry are used for hunting rifles. Varmint stocks are made with two types

Laminated target stocks are pre-shaped in Al Freeland's custom shop. Laminated stocks do not warp, but some shooters object to them, claiming that they lack eye appeal.

THIS THING CALLED ACCURACY

of lamination, one being walnut and maple, the other of 5/16-inch walnut and walnut lamination.

Mannlicher-type stocks, in which the wood of the forend extends to the muzzle of the barrel, originated in the Alps of Austria. Mountain troops and hunters there traditionally sling their rifles crossways over their backs to free their hands for mountain climbing. This meant that the unprotected barrel of a rifle was often banged up so much that it became useless. Extending the stock to protect the barrel made a lot of sense then, and it still does for some types of rifles, especially those made for sheep and goat hunters. When not properly bedded, however, or when the barrel channel has not been fully sealed, warping too often affects such a stock, making the cure worse than the ailment — better a banged-up and scratched-up barrel than an inaccurate rifle. Mannlicher stocks also permit the use of a slightly shorter and perhaps tapered barrel, but finding near-perfect stock blanks which are long enough for this type of stock is becoming more difficult each year, and you will have to pay premium prices for such stocks.

Some rifles are designed for specific purposes, and here the so-called survival or campers' rifles are of more than passing interest. The AR-7 sold by Charter Arms is a semiautomatic 22 LR gun that can be taken down by means of a single screw, and the metal parts can be stored in the plastic stock. The entire package floats, the action remains dry and functional, and now you can even get a scope mount for the AR-7. Other survival guns, not quite as compact as the AR-7, usually have a skeleton metal stock. Of course, this overcomes the problem of stock breakage and also reduces the weight of the rifle quite effectively.

A rather unusual stock design is found on rifles commonly known as bullpups. Short barreled, with a bolt action, the stock is designed so that the action is right under the shooter's nose, and the bolt cannot be operated unless the gun is dismounted from the shoulder. Every few

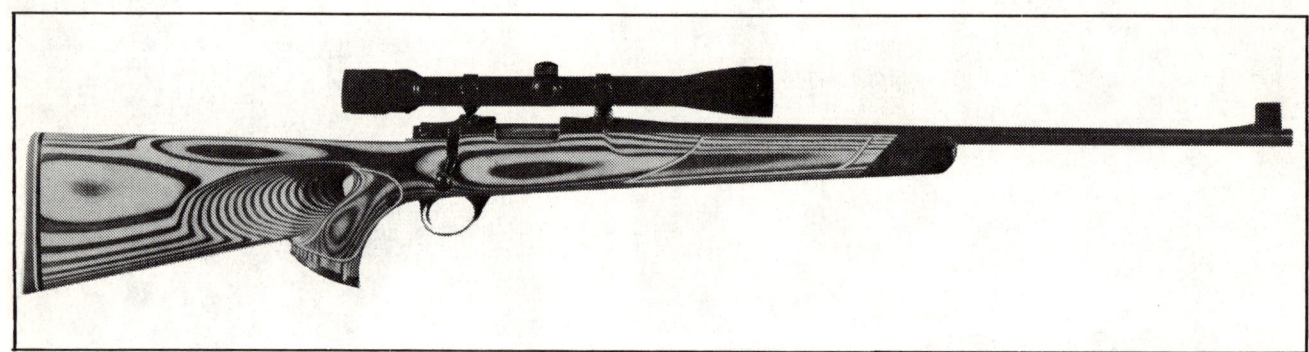

Fajen offers laminated stocks that do have eye appeal. This stock is laminated from walnut and maple.

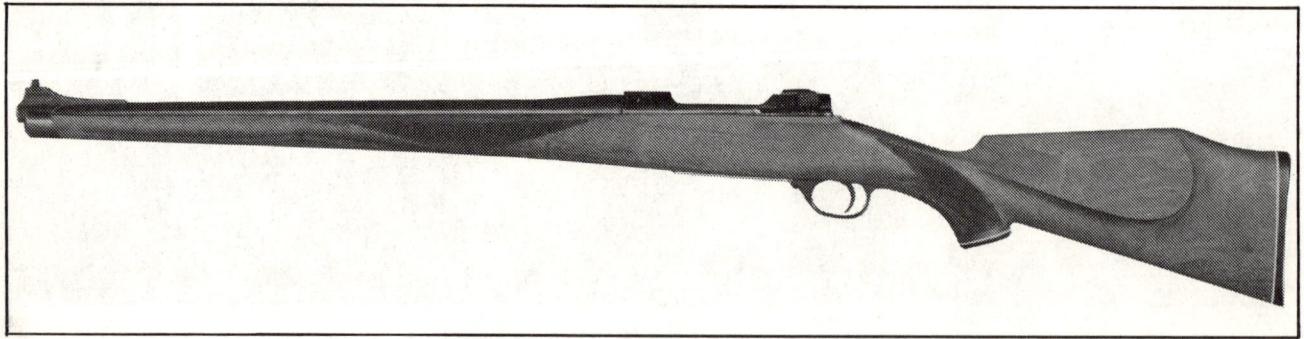

Mannlicher-style stock as offered by Fajen.

The weird rifle the late John Buhmiller holds is a lever-action single-shot match rifle that collected quite a few trophies in the mid-30s. Commercial production was unprofitable since action was too costly.

This takedown rifle, the AR-7, made and sold by Charter Arms, will float when barrel, action and magazine are stored in plastic buttstock and rubber butt plate has been pushed on butt.

years, the bullpup is "rediscovered" by someone, and according to the late John Buhmiller, the 'pup was designed for camping and saddle use when a regular-length rifle was too clumsy to use. Buhmiller, a barrel maker by profession and practical joker by avocation, designed and built a rifle monstrosity in the mid-30s: a single-shot lever action, chambered for a 30-caliber wildcat cartridge. He used the rifle in regional and national matches with some success, to the amazement of the other shooters.

Chapter Eight
Sights

Chapter Eight
Sights

When man still collected his dinner by throwing a rock at some edible animal, he found that he needed to guess at the trajectory of the missile he threw, and that he had to keep his eye on the target while throwing that rock. In short, primitive man learned to aim his projectile. Early bows and some of the more sophisticated crossbows have sights which are amazingly similar to those we use today.

Aiming at a target or sighting it is essentially a form of triangulation in which the three reference points are your eye, the intended target and the muzzle of your gun. Just look at the sights of a modern shotgun — a small bead or two on the upper surface of the barrel makes up the entire sighting equipment. Since greater accuracy was needed for a single projectile delivered at much longer ranges than a shot charge, special sighting devices were developed for rifles, and the sight we know today as a peep sight is actually a very early method of sighting. Just how effective these sights are can be easily shown. Take a strip of thin sheet metal, any size will do, then drill a small hole into the center of the strip at one end. Bend that end at a 90-degree angle to the base or long part of the strip, and you have just made your own peep sight. Put a refined version of this sight on your rifle after adding a windage and elevation adjustment system, and you have this metallic sight in its current form.

The sights found on most of the currently produced rifles consist of a front sight with a bead, the entire sight being mounted on a ramp, and a rear sight which, more often than not, is adjustable for windage and elevation. Elevation adjustments are usually by means of steps, and so these sights are sometimes called "elevator" type sights. The leaf of the rear sight is notched so that the front sight can be centered in the machined cutout during the sighting process. Open sights are adequate for short range hunting where the rifle is handled very much like a shotgun, for informal plinking with a 22 rimfire

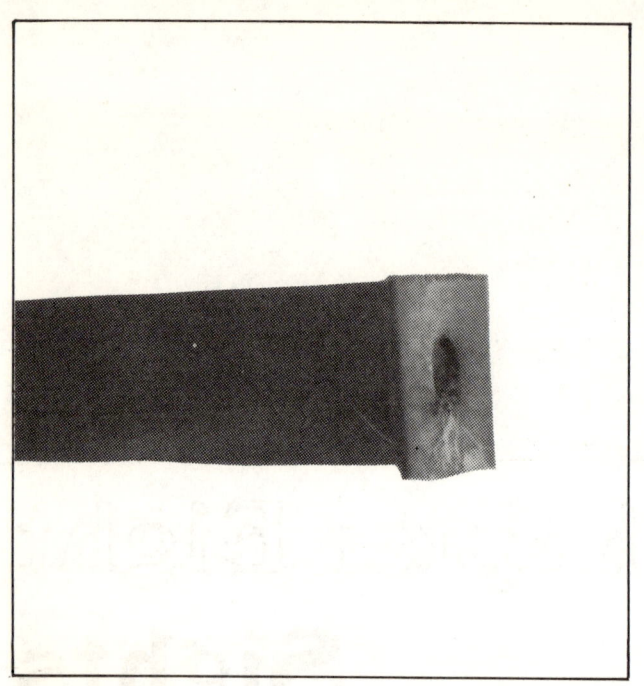 Fashioned in hunting camp, emergency peep sight was made from strip of tin can; hole was punched with a nail.

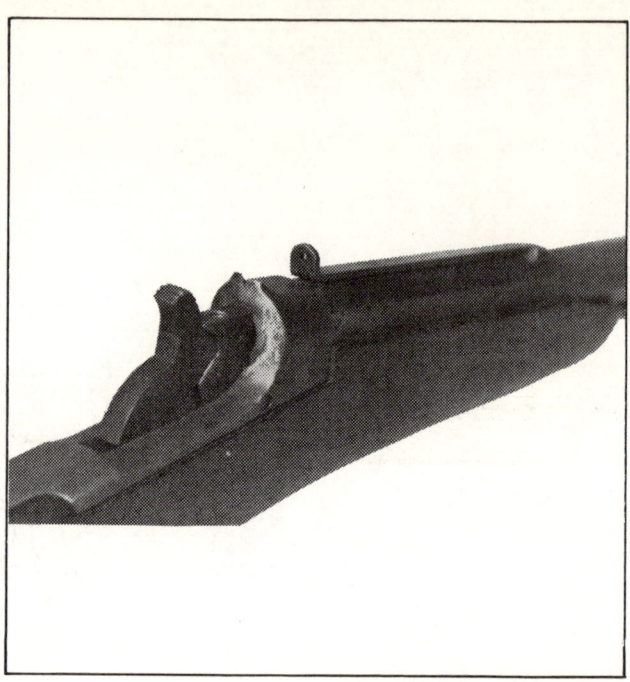 Belgian single-shot rifle has two rear sights. The open V-notch sight is part of action, while peep sight strongly resembles the emergency peep sight.

Simple open V-sight set into dovetail.

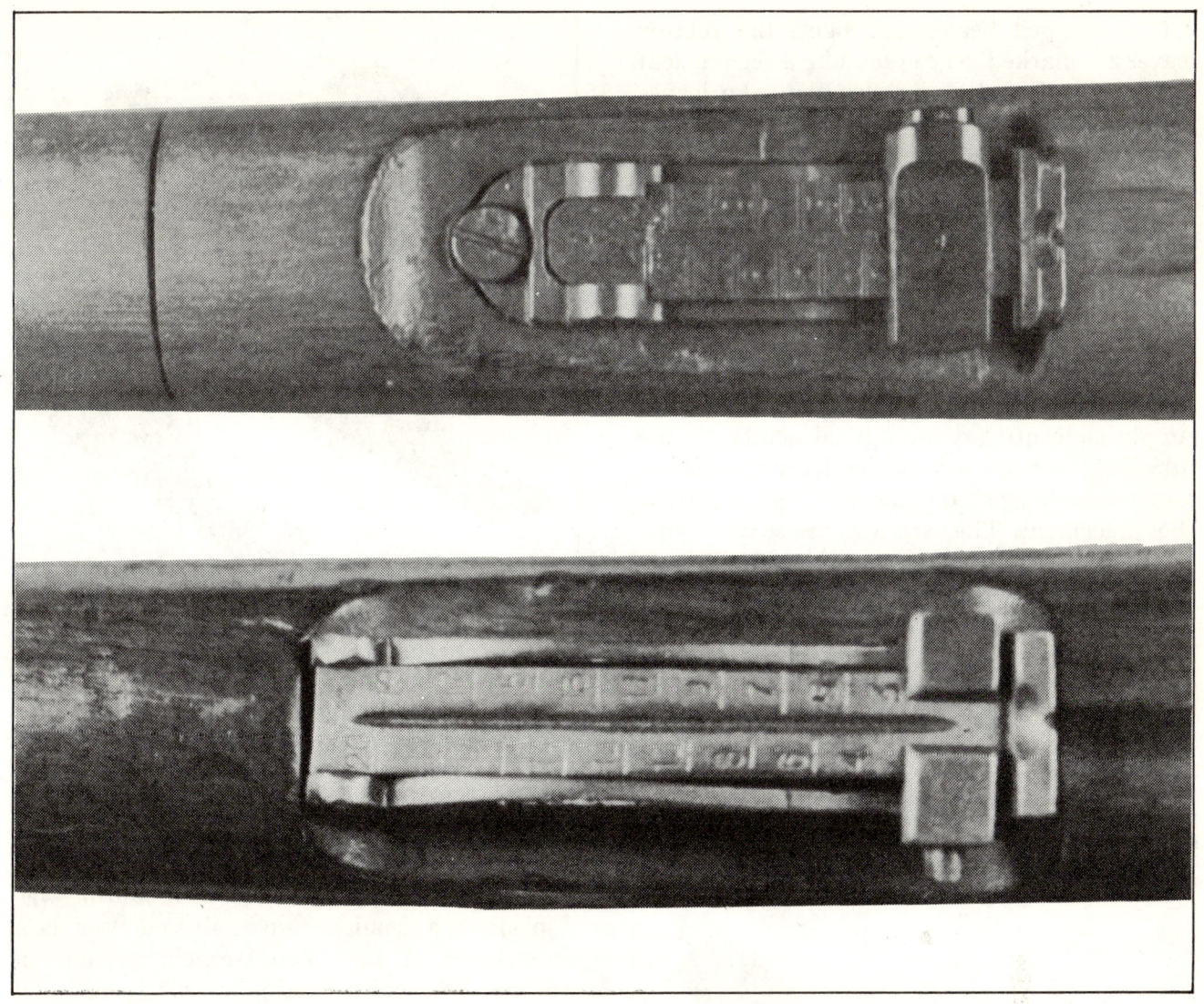

Military sights are adjustable for range as well as for windage.

rifle, and can also be used to good advantage should some accident befall your scope or other sighting system.

The principle of the peep sight is quite old. By moving the tiny hole in the piece of sheet metal close to your eye, the sight picture obtained appears to be sharpened. Then, when the front sight is aligned with the target in front and the eye in the rear, you are set to hit the bullseye, providing, of course, that you have sighted the rifle in. The old Schuetzen rifles had highly sophisticated and fully adjustable vernier peep sights which, when not in use, were folded down to keep them out of harm's way. The majority of the sights seen on military rifles use a combination of the features already mentioned. To obtain added elevation, the sight base might have steps, or the sighting leaf might be moved up or down on a collapsible frame, very much akin to the sight frame seen on Schuetzen rifles.

Military sights are usually marked for ranges, either in yards or in meters, on European rifles. Most of the military sights are not worth keeping around after a military rifle has been sporterized. If iron sights are needed or wanted, it is best to get a new set. A variation of the folding leaf rear sight is the British express sight. Unfortunately, these sights are neither imported nor manufactured here, but hopefully someone will one day do one or the other. In conjunction with a ramped bead front sight, the folding leaves are marked very much like a regular leaf sight; instead of steps for elevation, the leaves are built up so that, by erecting the suitable leaf and folding the others down, you have an automatically adjusted sight. This, of course, calls for precise sighting-in with a given load, which is true of all other sights, so the disadvantage is relatively small.

The very first of the telescopic sights, or scopes for short, were really sighting tubes without optics. These tubes acted somewhat like the peep or aperture sights and, in essence, simply concentrated the optical acuity in the tube. Add some lenses and suddenly the distant target looks bigger; this means a more certain shot placement. The variety of telescopic sights on the market today is staggering, and also confusing. The 1X or the 2X scope gives the eye a magnification of one or two times. Therefore, a scope that has a magnification factor of 20X gives you an image that is 20 times bigger than that of the 1X scope.

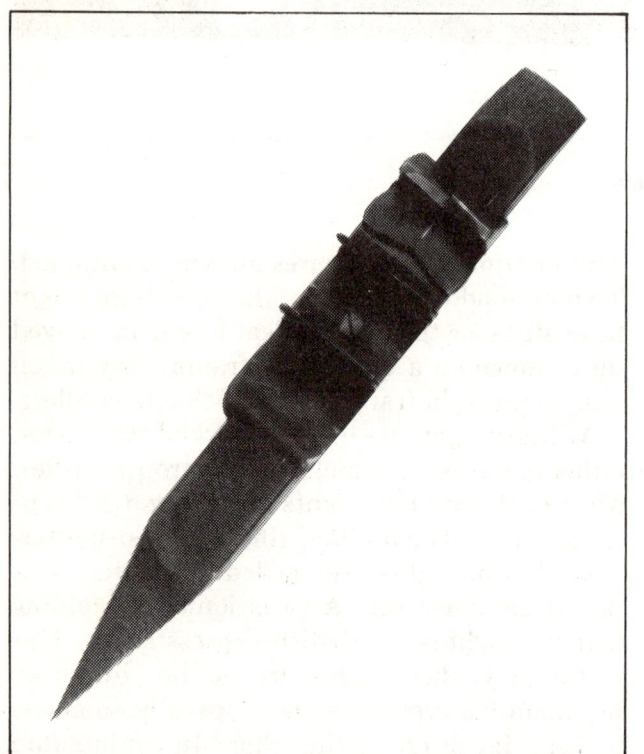

British express sight consists of folding leaf sights which are factory adjusted for range and marked suitably.

Two very early fully adjustable Lyman peep sights.

Scope selection must be governed by a number of factors. When you come to scope your 22-caliber rimfire rifle, the task will be easier because nearly all of the currently produced rifles come with a grooved receiver that makes scope mounting very simple. Once these rifles had to be drilled and tapped, and scope mounting was a job for a gunsmith. Now, all you need is a screwdriver or an Allen wrench, perhaps a collimator to make sighting-in easier, and you are set for plinking or hunting. Rimfire match rifles may also be equipped with a scope, but the type of match you are entering governs the type of sight you have to use for that course of fire.

For centerfire match rifles, the choice of scopes is wide and varied, and again, much will depend on the type of matches you compete in. For instance, the benchrest class of your rifle is determined by the weight of rifle plus scope — select a scope that is one or two ounces too heavy, and your rifle will compete in a class where the heavier guns have the edge over your benchrest rig. Silhouette shooting also requires a scope, and here you will want something a bit more powerful than your regular hunting scope. The Weaver T series of scopes, offered in 6, 10 and 16 power magnification, would be a good choice for this type of shooting. Target scopes

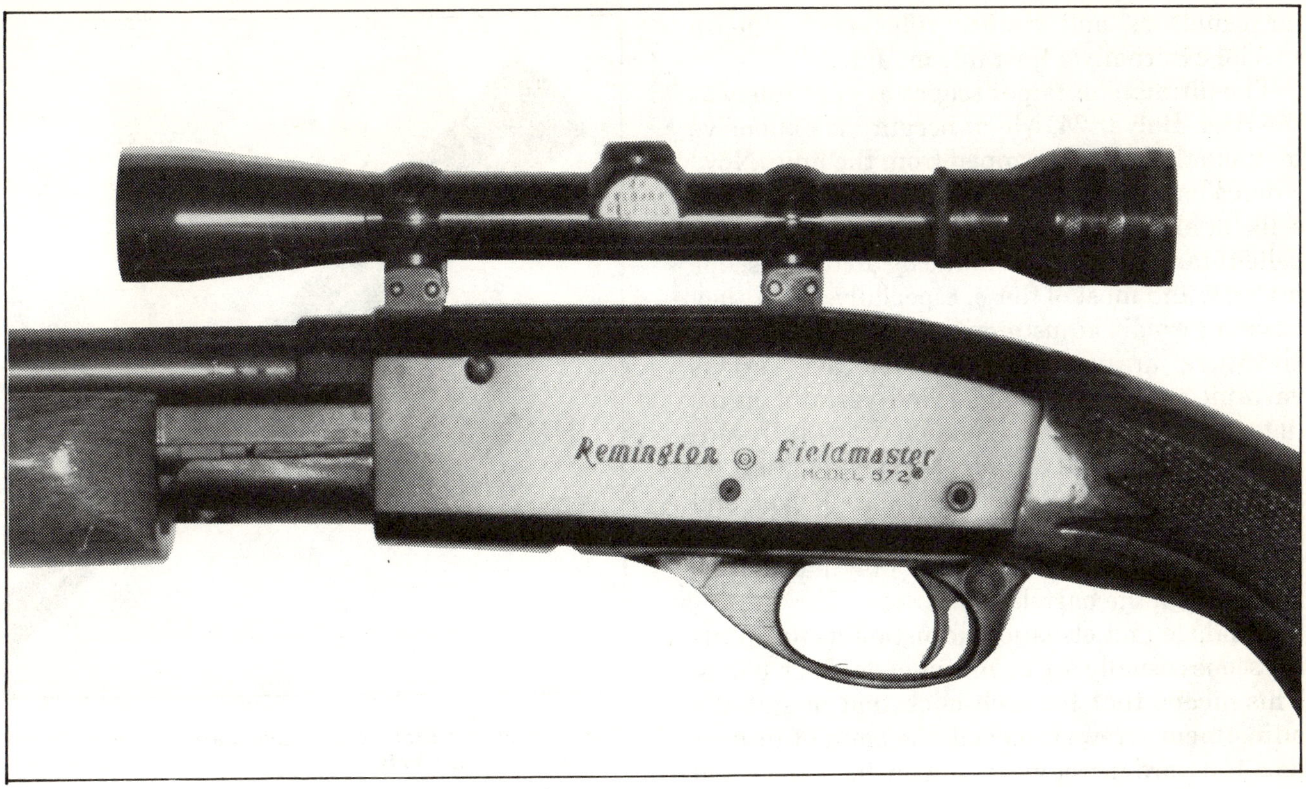

Nearly all 22 rimfire rifles come with grooved receiver which makes scope mounting very simple.

Weaver T-Scope, or Target Scope, has exposed windage and elevation adjustments.

SIGHTS

169

for centerfire and rimfire rifles may ride in special externally adjustable mounts.

The ultimate in target scopes at one time was the B&L Balvar 24, which became so expensive to make that it was dropped from the line. Now, when a used Balvar 24 appears on the market, it sells for about three times its original price. Excellent target scopes are made by all of the scope makers, and most of these, especially when they have internal adjustments for windage and elevation, are also suitable for the serious varmint hunter. The target and varmint hunting scope usually has a sun shade, is fully adjustable for parallax, has a magnification of 10X or more. Since such scopes are longer and heavier than the standard hunting scope, the forward scope mounting block may have to be mounted on the barrel.

Windage and elevation adjustments on hunting scopes usually are by means of one-inch clicks. This means that for each click that one of the adjustment screws is moved, the point of impact on a 100-yard target moves one inch. Target and varmint scopes have ¼-inch clicks, and this means that for each click an adjustment screw

Target and varmint scope have parallax adjustment in forward scope bell.

is moved, the point of impact on that 100-yard target changes ¼ inch. Some scope makers stick a little reminder about the click movement in the scope turret caps, and should this be lacking in your scope, you can easily make your own with a piece of masking tape or a small piece of self-adhesive label.

Some target and varmint scopes do not have internal windage and elevation adjustments. Here the adjustments are made in the rings, and whatever adjustment is made by this means actually moves the scope rather than the optics within the scope, as is the case with the internally adjustable scope. The externally adjustable scope is usually more resistant to the entry of dust and moisture into the scope tube since the tube has fewer holes in it, but on the other hand, the mounts are slightly more costly. The external system of mounting the adjustments for windage and elevation permits a somewhat more accurate click arrangement in the rings; some of the newer scopes now have internal adjustments which are every bit as accurate as the external ones.

The majority of the target and varmint scopes have fixed power magnification, although

Some scope makers have a label in the caps of the adjustment turrets indicating value each click has. On a 6x scope, each click or marked division on turret moves the point of bullet impact ½ inch.

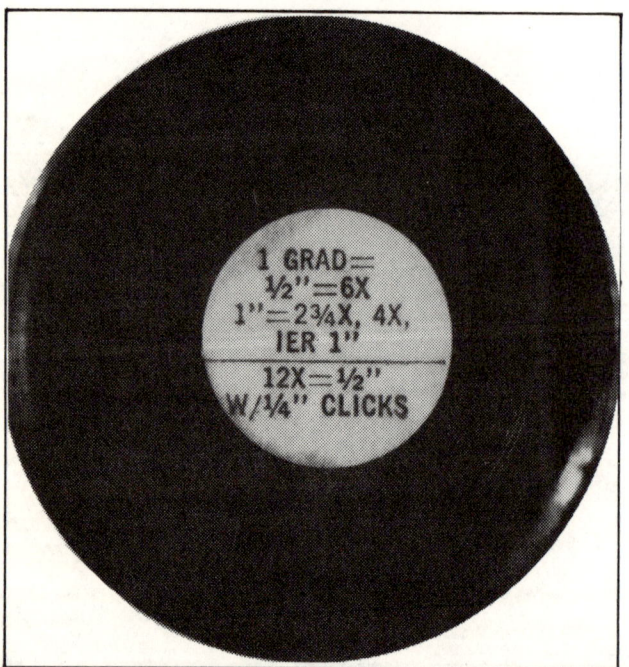

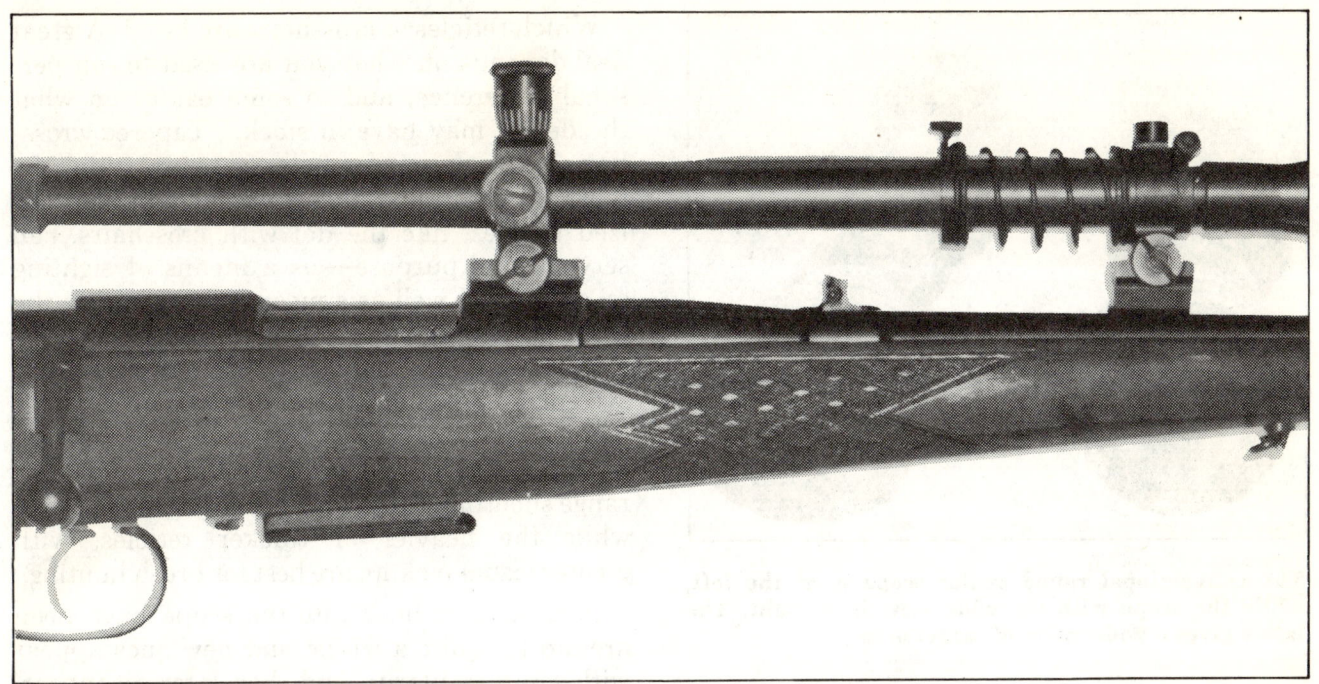

Rings for target scopes vary considerably from the rings used for hunting scopes.

a number of variable power scopes are also available. I favor the fixed power scope for varmint hunting and target shooting, since I found I did not need extra magnification and it was all too easy to forget to crank the power back up or down when the spotting was completed and I got ready to fire the next shot.

Variable power scopes for hunting have become very popular, and for good reason. A 3X–9X scope, for instance, can be set at 4X for hunting, and when the magnification is boosted to 9X, can be used for glassing a head or to spot game. The higher powered scopes must be held very steady, and high altitude climbing may make this more difficult. Be sure to turn the magnification back down after your glassing so that when a shot is offered, you don't have to readjust the magnification or perhaps miss a shot since the intended target does not show up too well in the scope.

Traditionally, the ocular bell, like the body of the scope, is round, and this gives you the classic view of the target. Rapidly moving game is sometimes hard to pick up visually in this type of scope configuration, and now the hunter has a choice — the classic round ocular bell on the scope or one that gives you a wide angle view of the area. The scope offering a wide angle view has some advantages, since you see more of the target and the immediate area around it, but it is also somewhat more expensive. I found that it took me a while to get used to the wide angle view of the field of view, but now I am so accustomed to both types that I am not even particularly aware of it when I switch from one to the other.

When you buy a scope you must also adjust the focus to suit your shooting eye. Scopes are factory adjusted for focus, but that in no way guarantees that the focus will be just right for you. When adjusting the focus, be sure the scope is resting solidly on a support; if the scope has been mounted, be sure to support the rifle so there is no wobble in either bench or rifle. The knurled ring is set against the front edge of of the ocular bell, locking the bell in position that way. Begin focusing by backing the bell off a turn or two, then run the ring up forward a bit. Rotate the bell toward the scope, watching all the time through the scope. When the focus is sharp and the image perfect, you have focused the scope. Next, run the ring back against the forward edge of the ocular bell, and you are all set.

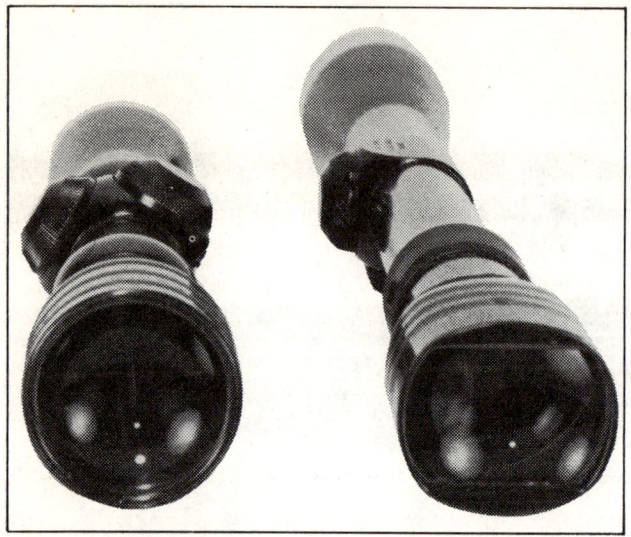

The conventional round ocular scope is at the left, while the scope with the wide view is at right. The latter gives a wider view of target area.

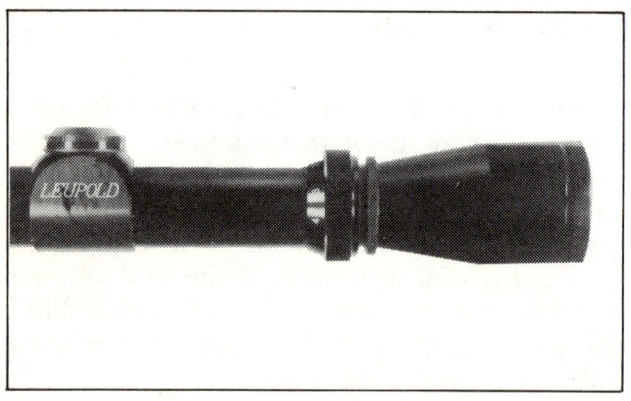

It is important to focus the scope. On this variable power scope, the smaller knurled ring near ocular bell is loosened, then ocular bell is rotated until sharpest possible picture is obtained. Finally, turn ring back against bell so that bell is locked in position.

Which reticles or crosshairs are best? A great deal depends on what you are used to, on personal preference, and to some extent on what the dealer may have in stock. Tapered crosshairs and plain crosshairs are probably the most widely used reticles, while some specialized reticles, like the dot with crosshairs, can serve a dual purpose — as a means of sighting on a target as well as a means of estimating the range or distance fairly accurately. The post-crosshair combination is another favorite reticle system, and each of the more common systems has its own devoted followers. As a general guide, thin crosshairs are preferred for long range shooting since they obscure the target less, while the heavier or thicker reticles, with greater visual pickup, are best for brush hunting.

Rangefinders built into the scope have been around for quite a while, and new ones appear with some regularity and then later disappear. All of the rangefinding scopes I have tested were well-designed and were accurate enough for hunting, but it always took too long to dope out the distance between target and shooter. If you must figure out the range and have the time to do so, a regular rangefinder will give you a very accurate reading in a second or two, and this can be important on the long shots, such as on antelope, goats or sheep. Rangefinders work on the split image system that is used in the focusing system of cameras, but the rangefinding reticles in scopes do require a bit of mental gymnastics to come up with the correct result.

The idea of seemingly projecting an aiming point on a distant target goes back 30 or perhaps even 40 years. One of the first of these non-

Shooters have a wide choice of crosshairs, and all of them have strong supporters. From left: (1) four posts with heavy crosshairs (2) four thinner posts with finer crosshairs (3) crosshairs with peep (4) fine crosshairs (5) medium thick crosshairs (6) tapered post with one crosshair (7) crosshairs with dot (8) Redfield's Accu-Range reticle.

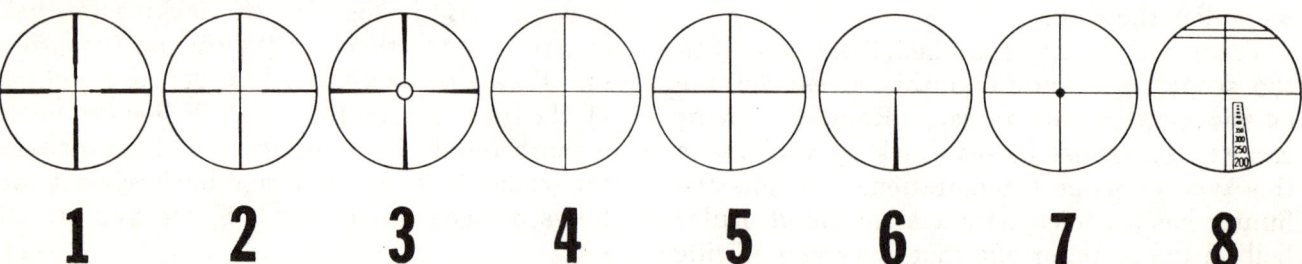

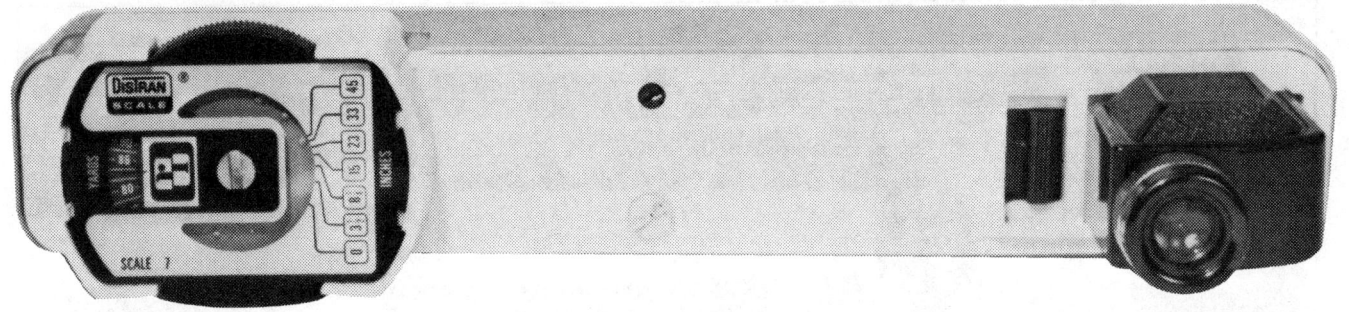

Rangefinder is helpful to those who cannot estimate distances too well.

magnifying optical sights was the Nydar Sight which used a system of optical prisms to capture the available light and then superimpose a means of aiming on the image of the target. The Nydar Sight was popular for rifles and shotguns, and I have used it with some success on a Remington XP-100 single-shot handgun. All of these sights have or had built-in elevation and windage adjustments, were mounted in the same way a scope is mounted today, and most of them were popular only for relatively limited periods. An exception is the Weaver Qwik-Point sight, especially useful for the deer hunter seeking his game in woods and brush. Three models of the Weaver sight are offered, for centerfire and rimfire rifles and for shotguns. When mounted on a 22 rimfire rifle, the Qwik-Point sight is a good choice, especially if magnifica-

Non-magnifying Weaver Qwik-Point sight is useful at the shorter ranges as well as for teaching young shooters. On a 22 rimfire, as shown here, the Qwik-Point sight is a great sighting system. Transparent bubble on front of sight is barely visible because camera does not record it on film.

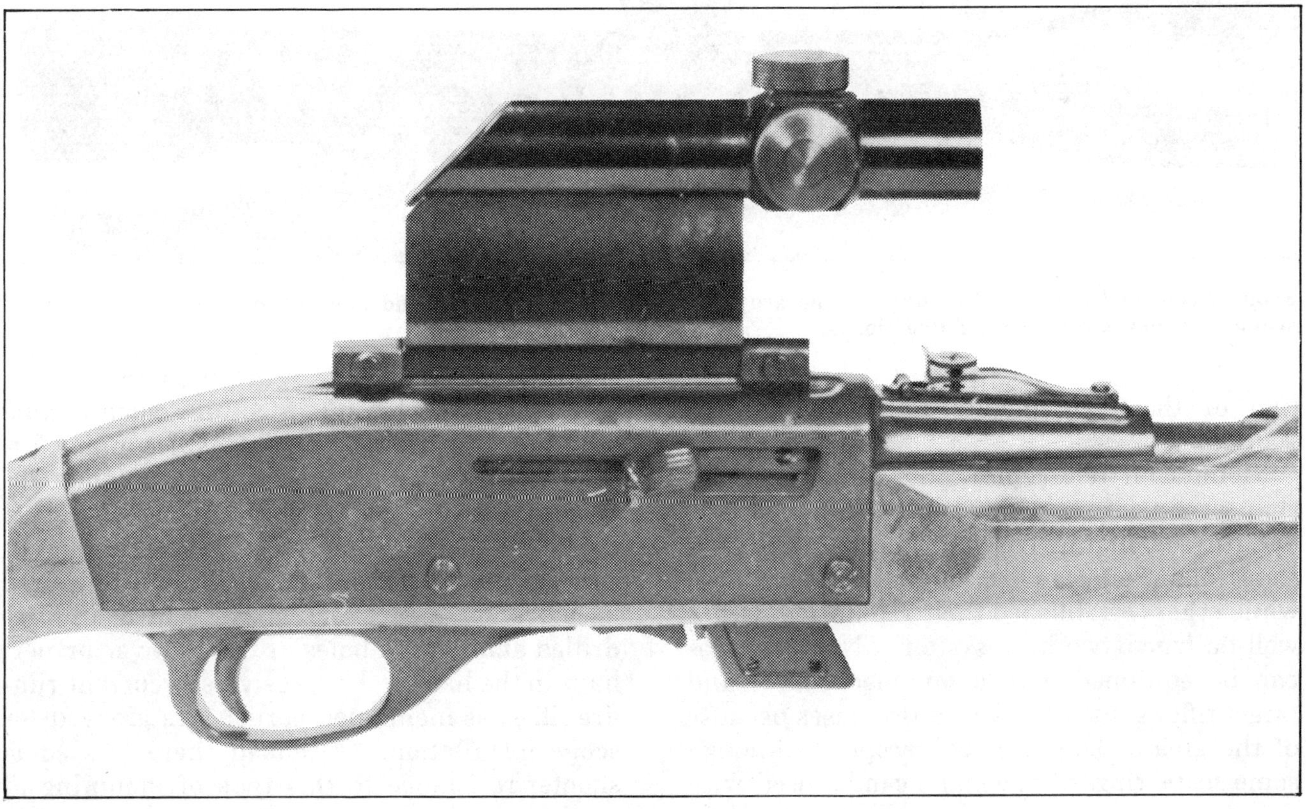

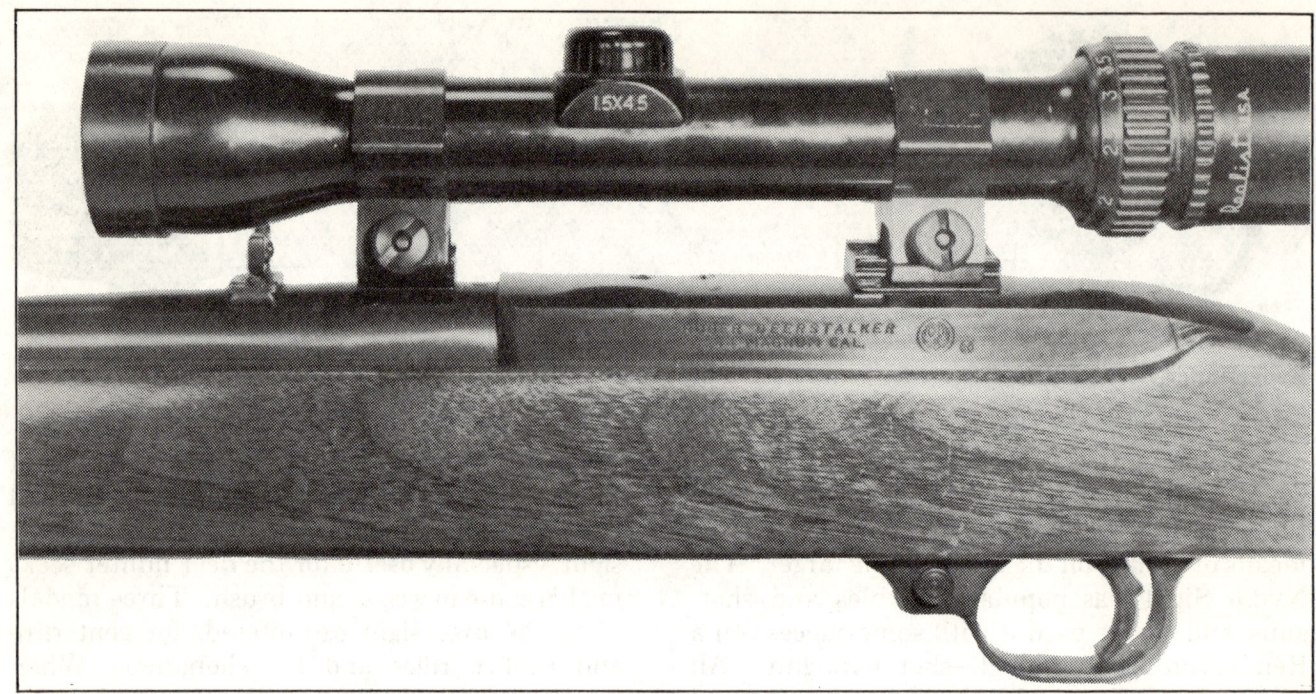

One-piece scope base was used on this Remington Model 700. Note that rings are too low and how rear sight butts up against scope. Higher rings allow rear sight to clear scope.

Scope bases on Ruger 44 Magnum carbine are the obsolete Realist bases and rings. Note that scope is anchored by means of two blocks.

tion of the sight picture is not needed or wanted.

Mounts for telescopic sights come in many shapes and forms. The most common differentiation is in the bases or blocks, and here some manufacturers lean to the one-piece base, while others established their reputation with a well-designed two-base system. Not all rifles can be equipped with a one-piece base, and target rifles generally require two bases because of the greater length of the scope. Although some scope rings of one make can be used with the bases of another manufacturer, such mixing of brands is often not successful since minor differences in tolerances may only become apparent when the effects of recoil have exerted their forces.

Scope mounts for centerfire rifles are anchored in place by means of screws seated in pre-drilled and tapped holes in the receiver or perhaps in the barrel. The receivers of current rimfire rifles, as mentioned earlier, are grooved for scope installation. Although there was some shooter resistance to this type of mounting at

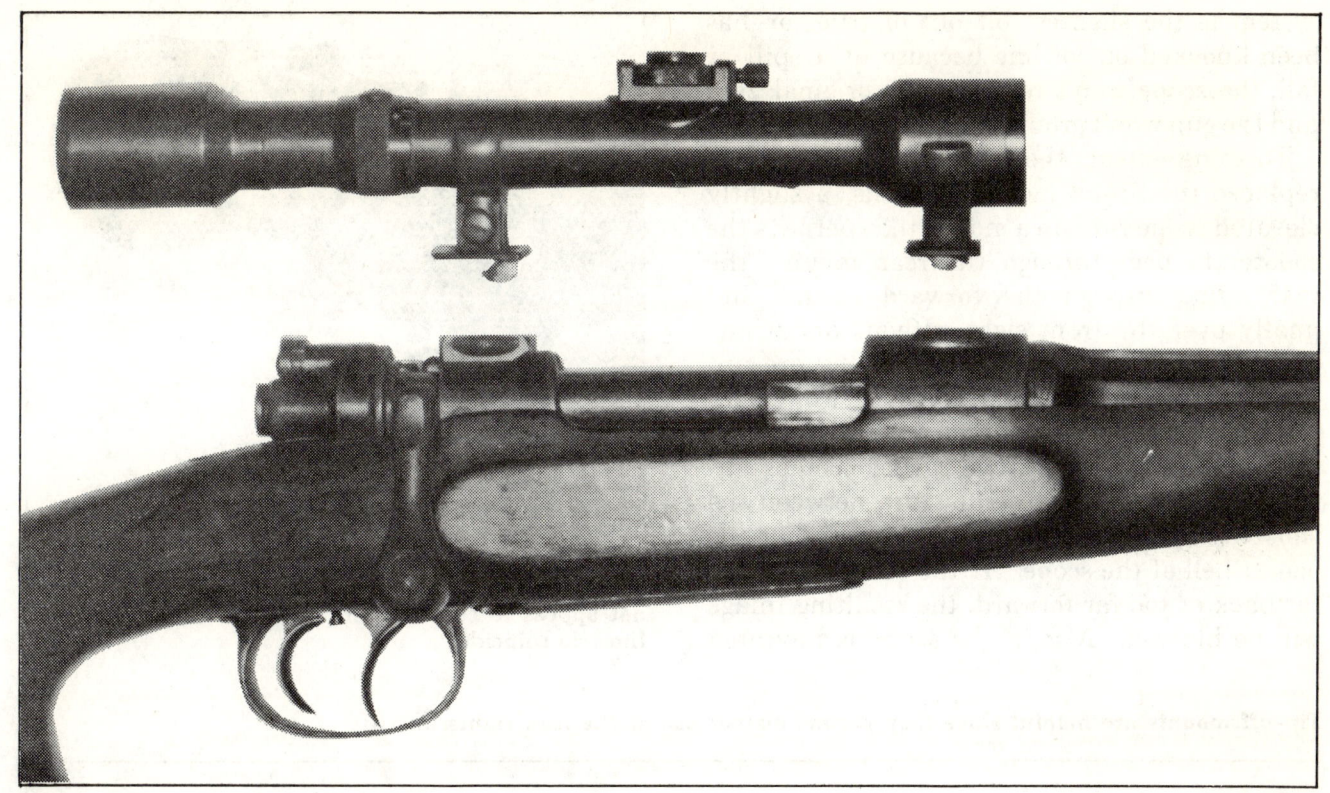

Claw mounts, seen mostly on rifles of German or Austrian origin, anchor scope securely, return it to perfect zero each time scope is detached from rifle.

first, it has shown itself to be excellent and trouble-free.

Some types of actions do not lend themselves to scope mounting as easily as others. The ultimate use of a rifle might also dictate the type of scope mounting method that is best for the purpose. For instance, a deer hunter's brush rifle may be used with a low powered scope, but when it is raining, such a scope becomes useless. A quick method of removing the scope may become important at that time, and should also be able to be accomplished without the use of tools. Weaver rings can be loosened with a dime, the rim of a cartridge case or the back edge of a hunting knife, and these rings with the scope in place are just as easily re installed as they are taken off the mounts. In Germany and Austria, claw mounts are popular, and once you have a chance to try these mounts, you may begin to wonder why they do not enjoy wider popularity.

Special scope mounting methods are needed for some actions, such as the Krag, the M94 Winchester, and several others. Scope mount manufacturers have produced special mounts for these rifles. Most of these actions require drilling and tapping, which is best left to the skilled hands of a gunsmith. Many of these scope mounts are offset — that is, the center of the scope or sight is not directly above the center of the bore, and the correction for this is built into the mount. Certain one-piece mounts have some degree of windage correction built into them, but most of these offset mounts lack any type of correction or adjustment; installation therefore can be critical.

The widespread use of the tip-off mount/ring combination is currently declining. The idea behind this design is simple and dates back a number of years. Should the hunter find himself in a position where the scope gets in his way of sighting the target, he simply swings the scope off the blocks or bases, then uses the open sights on the rifle. After being swung out of the way, tip-off mounts which are not re-seated properly will make the scope useless; if the swing-over system is the slightest bit out of true, or has been knocked out of line because of a spill or fall, the scope won't return to its original zero and the gun won't group where you aim.

To some extent, the see-through mount has replaced the tip-off mount. In this, a slightly elevated scope rides in a mount that permits the shooter to peer through the rear mount, the rear sight, through the forward mount and finally over the front sight without disturbing the position of the scope. All of this presupposes, of course, that the open or iron sight has been zeroed or sighted-in.

In mounting a scope, eye relief becomes important. Eye relief is the distance between the shooter's eye and the rear lens element in the ocular bell of the scope. If the scope is set too far back or too far forward, the resulting image will be blurred. Also, if the scope is mounted

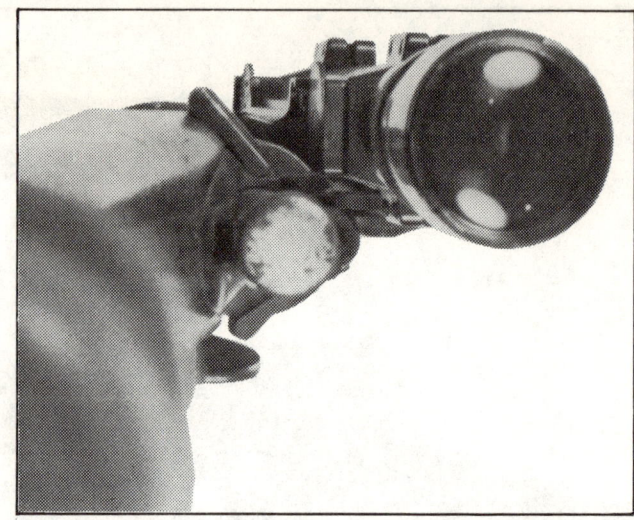

Offset scope mount is required for some actions, such as the Krag. Although line of sight and line of bore do not appear to coincide, the mount is adjusted so that lines do coincide.

Tip-off mounts are helpful since they permit instant use of the iron sights on rifle.

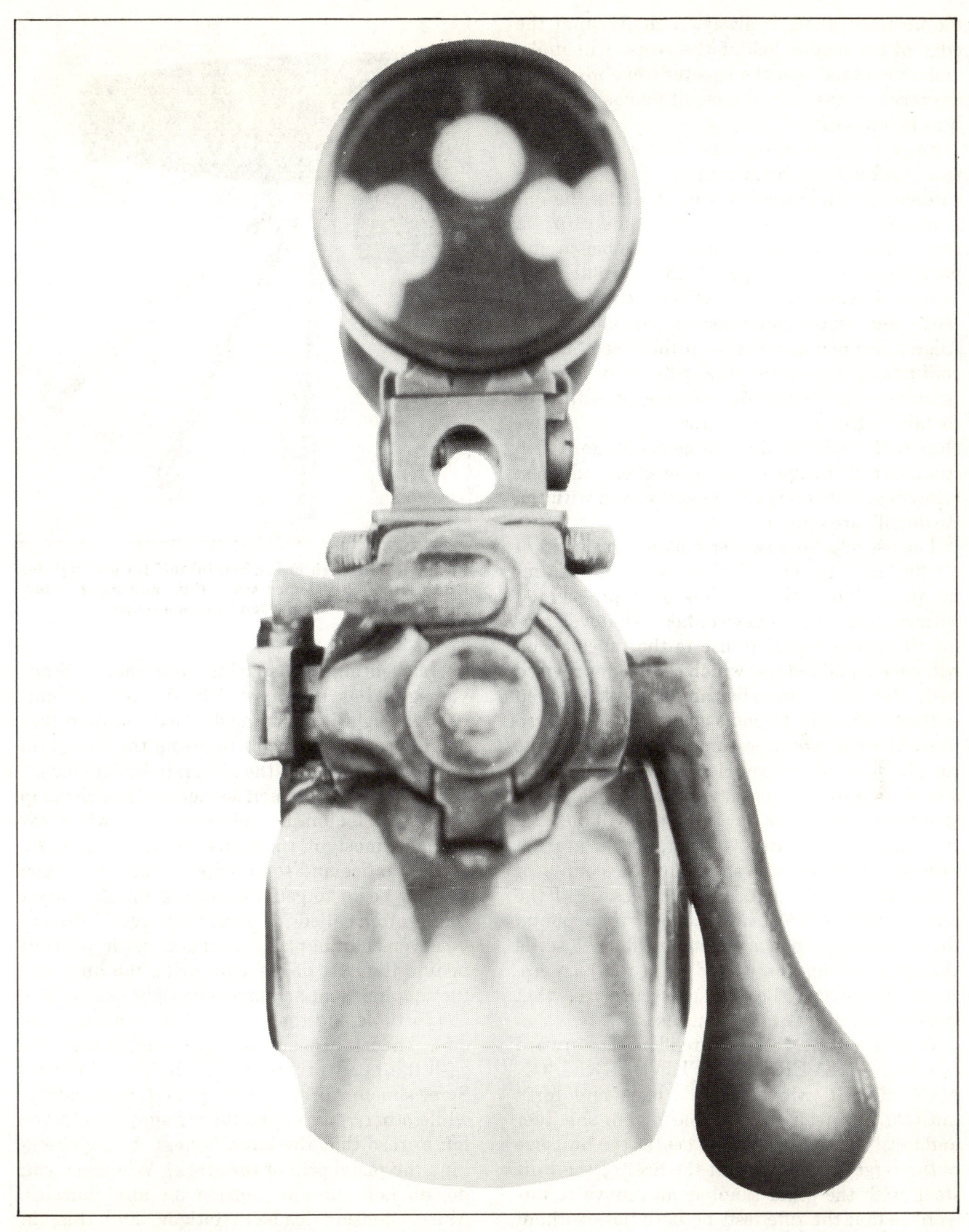
A see-through mount allows instant use of the iron sights.

too far back, there is always a chance that the edge of the ocular bell of the scope will make violent contact with the shooter's eyebrow during recoil of the rifle; the resulting gash usually bleeds copiously.

For years, gunsmiths have had a tool known as a collimator. Stick a spud of the suitable caliber into the muzzle of the rifle, afix the optical collimation system to the spud, turn a bench light on a target hung over the bench and peer through the scope in the normal way. You'll see two sets of crosshairs, those of the scope and those contained in the collimator. Align those of the scope with those seen in the collimator, and while the rifle may not be sighted-in for benchrest shooting, it will most certainly group on the paper, nearly always close to the point of aim. Large collimators with spuds for all calibers are expensive, and most hunters and shooters will be well served with the Bushnell bore sighter.

The use of a bore sighter makes sighting-in of a rifle much easier and also saves a lot of ammunition. Once the gun has been pre-sighted with such an optical device, take whatever ammunition you expect to use to the range. You will need a padded rest which can be improvised with a GI ammunition box and a blanket folded so that it gives the forend a good, soft support so that the wood won't be damaged when the rifle recoils. A set of commercial leather sandbags is a good investment if you expect to do a lot of shooting, but homemade sandbags will do. Fill the bags with fine dry sand, or, if you are not near a beach or lake shore, buy a couple of boxes of the sand used in bird cages. Fill the bags as full as you can get them, then pound them on a heavy bench or concrete floor to settle the sand, adding more sand until the bags are really full. Close the opening securely so that the sand won't leak out during use.

When shooting, rest the forend on the forward sandbag — NEVER REST THE BARREL ON ANYTHING! Move the rifle back and forth until the butt feels comfortable in your shoulder and until the sights or scope center the bullseye of the target. Now support the heel of the butt stock with the other sandbag and move it forward so that the rifle rests on both bags without tipping. Mention has already been made about

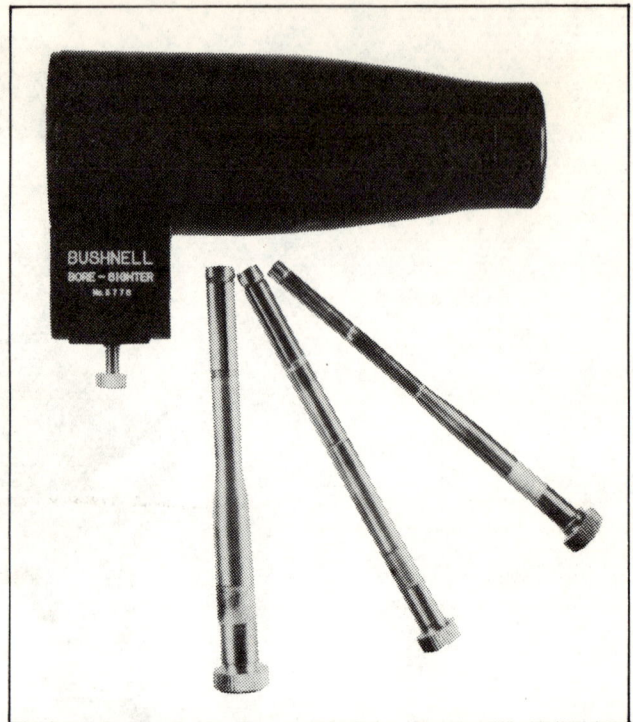

Bushnell Bore Sighter is a helpful tool for pre-sighting rifle. Use of this device saves time and money since only a few shots are needed to zero a scope.

barrel heating and spacing your shots. Since your gun has been pre-sighted, you can now begin to sight it in for good. Let's assume that you have a 270 and will be using the 130-grain bullet loads and also the 150-grain bullet loads.

Experienced riflemen sooner or later develop their own techniques of firing, but when examined, most of them are very much alike. With practice and some trips to the range, you too can begin to get that feeling for the target that is often called "reading the target." Before you even chamber the first round, settle yourself behind the butt of the gun, bring the butt into the shoulder and arrange your right arm so it is comfortable and there is no strain on the muscles. The left arm should lie parallel to the rifle, with the hand preferably not holding the rifle. Some shooters prefer to grasp the forend lightly, while others, myself included, simply fold the left arm so that the hand is near, below or behind the pistol grip of the stock. Whatever you do, do not put any tension on any muscles. Muscle tension leads to fatigue, and this, in turn, leads to muscle tremors or trembling.

Remington 40X-BR with Remington scope and target rings. Forend of rifle rests on sandbag which is lightly dusted with talcum powder, while butt of stock rests on eared sandbag.

All set? First, look at the target, but keep both eyes open. Again, squinting might seem to help, but it also induces muscle fatigue, and this leads to lacrimation, which makes sighting even more difficult. Unless range rules prohibit it, keep the bolt of the rifle closed, and rest the index finger of the right hand on the trigger — all of this applies to right-handed shooters; portsiders should simply reverse the directions given. Don't stare at the target, but look at it through the scope, note anything you see on it, even the bug or fly that might land on it. Slowly survey the entire target, then start again at the beginning.

Learn to concentrate so that you can align the the scope's crosshairs easily and steadily anywhere on or in a one-inch square drawn on the target with a felt-tipped pen. Once you learn to bisect the square with the crosshairs and can learn to hold that sight picture, you will be way ahead of the game. Now load the first round, put the safety on, and get settled again. Locate the target you want to shoot at and pick a spot on the bullseye where you think you'll want to place your shots. When you are all set and have a clear target picture, slip off the safety and gently apply pressure to the trigger. Chances are you'll barely feel the gun recoiling against your shoulder. An experienced rifleman will simply shove his right shoulder forward, relocating the rifle on the sandbags. Open the action and eject the fired case, unless you are shooting an autoloader, in which case the brass will already have been ejected.

Now, with the rifle back in position, again concentrate on the target. Where is the bullet hole in relation to your point of aim? Did the bullet print two inches high and three to the left or right? Never mind, you can adjust the scope later on. Fire a second and then a third shot, each time holding the same sight picture as you did with the first shot. This should give you a

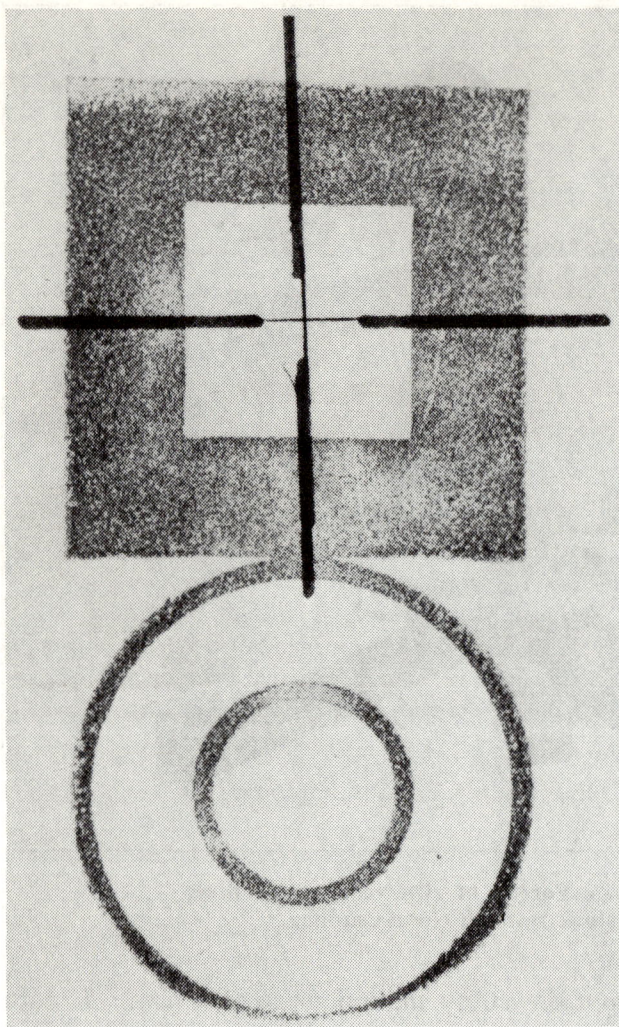

Rubber-stamped target has set of crosshairs superimposed to show what the shooter will actually see through the scope.

many inches or fractions of an inch each click of the windage and elevation adjustments will move the point of impact on the target. Make the needed scope adjustments. Now, using the same hold as before, repeat the two three-shot groups. This will not only show again where the loads group and their relationship with each other, but will also bring you one step closer to sighting-in.

The target shooter fires at known distances. Benchrest matches, for example, are fired at 100 and 200 yards. With the rifle carefully zeroed for 100 yards, the shooter can either adjust the elevation a known number of clicks when he fires at the longer range, or he can hold-over. The latter is a bit tricky since wind has to be taken into account as well, so it is better to adjust the scope for the longer ranges.

In contrast to this, the hunter fires at guessed-at distances, and he cannot pick his shot most of the time. This means that guessing range and the required hold-over, plus wind and possible

It took four shots, #1-#4, to move point of bullet impact so that shots would hit bullseye. Walking bullet impact across target is done by means of windage and elevation adjustments in scope.

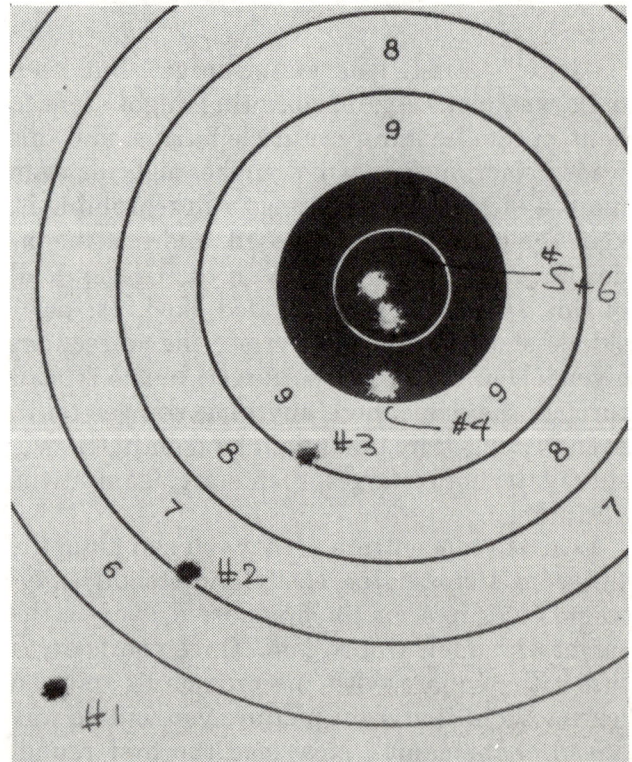

fairly decent group if you were shooting at 100 yards. If you have to sight-in at 50 yards, don't forget that your 100-yard group will be twice as large.

I like to keep a spare target on the bench and with a pen mark each hit on it that is not too readily visible when the target is later placed on the 100- or 200-yard target carrier. At this point, you have the group fired with the lighter load. Using the same hold, fire three rounds with the 150-grain loads, again watching your target and your timing of the shots. Now you can see where the two bullet weights will group in relation to each other. The instructions that came with your scope will tell you how

Scope mounting on AR-7 rimfire rifle.

obstructions to the bullet must be taken into account, all in a couple of seconds.

The late Warren Page, a superb shot who soundly trounced me more than once at benchrest matches, developed a method of sighting-in he called the Rule of Three. Follow this system, and you won't have to worry about hold-over unless you start shooting at extra long ranges, and this is neither sporting nor essential, excepting perhaps for sheep hunters. The Rule of Three applies to all calibers capable of delivering reasonably good groups beyond the 100-yard marker.

Sight the rifle so that the bullets will print three inches high at 100 yards. At ranges less than that, the bullet will certainly hit a lethal area if your aiming is right, excepting for head or neck shots where a dead-on hold would, of course, overshoot the point of aim. At 200 yards, the bullet will still be about three inches high, while at 300 yards, the bullet will print dead-on or on point of aim. At 400 yards, the bullet drop will be between 8–12 inches, depending on the ballistic coefficient of the bullet. In practice, a dead-on hold on a lethal area of a deer or elk at 350 yards will still place the bullet into the lethal area of the animal. The 308 Norma Magnum, the 300 Weatherby, the 300 Winchester Magnum, as well as the 7mm and the 8mm Remington Magnums will deliver predictable results providing your hold is correct and you are aiming at the right spot. For cartridges in the 30-06 and the 270 Winchester class, this range should be shortened, especially with the lighter bullets, to about 275–300 yards. Although the Rule of Three is just about foolproof, you should perform actual long-range shooting tests with the same type of ammo as you plan to use on the next big-game hunt.

Once the actual sighting-in has been completed, and if you have available safe range facilities, you should learn to shoot from the sitting, kneeling, offhand, and even prone positions. The knowledgeable hunter will assume any steady position that is available; here the use of the rifle sling will help immeasurably in getting a steadier and better sight picture.

Rimfire rifles are usually sighted-in at 50 yards, unless you know your shooting will require you to fire at perhaps 75 or even 100 yards. While recoil of the rimfire rifle won't affect you, the method of holding the sight picture is the same with all calibers.

Bolt-action rifles can be bore-sighted, but

lever-action, pump guns and autoloaders cannot. It is possible to bore-sight a top-break gun, but if the gun is scoped, this can be a bit difficult since the rifle — that is, barrel and scope, must be mounted so the gun can be rested on sandbags or some other sort of rest. In bore-sighting, you remove the bolt from the action and rest the rifle so the bullseye of the target is centered in the bore. Now, without touching the rifle, lift your head up and look through the scope or sight. If the sight also points to the center of the bullseye, you should be fairly close to your point of aim when you fire the first shot at the target. If the sight or scope is off, it will have to be adjusted so it points at the bullseye. Because bore-sighting is limited, for all practical purposes, to bolt-action rifles, and since collimators have become more widely available, bore-sighting has become something of a lost art.

So far, all of the shots discussed have been over more-or-less level land. What is the magic about shooting uphill or downhill? Rather than burden yourself with a lot of mathematics, with angle of departure and angle of flight, just remember that in both conditions — up or downhill shooting — the rifle will print high. To compensate for this, remember this simple rule of thumb. If the elevation is less than 20°, forget it and simply hold as you would over flat or level land. If the angle is somewhere between 25° to 40°, you can easily calculate your hold. If the target is 200 yards away, subtract 20 percent of the distance — that is, 200 minus 40, and

Spotting scope is important to target shooter; at one time it was also a "must" for big-game hunters. Spotting scope has been replaced to some extent by binoculars which are easier to handle and less heavy afield.

simply hold for 160 yards. If the distance seems to be 300 yards, hold for 240 yards.

This formula is based on ballistics tests for the medium calibers such as 270 Winchester and the 30-06, but can be used with the larger calibers such as the 8mm Remington Magnum, especially if the gun has been sighted-in by the Rule of Three. Those missed steep angle game shots, when analyzed later in camp, invariably result from the fact that the shooter held over rather than under.

Although not really a means of sighting at a distant target, the spotting scope should be mentioned here. A must for target shooters, and a great help when sighting-in a rifle, the spotting scope for the big-game hunter has taken a backseat in recent years. Meant to help the hunter to spot game and to evaluate heads, the weight, bulk and the nuisance of packing it safely aboard a packsaddle are among the reasons that the spotting scope has given way to binoculars. And these in turn, at least to some extent, gave way to variable power scopes. A good pair of binoculars, handled so that vibrations are excluded, is a lot easier to handle afield than a spotting scope; while it cannot always compete with the optical efficiency of the spotting scope, it is a far better means of spotting game and looking over possible trophy heads than the rifle scope. Although the rifle scope can be adjusted with respect to power of magnification, within limits, of course, the scope cannot be focused readily at a distant point while the binoculars can.

The hunter glassing a distant range while standing on top of a mountain makes for a nice photograph, but as far as seeing anything is concerned, such a practice is a waste of time and effort. Remember, the spotting scope uses a three-legged stand for maximum stability, and the same principle should be applied when using binoculars or a scope on a rifle — find a rest for it. Even the nearest log or rock makes a steadier rest than your unsupported arms!

Chapter Nine
Rifle Care and Tinkering

Chapter Nine
Rifle Care and Tinkering

I sometimes wonder why more good rifles are not ruined beyond repair by shooters who have read too much or heard too much about gun care and gun cleaning. Small bore match shooters consider cleaning the barrel of a match rifle tantamount to heresy, while benchrest shooters religiously clean the bores of their rifles after every relay. Although one group shoots rimfire ammo and the other centerfire ammo, the latter usually of the handloaded variety, both are quick to point out several facts which they consider important.

There is the matter of corrosive primers. Unless you latched onto some wartime military ammo, the primer mix found in today's primers is virtually noncorrosive. The smokeless powders used by factories and by handloaders burn as cleanly as modern chemistry can make them burn, and if the various 22-caliber rimfire bullets found in match ammunition don't ruin a rifle barrel, why should jacketed bullets?

So, bore cleaning can be a matter of controversy. As a very general rule of thumb, clean your gun after it has been exposed to bad weather, too much use and perhaps even abuse, and before prolonged storage. If you fired a centerfire rifle this afternoon and will fire the same rifle again tomorrow, and if the gun did not get soaked, dropped into the mud or the bore did not get filled with snow, you need not clean your rifle — unless, of course, you are a benchrest shooter.

Gun care and gun cleaning should be a matter of common sense. Clean when it is needed but don't get carried away. Too much is just as bad as too little.

First of all, gun care consists of, or should consist of, more than just running a solvent-soaked patch through the bore once in a while. Gun care should include cleaning of the action, the accessible parts of the magazine, the external metal parts of the gun, and care of the wood. Gun care should also include checking the scope-base mounting-screws, the tightness of scope rings, sling swivel studs, and perhaps even the grip cap or the recoil pad.

Metal fouling from either a jacketed or a lead bullet, plus the heat and friction created by the bullet as it moves along the lands and grooves, is the prime source of barrel fouling. Add to this particles and residue of the burned powder, dirt and foreign matter on the bullet and the debris that collects in a barrel, and a considerable amount of material is introduced that adds to the friction. More or less constant friction over a prolonged period will wear out the lands of any steel barrel, especially the edges of the lands, no matter what kind of steel is used. It is true that surgical instrument steel will outlast the type of stainless steel frequently used in rifle barrels, and this stainless steel, in turn, will outlast the type of steel used in most rifle barrels.

The velocity at which a bullet is driven also affects barrel fouling and the life expectancy of a barrel. Some calibers, such as the 220 Swift and the 264 Winchester, have acquired the reputation of being hard on barrels or of being barrel burners. Some wildcat cartridges with badly overbore capacity cases burn out barrels quickly, and some of the older loads which use lead bullets and black powder also present a barrel cleaning and maintenance problem.

Modern chemistry has given us what many consider to be the very best of the powder solvents. It makes relatively little difference what brand you use, as long as you use it regularly and follow any special directions on the label. I prefer the one-piece rods with plastic covering for gun cleaning at home, or in a pinch, any one-piece rod. If your shooting is limited and you don't clean your rifle more than three or four times a year, you can get along with a jointed rod. I also prefer the slotted or pull-through tip, but any other rod tip that will hold a cleaning patch securely is suitable.

Brass bristle brush tips, once by far the best to remove stubborn fouling and even traces of rust, are being replaced by brushes with extra tough and long-lasting plastic bristles. These seem to mat less, maintain the condition of the bristles better, and are easily cleaned. Suitable brushes for each caliber rifle you have are a small investment when you consider that regular care can save you the cost of a new barrel plus, of course, the gunsmithing costs of having the job done.

The days when shooters cut their own cleaning patches are a thing of the past, and few of us miss this tedious chore. If you shoot a lot, you'll clean guns frequently and, when buying patches, it is best to buy the large bulk packages rather than a dozen or so. Some time ago Hoppe's introduced a new type of patch which is based on DuPont's Reemay. A bit coarser than the usual flannel patch, these do a quick job of cleaning a rifle bore.

For barrels which don't respond to the usual patches with solvent treatment and also resist the solvent with brush treatment, you can resort to the J-B Bore Cleaning Compound. Put a bit

Bore solvent, powder fouling solvent—call it what you will, they all do a good job, but the choice must be yours. Shown here are just a few of the solvents used by author.

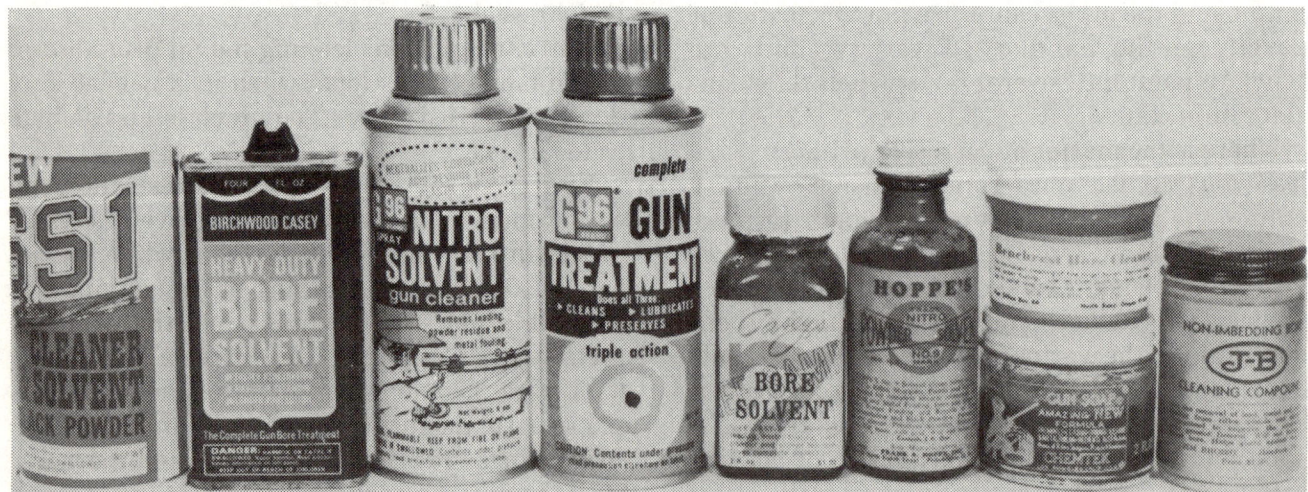

Storing cleaning rods can be a problem. Here, rifle rods are housed in rack underneath bookshelf, right above the bench where rifles are cleaned.

of the stuff on a patch and run it through the bore several times. Follow with a solvent-soaked patch to remove all of the compound, and check the bore. This product not only removes stubborn fouling, but also traces of rust, without affecting the lands of the rifling.

If you have a workbench with a vise, make this your rifle cleaning center. Rather than holding the rifle between your knees while going about the cleaning job, it is better to lock the rifle into the bench vise. Be sure to pad the jaws of the vise so that the wood of the stock will not be damaged. Special vise jaw pads are available from gunshops and such sources as Brownell's in Montezuma, Iowa. When locking the rifle into the vise, place it so the action area is being held by the jaws of the vise, and don't exert too much force on the stock or action since excessive force can damage the wood or even the metal beyond repair. If you do some of your own gun tinkering and perhaps some stock work, you can either make, or have made for you, an adjustable forend support which is worth its weight in gold when it comes to doing such work on your guns.

Another way of holding any long gun for cleaning is shown here. Such a cradle is easily made with a saw, a few pieces of scrap wood, a

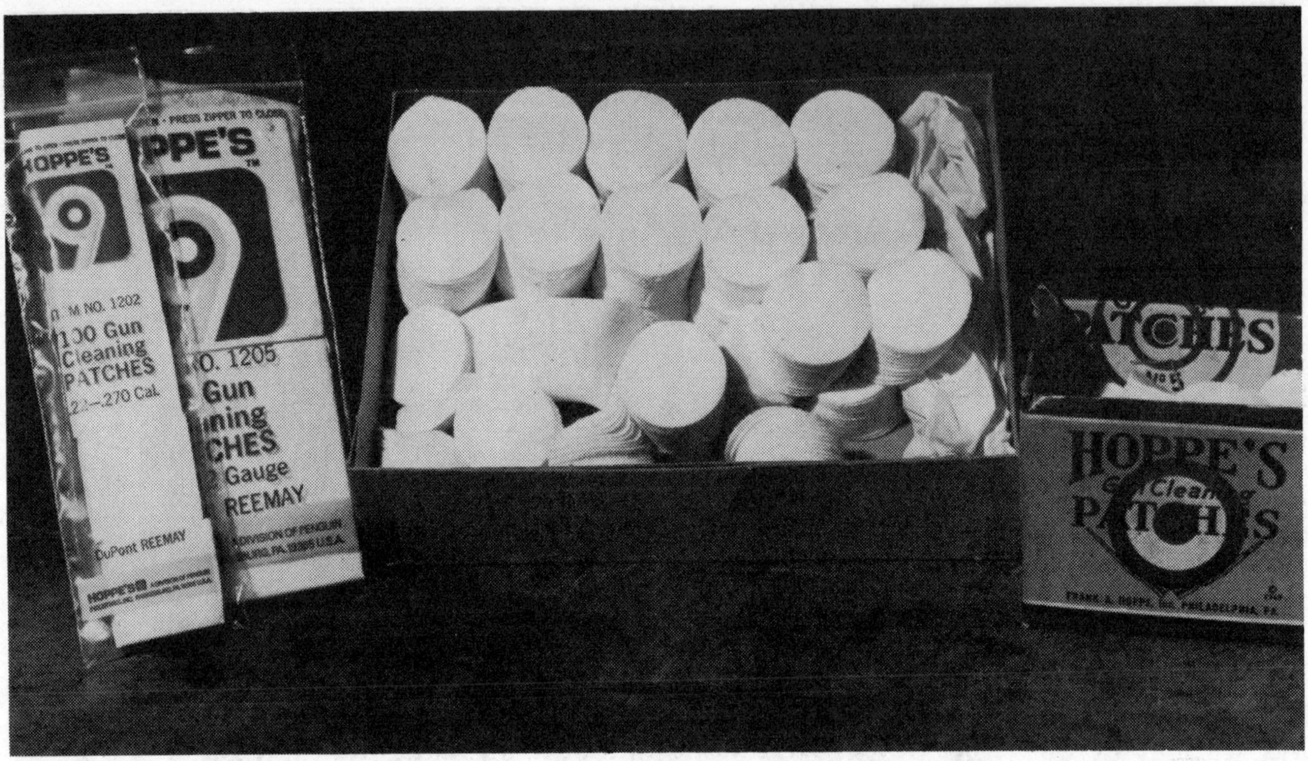

Cleaning patches are bought most economically in bulk. New Reemay patches may eventually replace the conventional flannel patches.

Rod tips, sorted by calibers, as well as mops, buttons and other cleaning tools such as brushes are kept handy by cleaning bench.

few nails and some padding, which can either be wool, flannel or even scraps of deer hide. Locked into the jaws of the bench vise, such a cradle will hold the gun securely and can easily be adjusted for special situations.

A few other items will prove helpful. A bore light, or even a flashlight with a barleycorn bulb on a long wire, will come in handy when you want to inspect the bore more closely. If neither is available, you can reflect quite a bit of light from the bench light into the chamber and bore by means of a dental mirror. Dentists are often glad to part with mirrors which they can no longer use, and you can fashion a suitable handle either from a dowel rod, drill rod or even a cut-off toothbrush. Simply locate and drill a hole, then either thread the handle if it's of metal, or set the mirror into the hole by means of some epoxy glue.

Benchrest shooters were among the first to discover that the friction of the cleaning rod on the lands can play hob with the rifling, and therefore with the accuracy of the rifle. I believe that Taylor & Robbins were the first to

Cradle, when locked into swivel base bench vise, is made from scrap lumber, tops are padded with several layers of soft cloth held in place by carpet tacks.

make a special chamber insert which was placed into the chamber and centered the cleaning rod in the bore so that there could be no contact between the steel cleaning rod and the rifling. Similar devices became popular, and now you can buy a plastic Bore Guide which is made by MTM, the same company that makes those sturdy plastic ammo boxes and other items for shooters.

Bolt-action rifles can be cleaned from the breech after the bolt has been removed. All other action types must be cleaned from the muzzle. Art Saunders (338 Somerset Street, North Plainfield, New Jersey 07060) produces a plastic gadget that is a necessity for those who must clean barrels from the muzzle. Called the Sav-Bore, it fits over the muzzle of the barrel, and like its cousins the chamber inserts, centers the moving cleaning rod neatly in the bore. Wear and tear of the rifling at the muzzle is a major complaint since it leads to a rapid loss of accuracy. Sav-Bore will prevent any such muzzle damage.

If you live in a very humid climate, and especially if guns are to be stored for some time, a rust preventive should be used on all metal parts, including the bore. A commercial product of Vaseline-like consistency called Rig has long been a favorite product for this. Various oils have been in vogue for years, but recently, a number of aerosol sprays have made inroads on the greases and oils. When using any of the aerosol sprays, be sure to study the label. Some of the products act not only as a rust inhibitor or preventive, but also as a lubricant which may be difficult to remove when the day comes that you want to head for the rifle range.

For removing fingerprints from metal, I prefer the various silicone-treated cloths. As a matter of fact, before I rack one of my cleaned guns, I give the stock a light going over with a silicone cloth. This restores some of the gloss to the wood finish and also cleans off any dirt and perspiration.

For cleaning internal action parts which cannot be reached with a cleaning rod, I use a solvent-soaked patch held by a dental forceps.

To prevent damage to throat or rifling of barrel, a throat or bore saver of some kind should be used. In a pinch, you can make your own from a de-headed cartridge case.

Again, your dentist might have one around that is no longer suitable for his office use. Most dentists refer to these forceps as "cotton pickers."

Once in a while it is a good idea, especially when it comes to hard-used hunting rifles, to take the barreled action out of the stock and clean the magazine well and all other parts of the action which normally do not see the light of day.

While out in the hunting fields, particularly on a prolonged big-game hunt, you should take along some basic gun cleaning equipment and perhaps even a small kit with a couple of screwdrivers and other stuff for emergency repairs. For field use, and I admit to being prejudiced, I prefer the collapsible cleaning rod known as the Shukra cleaning rod. Made abroad and imported by Kleinguenther's of Seguin, Texas, the collapsed rod can be carried in a shirt pocket, and in less than 30 seconds, you can have a solid one-piece rod that is long enough for all sporting rifles.

While on the subject of gun care afield, let me mention here the contents of the kit I carry on

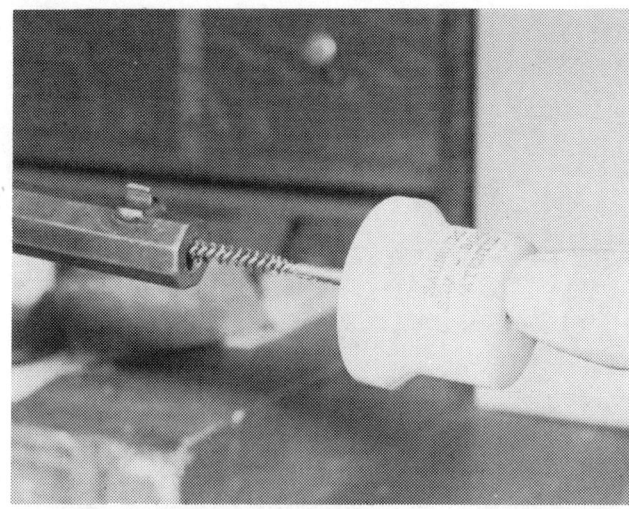

Saunders Sav-Bore is a helpful item when bore must be cleaned from muzzle since it prevents contact between cleaning rod and rifling.

major hunts: a screwdriver that fits the bedding screws of the rifle and a small screwdriver for the scope mounts, scope rings and other such screws. I also bring a couple of spare scope base mounting screws—I have had the misfortune of having the scope and blocks sheared off a rifle during a rock slide—plus a small tube of Loctite. For some models, such as the M98, and I have a number of wildcat rifles made up on that action, I take along an extra extractor since I have found that some extractors are just old and tired enough to break when used fast and furiously. Of course, cleaning patches, powder solvent, my Shukra cleaning rod, some dry lubricant and an extra set of scope covers all go into the ditty bag that holds such other items as compass and spare boot laces.

Collapsible cleaning rod from Germany is author's favorite for use afield. Can be used with all calibers.

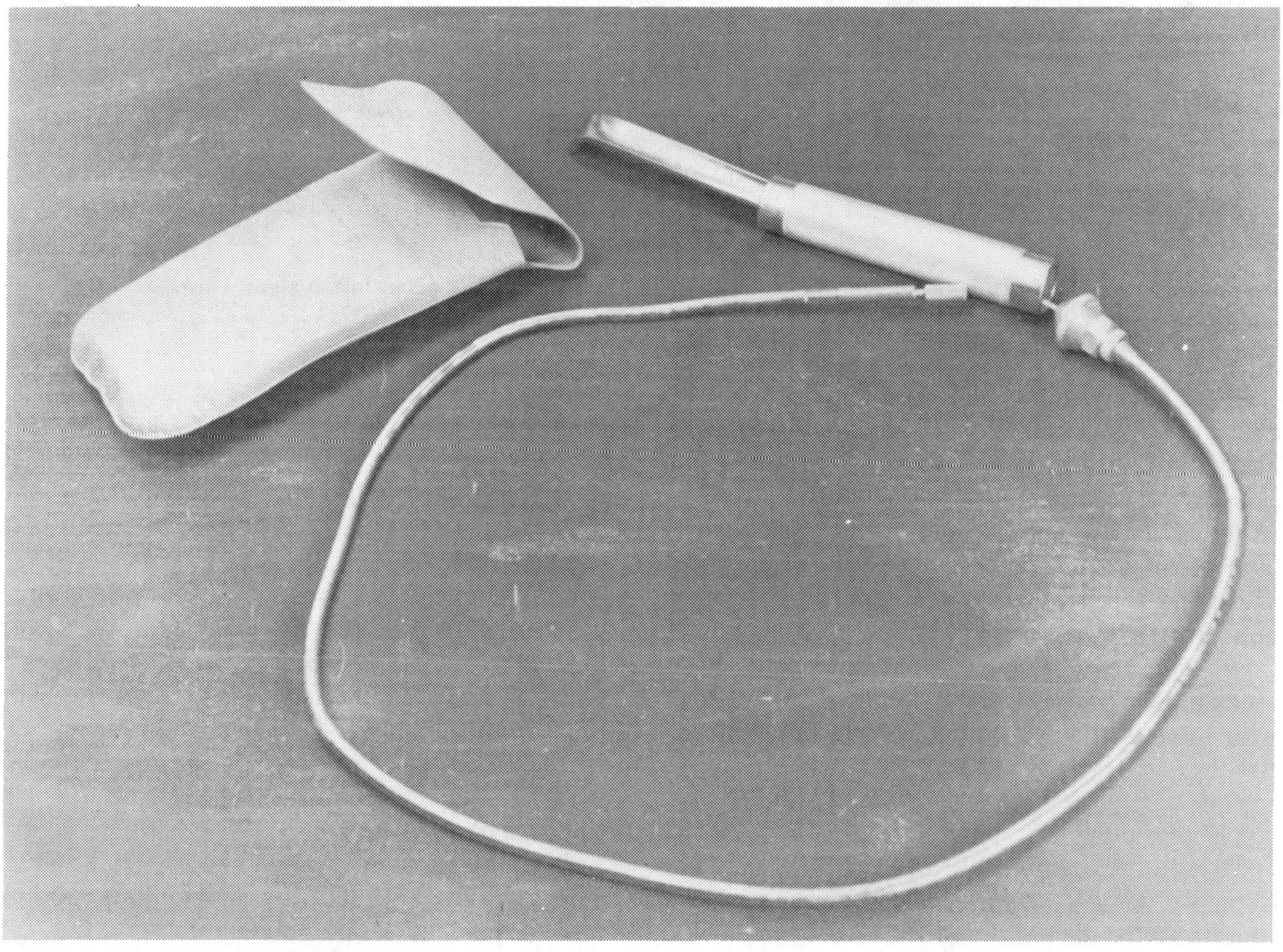

On hunting trips, this gun care kit is tossed into pannier, contains all the essentials for gun care and minor jobs while in hunting camp.

A word of caution is in order about gun lubrication: Old-fashioned gun oil in cans for use in action and barrel seems to have dropped in popularity, and the various aerosols, either with chemical compounds or oil, have taken over. The vast majority of these products are good to very good, but when used to excess, they too can gum up the works. Use any such spray sparingly and keep it away from the wood and stock finish. Some of these chemical sprays can even affect some of the stock finishes now being used.

GUN TINKERING

Many of the minor repairs on rifles can be done by almost anyone who knows how to handle a screwdriver properly. Nothing is more distressing to see than a rifle where each and every screw has fallen victim to an ill-fitting screwdriver blade. When working with gun screws and before putting the blade into the screwhead slot, make sure that the blade fits the screwhead slot.

Should you have the misfortune of messing up a screwhead, here is how you can hide your mistake. Using a fine Swiss file, remove all the burrs and while filing, try to maintain the contour of the screwhead. Polish with a buffing wheel, degrease with either a commercial degreasing agent, denatured alcohol or acetone, then use a touch-up blue.

Every so often a rifle will go sour. That is, where the gun grouped with a given handload or factory load at 1½ MOA, suddenly a five- or ten-shot group will look like a shotgun pattern. One's first inclination is to blame a shot-out barrel, but few barrels go to pot all of a sudden, and before either thinking of a new barrel or taking it to the local gunsmith, there are some things you can check.

If the rifle is scoped, check the scope rings as well as the screws that hold the blocks on the rifle. A loose screw that allows even the smallest amount of play in the mount can spoil the performance of a rifle faster than almost anything else you are likely to encounter. If there is one loose screw, chances are that there will be others, so check them all. Do not simply retighten a loose screw. Remove it completely, clean the screw thread with a wire brush, then apply a drop of Loctite to the screw thread and reseat the screw. When the screw is turned in all the way, keep the blade of the screwdriver in the slot and give the handle of the screwdriver a good whack with a rawhide or plastic mallet. This will allow you make at least another quarter turn of the screw, and once seated, this screw won't work loose.

If the screw has to be removed at some time in the future, lock the gun into the padded jaws of the bench vise, seat the screwdriver blade in the slot and give the handle of the screwdriver a couple of good whacks with the same mallet. Apply pressure gradually to the screwhead and it will turn out easily.

If a scope screw can work loose, so can one or both bedding screws. Although some gunsmiths use the same Loctite treatment on bedding screws as on scope screws, I prefer to hand-tighten these screws without the benefit of the Loctite. Of course, you can use the mallet treatment here, but be certain that the blade of the screwdriver fits the slot in width as well as in length.

As already mentioned, damage to the rifling at the muzzle will affect the accuracy of a rifle. If only the bluing is worn off from scabbard use, you can use touch-up bluing after degreasing the area. If the muzzle is worn and the rifling has been damaged, the gunsmith can recrown the muzzle, or if the damage is too extensive, he can cut off a bit of the muzzle, crown the new muzzle and reinstall the front sight.

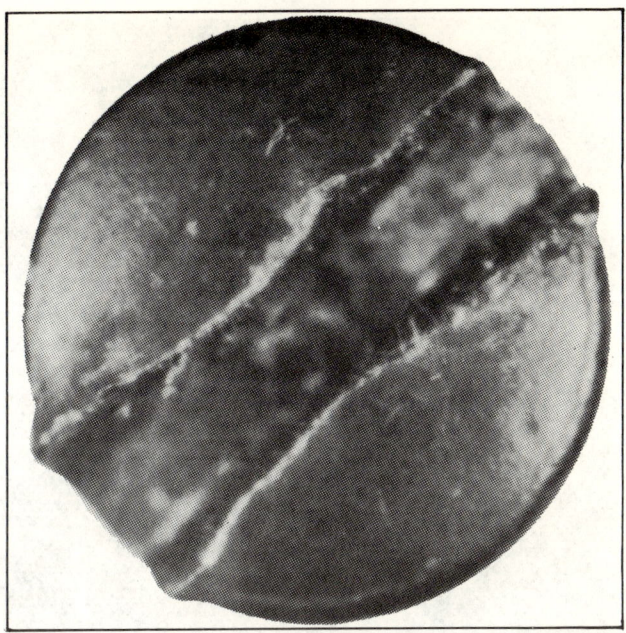

The use of a badly fitting screwdriver will do this to a screwhead. Properly ground and maintained screwdriver blades will forestall such damage.

Unless the barrel channel of a rifle stock is treated and made humidity- and moisture-resistant, it will warp, cup and twist, sometimes to such an extent that the wood will push a perfectly straight barrel clear out of the channel.

One year, when my hunting plans called for a major big-game hunt, I ordered a rifle in early spring so I would have ample time to work up loads, check the rifle out over the anticipated long ranges, and generally get used to it. Everything worked according to plan until the summer, which was hot and humid, and a sudden rush of work which prevented me from shooting that rifle for about two months. Then, just a week before the scheduled hunt, I took that gun out to the range, and was not even on the paper at 100 yards with the same ammo that had grouped beautifully at 200 and 300 yards. The moisture had warped the stock so much that the slender barrel was pushed out of the bedding, and I had to fall back on another rifle for the hunt.

Now, when I buy a rifle, the first thing I do is take the barreled action out of the wood and if the wood has not been sealed, I seal it with a couple of coats of shellac.

Seating rings or block screws is best done in this way. Apply one drop of Loctite to threads of screw, seat screw tight. Keep blade of screwdriver in slot of the screwhead, give handle of screwdriver a good whack with rawhide mallet, then turn in screw completely. To break bond, reverse procedure.

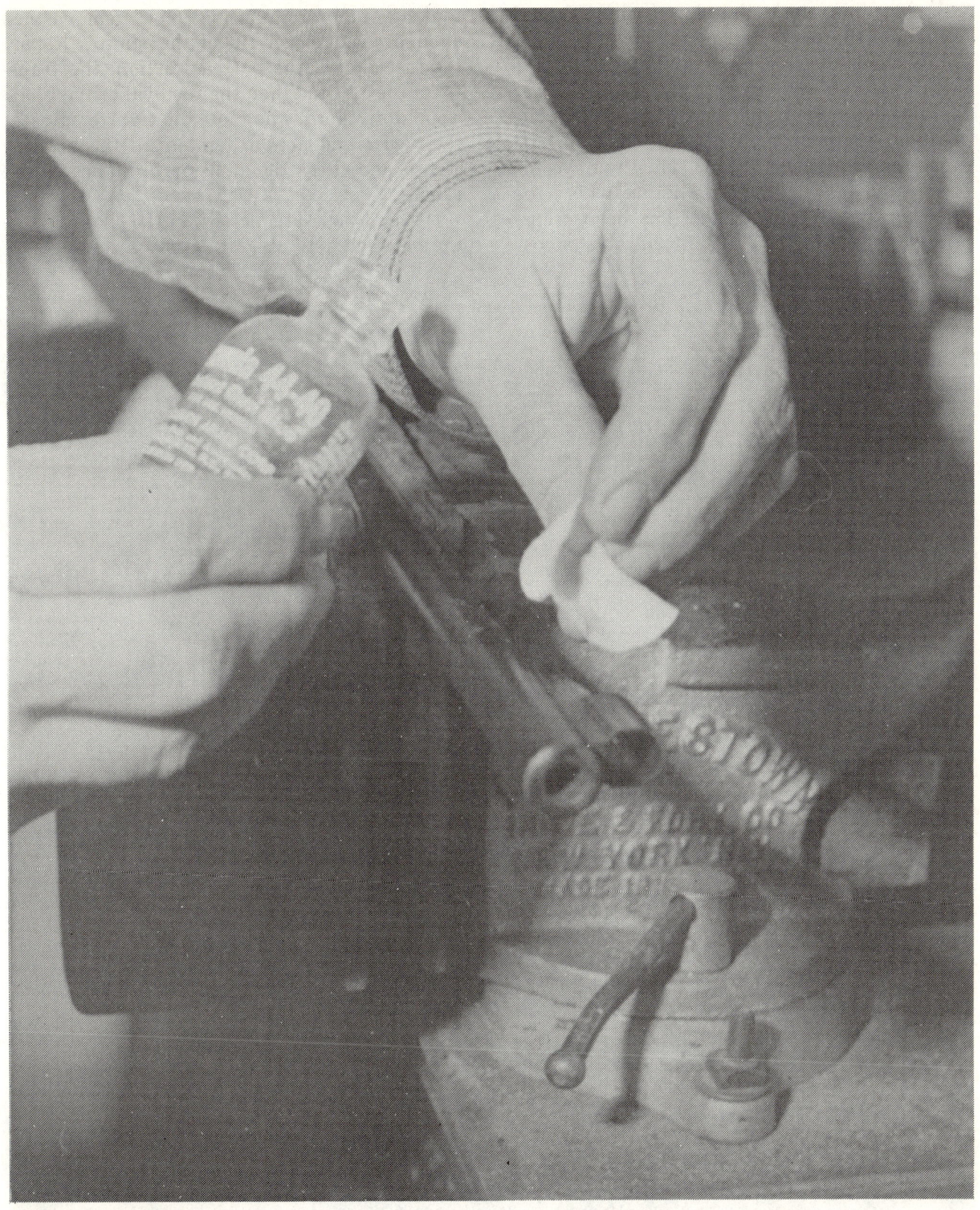

Touch-up bluings are simple to use and give good results if the instructions are followed carefully. Major reason for failure is usually because of incomplete removal of grease.

RIFLE CARE AND TINKERING

Such a minor stock job is done easily. To find out where the wood and metal make contact, apply some inletting blue to the metal parts you think make contact with the wood. Lower the barreled action into the wood and run the bedding screws in. Don't tighten them too much, just snug them down. Then remove the screws and barreled action and see where the inletting blue from the steel has been transferred to the wood. With a suitable stockmaker's tool or inletting tool, remove just enough wood to get rid of the stain. Repeat the insertion of the barreled action, the transfer of the die, and then the removal of the blued wood until there is no more die transfer. Reseat the barrel and action, tighten up the bedding screws and check the gun's performance on the range.

If groups are satisfactory, in the shop remove the barreled action again, apply a thin coat of

Inletting blue is essential to check fit between metal and wood. Here, inletting blue is applied to action to check fit of action to wood.

Glassbedding is not difficult, but care must be taken to be sure that there is enough space for the compound.

shellac, let it dry thoroughly and apply another coat. Let the second coat dry, then assemble the gun once more and head back to the range. You should get the same groups with the shellacked barrel channel as you got before you applied the shellac coats.

The easiest way to treat an ailing stock, providing the stock is sound and fits you well, is to glassbed the action and the barrel channel. Free-floated barrels are usually more accurate since there is no pressure point on them which can push the barrel out of alignment. For this reason, most target rifles are free-floated.

Glassbedding is not difficult, and although it is often described by professional stockmakers as the lazy man's way out, it is within the capabilities and the pocketbook of most shooters. It is true that many rifle stocks are glassbedded when the stocker made a mistake and took out too much wood, or when he had decided on doing the job the easy way by first chopping wood out, then making the needed

Compound is applied to action area of stock. Note how finish of wood is protected by paper walls or strips.

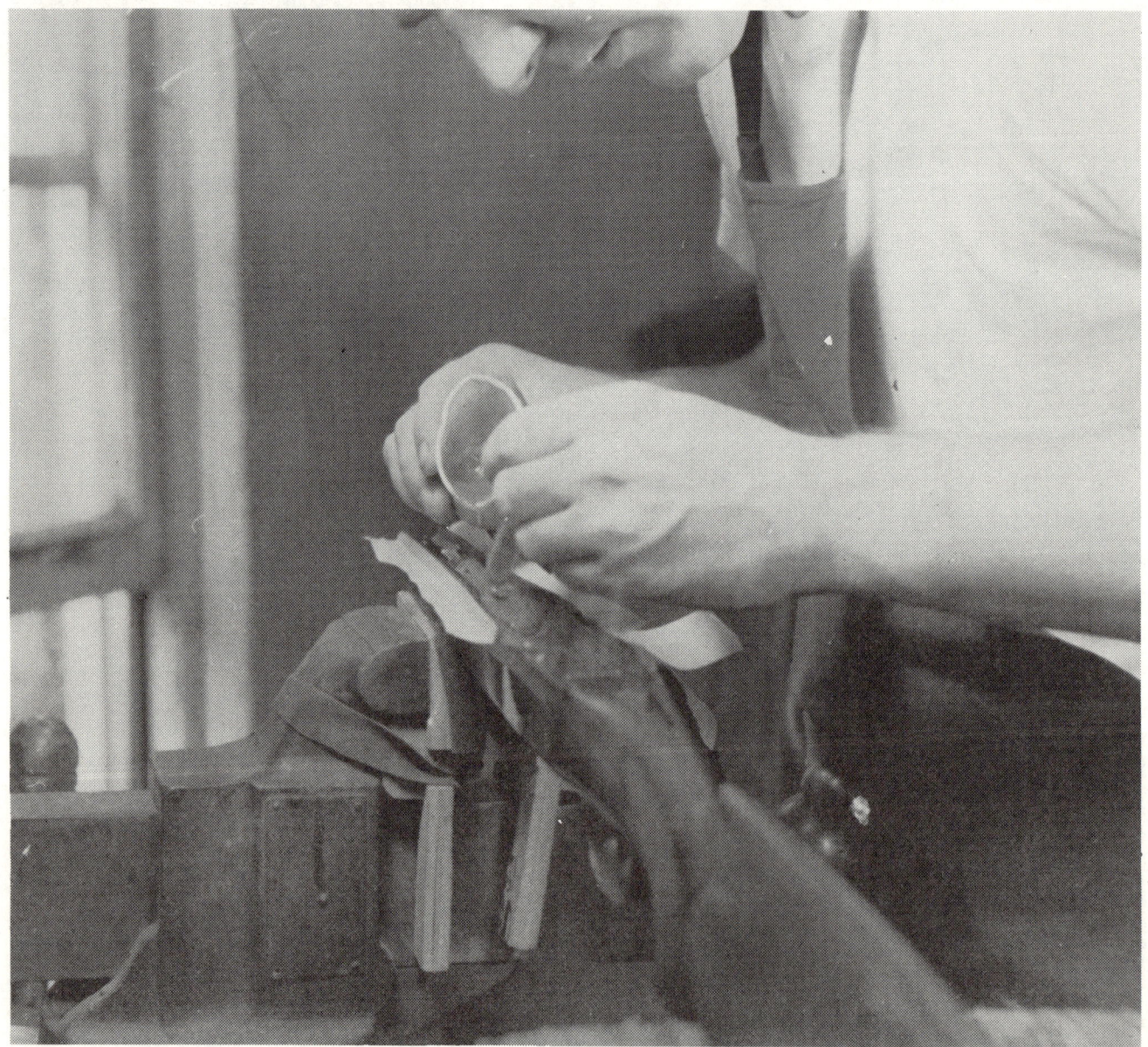

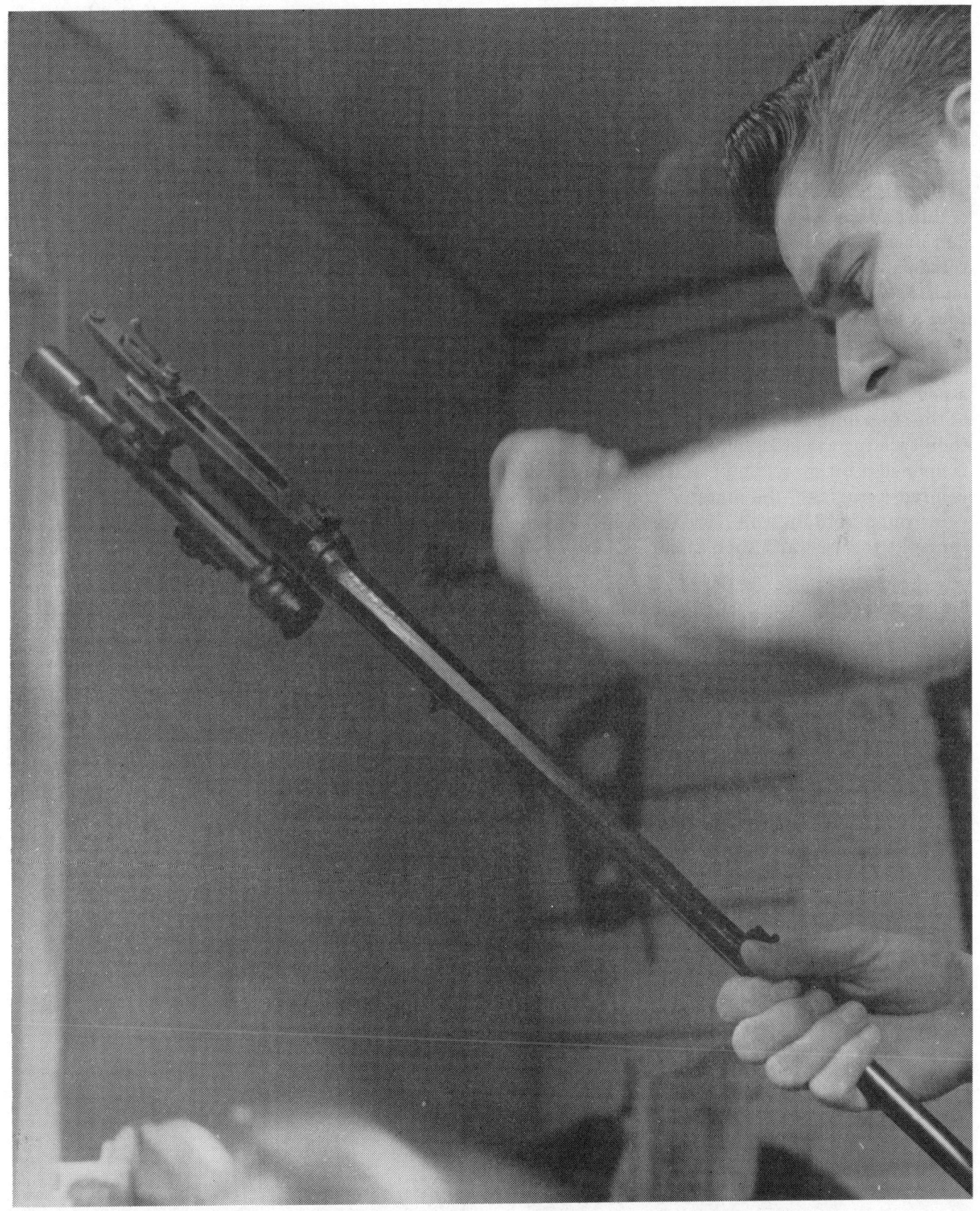

Release agent is applied to metal—forget this step and you will have a real problem on your hands.

adjustments by means of a glassbedding compound. A number of these compounds are on the market, and probably the easiest one to use is the Acraglas kit from Brownell's. If you follow the directions that come with it and work slowly so that there are no overruns or spills, you should encounter no problems with your very first job of glassbedding a stock.

Since Acraglas has great bonding strength, it can also be used for many repairs in the gun room as well as around the house. A split wrist on a stock used to be bad news — it either meant that a through bolt had to be installed, which often was difficult because the action interfered or the bolt made an unsightly mess, or it meant a new stock in most cases. By locking the butt of the stock into the padded jaws of the vise and then twisting the stock manually until the split is opened a bit more, you can flow in some precolored Acraglas — the material comes with the color you mix to match — into the split. Permit the split to close and then clamp it. In 24-48 hours, you will have an almost invisible repair. Touch up the stock finish and unless someone looks very closely, he won't be able to see the repair.

Although many shooters do much of their own stock work, it takes skill and patience before that dreamed-of stock looks the way you think it should look. But there are some stock or wood jobs that are not too difficult, and here are some of the more common ones.

Installation of a rubber recoil pad is fairly simple, especially if you use the B-Square recoil pad installation jig. Chances are that you will have to trim a bit of wood from the butt, and the cut should be as smooth as possible. If you have access to a bandsaw, use the finest blade possible. Measure your distance from the butt to see how much needs to be removed. Scribe a line with a steel scriber, and then apply masking tape to both sides of the line. Some stockmakers leave just enough space between the tapes for the scribed line to be visible, others

Job is finished, usefulness of rifle as well as accuracy have been restored.

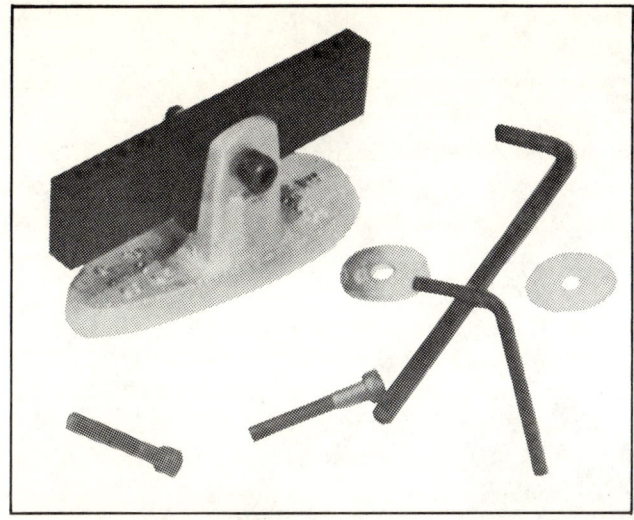

To install a recoil pad easily and quickly, use a B-Square jig which makes the job simple.

fasten a band of masking tape and make the scribe mark on the tape. If no bandsaw is available, use a fine dovetail saw, and saw right on the line. The tape prevents the splitting out of wood chips and also serves to keep the edge of the finish in perfect condition.

If the stock is just a trifle too short, you can either install a thicker recoil pad, or perhaps add a white spacer or two. Pre-trim spacers and pad before you do your final mounting; then use a sander to obtain that perfect fit.

Gun-stock checkering is an art requiring years of patient labor before most of us are good enough at it to admit having checkered our own gun stock. The impressed checkering that replaced hand checkering picks up a distressing amount of dirt which, because of perspiration, often sticks like glue in the checkering. This dirt can be cleaned out quite easily with either an old toothbrush or a very fine — and I mean very fine — steel or brass bristle brush, the type sold for the care of suede leather. Since some solvents used for this type of cleanup also affect the stock finish, it is best to avoid them and use either straight household ammonia or a little lukewarm water and a good soap. Do not use an abrasive soap since it may prove to be too hard on the fine edges of the checkering.

Recutting the impressed checkering requires patience and a steady hand, but it can be done in an evening or two with the help of one or two of the more common checkering tools. GunLine and Dembart offer the widest choice of tools, shapes and cuts, and most of these tools are carried in stock by Brownell's and others who serve the gunsmithing trade.

Dents in the wood and scratches in the finish can be repaired in the home workshop. Depending on the depth of the dent and the type of stock finish, you may have to refinish the entire stock. If a commercial finish was used, such as that seen on Remington guns, you may be able to repair the dent without having to refinish the stock. With some other commercial finishes, it is possible to touch up the repaired area and flow the new finish in so that the repair becomes all but invisible.

Dents in gun stocks are raised the same way they are in furniture — by heat and steam. Make up the smallest possible cotton or flannel pad and soak it in clear water — that is, water free of the usual chemicals or minerals found in most drinking water. Then apply the moist patch to the dent, and use a hot electric iron, without steam, on the patch until it is dry. Check to see whether the wood swells to fill the dent. Some of the epoxy finishes do not permit ready penetration of the steam; with others, the grain-raising process is a slow one. Once the dent has been raised and filled, you are practically done. Most woods require a very light sanding to smooth out the grain and then refinishing, but some woods and some finishes are best left at this stage unless you want to refinish the entire stock.

When working on a stock, especially when repairing checkering, raising dents or refinishing, it is essential to have a clear and unobstructed work area. For all of these jobs, as well as for the installation of a recoil pad, the barreled action must be taken out of the stock. For checkering and refinishing the stock, the recoil pad, spacers and grip cap must also be removed. The easiest way to handle the stock then is to lock it into a checkering cradle.

There are many very good commercial stock finishes. Some of them are quite simple to use, while others require a great deal of skill, to say nothing of spray equipment and other tools not usually found in the home workshop. The stock finishing products offered by Birchwood-Casey,

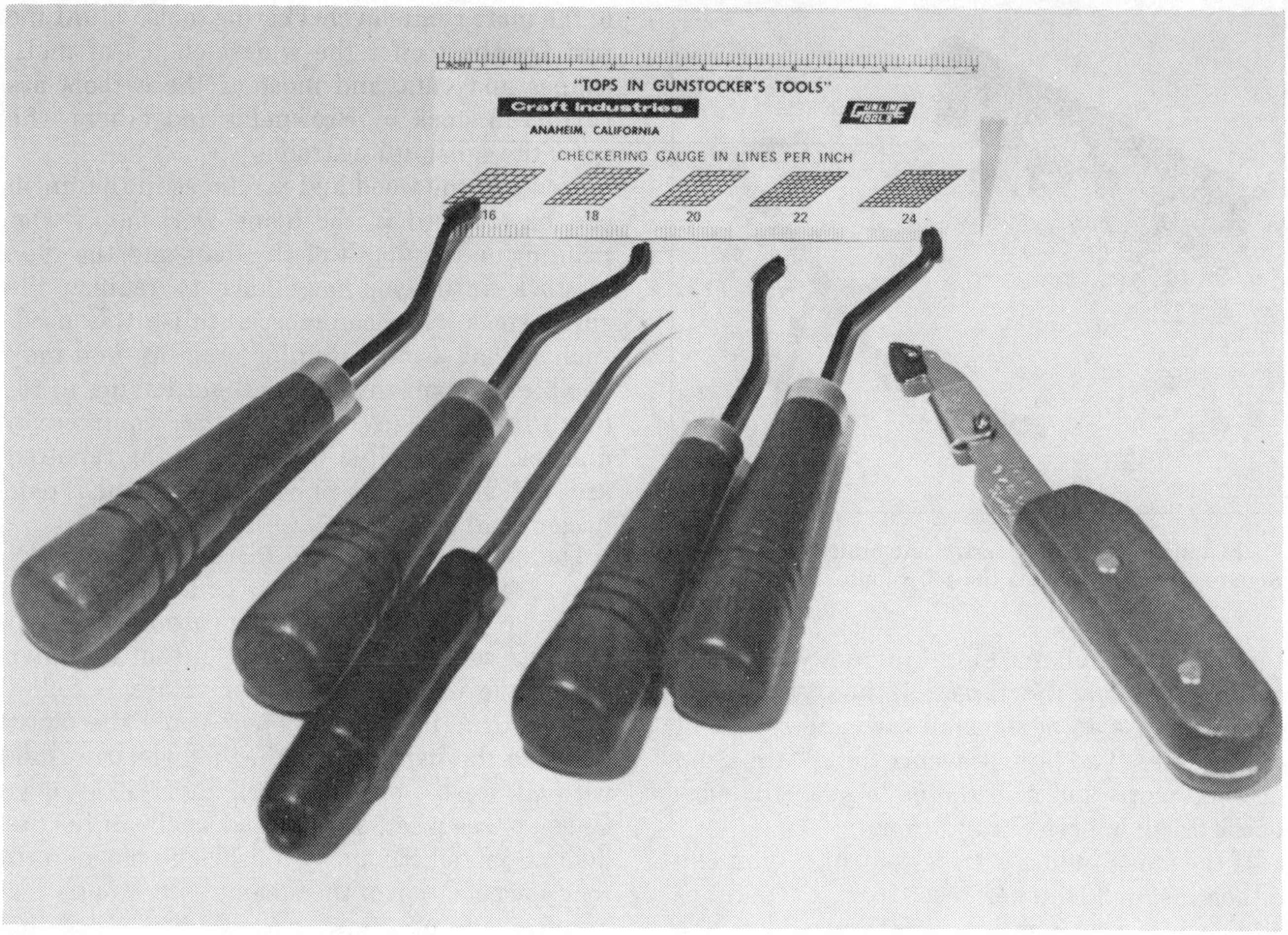

Checkering takes patience and a good place to work with ample light.

Dents in stocks should be removed providing the gun is not an antique. Small dents such as these are cosmetic faults.

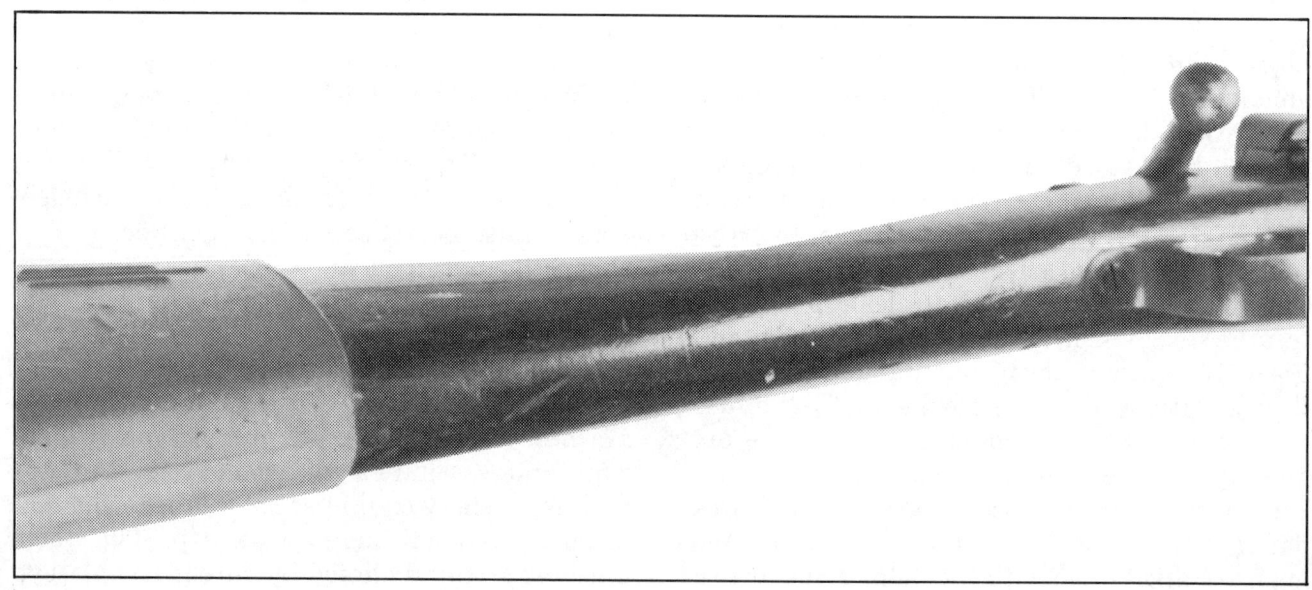

Brownell's checkering cradle is ideal to have since it takes up little space, works just as well as the bigger and more costly ones.

G-96, the famous Lin-Speed, as well as some of the Brownell stock finishing products, are suitable for amateur as well as for professional use.

Stripping the old finish is best done with a commercial finish remover, and the G-96 Stock Stripper, especially in the spray can, will do the job quickly and without harming the wood. Be sure to remove all the finish around the cheekpiece, the pistol grip, the areas where the action and barrel are inletted into the wood, as well as from the checkering. Should the checkering need some touching up, it is best done after the stock has been stripped of the old finish. Moisten the stock lightly with a cloth that has been wrung out in lukewarm water and move it over the stock to raise the grain. Sand the stock smooth with very fine sandpaper, then repeat the raising and sanding until the wood does not respond any longer to the moisture. Next comes a sealer and filler, and after this is completely dry, you can start the final finish of the wood. Some sealers and fillers, especially those designed for the professional, are applied after the final sanding, but after the filler-sealer has dried, the wood must be sanded again to get that super-smooth finish seen on professional jobs.

The gun tinkerer has a wide choice when it comes to finishes. Your choice will depend on your personal preference, as well as on how

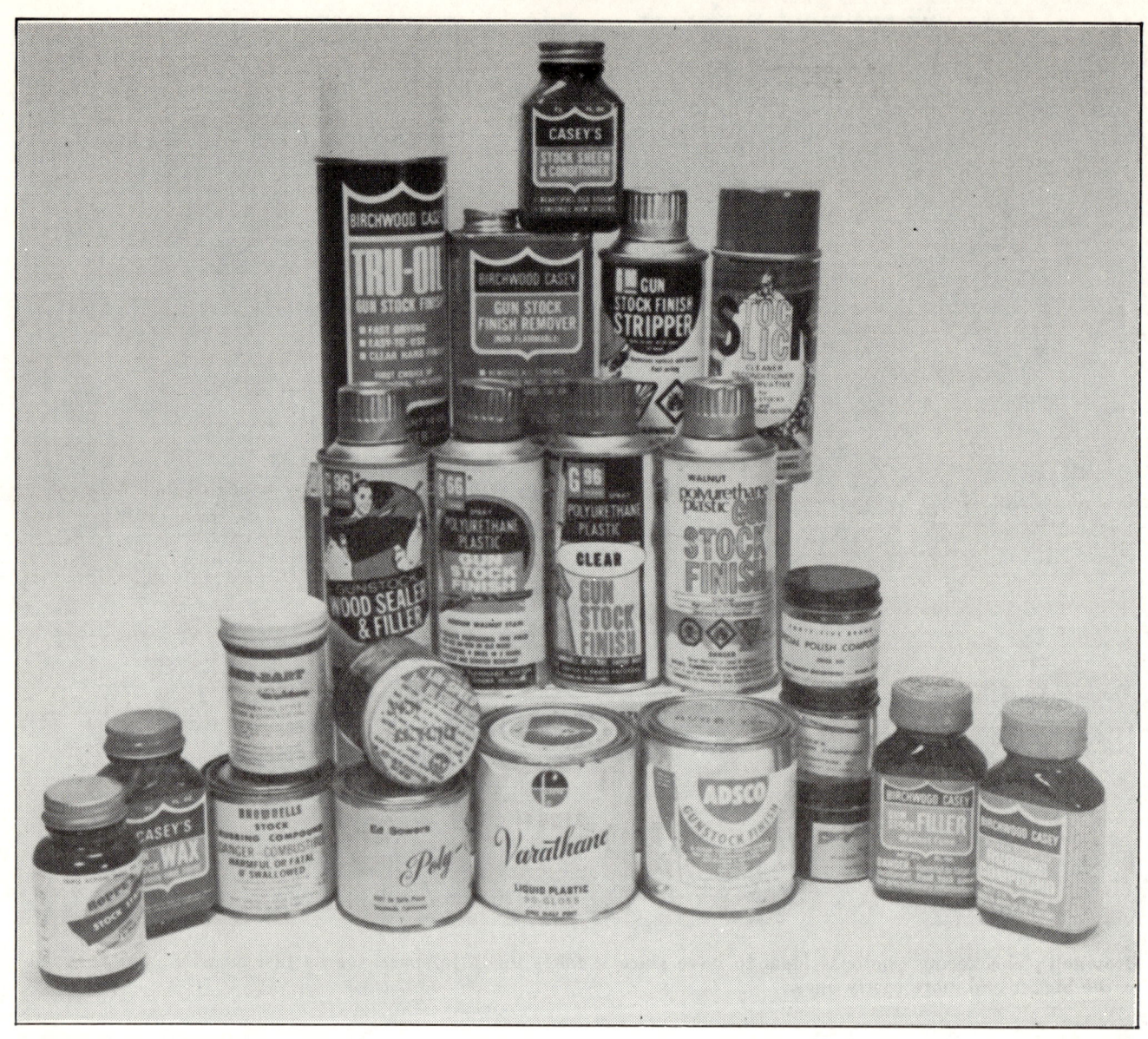

Which is the best stock finishing product? Shown here are a few of the ones that worked fine for author, and while some gun tinkerers develop a preference for one product or another, in practice it comes down to the skill and care with which the stuff is used.

much time and effort you want to spend on the project. Varnish is probably the easiest type of finish to use, providing you brush out each stroke with care, watch your overlaps, and like that kind of finish. The hand-rubbed oil or English finish takes a great deal of time, care and work, and perhaps even a special drying cabinet, but as far as I am concerned, there is nothing better. In between these two, there are roughly a dozen or so stock finishes, some applied with a brush, some with a rag, and even some which are sprayed on. Should your stock lack color before you start the finishing process, you can even get special dyes suitable for gun stocks.

A word of caution about gun-stock finishing—it takes some experience to get the job perfect, and perhaps also some trial and error until you decide which of the various finishes you like best. The nice thing about stock finishing is that you can always take off the newly applied finish and start over. There are some limita-

screw and start in on the muzzle. Again, be sure to pad the jaws of the vise holding the barrel. The main trick in recrowning is to hold the drill perfectly vertical and even with the muzzle.

Even in the most orderly gun cabinet, every so often a distressing sight appears—tiny rust spots all over a nicely blued custom rifle. Before running to the gunshop for a re-blue job, try this: Get some of the finest steel wool available and some very fine or light oil. Soak a small steel wool pad with oil and start rubbing the rust spots. They will disappear like magic and the treatment won't affect the bluing job.

Mention has already been made of touch-up bluing. Bluing is essentially a rusting process,

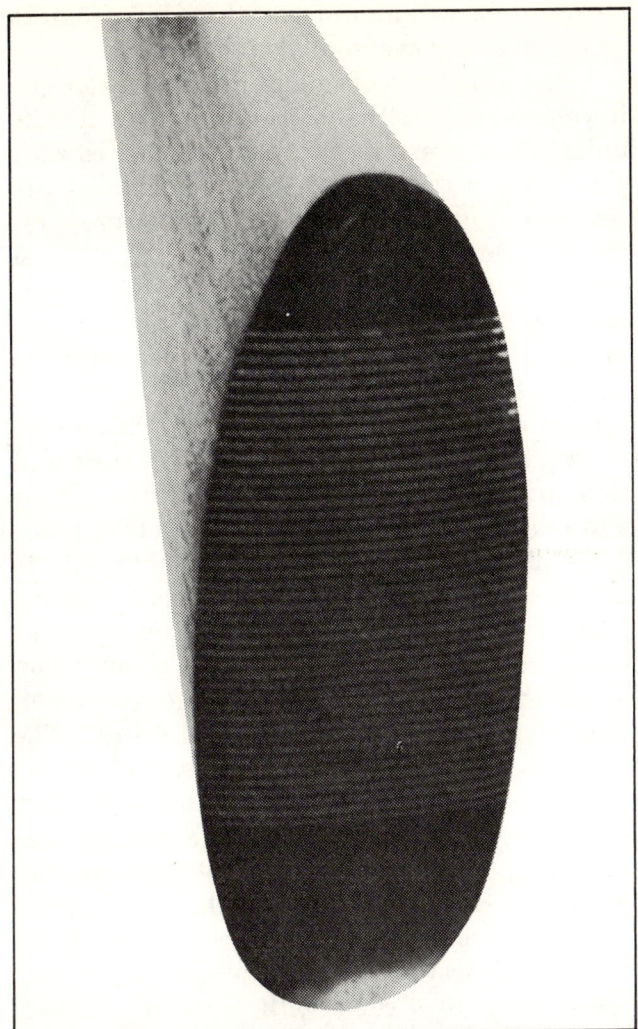

Horn, steel, or other butt plates—sometimes with an ammo trap—are sometimes seen on fine custom rifles. The butt of this one has only the serration of the wood.

Re-crowning a muzzle can be tackled, but go slowly and check your work often.

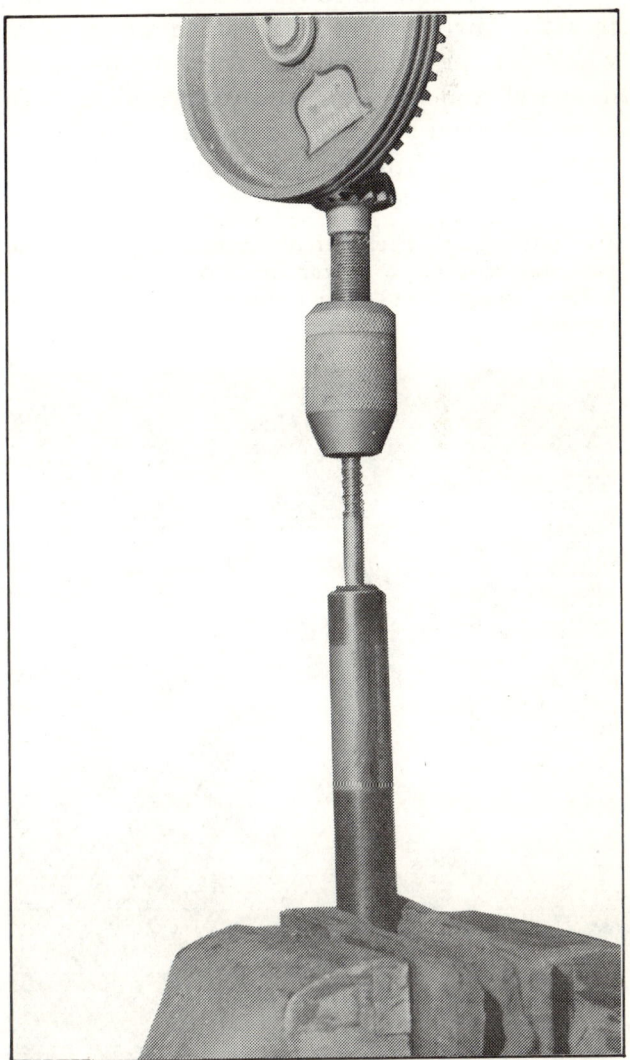

tions, of course, for frequent sanding will eventually affect some of the critical stock dimensions.

Most metal-working jobs are probably best left to a professional, unless you have the right tools, equipment and know-how. For instance, recrowning a barrel is not too difficult, but it is very easy to mess up the job. If you have an old barrel and want to practice, get a large round-headed brass screw, some fine valve grinding compound or the suitable dry abrasive flour mixed with cutting oil, and an old eggbeater drill from your tool chest. Fasten the threads of the brass screw into the chuck of the drill, apply some of the polishing material to the head of the

and commercial bluing is most often done by a hot process in which the perfectly polished and cleaned parts are given a bath in the hot bluing solution. Although the bluing process itself is not too difficult to master, it is a corrosive process, and the hot bluing tanks must be kept away from all other metals. In short, hot bluing is not for the home gun tinkerer unless he has the space and the facilities for it.

The secret of any bluing job lies in the initial polishing of the metal to be blued. The trick is to start with a fairly coarse polishing compound and work down to the finest one with the help of muslin polishing wheels, all without messing up the contours or sharp edges of the metal. Once a perfect polish is obtained, the parts, still in the white, of course, are degreased and then blued.

With some care and a lot of luck, it is possible to get a fairly decent cold bluing finish on a whole gun, providing all the polishing has been done well and the degreasing job was done with care. Cleaned and degreased areas should not be touched with bare hands since the residual perspiration will almost certainly leave marks on the steel and eventually on the bluing.

Touch-up bluing of small worn areas is simple if you remember that no bluing job will take unless the surface to be treated is almost surgically clean. Rust and spotty old bluing are best removed with one of the special preparations marketed for that purpose. While rust spots will disappear with the oil-steel wool treatment, old bluing won't — it will just become beautifully shiny where it was rubbed with the oily steel wool.

Over the years, I believe I have tried every instant touch-up blue on the market. Some of these products work well on three or four guns and fail to do the job on others. Another product will fail with two touch-up jobs, but will do a beautiful job on two or three other spots. Just what that efficiency depends on, I don't know. However, I suspect that the composition of the original bluing salts and the method of bluing may have something to do with it. The answer is to follow the directions, and if one product does not work, try another one — but save the first. It may do well on a gun that resists the product you just bought, the one that did such a nice touch-up job on that worn spot.

These days, all centerfire rifles are drilled and tapped for scope mounting, and nearly all of the rimfire rifles come with grooved receivers for easy scope mounting. I suggest that you do not attempt to drill and tap actions which have not been factory-prepared for scope mounting. This job calls not only for scope mounting jigs, but also for a drill press, a knowledge of steel, and a lot of skill. Some of the older military actions may be hardened to such a degree that a drill will not cut them, and then the spot where the hole is to be drilled and tapped must be annealed — and spot annealing is an art that is not learned quickly.

There is no trick to installing a scope on most of the newer rimfire rifles or even on some of the lower-powered 22-caliber centerfire rifles, since the receivers of those guns are grooved for ease of scope mounting. Again, start by locking the gun into the padded jaws of your bench vise, and this time use a small level, such as a Torpedo level, to make certain that the gun is level in the vise. Clean and degrease the

Use a polishing wheel with different grades of buffing compounds to get a mirror finish on all metal parts before bluing. Do not touch metal that has been degreased.

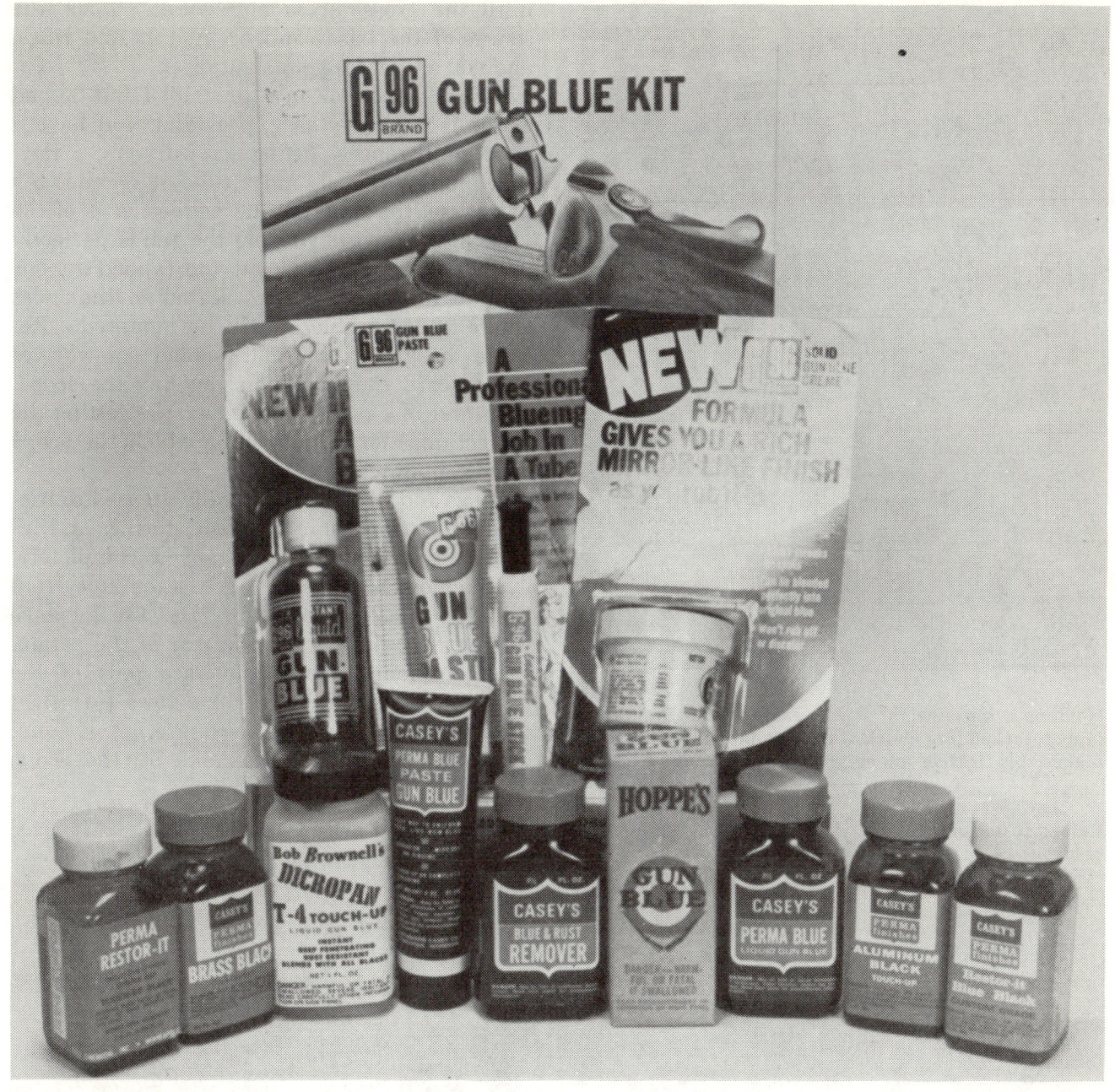

Another array of commercial products which are designed to make life easier for gun tinkerers.

mounts completely and thoroughly; if this was not done, you will not get a secure mounting job. Open the clamps or jaws of the bases wide, slip them over the grooves in the receiver and tighten the screws very lightly, just enough so that the scope or mounts won't slip off the receiver. Some of the rimfire scopes have their bases as integral units on the scope body or tube, others use conventional rings. If the latter are used, you can tighten the bases, but leave the rings on the loose side until you adjust the scope for proper eye relief.

Once the location of the scope in either the rings or the bases on the receiver has been determined for maximum eye relief, tighten the screws after making certain that the horizontal crosshair is really horizontal. If it is not, twist the scope tube lightly, one way or the other,

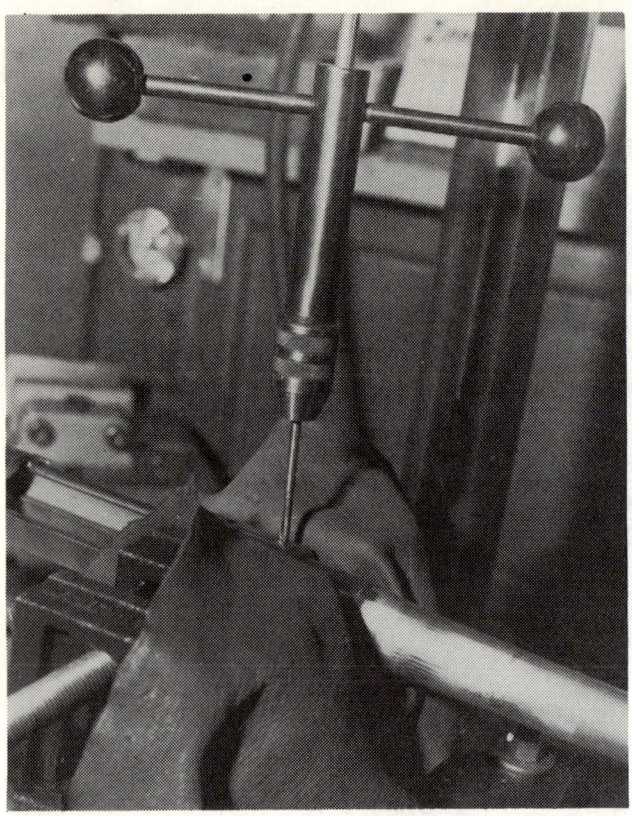

Holding a tap straight is not easy—so the **B-Square** tapper, locked into chuck of dead spindle of drill press, makes this ticklish job easy.

until the crosshair is horizontal. Lock the screws of the bases and/or mounts and rings, and you are set for your sighting-in.

Mounting a scope on a predrilled and tapped action is relatively easy, providing you have a couple of properly fitting screwdrivers, a rawhide mallet, a level, and a tube of Loctite. As before, set the rifle into the padded jaws of the vise, and make certain that the gun is perfectly level. Most factory-drilled and tapped actions contain four little screws seated in the holes where the scope blocks will be mounted. Remove those with a small bladed screwdriver and discard them. When you buy the scope, rings and blocks, make sure you are getting the correct ones for the action on which the scope is to be mounted.

Rings and blocks are liberally greased to prevent rust during shipping and storing, and all of this grease must be removed completely. Also remove any residual grease or lube from the four holes in the action. Be sure to place the rear scope mount on the rear of the action, the front mount on the forward part of the action. Sometimes, the four screws furnished for the mounting of the blocks are not of equal length. This is not a mistake by the scope

Before installing a scope, drilling, tapping or almost any other job, level gun in padded jaws of vise.

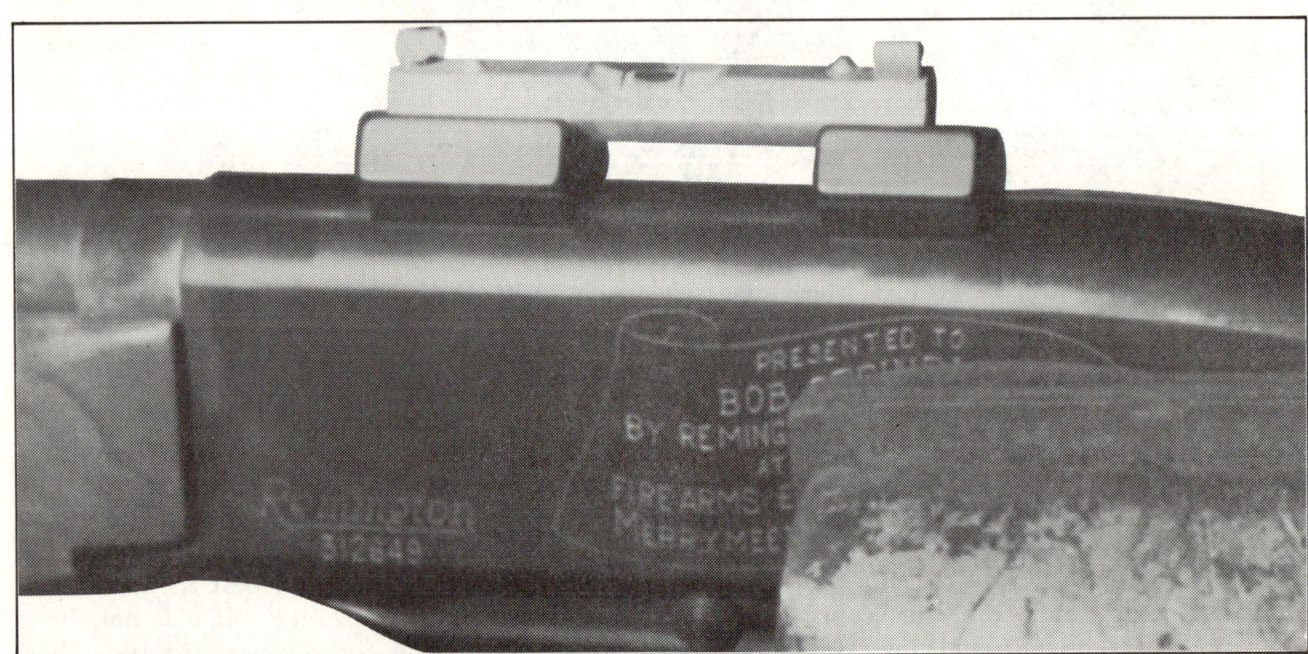

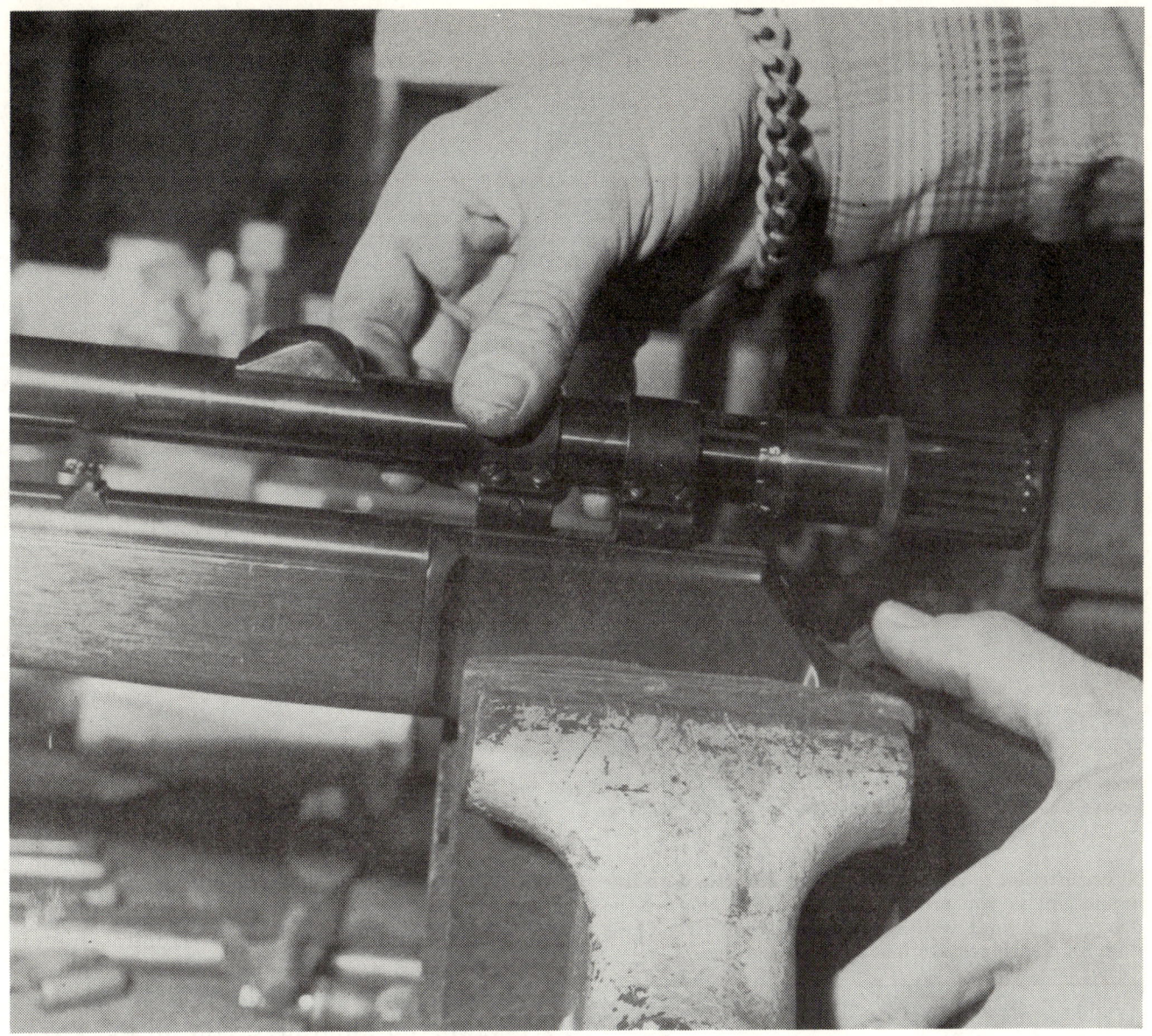

On rifles with exposed hammer, make sure that the hammer spur clears the ocular bell of the scope once it is mounted.

maker but is because one mount or the other, usually the rear one, is higher and therefore needs longer screws.

If you are scoping a lever action, pump action or an autoloader, you simply leave the action closed, but without any live round in the magazine or in the chamber. If at any time you want to ascertain whether or not a rifle functions properly while you are in your workshop or gun room, *never* use live ammo. Either make up dummy rounds with spent primers and without powder charge, or still better, buy a set of dummy cartridges. With a bolt-action rifle, you can either remove the bolt and check for bottoming screws, or you can leave the bolt in the action and find out the hard way whether one of the block mounting screws has bottomed out. If it has bottomed, you have the screws mixed up. Remember that such a screw will invariably lock up the bolt and therefore also the action.

Once you are sure that the blocks are in the right locations and that none of the screws have bottomed, run the screws into the blocks,

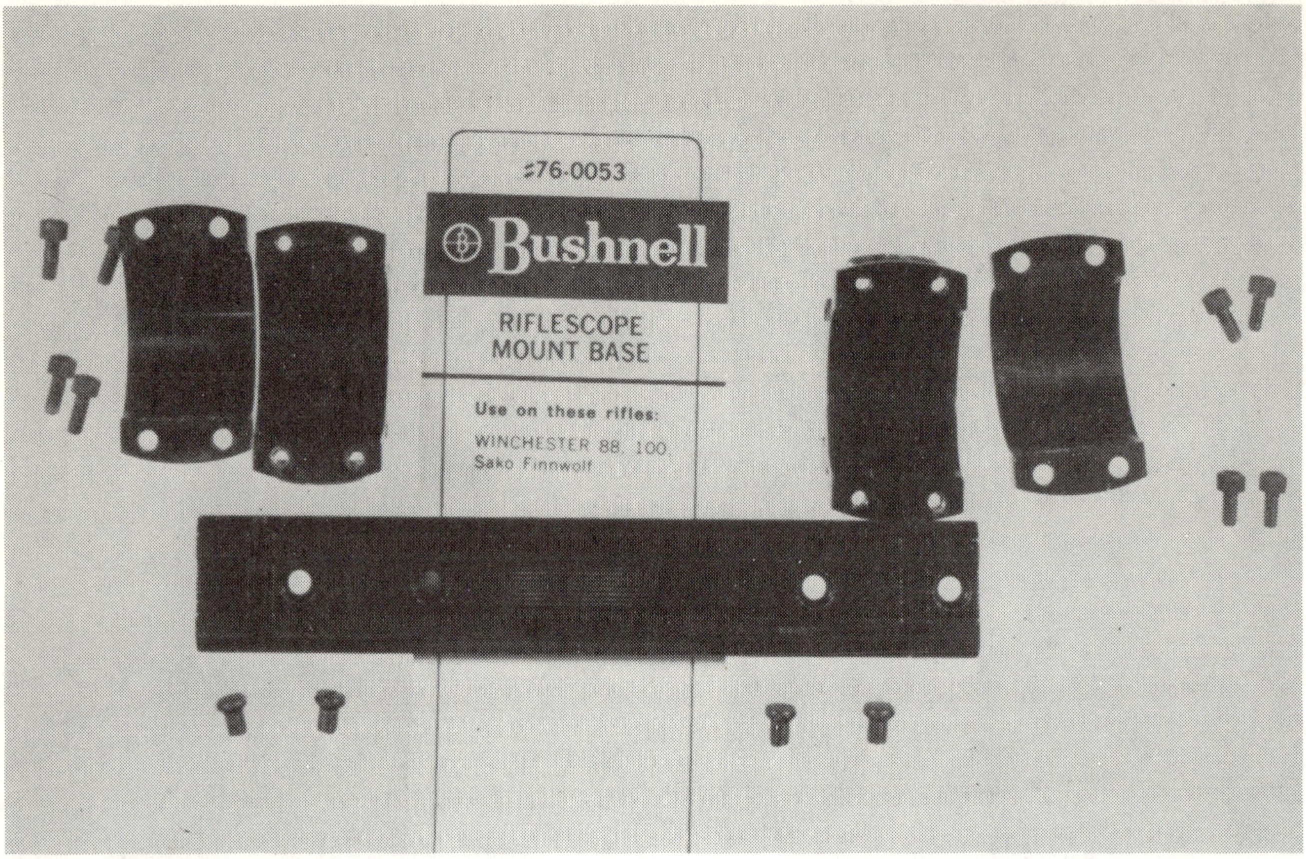

Scope base and rings laid out for installation. Be sure to degrease all surfaces since residual grease will allow slippage of parts.

Never attempt to check functioning of a rifle with live ammo unless you are on the range and there is no danger of anyone walking into the line of fire. These dummy cartridges are made by Winchester.

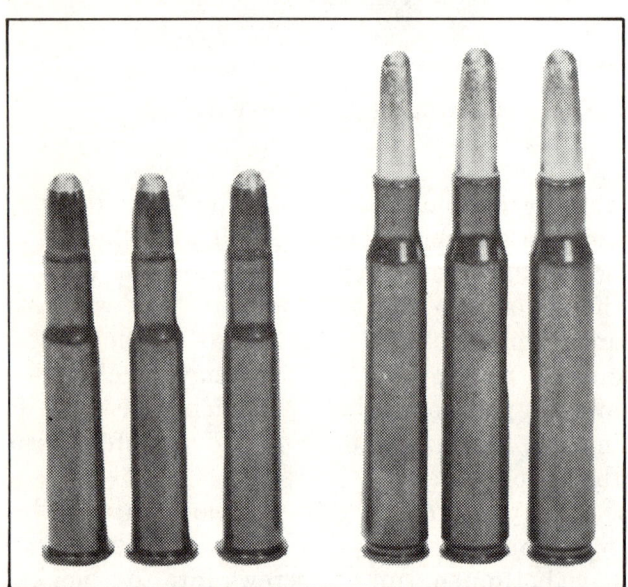

but do not cinch them tight. Again, check to see that the bolt moves freely and that the gun functions, without actually firing it. Dummy rounds are the easiest and safest way to check this. If everything is as it should be, remove each screw, apply a drop of Loctite to the thread of each screw, and turn each screw until it stops. Be sure that the screwdriver blade fits the slot of the screw.

Let the blade of the screwdriver rest in the slot of one of the screws, then give the handle of the screwdriver a healthy whack with a rawhide mallet. This allows you an extra quarter turn on the screw. Do the same thing with the other base screws. Next, seat the rings with the scope in the blocks, and again, make sure that your eye relief is correct and that the horizontal crosshairs are really horizontal. Now, before you tighten the screws in the rings, if you are working with a bolt-action rifle, make sure that the bolt handle clears the scope tube and the

Support rifle with a stand before installing scope. Never tighten jaws of vise too much since wood can be damaged and metal stressed.

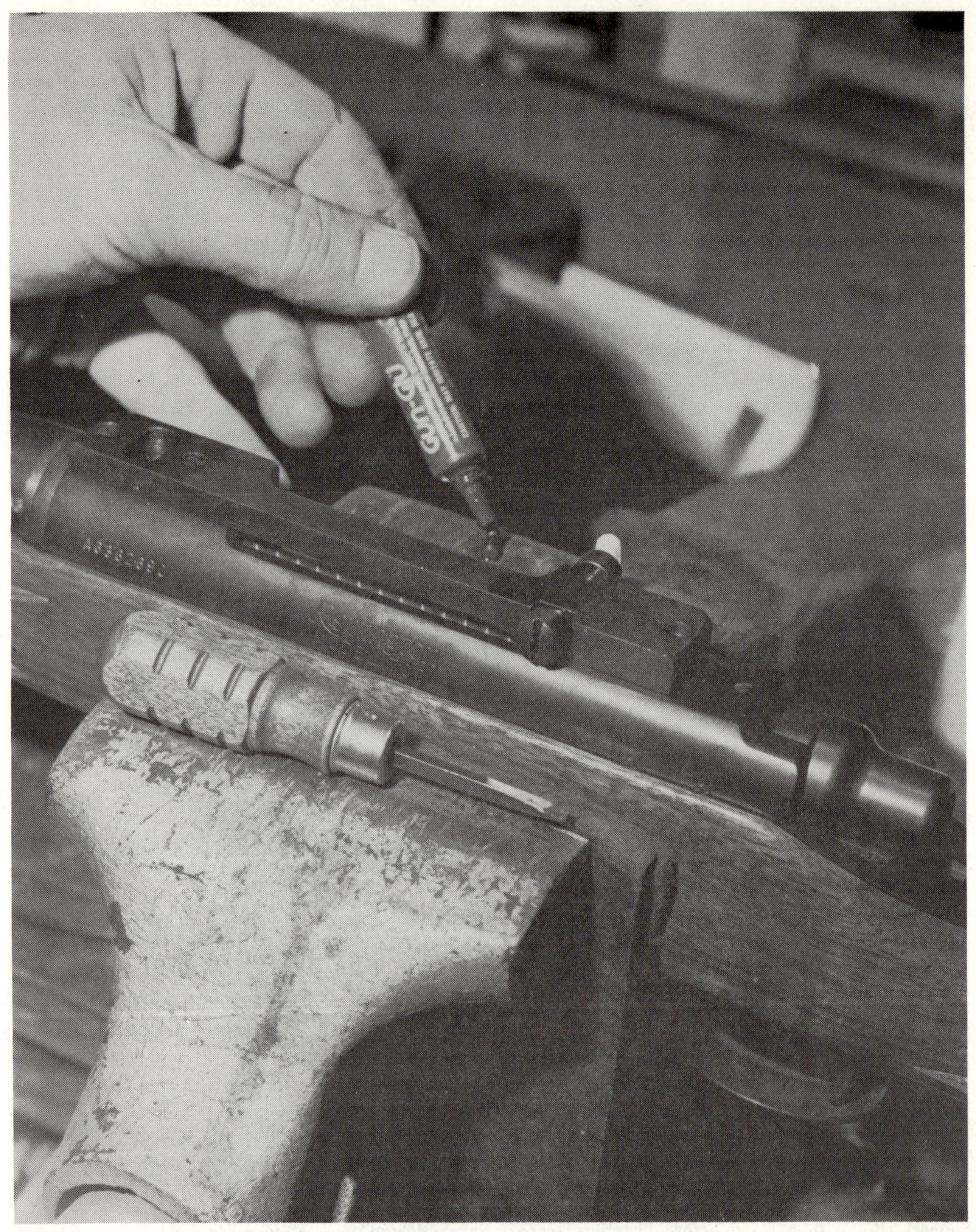
Gun-Glu or Loctite, one drop per screw, will give the best bonding of threads.

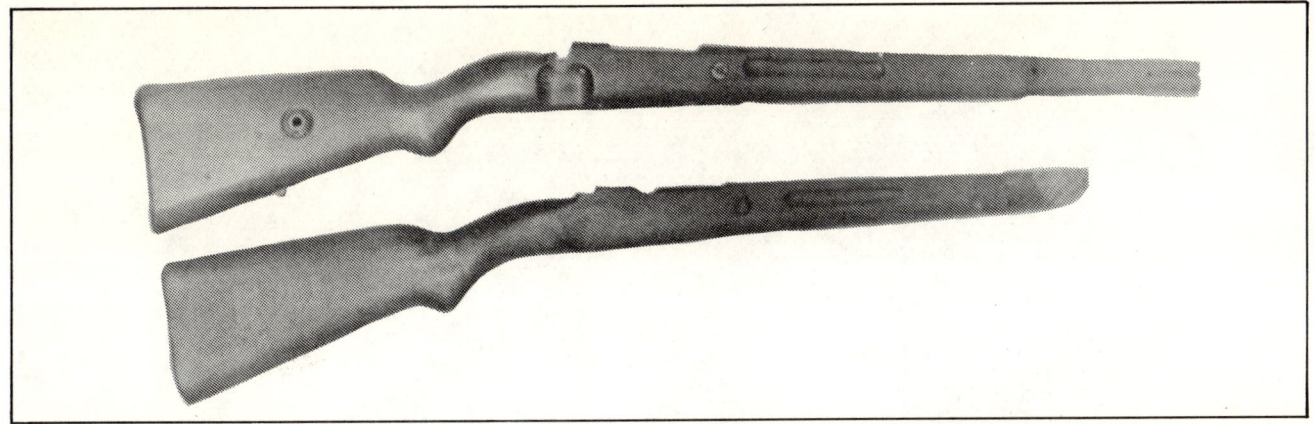

Two military stocks. Once cleaned, sanded and the military hardware removed, many of these hunks of wood have surprisingly nice wood which can be reshaped and finished to make a very acceptable sporter stock.

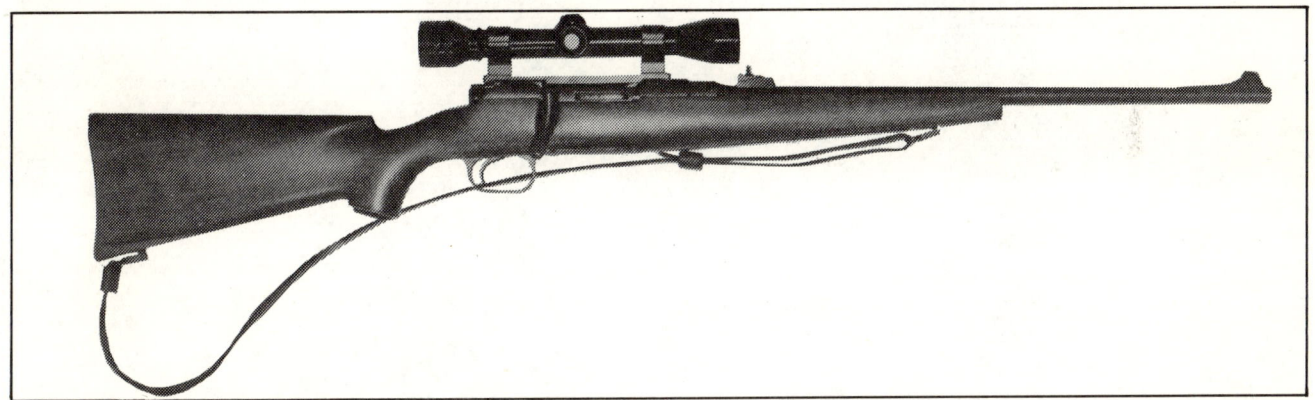

Military action, military stock, plus custom barrel, and presto, you have a sporting rifle.

ocular or rear bell of the scope. Some of the higher-powered scopes and some of the variable scopes have to be installed on extra-high bases so the bolt handle will clear.

Once everything is set, again Loctite all screws, grab a box or two of ammo and head for the range for scope sighting.

While on the subject of gun tinkering, we should consider one more point that is often raised when the talk turns to doing some of your own stock work. Time was when a military surplus gun, action or even a surplus stock could be acquired for very little money, and then could be sporterized or customized at the owner's leisure. Those days are gone, as a result of the Gun Control Act of 1968, but once in a while nice surplus stocks come on the market, and many of these can be customized without too much trouble. I have found that such a stock is ideal for learning to work with wood and stock finishes. If you do happen to mess up the job, you won't be losing a small fortune in stock wood.

By removing the military hardware, then altering the shape of the buttstock and even the pistol grip with the help of a coarse and then a medium rasp, you can salvage a nice looking piece of wood without much effort. You may not be able to shape a full pistol grip, but you can add a rubber recoil pad with a white spacer or two, and even a contrasting wood forend. Cut this at a slant, add some contrasting color wood spacers, anchor the new tip with dowel and glue, shape and sand to your liking, and presto, you have a stock that can cost you as little as five or ten dollars.

RIFLE CARE AND TINKERING

Chapter Ten
Military Rifles

Chapter Ten
Military Rifles

When peace broke out at the end of WW II, you could buy all sorts of military rifles, in all sorts of places, even in gas stations. The majority of these rifles were good buys since they were built to military standards which were usually quite high. At that time, a good German M98 could be bought for perhaps $25, a Springfield for as little as $45 or $50, while the various M1 30-caliber carbines went begging. The Gun Control Act of 1968 changed all of this, and now the once-glutted military surplus market is sadly depleted.

A Garand, once barely glanced at in a gunshop, now brings a fancy price, even when the inside of the barrel looks like an abandoned sewer pipe. An O3A3 Springfield or even an old British Enfield in fair condition will today cost you more than a suit of clothing, and some of the better-known military rifles have become so scarce that they command astronomical prices. In short, the military surplus rifle, once a shooter, a clunker, or something to be customized, sporterized and wildcatted, is now a treasured collector's gun.

The military rifles now on the market are of a vintage that escapes the GCA rules. Therefore, they are not suitable for rechambering since the steel in these guns is, or rather was, designed for semismokeless powders. The days when you could buy a military '06 rifle cheaply and have it rechambered for the 308 Norma Magnum are no more. Every so often, old German Model 88s appear, and they are best kept in the original 8mm J caliber (.318"). The few Schmidt-Rubins in the original 7.5mm chambering with their straight-pull actions are more curiosa than suitable for sporterizing, although the caliber is more than adequate for deer hunting if you can learn to live with the action.

Most of the military hardware of recent years, such as the Russian AK47, the SKS and similar rifles, fall under the control of the Bureau of Alcohol, Tobacco and Firearms (BATF), since many of them are capable of firing full as well as semiautomatic. Variations of Russian rifles, assault rifles and the like, coming from the various Asiatic factories in Communist-controlled countries are interesting subjects for study, providing you can afford them and can get the blessing of BATF.

Thanks to the lack of surplus military rifles and to increased collector interest, the "as issued" military rifle is usually more valuable than one that was customized and sporterized by a professional gunsmith. Twenty years ago, it was the accepted and sensible thing to do: buy a military rifle, then either have it customized and sporterized or do most of the work yourself, falling back on professional help for such matters as altering the bolt handle and changing the action so that it would cock on opening rather than on closing.

If you should run across one of these customized rifles, before grabbing for it and your checkbook, consider these points. If the wood and metal work was done by a top-notch gunsmith, perhaps even with a custom stock, if little or nothing is left of the original military appearance, if the work can be traced back to a top gunsmith, and if the gun is not in some kinky wildcat caliber, it can be a good buy. If, however, the customizing looks like it escaped from a blacksmith shop, if metal alterations are crude or poorly fitted, or if the gun is in some useless wildcat caliber and therefore may need rebarreling, you will probably find that it

Sporterizing military action with custom stock. If action is tuned and spruced up with engine turning, you won't be able to tell at glance if this action once was a military one.

Action of the Swiss Schmidt-Rubin service rifle.

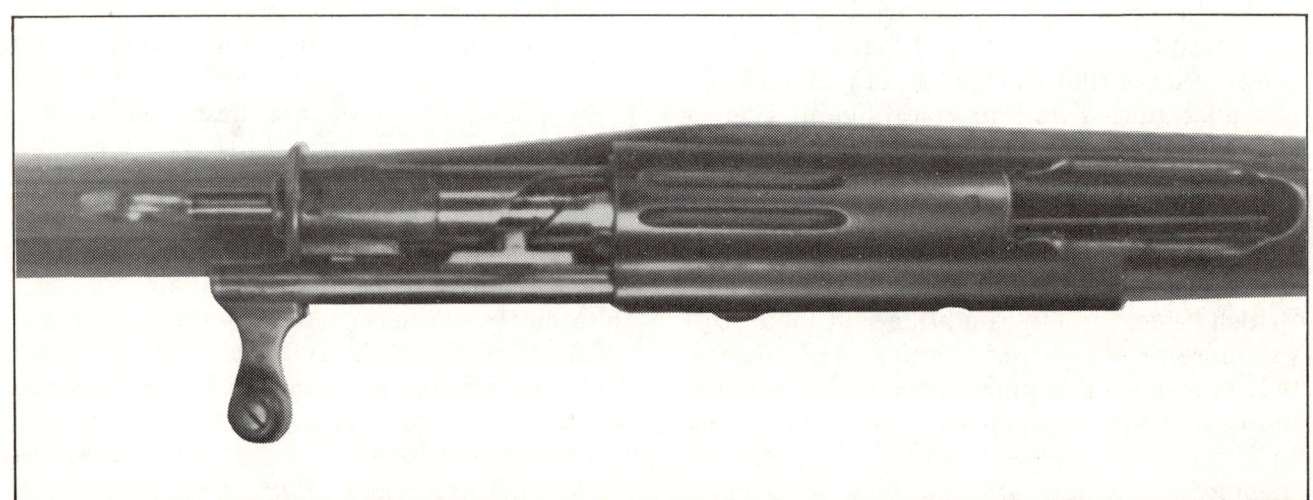

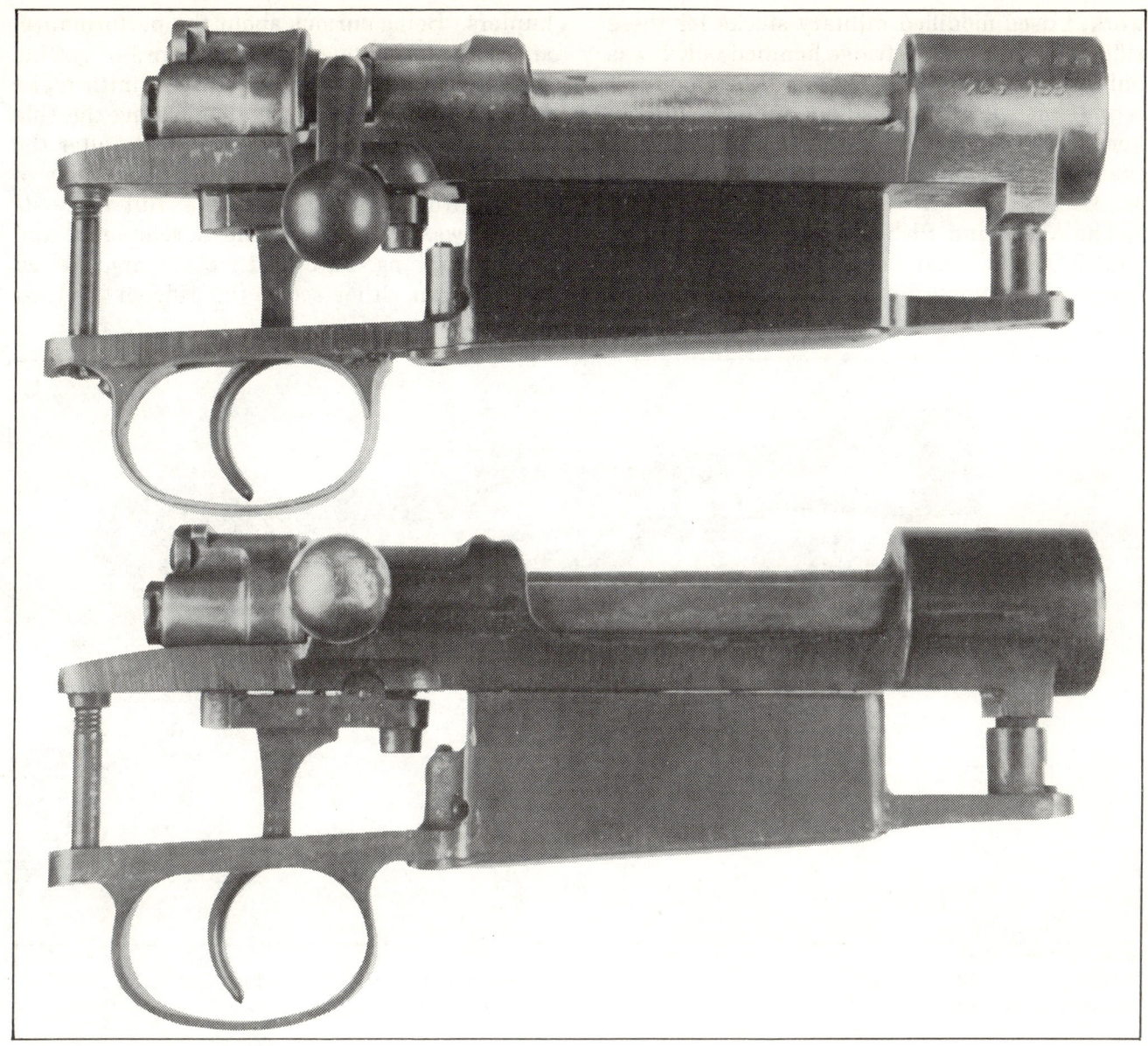

These two military actions have been set aside—one day both will be tuned, new triggers installed and then will serve as basis for custom rifles.

costs more to get the rifle into the shape and condition you want than a domestic or imported factory sporting rifle would cost you.

Springfield, German M98 and even Enfield actions, now as scarce as the proverbial hen's teeth, are sometimes encountered. Prices for these actions are often based on what the traffic will bear, and if you can afford one that is clean and has all the parts, it can well serve as the basis for a fine sporter rifle. Don't turn up your nose at a badly pitted M98 action — an hour or two with a stippling iron, an altered bolt handle and perhaps a Canjar or Timney trigger, and you have the makings of a genuine custom rifle.

Thanks to some military surplus dealers, barrels, stocks and even actions surface once in a while. Long ago, for instance, I learned that not every wildcat cartridge I dreamed up would perform the way my slide rule said it would. These rifles were usually made up on either M98 or Springfield actions, and to save money and work, I used modified military stocks for these rifles. If a wildcat cartridge bombed out, I was only out the cost of the barrel and the chambering. If the wildcat worked out and I decided to keep the rifle in one piece, then I would take off that modified clunker stock and make up a new stock for it.

The AK47 and SKS are chambered for the 7.62x39 round, a cartridge which really has not been fully explored by American shooters and hunters. Being curious about the performance, and not wanting to go to the expense of getting a Russian surplus rifle, I had a gunsmith make up a test rifle. I did not bother having the rifle blued, nor did I make any attempt to alter the trigger pull. The whole thing looks like a refugee from the scrap bucket. But it shoots and allows me to do my load development and chronographing. Later, if I feel the urgent need for it, I can either scope the rifle or at least

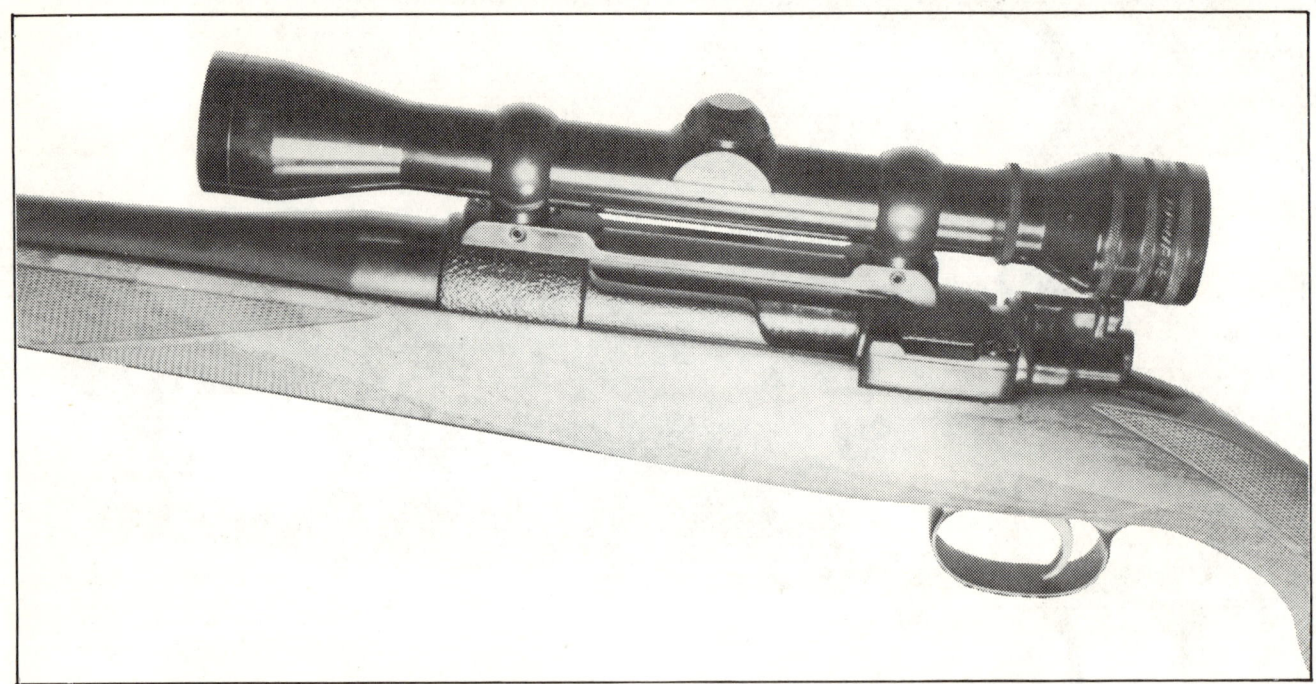

Badly pitted military action was heavy stippled when buffing did not remove pitting. Now action has the look of something special, thanks to an hour's work.

In order to test wildcat cartridge performance, many of the author's wildcats are made up from military components, such as this 7.62x39, which is based on an Italian action. Since many of these guns are rebarreled or rechambered after testing, no attempt has been made to give gun a beauty treatment.

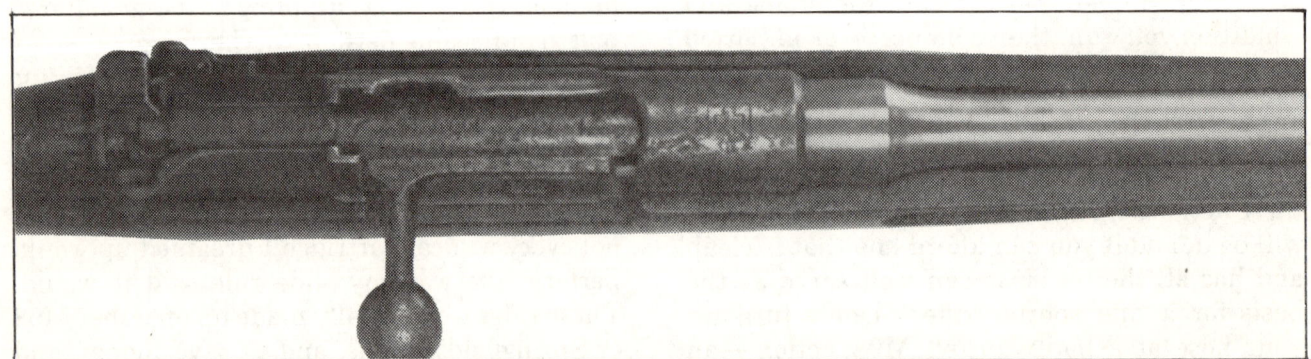

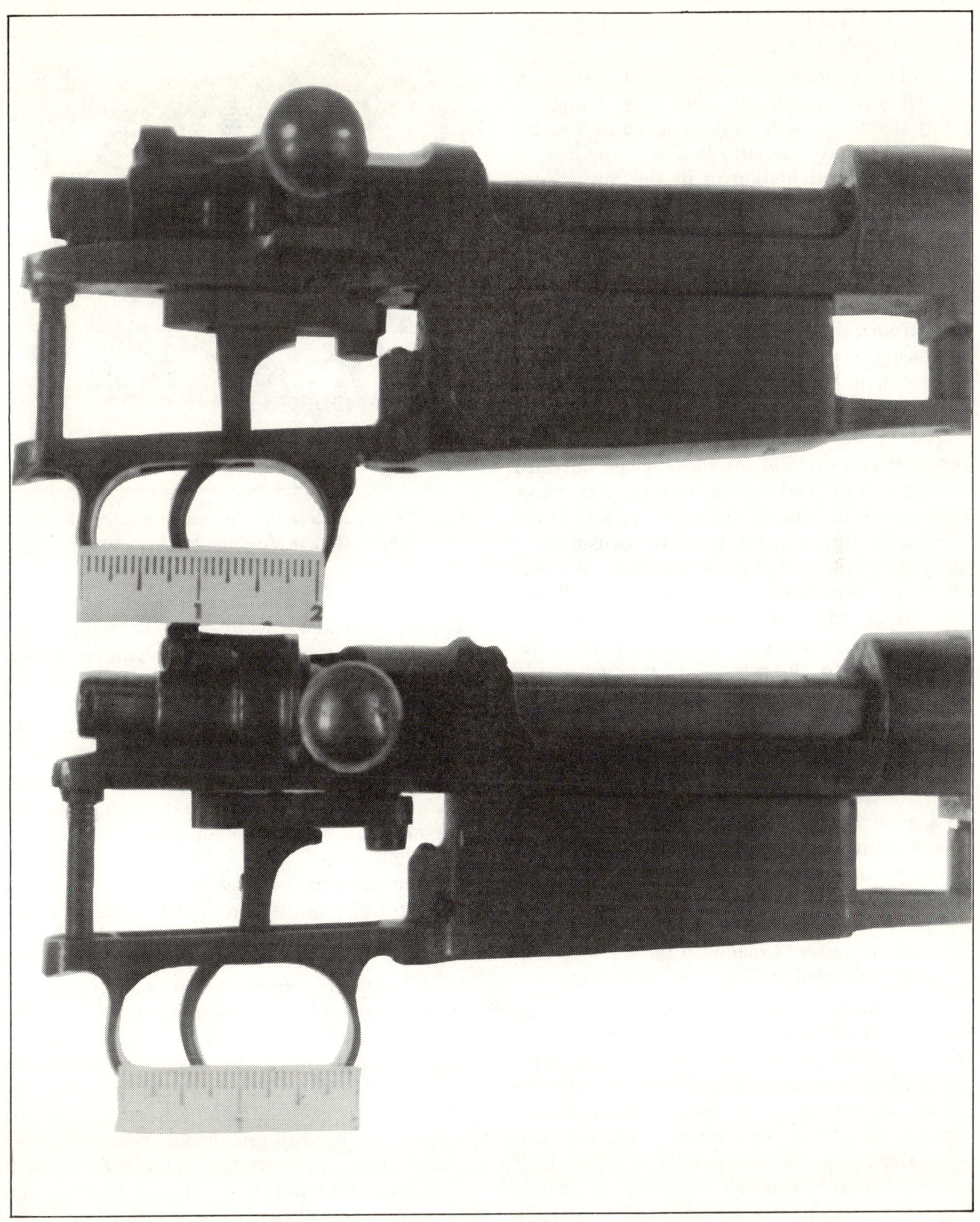

Upper action shows trigger position when action is cocked. Two-stage trigger pull is shown in lower action where trigger has been moved back until all the slack has been taken up.

MILITARY RIFLES

install iron sights, and of course, the exterior would undergo a face lifting too.

Military actions have the somewhat disturbing two-stage trigger pull which is strange to many shooters. Essentially designed as a safety or precautionary measure so that in the heat of battle or in anticipation of it, the raw recruit would be aware of the fact that the gun would not fire the moment he began his trigger pull. The two-stage pull is curable, but this job is best left in the hands of a gunsmith. The cock on opening feature can also be changed at the same time if the action needs it, and the follower can easily be ground down so that the bolt will close without having to depress the follower and the follower spring.

Today, the customized and sporterized military rifle is a thing of the past. Even barreled actions — if in good enough condition to make reworking economically feasible — cost so much that by the time you add the extra gunsmithing charges and the cost of the stock, you are better off buying a commercial sporting rifle. When sporterizing and customizing military rifles was at its height, a great many shooters were deluded into it by the promise of making a tidy profit when the gun was sold at some later date. But since every Tom, Dick and Harry heard the same story, the market was suddenly flooded with surplus hardware that often had been worked over by some amateur with an eye on a quick profit. Of course, every so often, a reworked military rifle in near-mint condition comes on the market, a gun worked on by an expert, a gun whose history alone is worth the asking price — such as a 257 Roberts on a Springfield that was made up for the late Col. Townsend Whelen.

Bolt handle alterations on many of the sporterized martial rifles can range from excellent to terrible, and if you should buy a rifle with a terrible bolt handle job, it is best to have the bolt handle cut off and replaced with a new one. The job should be done by someone who can weld and polish the new handle so it will look like it belongs to the bolt. Bolt handle bending — that is, using the original handle and only bending and reshaping it — can be done by any competent gunsmith.

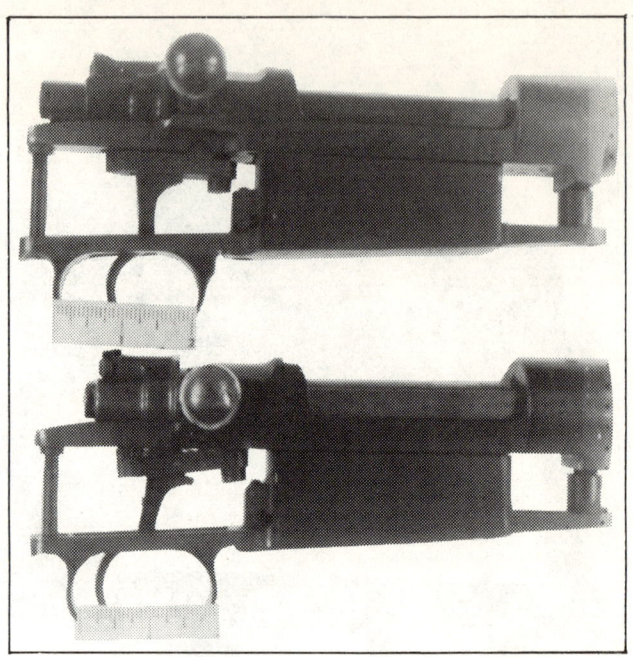

Upper action with trigger in normal position, lower action shows trigger after gun has been fired.

Before buying a military rifle in its original caliber, consider the question of caliber. Is commercial ammunition for it available, preferably the noncorrosive kind? If you reload, can brass and bullet availability become a problem? If you have to re-form brass to make cartridge cases, and maybe have to swage bullets up or down in diameter to get some shooting ammo, are you willing to go to all that trouble, and are the needed case and bullet altering dies going to be hard to get?

Norma is a good source for some of the European military caliber ammo that is being loaded into Boxer primed brass with modern smokeless powders. The larger European military calibers, from about 8mm up, date back to the old heavy bullet/black powder days. Ammo for those calibers is collector's stuff, cases are virtually impossible to find, and bullet molds would have to be custom-made in most instances. In short, unless you enjoy working with such hard-to-find components, or can make them yourself, an 11.4x50R Werndl M73 from Austria is best converted into a wall hanger, or perhaps a gunroom curio.

The greatest amount of research and innovative design originally took place in Europe,

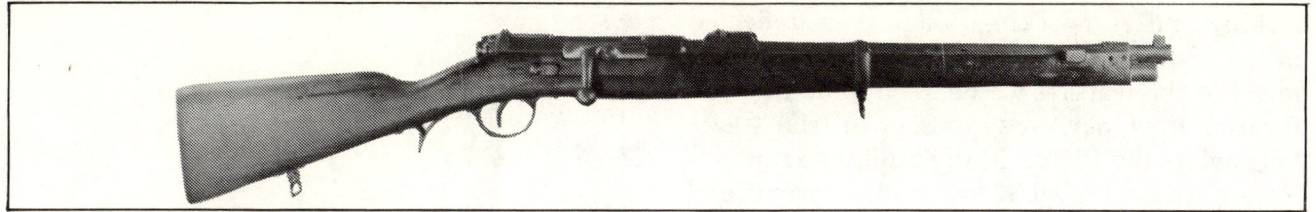

One of the earliest bolt-action rifles was the Kropatschek 8mm.

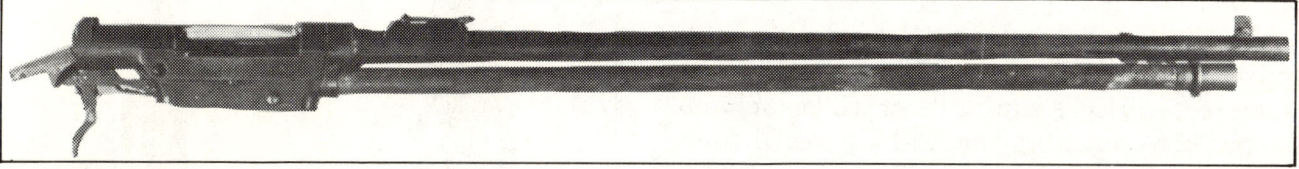

Stripped from wood, the rifle shows one of the earliest tubular magazines on a service rifle.

especially in the area of bolt-action rifles. Unfortunately, not much of the pertinent historical material has been translated, but enough of the military history of shoulder arms has come to us to make some interesting rediscoveries. So, for instance, the question of repeating rifles for troops was one that occupied European designers, and one of the first really usable ones was the Kropatschek rifle. This ten-shot arm used a tubular magazine, had a cut-off magazine lever, and was far ahead of its time in many of its features. Introduced in late 1874, the rifle was accepted by the Austro-Hungarian Ministry of War. Later, the entire Portugese army was equipped with Kropatschek rifles and carbines. These, however, were chambered for a modified 8mm round. And, believe it or not, these Kropatscheks found their way across the Atlantic some years ago and barely caused a ripple of interest here, even among the more knowledgeable gun writers and designers.

The Austrian M95 straight-pull Steyr rifle, chambered for the 8x50R round, shows up in gunshops every so often as a curio, and a cheap one, too, since ammunition for the rifle is not to be found. Many of these rifles were rechambered for the German 8mm round, but don't give up if you do have a gun with the original chambering. It is possible to use the 7.62 Russian brass, throat-expand the case mouth, and by using a .323-inch bullet loaded to Krag velocities, you should be able to use your Steyr M95 on the range — much to the astonishment of the other shooters.

Interest in military hardware ranges from the highly technical design features of full automatic weapons (there is a $200 BATF tax stamp needed for each gun) to the collector of straight-pull rifles. The whole controversy of forward-

Kropatschek ammo came with steel-jacketed bullet as well as with rounds topped off with wooden bullets.

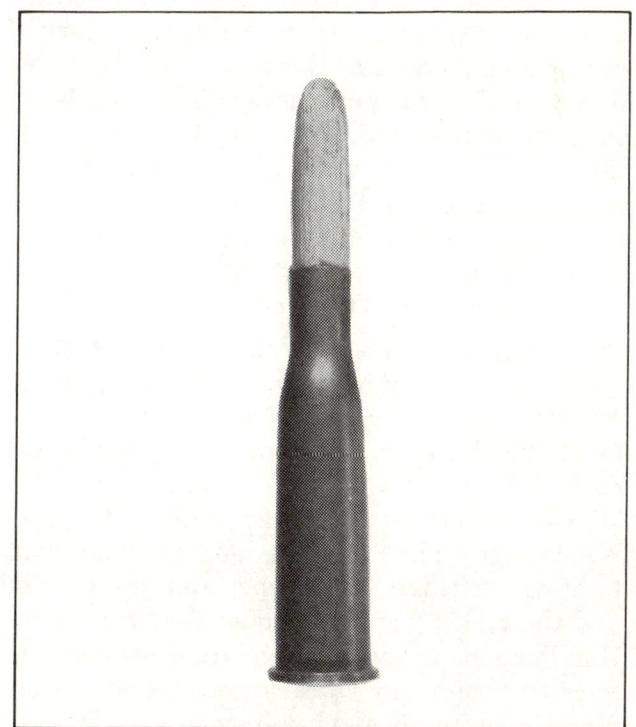

MILITARY RIFLES 225

locking and rear-locking bolt lugs is reflected in the history of military arms in Europe, and many of the features which seem to be new are far from it as they were in use or in trial stages long before the 1900s. Many military arms collectors are fascinated by the sundry designs, and thanks to this market, a new area of collecting has developed. Guns in good to very good condition are often hard to find, but clunkers are not.

So now we see, every so often, guns with mixed serial numbers which are the product of some enterprising gunsmith or collector who managed to construct one working model from the parts of two or more scrapped rifles. Purist collectors may well frown on this practice, but for study purposes, this would seem to be an excellent way of gathering a collection of representative specimens.

Perhaps a few comments about the development of military ammunition are in order. Take the caliber question, for example. For quite a few years, the 6mm Lee Navy was the smallest caliber military round. Then the thought that such a small caliber projectile really was not adequate came to the fore, and as a result, we wound up with the 30 calibers, while the European countries experimented with 6.5, the 7 and the 8mm rounds. Earlier military calibers, and these go back into the black powder era, were large caliber numbers, with the British Snider 577 or 14.7mm being the largest one. Now the trend is back to the small calibers, with the 5.56mm being the most widely accepted round. The British are working with a smaller caliber cartridge which might well be the next NATO round.

Military cartridge cases also have served as the basis for the development of new sporting rounds. The 7x57 or 7mm Mauser was the basis for the 257 Roberts. The 6mm Lee Navy, when necked down, became the 220 Swift, while the '06 case is, of course, the ancestor of the 270 Winchester. The 6.5s have long been popular hunting cartridges in Europe, and the 6.4x54 and the 6.5x55 have a devoted following here. Handloaders and wildcatters are especially interested in military cases since these are often plentiful in supply and low in cost — an unbeat-

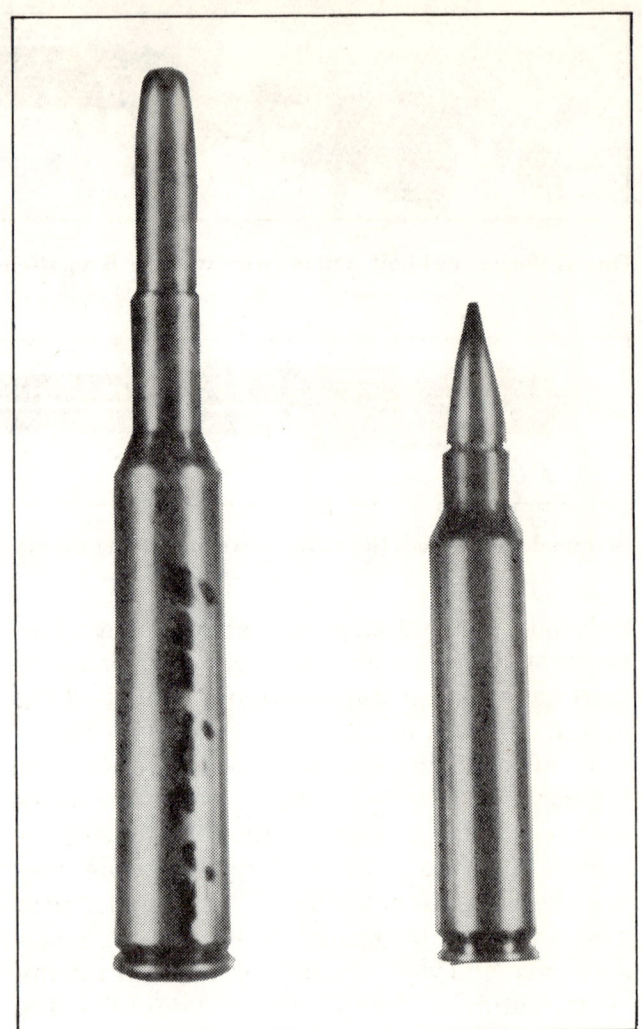

From the 6mm Lee Navy at left to the experimental 5.56mm round—the change was forecast by Kaisertreu in 1900, who also foresaw the use of automatic weapons.

able combination. Some military rounds have remained with us as sporting rounds. The 30-06, the 30-40 Krag and the 45-70 are outstanding domestic examples. The German 8mm, the 7mm Mauser, the 6.5s already mentioned, and the British 303 service round have continued to be popular, with the 303 British having its largest following in Canada, New Zealand and Australia.

Of continued interest are the service rifle matches, especially in Canada, Australia and, to some extent, New Zealand. In the United States, the big annual National Matches also include service rifle matches, although our shooters are not nearly as interested in those

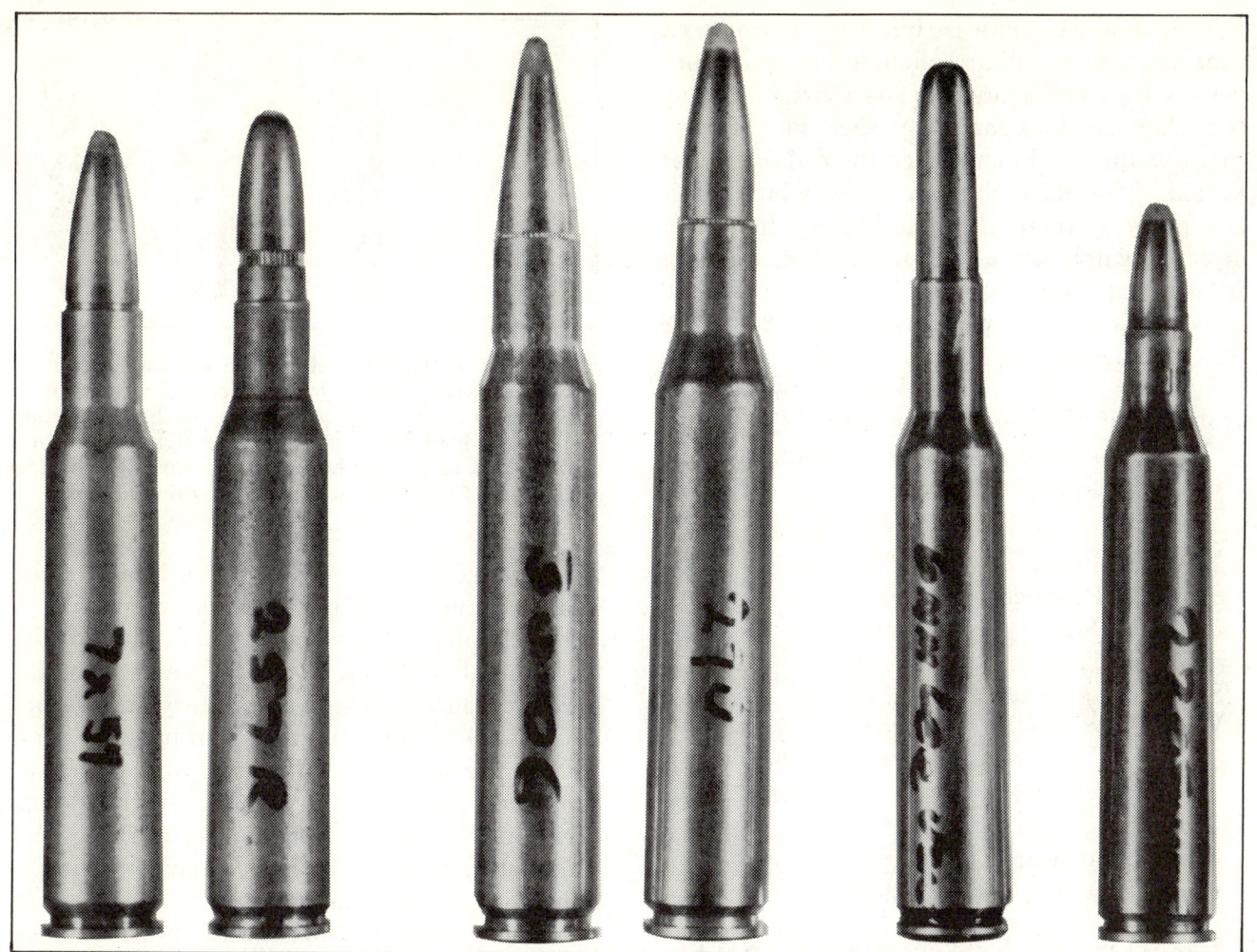

Because military brass is usually plentiful, it often serves as basis of wildcats. From left, in pairs: 7mm Mauser and 257 Roberts; the 30-06 and the 270; and the 6mm Lee U.S.N. and the 220 Swift.

events as are the British. The National Matches are held at Camp Perry under the auspices of the National Rifle Association. Every shooter should see this event at least once. Even if you don't compete, it is a sight not likely to be forgotten.

Mention should also be made of the M1 30-caliber carbine. GIs of WW II vintage will recall that it was originally meant to replace the 45 ACP pistol, but then somehow wound up as patrol and combat weapon. The ballistic efficiency of the cartridge has often been questioned when considered as a rifle round, and then, of course, it comes out on the bottom. A continued interest in the issue carbine has led to the production of guns which are essentially civilian copies of it. The easy availability of these carbines and GI weapons has led wildcatters to use the carbine as a basis for a number of wildcatting propositions. Jerry Yorks, a crackerjack gunsmith from Muskegon, Michigan, uses the M1 carbine for two highly efficient wildcats. One, based on the cut-off '06 case, is actually an elongated 357 AMP round. The 146-grain bullet, moved along by 27.0 grains of 4227, churns up about 2500 fps. The other is based on the 32 Remington case, which has been somewhat shortened and neck-expanded to 35 caliber and gives a 158-grain bullet a chronographed velocity of 2050 fps.

As issued, the carbine has in recent years become a highly specialized collector's item.

MILITARY RIFLES

During WW II, more carbines were produced than any other military shoulder weapon, and we now have collectors who specialize in finding legal M1 carbines made by each of the nine manufacturers who produced them during that period. The M1 carbine is the standard semi-automatic weapon, while the M2 carbine has a selector switch for full automatic fire, and the M3 is the M2 carbine with the infra-red Snooper Scope of sniper fame. The M2 and the M3 carbines require special BATF tax stamps, so you would be wiser and richer by concentrating your efforts on collecting the M1 carbine.

The breakdown on makers and numbers of carbines produced follows:

IBM	346,500		
Standard Products	247,155		
National Postal Meter	413,017		
Saginaw	739,136		
Winchester	809,451		
	17,500	M2s	
	1,108	M3s	
Underwood	545,616		
Quality Hardware	359,662		
Rock-Ola Mfg. Corp.	228,500		
Inland Mfg., Div. GM	2,625,000	M1s, M1A1s, M2s and some M3s	

This sure sounds like a lot of military hardware, but if you try to get one M1 carbine made by each of these companies you may spend the rest of your life hunting high and low for representative specimens.

Why this continuing interest in military rifles? Perhaps there is a little Walter Mitty in all of us. The fact remains that many

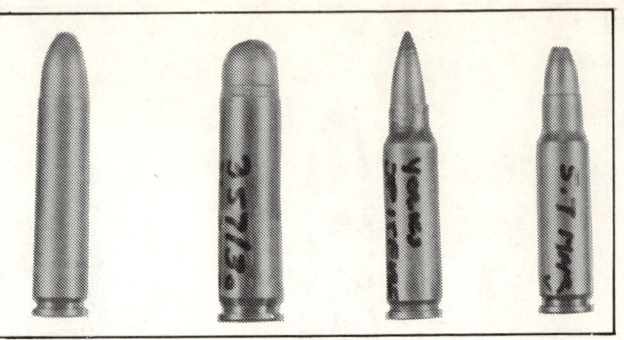

The action of the M1 carbine and the cartridge itself have been wildcatted widely. At far left, a South Korean 30M1 service round, a 357 based on the 25 Remington case which now functions through the carbine action, the 224/30 Carbine and the 5.7mmMMJ wildcat which also functions through the carbine action.

of the design features of the military rifles, both old and fairly new, are representative of the technological development. It should also be remembered that about 80 percent of the developmental research on military small arms has been done by individuals and by some arms companies, and that little of this work has come from military sources. It helps to know what went on in the past when you are working on a product that might be needed tomorrow to defend yourself and your country.

In looking at the history of military small arms, particularly rifles, the interested student can find many special features which are worth investigating. For instance, take the question of how to store ammunition in the rifle. The Kropatschek had a tubular feed magazine, then came the stripper clips, then the projecting magazine of the Enfield and the Italian Carcano, and finally the detachable magazine of the M16 and the 7.62mm M14 rifles. With the reduction in caliber and the size of the cartridge, what ammunition storage system will come next?

Chapter Eleven
Hints for Riflemen

Chapter Eleven
Hints for Riflemen

I fired my first rifle at the ripe old age of 10 or 11, and since then have shot in competition, have hunted, tested rifles (as well as handguns and shotguns), and every once in a while I even find time for that great American pastime known as "plinking."

The term "plinking" was coined by Elizabeth "Plinky" Toepperwein, perhaps the greatest woman trapshooter of all time. She used to call for her targets by calling "plink."

Since then, plinking has come to mean informal competitive shooting at some mark or target, with most of the plinking being done with the ubiquitous 22 rimfire cartridge because of its relatively low cost, the low noise level and minimal recoil.

* * * * *

The following collection of ideas, suggestions, hints and how-to's are in no particular order, but have been derived from practical experience and almost 50 years of shooting.

THOUGHTS ABOUT THE HUNTING RIFLE

If you are going to stalk elephants in the African bush with a large bore rifle, you will want a rifle that is about as heavy as you can handle. If the rifle is too light, the recoil of the big bore shoulder cannon will most likely deposit you on the seat of your pants and may well jar the fillings out of your teeth, not to mention the possibility of a dislocated shoulder. The first time I fired a 600 Nitro Express, I was conned into shooting for accuracy from the sitting position — fortunately, however, not from the shooting bench. The first shot was fired at 25 yards, the second one from 27 yards — the two extra yards resulted in my being dragged across the gravel on the range on the seat of my pants because of the recoil of the first barrel. When the second barrel was fired, I was moved back a bit more, and was then in need of a pair of pants with a whole bottom or perhaps a recoil pad on the seat of my pants.

Here's what plinking is all about. Low recoil and sound level make 22 rimfire the most suitable plinking round.

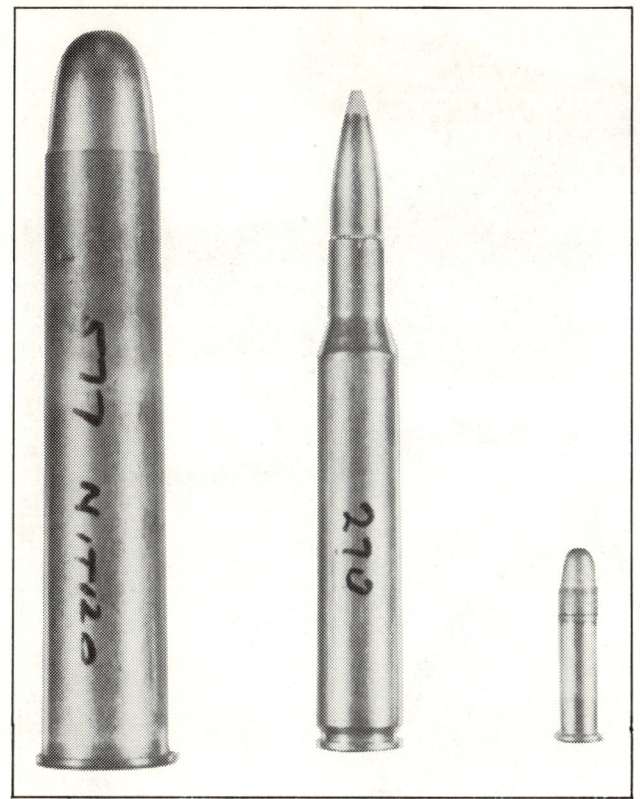

Cartridges come in all sizes and shapes. Here are three to show differences: the 577 Nitro, the 270 Winchester and a 22 Long Rifle rimfire round.

On the other hand, the hunter in pursuit of sheep and mountain goat will want as light a rifle as he can handle, considering that recoil and rifle weight go hand in hand. Thumbhole stocks have often been said to be the mountain hunter's best friend. I have used them, but I'll take the conventional pistol grip stock any time, any place. Maybe I simply don't have enough shooting practice with my two thumbhole rifles; I just don't feel at home on those stocks, and it takes me too long to get comfortable for that fast grab shot that is often needed for a trophy head.

* * * * *

I settled on the Latigo sling after I had tried every type of hasty sling, carrying strap and other such device known to man. With one pull of the leather strap, the Latigo sling becomes a hasty sling as well as a dandy carrying strap or sling. Pull it tight again, and it lies flat against the stock for convenient storage of the rifle in a rack.

If you have superb eyesight or simply don't want to use a scope on your hunting rifle or rifles, you can skip the next two or three paragraphs.

Once, in the Selway-Bitterroot area, when we had spotted a bull elk, I piled off the horse and yanked the rifle from the heavy leather scabbard. It had been snowing sporadically, we had been climbing, and the horse was steaming as she stood there watching the activities. Out of habit, I glanced through my scope and saw nothing but a mass of condensation on the inside of the lenses. The scope had fogged over, and this made it essential that I get the scope off the rifle as quickly as possible and fall back on the iron sights. Being somewhat of a pessimist, I had taken the time and trouble to adjust the rear sight of the rifle so it would print dead-on at 100 yards, and the Royal bull elk obligingly offered me a shot at about 85-90 yards.

* * * * *

During a six-week hunt in Alaska, I learned a hard lesson I am not likely to forget. A gunsmith friend had sold me on the virtues of one of his pet wildcats, and I decided to see just how good the 338-06 really was on big game. All summer I had worked up loads, had shot the rifle at various guessed-at ranges, and was ready for anything. I had asked my friend to install British Express sights on the rifle, but he did not do so, claiming that the clean lines of the rifle would be spoiled by the addition of the sights. A scope, perhaps a variable power one, would be more than adequate for anything I would care to shoot.

Before climbing up into sheep country, we double-checked our rifles, and my 338-06 was the envy of everyone — right on the button and shooting groups you could cover with a quarter at 200 yards. On the way up to sheep camp, we were caught in a miserable rock slide, more like an avalanche, and while trying to keep my footing, the rifle slipped off the GI packboard and crashed, scope first, against a passing boulder the size of a VW Beetle. The scope, rings, and

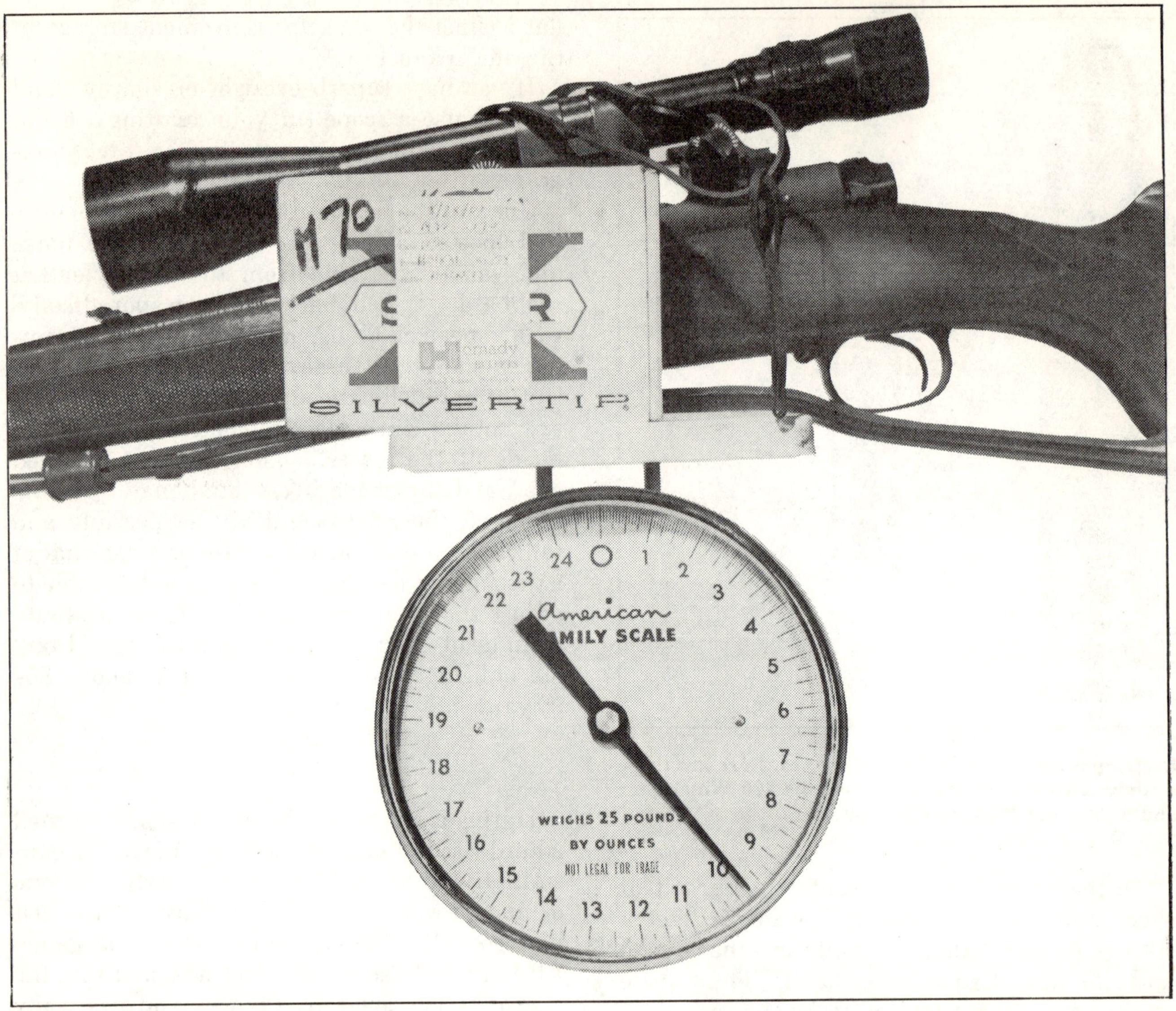

Mountain rifle, complete with scope, scope covers, sling and 20 rounds of ammo weighs just 9¾ pounds. This might seem to be on the heavy side, but so far author has not found a lighter rifle that is as accurate as this M70 in 270 Winchester.

Brownell's Latigo sling pulled tight for parade rest.

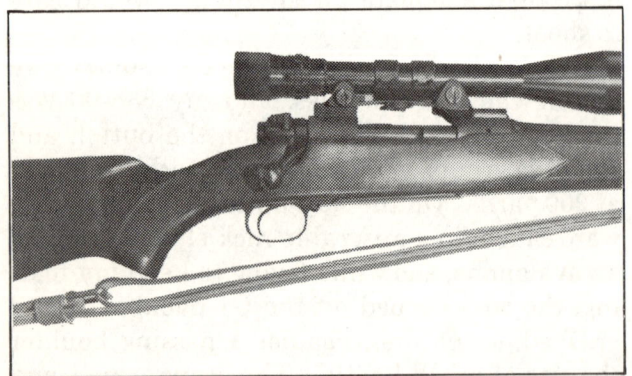

one of the blocks sheared off as cleanly as if cut by a power hacksaw. There I was without a scope, in the middle of the Alaskan mountains, and no way to get another scope, replace rings or blocks. Since then, I pack along a spare set of blocks or bases, and a pre-sighted scope, complete with rings. Should something like this ever happen again I'll be prepared for it.

* * * * *

Once, during a short visit to New Hampshire, a friend invited me to join him on a day's deer

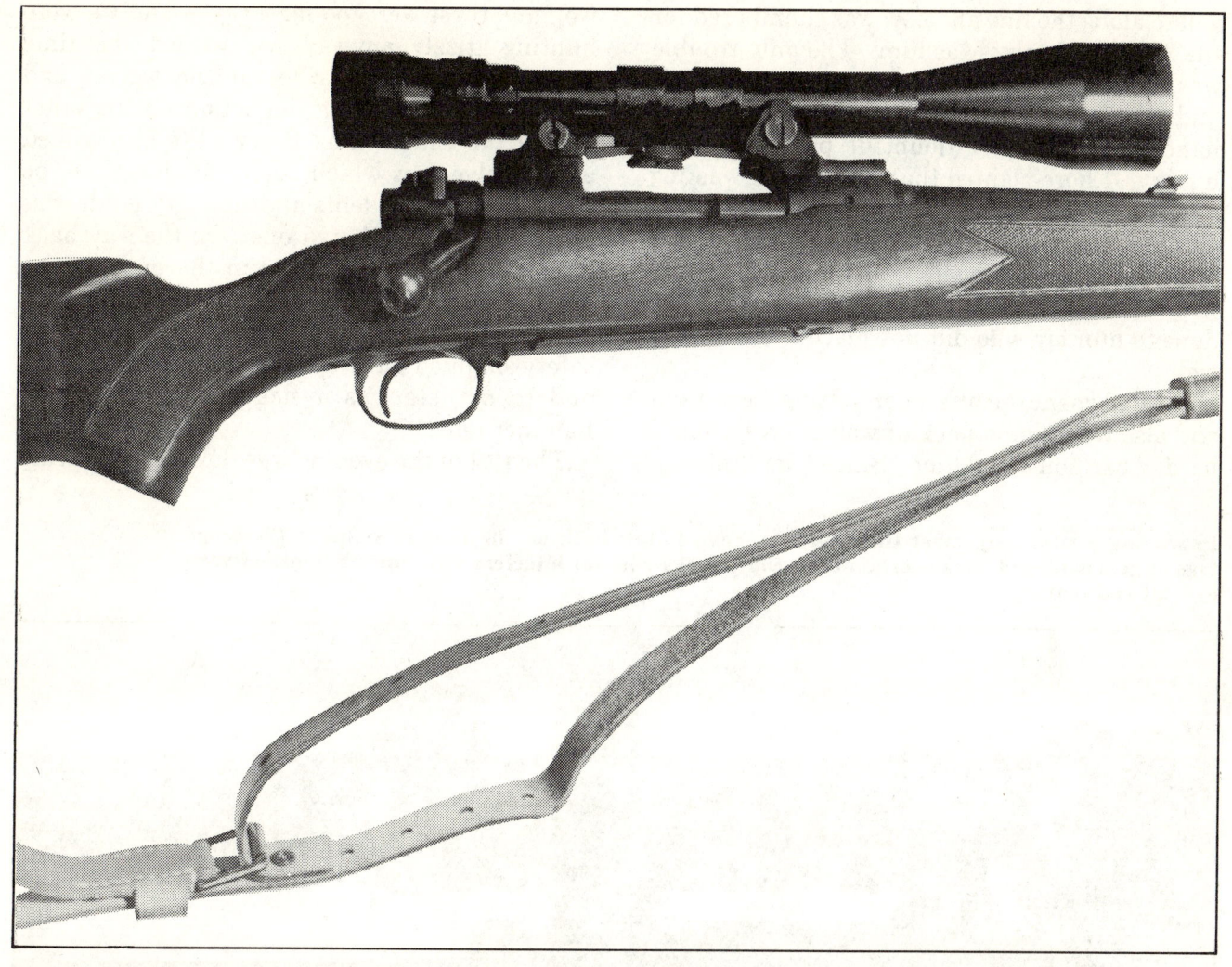

One quick pull on the Latigo sling, and you have either a carrying sling or one that will also double as hasty sling very well.

hunt. He offered not only to lend me the needed clothing, but also a rifle. Being a sucker for deer hunting, I took him up on the offer, and we got to the woods before dawn did. It was overcast and drizzling, but the forecast promised clearing weather. Instead, it began to rain harder and harder, and when we finally decided not to drown in our boots, I jumped the biggest whitetail buck I had seen in many a moon. Up came the rifle, and the water just poured off the scope — I could not even differentiate between a tree and a buck 15 feet away from me.

Since then, I equip each of my big-game hunting rifles with scope covers, and here I prefer the quick-detachable ones that can be flicked off with a finger from both ends of the scope. There are several good brands on the market, but the trick is to install the covers correctly and then learn how to flip them off as you bring the rifle to your shoulder and slide the safety off.

* * * * *

As a handloader, I prefer to use my own loads when hunting, and seldom use factory loads unless conditions require it. My guide and I were alone in the Alaskan wilderness, and we were concentrating on grizzly hunting. This was after I had broken the scope off my 338-06, and had borrowed a rifle from the outfitter. An old, pre-64 Model 70 originally chambered for the 300 H&H round, it had been reamed out some-

HINTS FOR RIFLEMEN

where along the line and now was chambered for the 300 Weatherby Magnum. The only trouble was, nobody knew where the rifle would print, and all the ammo we could scare up was two handloads of rather doubtful parentage and history. I bore-sighted the gun without wasting any ammo, and headed for the boonies. My guide, who was also a handloader, was packing a 7mm Remington Magnum, and entertained me with tales about what grizzlies can do and have done to hunters who did not place their bullets well.

We had spent the afternoon getting a good tan and also watching a pack of wolves give a small herd of caribou a bad time. Since I had taken a wolf and these were too far away — and we were hunting grizzly anyway, we whiled the time away by aiming our rifles at the wolves and caribou while following the action on the other side of the Chistochina River. We also talked about wolverines which could, at that time, be taken only by residents and how my guide was just dying to get a shot at one. On the way back to camp, we heard a sound in the bushes, and out came a wolverine — or at least, so the guide thought. Off the shoulder came the rifle, the safety snapped off, I could barely see him aim, and then there was a sickening click as the hammer fell.

The rest of the evening was devoted to tearing

In scoping a rifle, remember that you may have to fall back on the factory sights if the scope fogs or gets damaged. Make certain that scope blocks will not interfere with line of sight between eyeball and rear sight.

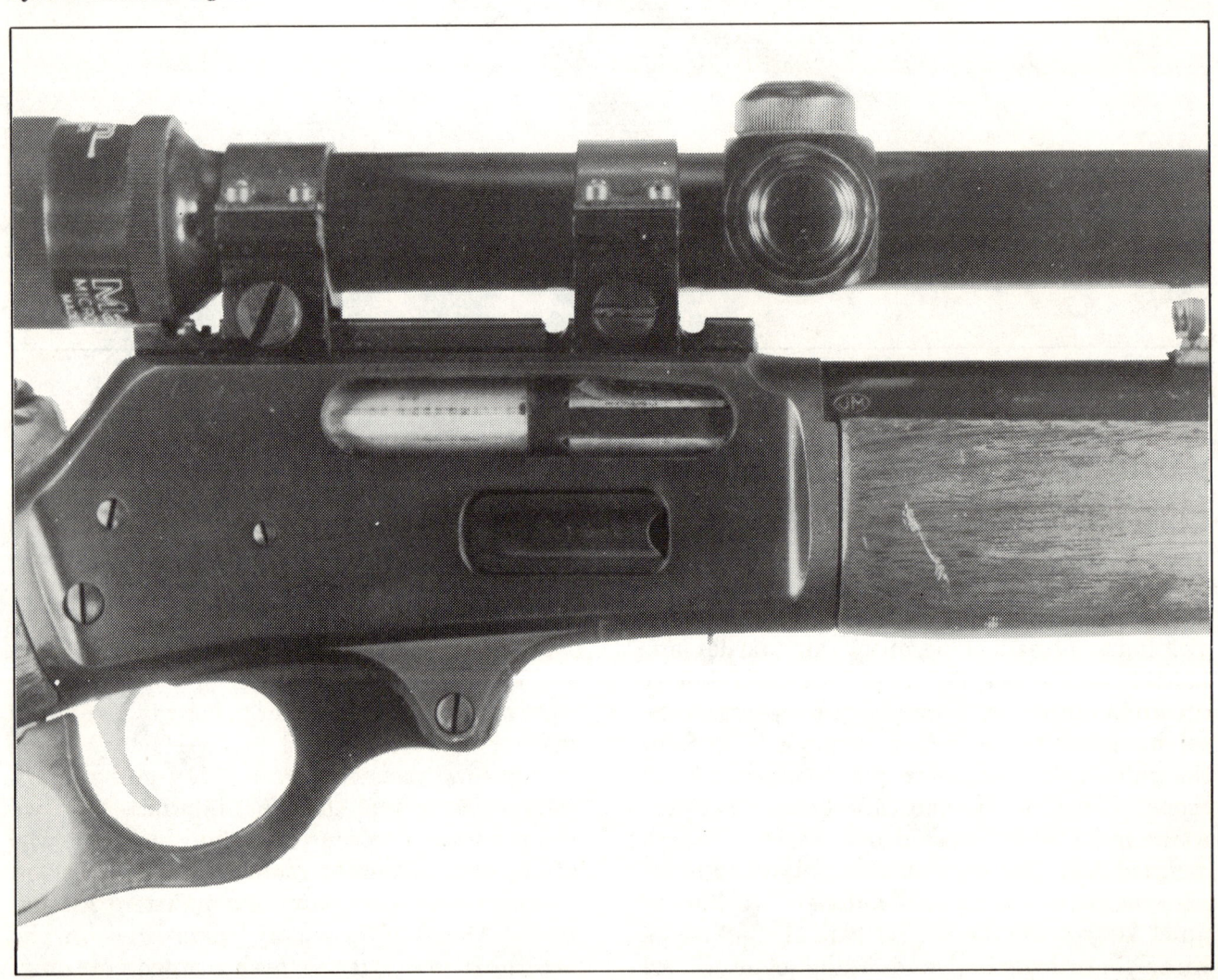

Spring grizzly hunt was accompanied by this first-class snowstorm—scope caps are essential for this sort of hunting weather.

apart his ammo, the same ammo he was going to use as backup for me should anything go wrong with my two handloaded rounds in a confrontation with a grizzly. Bullet pullers are not part of camp equipment; there is an easy way to remove bullets from loaded cartridges without using a bullet puller. Find a flat rock, place the cartridge on it so that bullet and case neck rest on the rock. With another rock, begin to tap on the case neck, but do it gently so that the brass does not get too much out of shape. Rotate the case, and soon the bullet will be loosened enough to be removed.

Better than half my guide's loads did not contain a powder charge...the lesson here is simple: Pay attention when you load ammo.

* * * * *

Muzzle caps are almost unheard of here, but once you have used one, or at least a substitute, you won't want to be without one while hunting in the rain. The commercial ones offered by some British and German gunmakers are a bit too fancy and costly for my taste. By applying two pieces of transparent tape criss-cross over

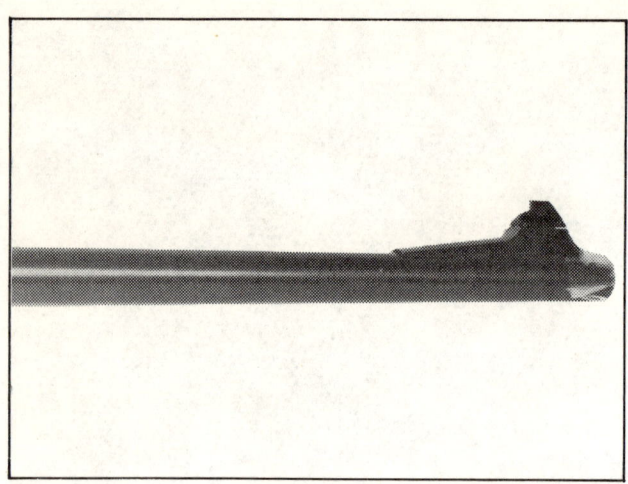

If it rains or snows and you want to keep foreign objects out of the barrel of your rifle, tape some Scotch tape over it—it shoots away without creating pressure problems, is cheap and easy to replace.

the muzzle, you can keep rain and woods debris out of the muzzle. A toy balloon or a similar substitute slipped over the muzzle will accomplish the same thing, and when you want to fire, you simply disregard the existence of the muzzle covering you use. It will not affect the ballistic performance of the bullet, nor will it raise pressures to dangerous levels, since such a muzzle covering is not at all tight and seems to fracture or blow away even before a bullet nose makes contact with it.

* * * * *

Just how finely tuned should the trigger of a hunting rifle be? That is a loaded question, somewhat akin to asking someone whether he has stopped beating his wife. Some factory rifles come with adjustable triggers; others don't, and the latter are often considered inferior because they lack this mechanical refinement.

A lot depends on the trigger pull to which you are accustomed. If you shoot a rifle with a two-stage military trigger pull quite frequently, you have most likely become very proficient in the use of the trigger. Then, a trigger tuned to break or release at three or four pounds of pressure will seem like a hair trigger to you, while to the target shooter, the same trigger pull will appear to be extraordinarily heavy.

Of course, you can have a gunsmith install adjustable triggers in any of your rifles that do not have this feature, and you then tune the triggers of the rest of your rifles yourself until all have the desired pull. If you switch guns often, from a deer-brush rifle, to another one for antelope, sheep and goat, to perhaps a bigger caliber for moose, elk and bear, the triggers of these rifles should be tuned identically.

A nice, light trigger pull impresses your friends and may please you mightily on the range, but the hunting fields are no place for a hair trigger. Don't forget that a severe jolt can release the sear, that safeties can be slipped off accidentally or perhaps while the rifle is being pulled out of the scabbard.

In testing trigger pull, be certain that there is no live ammunition in the gun, and don't rely on having an educated index finger — use a trigger pull scale. By using a scale, you can tune triggers to a greater degree of uniformity, but don't overlook the fact that few rifles will register an identical pull each and every time. To get a valid reading from your trigger pull scales, you should perform ten such tests on each rifle and then average these figures for a median or average trigger pull.

* * * * *

If you pack an extra rifle scope, a spotting scope or a pair of binoculars on a hunting trip, pack them either in the center of your bedroll or the center of your pannier. This way, they are least likely to suffer any damage either en route or on a pack horse. Never put all your ammunition into one piece of luggage, whether you fly or drive to your jumping-off point. Should one duffle bag, pannier or suitcase be lost, broken into and cleaned out, or not arrive at your destination when you do, you can always fall back on the ammo elsewhere in your luggage.

* * * * *

If you fly, the FAA regulations are becoming more and more stringent, and even border on the ridiculous. Your rifle or rifles should be transported in special hard plastic cases, or in even more ruggedly made aluminum cases, both

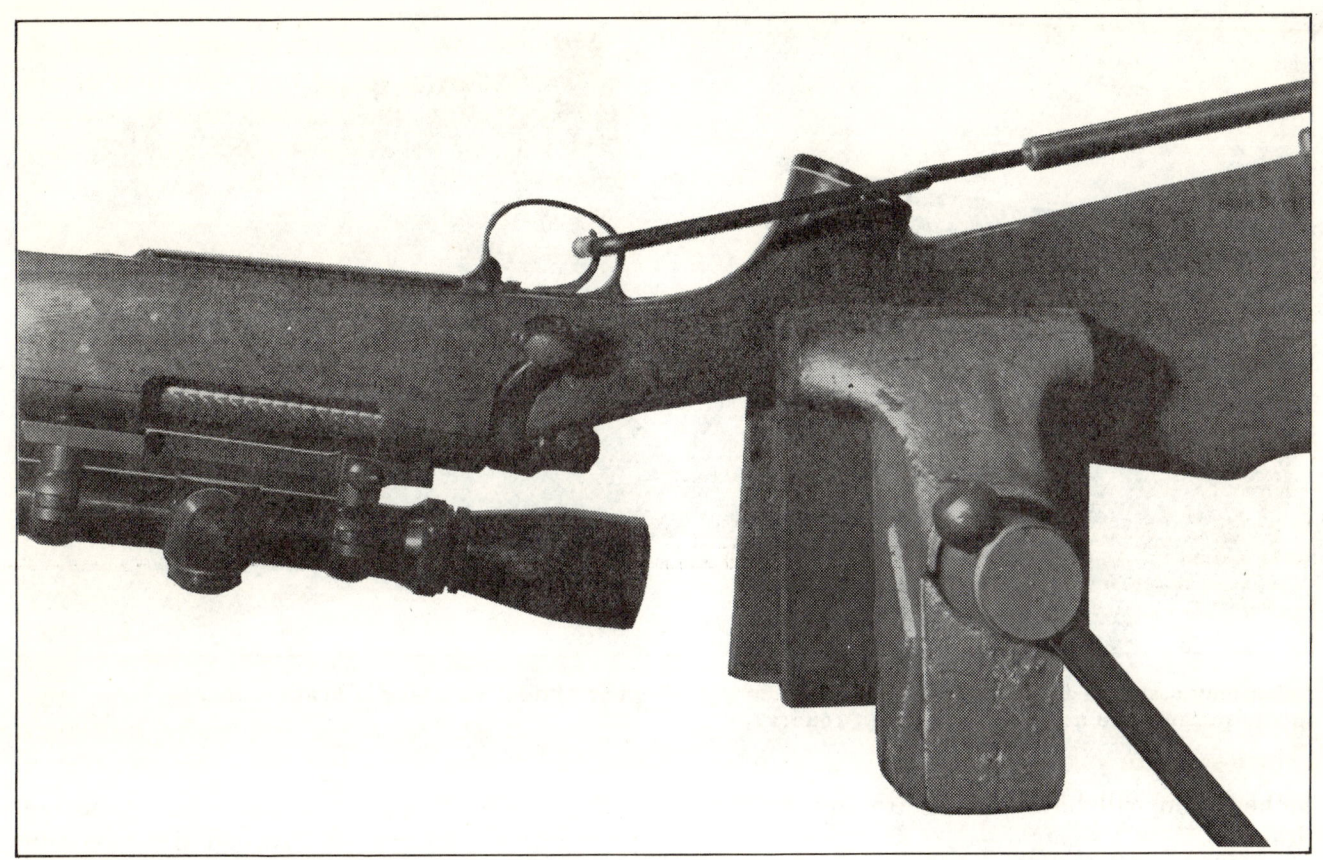

Checking trigger pull can be done either with spring-loaded scale as shown or by means of dead weights—the more accurate way of doing the job.

of which are lined with a synthetic foam material. These cases come in one and two gun models, and even though the cased gun or guns will ride in the baggage compartment of the plane, you must notify the ticket agent that you are transporting firearms. If you are carrying a bolt-action rifle, I suggest that you remove the bolt and store it somewhere else in your luggage. By law, the ticket agent can ask you to disassemble the rifle, and if you are carrying a Model 99 or Model 94, you then have the job of explaining that the rifle is not taken apart that easily.

Be sure to note all serial numbers of licenses, scopes, cameras and rifles if you cross international borders, and check with the U.S. or Canadian Customs before leaving the country. You may need a special re-entry permit for some items.

When taking gun cases to the airport, be sure that the now-required name and address stickers are securely fastened, and that the lock or locks on the case are functional. Do not pack ammunition, extra scope or cleaning paraphernalia with the guns—the less extraneous material you carry in the gun case, the easier it will be for you. Under no circumstances should you attempt to transport any gun on a commercial aircraft that is not in a hard case. The soft cases are less costly, but cannot afford your guns the protection they get from the hard plastic or aluminum case.

* * * * *

If you are heading for the boonies and will be using a pack string, be sure your outfitter has a suitable scabbard for your rifle. If you decide to take your own scabbard, send it along with the rest of your gear as a separate item and do not attach it to the outside of a gun case, duffle bag or pannier. Should such items become de-

Extra ammo should be carried on belt, never in pocket where bullet tips take a beating, and the noise can scare a buck into the next county.

tached, you will have trouble tracing the lost item.

* * * * *

It is better to hand-carry your camera equipment onto the plane. You should carry only photographic equipment in the camera case, so take out that forgotten round of ammunition, that spent shotshell hull or anything else that looks like it might be related to shooting or hunting. Get some blaze orange stickers from your camera store and fasten them to your camera case. These stickers caution that there is live photographic material in the camera case and that hand inspection is desired. If you don't insist on hand inspection, however, you are very likely to have your film and camera X-rayed anyway. And no matter what the attendants at the gate tell you, film may fog completely even though the X-ray machines are called "low-level output."

Transport all exposed as well as unexposed film in special lead foil bags you can buy in any of the better camera stores. These bags completely protect all film and I have never had the slightest bit of trouble with X-ray fogging when using one of these lead foil bags.

When returning from a hunting trip, do not pack either cameras or exposed film in your luggage, but again hand-carry these items onto the plane. A friend of mine coming back from an African safari decided to pack his camera and film in his luggage — he got his dirty laundry back, but not the films and camera.

THE TARGET RIFLE

Your equipment needs will differ, depending on the type of target shooting you favor. The small bore shooter, especially in the four-position course of fire, needs a shooting mat, special sling, glove, ammo box, with perhaps a stopwatch and a rifle rest.

* * * * *

When buying match ammo do not buy one or two boxes at a time. Buy at least 500 rounds, or better yet, a whole case. This will ensure that you get all ammo from one production lot, and although modern match ammunition is the most accurate type of ammunition that can be assembled, small variations are excluded when you buy your ammo in larger lots.

This lead bag can be bought in most camera stores and will prevent fogging of film when it has to go through X-ray machine at airport.

Although small bore shooters do not clean their rifles on the firing line or during relays, it is a good idea to have a cleaning rod in the rifle case. It can happen that a case will not extract, and then the rod can be used to push the recalcitrant case out of the chamber.

* * * * *

Sanctioned matches also call for a score book, and the other equipment needed will vary somewhat with the type of match you are firing, whether it is a centerfire or rimfire event. On the whole, your equipment needs will be dictated by the match rules prevailing at the time.

* * * * *

In benchrest competitions, the weight of the gun is regulated, and the classification in which your rifle falls depends on the gun-with-scope weight. Most dedicated benchrest competitors drive to the matches, and then carry with them complete loading equipment, tent, portable loading bench and other gear. Some of these loading setups are quite simple, and the trunk of the family sedan is converted for this use during the shoot; others use a trailer for their equipment and the omnipresent coffee pot.

* * * * *

Most small bore shooters leave their match rifles in the carrying boxes they use to move the gun from the house to the car and from the car to the range. If the gun is stored for more than a day or two, small rust spots are almost certain to appear unless you place an antirust agent in the case.

* * * * *

Target rifles should be placed in a rack between shoots in the same fashion as hunting rifles; of course, a closed gun cabinet is better than an open rack since it helps keep dust off the rifle. When the cabinet is locked, it also keeps unauthorized and inquisitive fingers away from the guns. When racking up rifles in an open rack, it is a good idea to use scope covers or some other protection from dust, soot and other dirt that accumulates, especially in a basement where most shooters store their guns and have their workshop.

Because many of the target rifles are scoped with high-power scopes and are often mounted on extra-high blocks, you may find that a gun rack with an open back is a better choice than one with a plywood back. The latter does not allow the target guns to be racked properly and therefore, these match rifles tend to rest on only a small portion of the butt. If you are stuck with a solid-back cabinet, simply cut a piece of plywood, at least ½-inch thick, and fasten it on the base of the rack where the butt of the rifle rests. Make the board wide enough to permit the gun to lean securely in the rack, and then apply some non-slip rubber, which is sold for kitchen use, to the plywood.

* * * * *

When placing rifles with large scopes into a gun rack or cabinet, be certain that the weight of the gun does not rest on the scope. The scope can take the strain, but the finely adjusted scope mounts may not.

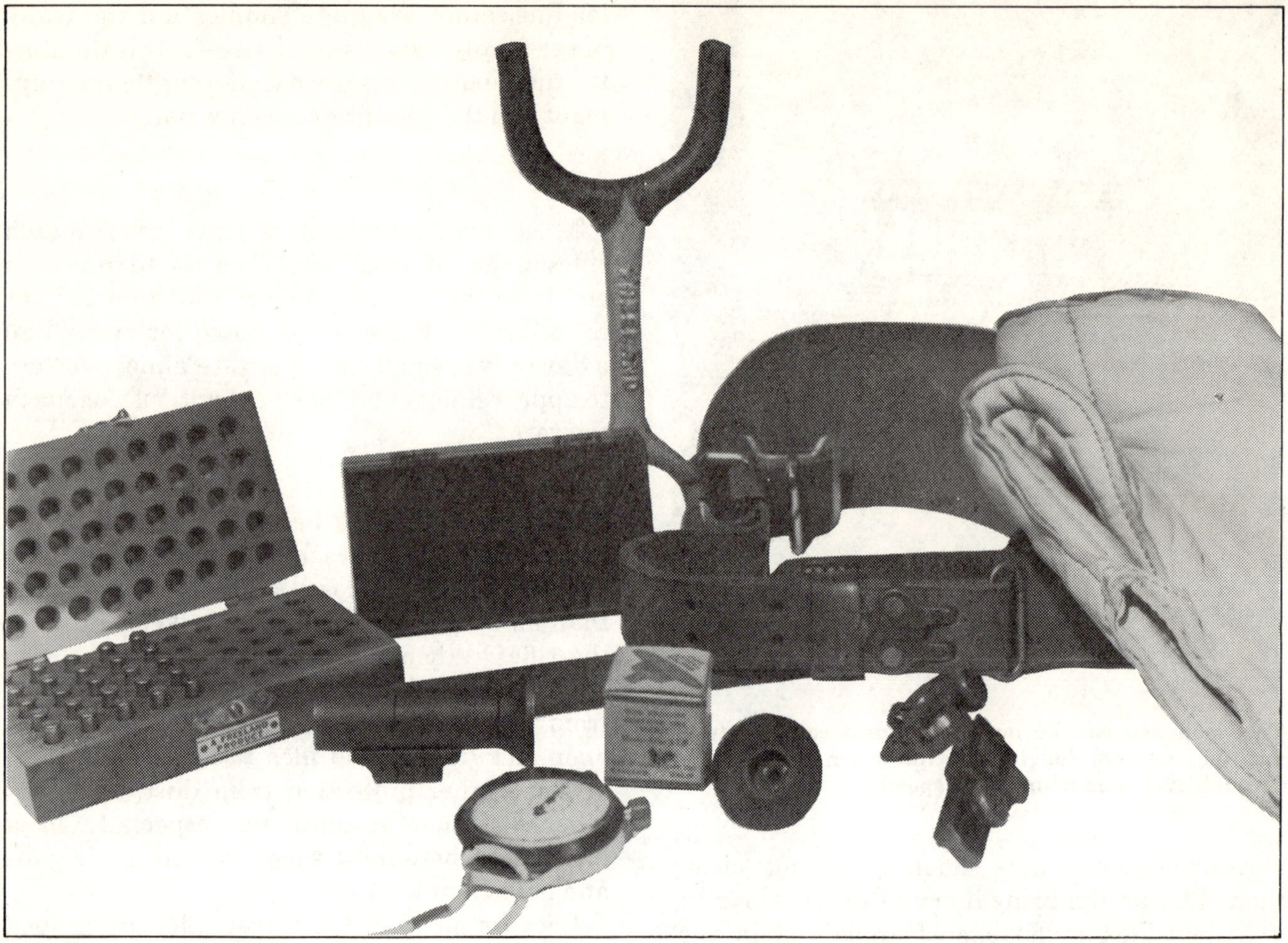

Target shooters collect all sorts of gear—special sling, shooting glove, etc., but it did not help author in his four-position match shooting days, and he never reached the magic 100 number.

New benchrest handloading dies are now being produced in all factory calibers for shooters by Central Products of East Brunswick, N.J. Dies are custom made, neck size cartridge case only.

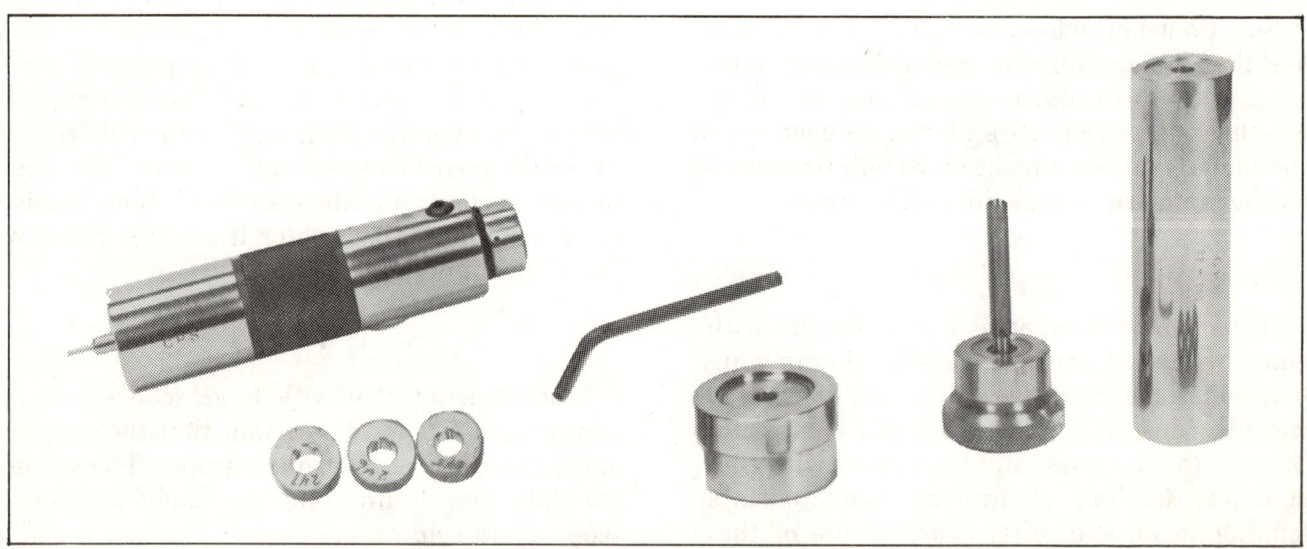

Overview of part of the rifle collection in author's gun room.

Traditionally, rifles are stood upright in racks with butt down. In the past, after cleaning a rifle, an oily patch was run through the bore. As the rifle stood in the rack, the oil would tend to run down the bore and into the action, and eventually penetrate the wood. Sooner or later this would ruin a fine stock. With the new cleaning products, nobody seems to worry about this any more, and gummed actions from the oil which evaporated seem to be a thing of the past.

Old-timers, in the oil-the-bore days, got into the habit of standing rifles on the muzzle so that oil and solvent would run out of the muzzle. Unless the rifle was carefully balanced, it was all too easy to have the rifle come tumbling out of the rack. I tried the system, but did not like it.

* * * * *

The matter of dry firing any rifle, especially a match rifle, is still very much disputed. Dry firing a rimfire rifle or handgun is said to be bad for the firing pin because the tip of the pin does not make contact with the soft brass of the cartridge case, but with the steel of the rim of the chamber. Dry firing a centerfire rifle does not damage the firing pin, although there are some purists who leave a fired case with the spent primer in place in the chamber so the firing pin will fall on the spent primer when the trigger is pulled. Some small bore shooters also leave a spent case in the chamber of a match rifle, while others blithely disregard the warning about damaging the firing pin and continue to snap the trigger.

In double-barreled shotguns I always use snap caps, but years ago gave up the habit of leaving spent cases in rifle chambers so that the firing pin would not be damaged. First of all, when a visitor wants to look at one of my rifles, I open the action, and when the other fellow sees that brass sliding out of the chamber, he automatically assumes that all guns are kept loaded and suddenly finds that he has urgent business elsewhere. Secondly, I got sick and tired of chasing brass all over the gun room floor after yanking an action open and thirdly, I too decided that if the firing pin could not take an occasional dry firing, I should either get a new firing pin or a whole new gun.

* * * * *

Perhaps the best way to keep track of the performance of a rifle is to save either the whole target or just the section of it that shows group size, range data and loads or type of ammunition used. For a hunting rifle, this can save time and costly ammo, especially if you use more than one load in that same rifle, perhaps one load with a light bullet and one with a heavy bullet. From a target, you can see where one load prints in relation to the other, where the point of aim was for both loads and, if you have a 200-yard range near you, you can also record on such targets how any load groups and where it prints at the longer range.

If you take the time and trouble to keep track of such things, including scope data, you will find it a simple matter to take your chuck rifle out of the rack, double-check the zero on the range and head for chuck country while your shooting cronies are still trying to sight-in their varmint rifles.

Chapter Twelve
Reading for Riflemen

Chapter Twelve
Reading for Riflemen

The easiest way to acquire knowledge and understanding is through reading... yesterday's novice is tomorrow's expert.

Here, you will find the most important books in the area of rifle design and rifle shooting. Some of these titles are out of print, but can be found once in a while in second-hand bookstores.

Ackley, P.O. *Home Gun Care & Repair.* Stackpole, 1969.
Anonymous. *Textbook of Small Arms 1909.* Harrison, 1909.
_____ *Textbook of Small Arms 1929.* Holland Press, 1961.
_____ *U.S. Army Special Forces Foreign Weapons Handbook.* U.S. Army John F. Kennedy Center for Special Warfare, 1967.
Arnold, R. *The Book of the .22.* Barnes, 1962.
Askins, C. *Rifles and Rifle Shooting.* Macmillan, 1923.
_____ *Shooting Fact.* Recreation Library, 1935.
Baker, C. *Modern Gunsmithing.* Small Arms Technical Publishing, 1933.
Barnes, F.C. *Cartridges of the World.* Gun Digest, 1969.
Bearse, R. *Centerfire American Rifle Cartridges, 1892–1963.* Barnes, 1966.
Bevis, J.R. and Donovan, J.A. *Modern Rifle, Vol. 1, Practical Exterior Ballistics.* privately published, 1917.
Blackmore, H.L. *British Military Firearms, 1650–1850.* Jenkins, 1961.
Bosworth, N. *The Rifle.* Redfield, 1846.
Brownell, F.R. *Gunsmith Kinks.* Brownell, 1969.
Burrard, G. *Notes on Sporting Rifles.* Arnold, 1958.
Butler, J.G. *Systems of Projectiles and Rifling.* Van Nostrand, 1875.
Campbell, C.S. *The '03 Springfields.* Riling, 1971.
Carmichel, J. *The Modern Rifle.* Stoeger, 1976.
Caswell, J. *Sporting Rifles and Rifle Shooting.* Appleton, 1920.

Cleveland, H.W.S. *Hints to Riflemen*. Compton, reprint, 1948.

Corner, J. *Theory of the Internal Ballistics of Guns*. Wiley, 1950.

Crossman, E.C. *Military and Sporting Rifle Shooting*. Samworth, 1932.

_____ *The Book of the Springfield*. Samworth, 1951.

Cummings, C.S.2nd. *Everyday Ballistics*. Stackpole & Heck, 1950.

de Haas, F. *Single Shot Rifles and Actions*. Digest Books, 1969.

_____ *Bolt Action Rifles*. Digest Books, 1971.

Donaldson, H.A., Whelen, T., and Hubbard, F.E. *The Ultimate in Rifle Precision*. Sportsman's Press, 1949.

Dunlap, R.F. *Gunsmithing*. Stackpole, 1963.

Fremantle, T.F. *The Book of the Rifle*. Longmans, Green & Co., 1901.

George, J.N. *English Guns and Rifles*. Stackpole, 1947.

Gould, A.C. *Modern American Rifles*. Samworth reprint, 1946.

Grant, J. J. *Single Shot Rifles*. Morrow, 1947.

_____ *More Single Shot Rifles*. Morrow, 1959.

_____ *Boys' Single Shot Rifles*. Morrow, 1967.

Greener, W.W. *Modern Breechloaders*. Cassell, 1871.

_____ *The Gun and its Development*. Cassell, 9th ed., 1910.

Hatcher, J.S. *Book of the Garand*. Infantry Journal Press, 1948.

_____ *Hatcher's Notebook*. Stackpole, 1966.

Hayes, T. *The Modern Hunting Rifle*. Barnes, 1964.

Howe, J.V. *The Modern Gunsmith*. Funk & Wagnalls, 1934.

Howe, W. *Professional Gunsmithing*. Small Arms Technical Publishing, 1946.

Hübner, S.F. *Waffentechnik*. Journal-Verlag Schwend, 1974.

Ingalls, J.M. *Exterior Ballistics in the Plane of Fire*. Van Nostrand, 1886.

James, E. *The Golden Age of Single-Shot Rifles*. Pioneer Press, 1974.

Johnson, M.M. and Haven, C.T. *Automatic Arms*. Morrow, 1941.

_____ *Ammunition*. 1943.

Keith, E. *Big Game Rifles and Cartridges*. Samworth, 1936.

_____ *Rifles for Large Game*. Standard Publications, 1946.

Kelver, G.O. *Schuetzen Rifles*. Paddock, 1972.

Korn, R.H. *Mauser Gewehre und Mauser Patente*. Ecksteins, 1908.

Landis, C.S. *.22 Caliber Rifle Shooting*. Samworth, 1932.

_____ *Twenty-Two Caliber Varmint Rifles*. Samworth, 1947.

_____ *Woodchucks and Woodchuck Rifles*. Greenberg, 1951.

Lee, K. F. *Big Game Hunting and Marksmanship*. Samworth, 1941.

Lenz, E.C. *Rifleman's Progress*. Standard Publications, 1932.

_____ *Muzzle Flashes*. Standard Publications, 1944.

Lowry, E.D. *Exterior Ballistics of Small Arms Projectiles*. Olin Mathieson, 1965.

_____ *Interior Ballistics*. Doubleday, 1968.

MacFarland, H.E. *Gunsmithing Simplified*. Combat Forces Press, 1953.

_____ *Introduction to Modern Gunsmithing*. Stackpole, 1965.

MacKenty, J.G. *Getting the Most out of Your .22*. Prentice-Hall, 1957.

Madis, G. *The Winchester Book*. Taylor Publishing, 1961.

Mann, F.W. *The Bullet's Flight*. Riling, reprint, 1965.

Mattern, J.R. *Handloading Ammunition*. Small Arms Technical Publishing, 1926.

Moulton, F.R. *Methods in Exterior Ballistics*. Dover Publications, 1962.

Musgrave, D.D. and Nelson, T.B. *The World's Assault Rifles and Automatic Carbines*. T.B.N. Enterprises, 1967.

Naramore, E. *Principles and Practice of Loading Ammunition.* Samworth, 1954.

Nelson, T.B. and Lockhoven, H.B. *The World's Submachine Guns.* International Small Arms Publishers, 1963.

Ness, F.E. *Practical Dope on the Big Bores.* Stackpole & Heck, 1948.

———— *Practical Dope on the .22.* Stackpole, 1955.

O'Connor, J. *The Hunting Rifle.* Stoeger, 1975.

———— *The Rifle Book.* Knopf, 1964.

Olson, L. *Mauser Bolt Rifles.* Brownell, 1976.

Ommundsen, E. and Robinson, E.H. *Rifles and Ammunition.* Waverly, 1915.

Otteson, S. *The Bolt Action.* Winchester Press, 1976.

Page, W. *The Accurate Rifle.* Stoeger, 1975.

Petzal, D. *The .22 Rifle.* Winchester Press, 1973.

Reynolds, E.G.B. *The Lee-Enfield Rifle.* Arco, 1962.

———— *Essentials of Marksmanship.* Marshall, 1964.

Richardson, P.W. *Exterior Ballistics and Miscellaneous Notes.* Published for private circulation, 1918.

Roberts, N. and Waters, K. *The Breech-Loading Single-Shot Match Rifle.* Van Nostrand, 1967.

Roberts, N.H. *Big Game Hunting.* Paul, Richmond & Co., 1947.

———— *The Muzzle-Loading Cap Lock Rifle.* Stackpole, 1952.

Sauer, von K. Th. *Bilderatlas zun Grundriss der Waffenlehre.* Pawlas, reprint, n.d.

Schmidt, R. *Die Handfeuerwaffen* (2 Vols.). Akademische Druck u. Verlaganstalt, 1968.

Schmuderer-Maretsch, M. *Jagd- und Sport-Waffenkunde.* Paul Parey, 1928.

Sharpe, P.B. *Complete Guide to Handloading.* Funk & Wagnalls, 1953.

———— *The Rifle in America.* Funk & Wagnalls, 1958.

Simmons, R.F. *Wildcat Cartridges.* Morrow, 1947.

———— *Custom Rifles.* Stackpole, 1955.

Smith, W.H.B. *The Book of Rifles.* Stackpole, 1960.

———— *Mauser, Walther & Mannlicher Firearms.* Stackpole, 1971.

———— *Small Arms of the World.* various editions.

Stebbins, H.M. *Rifles, a Modern Encyclopedia.* Stackpole, 1958.

Steindler, R.A. *Modern ABC's of Guns.* Stackpole, 1965.

———— *The Firearms Dictionary.* Paladin Press, reprint, 1975.

———— *Reloader's Guide, 3rd edition.* Stoeger, 1975.

———— (translator). *Standard Directory of Proof Marks.* Jolex, 1975.

Suydam, C.R. *The American Cartridge.* G.R. Lawrence, 1960.

Taylor, J. *African Rifles and Cartridges.* Stackpole, 1948.

Vickery, W.F. *Advanced Gunsmithing.* Samworth, 1955.

Wallack, L.R. *Modern Accuracy.* Greenberg, 1951.

———— *The Anatomy of Firearms.* Simon & Schuster, 1965.

Whelen, T. *The American Rifle.* Century, 1920.

———— *Small Arms Design and Ballistics* (2 Vols.). Samworth, 1946.

———— *The Hunting Rifle.* Stackpole & Heck, 1950.

———— (editor). *The Ultimate in Rifle Precision.* Stackpole, 1958.

Appendices

Good Starting Loads

The following loading tables were developed over the years in testing rifles. Also incorporated are loads which were worked up for custom rifles and wildcats. The loading data presented here do not constitute an endorsement for either the loading components or firearms manufacturers mentioned. Good handloading practice dictates that, if you decide to use any of these loads for your own guns, you should start your first test load about five per cent below the listed powder charge. The following loads are believed to be safe in modern firearms of sound construction, but neither the publisher nor the author can assume any responsibility, since choice of components, arms and individual loading technique is beyond our control. Guns of doubtful vintage, or firearms that have seen considerable service should be checked by a competent gunsmith for soundness, headspace, and functioning before being used with any handloaded ammunition.

Bullet Weight	Powder Charge	Muzzle Velocity	Remarks
.17 Mach IV (.17/221)			
25 gr. HP	630 13.1 gr.	3690	
	4198 15.4 gr.	3710	
.17/222			
25 gr. HP	4198 16.7 gr.	3690	
	4320 22.0 gr.	3840	
	760 25.3 gr.	3800	
.17/223			
25 gr.	4064 24.5 gr.	—	
	N-203 19.5 gr.	—	CCI 450 primer
	4198 22.0 gr.	3995	
	4895 21.7 gr.	—	
	3031 23.0 gr.	4067	

Bullet Weight	Powder Charge	Muzzle Velocity	Remarks
.17 Rem.			
25 gr.	4064 23.6 gr.	3412	Rem 7½ primer
	4198 18.2 gr.	3556	"
	N-203 19.3 gr.	3290	"
	4320 25.0 gr.	4000	"
.218 Bee			
45 gr.	H-4227 12.0 gr.	2550	Good Load
48 gr.	H-4227 11.0 gr.	2440	
43 gr.	H-4227 10.5 gr.	2200	Lyman G. C. 225438
46 gr.	Factory load	2754	
.219 Zipper			
40 gr.	3031 25.5 gr.	3550	
50 gr.	4064 28.0 gr.	3480	
55 gr.	4064 27.5 gr.	3100	
43 gr.	2400 9.5 gr.	1980	Lyman G. C. 225438
56 gr.	Factory load	3110	
.219 Zipper Imp.			
45 gr.	4064 34.5 gr.	3850	
50 gr.	4064 33.5 gr.	3700	
55 gr.	3031 30.5 gr.	3400	
.219 Donaldson Wasp			
40 gr.	4064 29.0 gr.	3540	
45 gr.	4064 28.0 gr.	3350	
50 gr.	4895 28.0 gr.	3300	
52 gr.	4895 28.5 gr.	3315	
55 gr.	H-375 32.5 gr.	3590	
55 gr.	4895 27.0 gr.	3140	
.22 Hornet			
46 gr.	H-110 6.6 gr.	2200	
50 gr.	2400 9.3 gr.	2400	
	4227 11.2 gr.	2600	
55 gr.	4227 10.7 gr.	2350	
43 gr.	2400 7.2 gr.	1900	Lyman G. C. 225438
48 gr.	H-4227 9.5 gr.	2380	Lyman G. C. 225450
	2400 8.5 gr.	2380	"
	4227 9.5 gr.	—	"
46 gr.	Factory load	2550	
.22-250 Rem.			
45 gr.	4320 38.0 gr.	3670	
	3031 35.5 gr.	3760	
	4895 38.0 gr.	3745	
	748 38.0 gr.	3910	Accurate, max Magnum primer
	H-380 38.3 gr.	3700	Magnum primer
50 gr.	4895 36.5 gr.	3800	
	H-380 38.0 gr.	3700	
	4064 36.0 gr.	3700	Near max
	748 34.9 gr.	3670	Magnum primer
	760 39.3 gr.	3650	Magnum primer

(cont'd)

Bullet Weight	Powder Charge	Muzzle Velocity	Remarks
55 gr.	4895 37.0 gr.	3610	
	H-375 37.0 gr.	3600	
	748 34.6 gr.	3500	Magnum primer
	760 39.0 gr.	3540	Magnum primer
55 gr.	Factory load	3760	

.220 Swift

40 gr.	4895 40.0 gr.	3850	
45 gr.	4320 39.5 gr.	3800	
	H-380 42.0 gr.	3960	
50 gr.	BL-C(2) 37.5 gr.	3850	
	H-380 41.5 gr.	3700	
55 gr.	H-380 42.0 gr.	3700	
	4831 45.0 gr.	3560	
60 gr.	H-375 36.5 gr.	3300	
	H-450 42.0 gr.	3470	
63 gr.	H-380 40.0 gr.	3480	
	4831 45.0 gr.	3510	
48 gr.	Factory load	3861	

.22 K Hornet

40 gr.	4227 12.5 gr.	3030	This wildcat is becoming obsolete, was one of the first improved versions of the Hornet.
	2400 11.5 gr.	3060	
45 gr.	2400 11.0 gr.	2890	
	4227 12.2 gr.	2860	
50 gr.	4198 11.6 gr.	2420	
	2400 10.3 gr.	2640	
	4227 11.0 gr.	2520	
55 gr.	4227 11.0 gr.	2410	
	2400 10.0 gr.	2450	
	4198 12.0 gr.	2420	

.22-3000 Lovell

50 gr.	4227 15.5 gr.	3000	This is another, now almost obsolete wildcat.
55 gr.	4227 13.4 gr.	2600	

2-R Lovell

50 gr.	4198 16.5 gr.	2930	Maximum!!! This is a wildcatted .22-3000 Lovell.
	4198 15.0 gr.	2700	
55 gr.	4198 15.0 gr.	2600	
	2400 10.0 gr.	2440	

.222 Rem.

40 gr.	4198 19.8 gr.	3360	
	H-335 23.0 gr.	3280	
	4320 25.3 gr.	3400	
	4895 25.0 gr.	3200	
45 gr.	BL-C(2) 23.0 gr.	3200	
	4320 25.3 gr.	3300	
	4895 24.7 gr.	3400	
	4198 19.8 gr.	3220	
50 gr.	BL-C(2) 22.5 gr.	3090	
	H-335 22.0 gr.	3010	
	4320 25.1 gr.	3050	
	4895 24.7 gr.	3200	
	4198 19.6 gr.	3220	

(cont'd)

GOOD STARTING LOADS

Bullet Weight	Powder Charge	Muzzle Velocity	Remarks
52 gr.	BL-C(2) 22.5 gr.	3100	
	4198 18.0 gr.	3025	
	4320 25.1 gr.	3000	
	4895 24.7 gr.	3150	
53 gr.	H-335 21.0 gr.	3000	
	4895 18.0 gr.	3020	
55 gr.	H-380 26.6 gr.	3010	
	4198 18.0 gr.	3020	
	BL-C(2) 22.7 gr.	3040	
	4895 24.0 gr.	2999	
	4320 24.6 gr.	3000	
	748 24.0 gr.	2900	
63 gr.	4895 20.3 gr.	2700	
	4831 23.4 gr.	2600	
70 gr.	748 21.5 gr.	2650	Magnum primer
	4320 22.8 gr.	2700	
	4064 22.0 gr.	2800	
43 gr.	4227 9.7 gr.	2030	Lyman G. C. 225438
	4198 12.5 gr.	2000	"
	Unique 5.0 gr.	1448	"
48 gr.	AL-5 7.7 gr.	2000	Lyman G. C. 225450
	Unique 6.2 gr.	1430	"
	4227 9.7 gr.	1900	"
	4198 11.5 gr.	1900	"
55 gr.	AL-5 7.7 gr.	1965	Lyman G. C. 225462
	Unique 6.6 gr.	1800	"
	2400 8.7 gr.	1800	"
	4198 10.1 gr.	1770	"
50 gr.	Factory load	3150	

.222 Rem. Mag.

Bullet Weight	Powder Charge	Muzzle Velocity	Remarks
40 gr.	H-4227 17.0 gr.	3045	
	4759 19.5 gr.	3400	
	H-335 29.0 gr.	3760	
	3031 26.5 gr.	3500	
	4895 28.5 gr.	3470	
	4320 28.4 gr.	3360	
	4198 23.0 gr.	3460	
45 gr.	H-335 28.5 gr.	3610	
	4895 28.0 gr.	3400	
	3031 26.6 gr.	3490	
	4064 27.0 gr.	3425	
	H-380 31.0 gr.	3175	
	4198 23.3 gr.	3537	
	4320 28.4 gr.	3300	
	BL-C(2) 27.0 gr.	3400	Magnum primer
50 gr.	H-335 28.0 gr.	3545	
	4895 28.0 gr.	3330	
	3031 25.5 gr.	3300	
	4064 26.8 gr.	3330	
	H-380 30.6 gr.	3329	
	4198 22.0 gr.	3315	
	4320 28.5 gr.	3300	
	BL-C(2) 26.5 gr.	3300	Magnum primer
52 gr.	3031 25.5 gr.	3300	
	4198 21.0 gr.	3230	
	4895 27.5 gr.	3300	
	4064 26.0 gr.	3240	
	H-380 29.5 gr.	3220	
55 gr.	H-335 27.5 gr.	3350	
	4895 27.0 gr.	3200	
	H-380 29.5 gr.	3160	
	4198 20.0 gr.	3115	
	4320 28.0 gr.	3230	
	4064 26.8 gr.	3200	
	BL-C(2) 25.5 gr.	3100	Magnum primer (cont'd)

Bullet Weight	Powder Charge	Muzzle Velocity	Remarks
63 gr.	4895 25.5 gr.	3000	
	H-380 29.4 gr.	2960	
70 gr.	H-380 28.5 gr.	2880	Magnum primer
	H-414 28.2 gr.	2880	Magnum primer
	4320 26.0 gr.	2880	
55 gr.	Factory load	3240	

.223 Rem. (5.56mm)

Bullet Weight	Powder Charge	Muzzle Velocity	Remarks
40 gr.	4895 26.0 gr.	3330	
	H-335 27.4 gr.	3498	
	4320 28.0 gr.	3350	
	4064 27.1 gr.	3400	
45 gr.	4320 28.0 gr.	3320	
	H-335 27.0 gr.	3600	Magnum primer
	BL-C(2) 27.0 gr.	3490	Magnum primer
50 gr.	4895 26.5 gr.	3300	
	H-335 27.4 gr.	3305	
	4320 27.9 gr.	3250	
	4064 26.7 gr.	3280	
	3031 25.7 gr.	3400	
55 gr.	4895 25.7 gr.	3260	
	H-335 26.0 gr.	3215	
	4320 27.7 gr.	3120	
	4064 25.4 gr.	3090	
	3031 25.0 gr.	3300	
63 gr.	H-335 24.4 gr.	2970	
70 gr.	4320 25.8 gr.	2900	
	4064 24.7 gr.	3000	
	H-335 24.0 gr.	2950	Magnum primer

Johnson "Spitfire" (5.7 mm)

Bullet Weight	Powder Charge	Muzzle Velocity	Remarks
40 gr. Sisk (0.2235")	4227 12.5 gr.	—	.30 carbine case necked down — #6½ primer small rifle, use cases only three times!
45 gr. Sisk (0.2235")	4227 12.0 gr.	—	
	4198 13.0 gr.	—	

.224 Weatherby Mag.

Bullet Weight	Powder Charge	Muzzle Velocity	Remarks
50 gr.	4895 30.5 gr.	3790	
	3031 29.5 gr.	3700	
	4350 31.6 gr.	3715	
55 gr.	3031 27.3 gr.	3430	
	4064 29.5 gr.	3337	
	4895 30.0 gr.	3500	
50 gr.	Factory load	3750	
55 gr.	Factory load	3650	

.225 Winchester

Bullet Weight	Powder Charge	Muzzle Velocity	Remarks
45 gr.	4895 32.3 gr.	3590	
	4064 31.6 gr.	3630	
	4350 36.0 gr.	3400	Accurate
	760 36.2 gr.	3500	Near max, magnum primer
	H-380 36.1 gr.	3520	Magnum primer
50 gr.	4320 32.0 gr.	3600	
	4895 31.0 gr.	3600	
	4064 31.5 gr.	3550	
	N-203 32.0 gr.	3660	Norma powder
	4350 35.7 gr.	3350	
	760 35.0 gr.	3400	Magnum primer

(cont'd)

Bullet Weight	Powder Charge	Muzzle Velocity	Remarks
52 gr.	H-380 34.5 gr.	3565	
	4320 31.6 gr.	3560	
	4064 30.5 gr.	3500	
	4895 31.0 gr.	3600	
55 gr.	4064 31.5 gr.	3510	
	4895 31.6 gr.	3520	
	4350 34.0 gr.	3440	
	4320 31.6 gr.	3460	
	760 35.0 gr.	3430	Near max, magnum primer
	3031 29.5 gr.	3400	
63 gr.	BL-C(2) 33.0 gr.	3430	
	4831 35.5 gr.	3040	
70 gr.	4831 35.7 gr.	3100	
	4350 34.0 gr.	3000	
	760 33.7 gr.	3100	Magnum primer
55 gr.	Factory load	3580	

.240 Page Super Pooper

Bullet Weight	Powder Charge	Muzzle Velocity	Remarks
75 gr.	4831 52.0 gr.	3478	Designed by Warren Page, gun editor of Field & Stream. Data are those developed by Speer, Inc.
	4350 48.0 gr.	3434	
	4320 42.0 gr.	3418	
	4895 42.0 gr.	3416	
	4064 41.0 gr.	3403	
	3031 38.0 gr.	3412	
80 gr.	4831 51.0 gr.	3374	
	4350 48.0 gr.	3363	
	4320 42.0 gr.	3320	
	4064 40.0 gr.	3325	
	3031 37.0 gr.	3288	
	4895 41.0 gr.	3324	
90 gr.	4831 49.0 gr.	3215	
	4350 46.0 gr.	3217	
	4320 40.0 gr.	3178	
	4895 39.0 gr.	3182	
	4064 39.0 gr.	3177	
	3031 35.0 gr.	3010	
105 gr.	4831 46.0 gr.	2959	
	4350 43.0 gr.	2965	
	H-380 39.0 gr.	2857	
	4895 36.0 gr.	2830	
	4064 36.0 gr.	2824	
	4320 37.0 gr.	2876	

.243 Rockchucker

Bullet Weight	Powder Charge	Muzzle Velocity	Remarks
75 gr.	4831 53.0 gr.	3432	This cartridge was designed by Fred Huntington of RCBS. Data are those of Speer, Inc., and have been verified by Fred. Barrel length is 26".
	4350 51.0 gr.	3615	
	4320 44.0 gr.	3519	
	4895 44.0 gr.	3505	
	4064 44.0 gr.	3610	
	3031 42.0 gr.	3540	
90 gr.	4831 53.0 gr.	3339	
	4350 48.0 gr.	3322	
	4320 42.0 gr.	3281	
	4895 41.0 gr.	3251	
	4064 41.0 gr.	3295	
	3031 38.0 gr.	3170	
105 gr.	4831 51.0 gr.	3112	
	4350 46.0 gr.	3030	
	4320 40.0 gr.	2983	
	4895 40.0 gr.	2889	
	4064 40.0 gr.	2910	
	3031 37.0 gr.	2805	

.243 Winchester

Bullet Weight	Powder Charge	Muzzle Velocity	Remarks
60 gr.	4895 42.5 gr.	3680	
70 gr.	4320 41.8 gr.	3487	
	4064 38.0 gr.	3390	(cont'd)

Bullet Weight	Powder Charge	Muzzle Velocity	Remarks
75 gr.	4895 40.2 gr.	3400	
	4831 47.7 gr.	3262	
	4350 44.5 gr.	3321	
	H-380 40.5 gr.	3280	
	4320 39.6 gr.	3327	
	4064 38.0 gr.	3380	
	3031 37.5 gr.	3350	
	760 43.0 gr.	3300	Magnum primer
80 gr.	4895 38.5 gr.	3245	
	4831 46.7 gr.	3200	
	4350 42.6 gr.	3300	
	BL-C(2) 34.0 gr.	3100	
	4064 36.5 gr.	3260	
	H-380 38.1 gr.	3150	
	4320 37.5 gr.	3225	
	3031 33.7 gr.	3130	
	760 43.0 gr.	3250	Magnum primer
85 gr.	4064 37.0 gr.	3110	
	4350 43.0 gr.	3150	
90 gr.	H-375 36.0 gr.	2831	
	4831 45.2 gr.	2920	
	4350 41.5 gr.	3128	
	H-380 37.3 gr.	2960	
	4320 36.6 gr.	3000	
	3031 33.0 gr.	2940	
	4064 35.5 gr.	3000	
	4895 36.6 gr.	3000	
	760 41.9 gr.	3100	Magnum primer
100 gr.	4350 40.0 gr.	2965	
	4831 42.0 gr.	2760	
	4895 37.7 gr.	2950	
105 gr.	4831 41.0 gr.	2700	
	4895 34.5 gr.	2725	
	H-570 34.0 gr.	2620	
	4350 37.0 gr.	2740	
	4320 34.5 gr.	2720	
	4064 33.5 gr.	2675	
	3031 31.5 gr.	2727	
85 gr.	2400 11.0 gr.	1775	Lyman G. C. 245496
	4198 14.5 gr.	1760	,,
	AL-5 9.5 gr.	1721	,,
	H-240 11.0 gr.	1800	,,
95 gr.	Unique 9.5 gr.	1727	Lyman G. C. 245497
	H-240 13.0 gr.	1835	,,
	4227 13.0 gr.	1795	,,
	4759 12.0 gr.	1720	,,
	4198 15.0 gr.	1810	,,
80 gr.	Factory load	3450	
100 gr.	Factory load	3050	

6 x 47 Benchrest (6mm/222)

Bullet Weight	Powder Charge	Muzzle Velocity	Remarks
75 gr.	H-335 28.7 gr.	3010	Rem. 7½ primer, near max
	BL-C(2) 28.1 gr.	2900	Rem. 7½ primer
	4320 28.7 gr.	2800	Rem. 7½ primer, near max
	4895 27.3 gr.	2900	Rem. 7½ primer
80 gr.	H-335 27.7 gr.	2900	Rem. 7½ primer
	BL-C(2) 27.3 gr.	2910	Rem. 7½ primer
	4320 27.3 gr.	2700	Rem. 7½ primer
	4895 26.8 gr.	2800	Rem. 7½ primer, near max
90 gr.	H-380 26.7 gr.	2440	Rem. 7½ primer
	4320 26.3 gr.	2610	Rem. 7½ primer
	4895 26.0 gr.	2740	Rem. 7½ primer, maximum
	BL-C(2) 26.4 gr.	2790	Rem. 7½ primer

6mm Intl. Benchrest (6mm/250 Sav.)

Bullet Weight	Powder Charge	Muzzle Velocity	Remarks
75 gr.	4350 39.5 gr.	3300	(cont'd)

GOOD STARTING LOADS

Bullet Weight	Powder Charge	Muzzle Velocity	Remarks
75 gr.	760 38.1 gr.	3200	Magnum primer
	4064 34.0 gr.	3260	
	4895 32.8 gr.	3240	
80 gr.	4831 39.0 gr.	3200	
	4350 39.0 gr.	3200	
	760 36.9 gr.	3100	Magnum primer
	4064 33.5 gr.	3200	
90 gr.	4831 38.4 gr.	3110	
	4350 38.4 gr.	3000	
	760 35.0 gr.	2840	Magnum primer
	4064 32.3 gr.	3000	Maximum charge

.240 Weatherby Magnum

Bullet Weight	Powder Charge	Muzzle Velocity	Remarks
80 gr.	N-205 58.0 gr.	3680	
	4350 52.0 gr.	3520	
85 gr.	4350 53.0 gr.	3500	
	4831 58.0 gr.	—	Near max
	N-205 58.0 gr.	—	"
100 gr.	4350 51.0 gr.	3250	Near max
	4831 55.0 gr.	3380	Near max
	N-205 55.0 gr.	3360	Near max
	4320 45.8 gr.	3200	Near max
	760 49.0 gr.	3130	Federal 215 primer

.244 Rem. (6mm Rem.)

Bullet Weight	Powder Charge	Muzzle Velocity	Remarks
70 gr.	4320 45.0 gr.	3610	
	4064 41.5 gr.	3370	
	4895 40.5 gr.	3585	
	H-380 46.0 gr.	3680	
75 gr.	4064 38.0 gr.	3370	
	4831 49.5 gr.	3340	
	4350 46.3 gr.	3440	
	H-380 39.0 gr.	3200	
	4320 40.0 gr.	3419	
	4895 38.5 gr.	3260	
	3031 35.5 gr.	3300	
80 gr.	4350 45.5 gr.	3400	
	4064 35.5 gr.	3030	
	4831 50.5 gr.	3363	
	4895 38.5 gr.	3258	
	H-380 38.0 gr.	3120	
	4320 38.5 gr.	3310	
	3031 34.0 gr.	3211	
85 gr.	4064 40.0 gr.	3175	
	H-380 42.0 gr.	3180	
	4350 43.0 gr.	3290	
	H-375 39.0 gr.	3030	
	4895 39.0 gr.	3310	
	3031 37.0 gr.	3175	
90 gr.	3031 33.5 gr.	2955	
	4895 36.5 gr.	3045	
	4064 35.7 gr.	3005	
	4320 37.0 gr.	3100	
	4831 48.2 gr.	3200	
	4350 42.5 gr.	3130	
	H-380 38.5 gr.	2999	
100 gr.	4350 39.0 gr.	2800	
	H-380 36.0 gr.	2750	
	4831 45.0 gr.	3005	
	4895 34.0 gr.	2940	
105 gr.	3031 30.5 gr.	2620	
	H-380 33.5 gr.	2610	

(cont'd)

Bullet Weight	Powder Charge	Muzzle Velocity	Remarks
105 gr.	4895 33.5 gr.	2660	
	4064 32.0 gr.	2610	
	4320 33.5 gr.	2710	
	4350 37.2 gr.	2705	
	4831 42.0 gr.	2815	
85 gr.	2400 11.5 gr.	1768	Lyman G. C. 245496
	4759 12.0 gr.	1910	”
	4198 13.7 gr.	1800	”
	H-240 11.0 gr.	1783	”
95 gr.	H-240 11.0 gr.	1730	Lyman G. C. 245497
	4198 13.0 gr.	1692	”
	4759 12.5 gr.	1910	”
	2400 11.0 gr.	1710	Lyman G. C. 245497
	4227 12.0 gr.	1548	”
75 gr.	Factory load	3500	
90 gr.	Factory load	3200	

.25-20 WCF

Bullet Weight	Powder Charge	Muzzle Velocity	Remarks
70 gr.	Unique 4.0 gr.	1489	Lyman G. C. 257420
	4759 7.5 gr.	1750	”
	2400 7.0 gr.	1600	”
	4227 8.5 gr.	1680	”
75 gr.	Unique 4.2 gr.	1450	Lyman G. C. 257463
	4759 7.5 gr.	1701	”
	2400 8.0 gr.	1671	”
	4227 8.3 gr.	1632	”
	H-240 7.5 gr.	1600	”
85 gr.	H-240 7.5 gr.	1600	Lyman 257283
	2400 7.6 gr.	1542	”
	4227 8.1 gr.	1467	”
	Unique 4.8 gr.	1279	”
60 gr.	Factory load	2250	

.25 Souper

Bullet Weight	Powder Charge	Muzzle Velocity	Remarks
60 gr.	4831 49.0 gr.	3123	Designed by P. F.
	4350 50.0 gr.	3455	Lambert, the .25
	4320 47.0 gr.	3755	Souper is said to
	4895 47.0 gr.	3715	be somewhat better
	4064 47.0 gr.	3755	than the .257
	3031 44.0 gr.	3779	Roberts. Data
	4198 38.5 gr.	3767	furnished by
87 gr.	4831 49.5 gr.	3091	Speer, Inc.
	4350 48.5 gr.	3262	
	4064 42.5 gr.	3238	
	3031 41.5 gr.	3295	
	4320 42.0 gr.	3095	
87 gr.	4895 42.0 gr.	3133	
	4198 35.5 gr.	3169	
100 gr.	4831 48.0 gr.	3022	
	4350 44.5 gr.	3092	
	4064 39.0 gr.	2958	
	3031 37.5 gr.	2981	
	4320 37.0 gr.	2825	
	4895 41.0 gr.	3008	
120 gr.	4831 42.5 gr.	2873	
	4350 42.5 gr.	2797	
	4320 33.0 gr.	2500	
	4895 36.5 gr.	2688	
	4064 34.0 gr.	2558	
	3031 36.0 gr.	2713	

Bullet Weight	Powder Charge	Muzzle Velocity	Remarks
.25/284			
60 gr.	4320 56.0 gr.	4080	
	4350 56.7 gr.	3713	
75 gr.	4350 57.0 gr.	3790	
87 gr.	4350 56.0 gr.	3590	
100 gr.	4350 53.0 gr.	3250	Max load
117 gr.	4350 49.5 gr.	3002	
	4831 53.0 gr.	2990	
120 gr.	4350 50.0 gr.	2931	
.25 Niedner (.25-06)			
87 gr.	4831 59.0 gr.	3404	Based on the .30-06
	4350 54.0 gr.	3345	case, this cartridge
	H-380 42.0 gr.	3055	is also known as
	4320 45.0 gr.	3307	the .25-06 and is
	4895 45.0 gr.	3336	one of the best and
	4064 45.0 gr.	3299	most long-lived
100 gr.	H-570 61.0 gr.	3150	wildcats. Data are
	4831 58.0 gr.	3245	from Speer, Inc.
	4350 53.0 gr.	3188	
	4320 44.0 gr.	3064	
	4895 44.0 gr.	3094	
	4064 44.0 gr.	3094	
115 gr.	H-870 63.0 gr.	3050	CCI 250 primer
120 gr.	H-570 61.0 gr.	3021	
	4831 55.0 gr.	3038	
	4350 50.0 gr.	2935	
	4320 43.0 gr.	2805	
	4895 43.0 gr.	2807	
	4064 42.0 gr.	2823	
.25-06 RCBS IMP.			
75 gr.	H-335 46.0 gr.	3350	
100 gr.	4350 59.0 gr.	3595	
	4831 60.5 gr.	3525	
	4831 57.0 gr.	3045	Very accurate
	H-450 46.0 gr.	2810	
117 gr.	4831 54.0 gr.	—	
	4350 52.0 gr.	—	
120 gr.	H-450 50.0 gr.	—	
	4350 52.0 gr.	—	
	4831 57.0 gr.	—	
.25-06 Remington			
87 gr.	4831 58.0 gr.	3600	
	4350 55.2 gr.	3500	
	4064 48.3 gr.	3450	
	4320 45.3 gr.	3300	
100 gr.	4831 55.3 gr.	3380	
	4350 51.9 gr.	3200	Accurate
	4064 46.8 gr.	3300	Near max
	4320 44.7 gr.	3100	
117 gr.	4831 56.0 gr.	3100	
	4350 49.9 gr.	3000	
	4064 45.1 gr.	3020	Near max
120 gr.	4831 49.3 gr.	3000	
	4350 48.2 gr.	3000	Near max
	4064 43.4 gr.	2900	Near max
	4895 40.0 gr.	2700	Near max

Bullet Weight	Powder Charge	Muzzle Velocity	Remarks
.250-3000			
60 gr.	4895 40.0 gr.	3542	
	4064 38.6 gr.	3400	
	4350 41.0 gr.	3170	
	4320 39.5 gr.	3420	
	4198 32.0 gr.	3420	
	3031 35.0 gr.	3465	
87 gr.	4895 37.0 gr.	3000	
	4064 35.5 gr.	2940	
	4350 39.5 gr.	2906	
	4320 36.3 gr.	2890	
	3031 32.6 gr.	2880	
	H-380 36.0 gr.	2835	
	4831 41.5 gr.	2785	
100 gr.	4831 42.0 gr.	2800	
	4895 35.0 gr.	2876	
	3031 30.0 gr.	2600	
	H-380 33.5 gr.	2615	
	4320 36.0 gr.	2841	
120 gr.	4831 41.5 gr.	2683	
	3031 28.0 gr.	2430	
	4895 33.2 gr.	2500	
	4064 32.0 gr.	2540	
	4320 34.6 gr.	2668	
	4350 37.5 gr.	2694	
	H-380 29.0 gr.	2200	
	4320 36.0 gr.	2800	
	4895 34.5 gr.	2600	
70 gr.	4227 14.0 gr.	1760	Lyman G. C. 257420
	4198 14.5 gr.	1710	,,
	4895 14.3 gr.	1600	,,
	2400 11.1 gr.	1700	,,
	Unique 8.1 gr.	1640	,,
	H-240 11.8 gr.	1747	,,
80 gr.	4227 16.0 gr.	1900	Lyman G. C. 257388
	4198 15.5 gr.	1800	,,
	2400 15.4 gr.	1945	,,
	Unique 8.4 gr.	1800	,,
	H-240 15.2 gr.	1966	,,
100 gr.	4198 15.6 gr.	1693	Lyman G. C. 257418
	4227 17.0 gr.	2000	,,
	2400 14.2 gr.	1900	,,
87 gr.	Factory load	3030	
100 gr.	Factory load	2820	
.250-3000 Bolt Action Rifle Only			
87 gr.	4350 43.2 gr.	3200	The revival of the bolt action .250 Savage allows handloaders to make ammo which delivers higher velocities than permissible for acceptable pressure levels in lever action rifles. Loads were developed in custom rifle and care must be taken when developing your own loads for your rifle. Start with lever action loads and work up.
	4064 38.4 gr.	3100	
100 gr.	4831 42.8 gr.	3100	
	4350 41.2 gr.	3000	
120 gr.	4831 39.4 gr.	2850	
	4350 38.4 gr.	2750	
.256 Win.			
60 gr.	4198 17.6 gr.	2740	Originally designed as a pistol cartridge, the .256
	2400 14.1 gr.	2705	
	4227 15.8 gr.	2640	

(cont'd)

GOOD STARTING LOADS

Bullet Weight	Powder Charge	Muzzle Velocity	Remarks
87 gr.	4198 15.3 gr.	2100	Winchester also
	4227 14.6 gr.	2137	found acceptance
	2400 12.7 gr.	1945	as a rifle cartridge.
60 gr.	Factory load	2800	

.257 Roberts

Bullet Weight	Powder Charge	Muzzle Velocity	Remarks
60 gr.	4895 43.5 gr.	3600	
	4198 33.6 gr.	3589	
	4064 42.4 gr.	3600	
	4320 44.7 gr.	3534	
	H-380 45.2 gr.	3600	
	3031 38.5 gr.	3613	
87 gr.	4895 41.0 gr.	3260	
	3031 35.6 gr.	3100	
	4320 41.6 gr.	3255	
	4350 44.0 gr.	3175	
	4064 40.0 gr.	3171	
	H-380 41.6 gr.	3123	
	BL-C(2) 35.8 gr.	2900	
100 gr.	4320 37.6 gr.	2872	
	4350 42.2 gr.	2921	
	4064 37.0 gr.	2961	
	4831 46.6 gr.	2986	
	4895 37.6 gr.	2923	
120 gr.	4831 42.0 gr.	2701	
	4895 35.0 gr.	2635	
	4320 34.6 gr.	2526	
	4350 39.0 gr.	2681	
	4064 33.5 gr.	2541	
	3031 30.3 gr.	2498	
85 gr.	4227 14.2 gr.	2006	Lyman G. C. 257312
	4198 13.6 gr.	1700	”
	2400 13.3 gr.	2011	”
100 gr.	4227 15.3 gr.	2006	Lyman G. C. 257418
	4198 22.2 gr.	2145	”
	2400 13.1 gr.	1967	”
87 gr.	Factory load	3200	
100 gr.	Factory load	2900	
117 gr.	Factory load	2650	

.257 Imp.

Bullet Weight	Powder Charge	Muzzle Velocity	Remarks
60 gr.	3031 47.5 gr.	3682	This is the .257
	4320 51.4 gr.	3700	Roberts wildcatted
	4064 49.6 gr.	3602	by P. O. Ackley.
	4895 50.4 gr.	3591	
87 gr.	3031 41.0 gr.	3178	
	4064 47.0 gr.	3280	
	4320 47.4 gr.	3326	
	4350 53.0 gr.	3333	
	4895 47.6 gr.	3278	
	H-380 42.0 gr.	3002	
100 gr.	4064 44.0 gr.	3090	
	3031 40.0 gr.	2903	
	4350 49.7 gr.	3226	
	4320 43.5 gr.	2917	
	4831 53.6 gr.	3036	
	H-380 42.0 gr.	2857	
117 gr.	4350 48.0 gr.	3009	
120 gr.	4831 49.9 gr.	2746	
	4064 40.5 gr.	2801	
	3031 36.4 gr.	2675	
	4895 41.0 gr.	2683	
	4320 41.4 gr.	2697	
	4350 46.3 gr.	2776	
	H-380 39.0 gr.	2505	

Bullet Weight	Powder Charge	Muzzle Velocity	Remarks
.257 Weatherby Magnum			
87 gr.	3031 53.0 gr.	3597	Because of the high velocity attained, bullets lighter than 87 gr. are not very practical.
	4320 58.6 gr.	3667	
	4350 66.3 gr.	3681	
	4064 56.0 gr.	3597	
	4895 58.0 gr.	3580	
	4831 70.6 gr.	3700	
	H-450 71.0 gr.	3700	CCI 250 primer
100 gr.	4895 56.0 gr.	3313	
	4064 53.0 gr.	3244	
	4320 55.0 gr.	3278	
	4350 63.2 gr.	3483	
	4831 68.0 gr.	3472	
	H-570 76.8 gr.	3240	
	H-450 68.0 gr.	3400	CCI 250 primer
117 gr.	4831 67.0 gr.	3345	
	4350 62.0 gr.	3188	
	H-870 75.0 gr.	3267	Use magnum primer
120 gr.	4831 64.0 gr.	3170	
	4350 60.0 gr.	3144	
	4320 52.4 gr.	3000	
	4895 52.0 gr.	3025	
	4064 50.0 gr.	2987	
	H-870 75.0 gr.	3138	Use magnum primer
	H 570 77.0 gr.	3200	
100 gr.	Factory load	3300	
117 gr.	Factory load	3550	
6.5 x 55 Swedish Mauser			
87 gr.	4320 46.7 gr.	2971	Most 6.5 x 55 military Mauser rifles are proofed for about 45,000 psi. Therefore, care should be taken in working up loads.
	4350 51.0 gr.	2963	
	4064 45.5 gr.	3002	
	4895 45.7 gr.	3044	
	3031 42.8 gr.	3101	
120 gr.	4350 51.0 gr.	2623	
	4320 41.0 gr.	2675	
	4831 51.6 gr.	2681	
	4895 40.5 gr.	2625	
	4064 41.0 gr.	2643	
	3031 38.6 gr.	2658	
140 gr.	4350 46.0 gr.	2520	
	4320 36.5 gr.	2315	
	4831 49.4 gr.	2600	
	4895 37.0 gr.	2312	
	4064 35.5 gr.	2300	
	3031 31.6 gr.	2100	
160 gr.	4350 41.0 gr.	2410	
139 gr.	Factory load	2789	
6.5 Japanese (6.50 x 50mm Arisaka)			
100 gr.	3031 34.2 gr.	2850	Near max
	4064 37.0 gr.	3000	Near max
	4320 38.0 gr.	2700	Near max
120 gr.	3031 34.0 gr.	—	Near max
	4064 36.5 gr.	2600	
140 gr.	3031 32.5 gr.	—	Max load
156 gr.	3031 26.0 gr.	—	Max load
6.5 x 54 M-S			
100 gr.	3031 33.0 gr.	2490	Near max

(cont'd)

GOOD STARTING LOADS

Bullet Weight	Powder Charge	Muzzle Velocity	Remarks
100 gr.	4895 37.1 gr.	2580	
	4320 37.1 gr.	2570	
140 gr.	4350 39.8 gr.	2380	
	4831 43.2 gr.	2400	
	4320 35.4 gr.	2290	
160 gr.	4350 38.7 gr.	2220	
	4831 40.3 gr.	2230	Near max
	N-204 42.1 gr.	2240	Max load

6.5 x 284

Bullet Weight	Powder Charge	Muzzle Velocity	Remarks
100 gr.	4350 59.0 gr.	3540	RCBS data
120 gr.	4350 57.0 gr.	3320	” ”
139 gr.	4350 55.0 gr.	3150	” ”
140 gr.	4350 55.0 gr.	3120	” ”
160 gr.	4350 50.0 gr.	2780	” ”

6.5 Carcano (6.5 x 52 Mannlicher-Carcano)

Bullet Weight	Powder Charge	Muzzle Velocity	Remarks
100 gr.	3031 31.6 gr.	2500	Near max
	4320 35.1 gr.	2500	Near max
	4350 41.3 gr.	2500	Near max
140 gr.	4895 31.8 gr.	2190	
	4064 32.0 gr.	2200	
	4320 32.8 gr.	2200	
160 gr.	4350 38.1 gr.	2200	Accurate, max load
	4895 31.8 gr.	2100	Near max

6.5 Remington Magnum

Bullet Weight	Powder Charge	Muzzle Velocity	Remarks
100 gr.	4895 51.0 gr.	3475	26" test barrel Alcan primer
	4831 58.2 gr.	3400	Near max
	4350 55.7 gr.	3280	
	4320 50.0 gr.	3200	Near max
120 gr.	4350 54.5 gr.	2900	Near max, CCI 250 primer
	4831 57.5 gr.	2870	CCI 250 primer
	H-450 55.2 gr.	3000	Near max
	4895 45.0 gr.	3000	Near max
	4320 46.0 gr.	2800	
	H-380 52.0 gr.	2900	CCI 250 primer
140 gr.	4350 52.0 gr.	2800	CCI 250 primer
	4831 56.0 gr.	2765	CCI 250 primer
	N-205 54.4 gr.	2800	
	H-450 52.0 gr.	2800	
	4064 43.7 gr.	2630	
	4320 44.0 gr.	2600	
	H-380 48.5 gr.	2620	CCI 250 primer

.264 Winchester Magnum

Bullet Weight	Powder Charge	Muzzle Velocity	Remarks
87 gr.	4350 64.0 gr.	3559	
	4320 56.3 gr.	3600	
	4831 70.0 gr.	3698	
	4895 56.0 gr.	3591	
	4064 55.6 gr.	3657	
	3031 51.0 gr.	3568	
	H-450 68.0 gr.	3662	Use magnum primer.
100 gr.	4350 56.1 gr.	3164	
	4320 55.0 gr.	3375	
	4831 65.0 gr.	3427	
	4895 53.0 gr.	3388	
	4064 52.9 gr.	3309	

(cont'd)

Bullet Weight	Powder Charge	Muzzle Velocity	Remarks
100 gr.	H-450 66.0 gr.	3426	Use magnum primer.
120 gr.	4350 59.0 gr.	3241	
	4320 51.5 gr.	2997	
	4064 50.0 gr.	3100	
	4831 65.0 gr.	3349	
	4895 51.5 gr.	2990	
	5010 78.0 gr.	3363	
	H-870 76.0 gr.	3370	Use magnum primer.
	H-570 76.0 gr.	3301	
	H-450 62.0 gr.	3264	Use magnum primer.
140 gr.	4350 56.0 gr.	3017	
	4320 49.0 gr.	2888	
	4831 61.0 gr.	3071	
	4895 50.0 gr.	2890	
	5010 73.5 gr.	2915	
100 gr.	Factory load	3700	
140 gr.	Factory load	3200	

6.5/280 Remington IMP

Bullet Weight	Powder Charge	Muzzle Velocity	Remarks
100 gr.	4350 55.0 gr.	3210	RCBS data
120 gr.	4350 55.0 gr.	3240	" "
125 gr.	4350 56.0 gr.	3300	" "
140 gr.	4350 50.0 gr.	2880	" "

6.5 x 61 Magnum (6.5/300 H&H)

Bullet Weight	Powder Charge	Muzzle Velocity	Remarks
85 gr.	4831 70.0 gr.	3800	½ MOA, Federal 210 primer
	4350 69.0 gr.	3870	— " " "
100 gr.	4350 65.5 gr.	3580	¾ MOA, " " "
120 gr.	4350 63.5 gr.	3400	MOA, " " "
139 gr.	N-202 89.4 gr.	3500	¾ MOA, " " "
	H-870 86.4 gr.	3580	¾ MOA, " " "
140 gr.	4350 60.5 gr.	3240	½ MOA, " " "
160 gr.	4350 57.0 gr.	2890	MOA, " " "

.270 Winchester

Bullet Weight	Powder Charge	Muzzle Velocity	Remarks
100 gr.	4831 62.7 gr.	3400	
	4895 51.5 gr.	3400	
130 gr.	4350 54.0 gr.	3035	
	4320 47.0 gr.	2810	
	4831 58.0 gr.	3100	
	4895 47.5 gr.	2951	
	4064 46.3 gr.	2942	
	3031 43.5 gr.	2876	
150 gr.	4350 51.0 gr.	2721	
	4320 45.5 gr.	2750	
	4831 57.0 gr.	3013	
	4895 45.5 gr.	2763	
	4064 44.3 gr.	2744	
	H-570 62.0 gr.	2720	
170 gr.	4350 49.5 gr.	2516	
	4320 43.0 gr.	2445	
	4831 53.7 gr.	2700	
	4895 43.5 gr.	2457	
	4064 42.0 gr.	2403	
	H-570 62.0 gr.	2652	
125 gr.	Unique 7.5 gr.	1200	Lyman G. C. 280473
	4198 17.5 gr.	1522	"
135 gr.	Unique 7.3 gr.	1200	Lyman G. C., H.P. 280412
	4198 19.0 gr.	1591	"
100 gr.	Factory load	3700	
130 gr.	Factory load	3140	
150 gr.	Factory load	2800	

Bullet Weight	Muzzle Velocity	Powder Charge	Remarks
.270 Weatherby Magnum			
100 gr.	4831 78.0 gr.	3700	
	4350 74.2 gr.	3710	Near max.
	4895 65.5 gr.	3600	
130 gr.	4350 67.0 gr.	3312	
	4320 59.5 gr.	3175	
	4831 71.0 gr.	3277	
	4895 59.3 gr.	3202	
	4064 57.5 gr.	3150	
	3031 53.5 gr.	3100	
	H-570 80.0 gr.	3200	
150 gr.	4350 65.0 gr.	3122	
	4320 56.5 gr.	2917	
	4831 70.0 gr.	3128	
	4895 56.5 gr.	2900	
	5010 80.5 gr.	2999	
	4064 56.5 gr.	2903	
	H-570 80.0 gr.	3131	
170 gr.	4350 60.0 gr.	2742	
	4320 52.5 gr.	2617	
	4831 65.6 gr.	2766	
	4895 52.0 gr.	2602	
	4064 51.4 gr.	2587	
	5010 78.0 gr.	2929	
	H-570 76.4 gr.	2953	
130 gr.	Factory load	3375	
150 gr.	Factory load	3245	
7 mm Mauser (7 x 57)			
130 gr.	4350 49.5 gr.	2816	
	4320 44.0 gr.	2875	
	4831 52.5 gr.	2857	
	4895 43.6 gr.	2844	
	4064 42.5 gr.	2800	
	3031 39.4 gr.	2748	
145 gr.	4350 47.5 gr.	2696	
	4320 41.4 gr.	2653	
	4831 51.2 gr.	2749	
	4895 41.0 gr.	2666	
	4064 41.0 gr.	2681	
	3031 37.3 gr.	2564	
160 gr.	4350 46.0 gr.	2615	
	4064 41.0 gr.	2600	
	4320 40.6 gr.	2509	
	4831 51.2 gr.	2660	
	4895 39.0 gr.	2500	
	3031 36.8 gr.	2481	
130 gr.	2400 14.2 gr.	1710	Lyman G. C. 287346
	4227 15.0 gr.	1710	”
	4198 17.5 gr.	1487	”
	H-240 14.3 gr.	1800	”
150 gr.	2400 12.4 gr.	1387	Lyman G. C. 287377
	4227 13.0 gr.	1463	”
	4198 17.6 gr.	1521	”
	H-240 12.6 gr.	1401	”
150 gr.	Factory load (Norma)	2756	
.280 Remington			
130 gr.	4350 56.0 gr.	3160	These loads are for bolt actions only!
	4320 48.6 gr.	3000	
	4831 59.6 gr.	3000	
	4895 47.3 gr.	3001	

(cont'd)

Bullet Weight	Powder Charge	Muzzle Velocity	Remarks
130 gr.	4064 47.5 gr.	3006	
	3031 45.0 gr.	3000	
	H-380 48.0 gr.	2829	
145 gr.	4350 52.0 gr.	2930	
	4320 46.0 gr.	2767	
	4831 56.5 gr.	2900	
	4895 46.0 gr.	2800	
	4064 45.3 gr.	2801	
	3031 42.6 gr.	2763	
160 gr.	4350 51.4 gr.	2797	
	4320 45.0 gr.	2641	
	4831 55.4 gr.	2736	
	4895 44.0 gr.	2603	
	4064 44.0 gr.	2680	
	3031 40.7 gr.	2625	
125 gr.	Factory load	3190	
150 gr.	Factory load	2890	
165 gr.	Factory load	2820	

.280 Remington Imp.

Bullet Weight	Powder Charge	Muzzle Velocity	Remarks
140 gr.	4350 63.0 gr.	3320	This is Fred Huntington's pet caliber and with it, he has taken a great many heads of game in the U.S., Canada, and Africa. Data from Fred Huntington, RCBS, Inc.
145 gr.	4831 61.0 gr.	3120	
154 gr.	4831 60.0 gr.	2920	
	4350 60.0 gr.	3070	
175 gr.	4350 58.0 gr.	2850	

.284 Winchester

Bullet Weight	Powder Charge	Muzzle Velocity	Remarks
130 gr.	4350 55.0 gr.	2991	Ballistically similar to the .270, the cartridge was designed for use in lever action rifles.
	4320 46.4 gr.	2789	
	4831 58.8 gr.	2799	
	4895 45.6 gr.	2743	
	3031 43.0 gr.	2764	
	BL-C(2) 47.6 gr.	2830	
	H-380 49.5 gr.	2788	
	4064 46.0 gr.	2775	
	760 55.7 gr.	3000	Magnum primer
	N-205 58.0 gr.	2900	
145 gr.	4350 53.0 gr.	2783	
	4320 46.0 gr.	2673	
	4831 57.0 gr.	2668	
	4895 45.5 gr.	2713	
	3031 41.6 gr.	2650	
	BL-C(2) 47.6 gr.	2876	
	H-380 49.5 gr.	2763	
	4064 47.0 gr.	2687	
	760 53.8 gr.	2840	Magnum primer
	N-205 56.0 gr.	2800	
160 gr.	4350 52.5 gr.	2700	
	4320 43.0 gr.	2491	
	4831 56.5 gr.	2603	
	4895 44.0 gr.	2597	
	4064 45.5 gr.	2577	
	H-380 49.4 gr.	2561	
175 gr.	4831 52.3 gr.	2630	
	4350 52.0 gr.	2640	
	N-205 53.7 gr.	2600	
125 gr.	Factory load	3200	
150 gr.	Factory load	2900	

GOOD STARTING LOADS

Bullet Weight	Powder Charge	Muzzle Velocity	Remarks
7 x 61 Sharpe and Hart			
130 gr.	4350 61.3 gr.	3200	
	4320 54.6 gr.	3143	
	4831 66.5 gr.	3214	
	4895 55.0 gr.	3155	
	4064 53.7 gr.	3161	
	3031 50.6 gr.	3101	
	H-380 51.0 gr.	2922	
145 gr.	4350 60.3 gr.	3035	
	4320 54.0 gr.	3036	
	4831 65.5 gr.	3103	
	4895 53.6 gr.	3108	
	4064 53.0 gr.	2998	
	5010 75.0 gr.	2957	
160 gr.	4350 59.4 gr.	2923	
	4320 52.4 gr.	2840	
	4831 64.0 gr.	2987	
	4895 52.5 gr.	2860	
	4064 52.0 gr.	2860	
	5010 75.0 gr.	2900	
	Factory load	3100	
7 mm Weatherby Magnum			
130 gr.	4350 68.3 gr.	3358	
	4320 61.0 gr.	3251	
	4831 73.5 gr.	3310	
	4895 59.0 gr.	3200	
	4064 58.5 gr.	3201	
	3031 55.7 gr.	3258	
	H-570 81.0 gr.	3050	
145 gr.	4350 65.0 gr.	3120	
	4320 58.5 gr.	3054	
	4831 70.6 gr.	3251	
	4895 57.4 gr.	3054	
	5010 80.0 gr.	2922	
	H-570 79.6 gr.	3010	
160 gr.	4350 64.5 gr.	3100	
	4320 56.7 gr.	2912	
	4831 69.3 gr.	3065	
	4895 56.6 gr.	2903	
	4064 54.0 gr.	2881	
	5010 79.8 gr.	2919	
	H-570 80.0 gr.	2981	
139 gr.	Factory load	3300	
154 gr.	Factory load	3160	
7mm Remington Magnum			
130 gr.	4350 66.5 gr.	3242	Use of
	4320 55.0 gr.	3180	magnum primers
	4831 72.4 gr.	3300	is recommended
	4895 54.0 gr.	3001	for this caliber.
	4064 54.5 gr.	3100	
	H-450 68.7 gr.	3160	
	H-570 80.6 gr.	3122	
	N-205 67.0 gr.	3260	
145 gr.	4350 64.4 gr.	3116	
	4320 53.5 gr.	2981	
	4831 70.5 gr.	3151	
	4895 53.6 gr.	2911	
	5010 80.8 gr.	3037	
	H-570 80.3 gr.	3027	
	H-450 66.2 gr.	3000	
	N-205 65.0 gr.	3200	Max load (cont'd)

Bullet Weight	Powder Charge	Muzzle Velocity	Remarks
154 gr.	4350 59.0 gr.	2900	
	4320 51.5 gr.	2665	
	4831 65.0 gr.	3007	
	4895 50.5 gr.	2691	
	5010 76.0 gr.	2981	
	H-570 86.6 gr.	3023	
	H-450 62.0 gr.	2889	
160 gr.	4350 63.0 gr.	3035	
	4320 53.8 gr.	2840	
	4831 65.6 gr.	3035	
	4895 51.5 gr.	2741	
	5010 80.6 gr.	3018	
	H-570 80.6 gr.	3019	
	H-450 65.0 gr.	2860	
	H-870 77.1 gr.	2980	
175 gr.	4831 57.8 gr.	2750	
	4350 56.6 gr.	2770	
	4320 50.4 gr.	2640	
	H-870 75.0 gr.	2830	
150 gr.	Factory load	3260	
175 gr.	Factory load	3020	

7.5mm Swiss (7.5mm Schmidt-Rubin)

Bullet Weight	Powder Charge	Muzzle Velocity	Remarks
130 gr.	3031 42.6 gr.	2930	Use Norma brass,
	4064 44.7 gr.	2920	.3085" bullets for
	4895 45.0 gr.	2920	all rounds
150 gr.	3031 44.0 gr.	2820	
	4064 46.0 gr.	2830	Max load
	4895 46.2 gr.	2830	Near max
165 gr.	3031 42.7 gr.	2740	
	4064 45.2 gr.	2730	
	4895 45.0 gr.	2740	

.30 M1 Carbine

Bullet Weight	Powder Charge	Muzzle Velocity	Remarks
93 gr.	2400 13.6 gr.	1987	Use CCI 400 primer.
100 gr.	H-4227 16.0 gr.	2106	
	2400 15.0 gr.	2043	
	AL-7 12.0 gr.	2108	
115 gr.	H-240 13.5 gr.	2103	Lyman G. C. 311359
	2400 13.5 gr.	2068	"
	4227 13.4 gr.	1937	"
130 gr.	H-240 10.5 gr.	1800	Lyman G. C. 311410
	2400 11.6 gr.	1731	"
	4227 12.0 gr.	1800	"
110 gr.	Factory load	1980	

.30-40 Krag

Bullet Weight	Powder Charge	Muzzle Velocity	Remarks
100 gr.	4895 47.6 gr.	3061	Also known as
	4759 16.3 gr.	1875	.30 Army, .30
	4064 46.0 gr.	3115	USA; maximum
	3031 41.0 gr.	3020	pressure is 40,000
	4198 35.3 gr.	2693	psi.
110 gr.	4350 52.5 gr.	3300	
	4320 46.0 gr.	3017	
	4895 46.8 gr.	3030	
	4064 45.4 gr.	3041	
	3031 42.0 gr.	3063	
	H-380 46.8 gr.	3029	
130 gr.	4350 52.0 gr.	2823	
	4320 45.0 gr.	2827	
	4895 46.0 gr.	2840	
	3031 40.5 gr.	2877	
	4064 44.6 gr.	2891	

(cont'd)

GOOD STARTING LOADS

Bullet Weight	Powder Charge	Muzzle Velocity	Remarks
130 gr.	BL-C(2) 41.0 gr.	2703	
	H-380 45.0 gr.	2784	
150 gr.	4350 48.3 gr.	2641	
	4320 44.0 gr.	2650	
	4895 43.3 gr.	2633	
	4064 42.6 gr.	2645	
	3031 39.0 gr.	2641	
	BL-C(2) 37.0 gr.	2348	
	H-380 43.3 gr.	2600	
165 gr.	4350 46.0 gr.	2300	
	4320 41.0 gr.	2403	
	4831 48.5 gr.	2163	
	4895 40.6 gr.	2391	
	3031 37.0 gr.	2473	
	H-380 41.0 gr.	2345	
180 gr.	4350 44.0 gr.	2205	
	4320 40.6 gr.	2241	
	4831 47.8 gr.	2173	
	4895 39.3 gr.	2292	
	3031 37.0 gr.	2281	
	H-380 40.0 gr.	2274	
200 gr.	4350 42.0 gr.	2041	
	4320 37.6 gr.	2035	
	4831 45.4 gr.	2027	
	4895 38.0 gr.	2151	
	4064 36.5 gr.	2143	
	3031 33.4 gr.	2100	
	H-380 37.0 gr.	2037	
110 gr.	2400 13.7 gr.	1537	Lyman G. C. 311316
	Unique 7.6 gr.	1241	”
	4227 15.0 gr.	1528	”
	4759 15.5 gr.	1621	”
	H-240 13.3 gr.	1561	”
125 gr.	2400 14.0 gr.	1540	Lyman G. C. 311241
	Unique 8.6 gr.	1336	”
	4227 14.5 gr.	1483	”
	4759 14.0 gr.	1386	”
	H-240 13.5 gr.	1563	”
150 gr.	2400 15.0 gr.	1481	Lyman G. C. 311464 or Lyman 311241
	Unique 6.3 gr.	1141	”
	4227 16.3 gr.	1581	”
	4759 16.3 gr.	1466	”
	H-240 15.6 gr.	1544	”
165 gr.	2400 18.7 gr.	1671	Lyman G. C. 311413 or
	Unique 11.0 gr.	1400	Lyman G. C. 311291 or
	4227 18.6 gr.	1650	Lyman G. C. 31141
	4759 17.6 gr.	1623	”
	H-240 17.4 gr.	1643	”
	4198 23.0 gr.	1475	”
180 gr.	Factory load	2470	
220 gr.	Factory load	2200	

.30-30 Winchester

Bullet Weight	Powder Charge	Muzzle Velocity	Remarks
100 gr.	4759 13.7 gr.	1763	Pressure limit is 40,000 psi. Bolt action rifles chambered for this round deliver somewhat higher velocities with slightly stiffer charges. Work up loads slowly and be sure never to fire reloads for such a rifle in a lever
	4198 32.5 gr.	2710	
	4895 38.5 gr.	2705	
	3031 38.0 gr.	2866	
	BL-C(2) 39.0 gr.	2641	
110 gr.	4350 39.7 gr.	2440	
	4064 36.4 gr.	2600	

(cont'd)

Bullet Weight	Powder Charge	Muzzle Velocity	Remarks
110 gr.	N-201 35.0 gr.	2600	action gun.
150 gr.	4895 35.4 gr.	2209	Max load
	4320 35.5 gr.	2241	
	4198 26.0 gr.	2225	
	4064 34.8 gr.	2300	
	3031 31.6 gr.	2237	
	H-380 35.5 gr.	2172	
	748 34.0 gr.	2300	
170 gr.	BL-C(2) 32.5 gr.	2155	Magnum primer
	4895 29.5 gr.	1893	
	H-380 34.6 gr.	2120	
	3031 28.6 gr.	2000	Magnum primer, near max
150 gr.	4895 28.5 gr.	1847	Lyman G. C. 311466
150 gr.	Factory load	2410	
160 gr.	Factory load	2220	
170 gr.	Factory load	2220	

.300 Savage

Bullet Weight	Powder Charge	Muzzle Velocity	Remarks
100 gr.	3031 41.0 gr.	2931	
	4064 44.5 gr.	3009	
	4198 35.3 gr.	3000	
	4759 14.1 gr.	1803	
	4895 45.7 gr.	2862	
130 gr.	BL-C(2) 41.2 gr.	2678	
	3031 40.3 gr.	2835	
	4064 44.6 gr.	2789	
	4198 35.0 gr.	2780	
	4895 45.4 gr.	2750	
	4320 45.8 gr.	2797	
	H-380 46.3 gr.	2718	
150 gr.	4350 46.6 gr.	2530	
	4320 42.6 gr.	2540	
	4895 41.0 gr.	2470	
	4064 41.4 gr.	2655	
	H-380 43.0 gr.	2482	
	BL-C(2) 38.7 gr.	2400	
165 gr.	4350 46.0 gr.	2455	
	4320 41.5 gr.	2508	
	4895 40.7 gr.	2391	
	4064 40.3 gr.	2513	
	3031 37.4 gr.	2488	
	H-380 42.5 gr.	2349	
	BL-C(2) 38.0 gr.	2300	
180 gr.	4350 44.0 gr.	2385	
	4320 40.5 gr.	2303	
	4895 39.4 gr.	2210	
	4064 39.6 gr.	2312	
	3031 36.6 gr.	2301	
	H-380 40.0 gr.	2254	
200 gr.	4350 42.0 gr.	2250	
	4320 37.0 gr.	2200	
	4895 36.3 gr.	2200	
	4064 36.2 gr.	2206	
	3031 34.0 gr.	2222	
	H-380 37.0 gr.	2065	
85 gr.	Unique 4.6 gr.	1226	Lyman G. C. 311419
	2400 16.0 gr.	2122	"
	4227 16.3 gr.	2100	"
	4759 13.6 gr.	1711	"
	H-240 15.0 gr.	2138	"
120 gr.	Unique 9.3 gr.	1962	Lyman G. C. 311465
	2400 15.4 gr.	1933	"
	4227 17.6 gr.	1847	"
	4759 11.4 gr.	1331	"
	H-240 15.0 gr.	2040	"
150 gr.	H-240 15.0 gr.	1505	Lyman G. C. 311466

(cont'd)

Bullet Weight	Powder Charge	Muzzle Velocity	Remarks
150 gr.	2400 16.0 gr.	1540	
	4759 14.5 gr.	1430	"
	4198 23.0 gr.	1832	"
	4227 16.0 gr.	1516	"
	Unique 9.5 gr.	1448	"
165 gr.	H-240 15.0 gr.	1498	Lyman G. C. 311413
	2400 16.0 gr.	1525	"
	4759 14.5 gr.	1634	"
	4198 23.6 gr.	1788	"
	4227 16.3 gr.	1518	"
	Unique 6.6 gr.	1188	"
150 gr.	Factory load	2670	
180 gr.	Factory load	2370	

.308 Winchester (7.62 NATO)

Bullet Weight	Powder Charge	Muzzle Velocity	Remarks
100 gr.	3031 44.0 gr.	3083	
	4198 35.0 gr.	2962	
	4895 44.5 gr.	2745	
	4759 16.6 gr.	1821	
	4320 52.0 gr.	2968	
	2400 24.0 gr.	2499	
	BL-C(2) 48.0 gr.	2979	
	H-380 54.0 gr.	3067	
110 gr.	4320 52.0 gr.	3129	
	4198 38.0 gr.	3100	
	4895 50.5 gr.	3112	
	4064 49.6 gr.	3200	
	3031 45.3 gr.	3101	
	H-380 52.0 gr.	3103	
	4831 49.0 gr.	2472	
	H-335 50.0 gr.	3275	
130 gr.	4320 50.0 gr.	2981	
	4064 49.0 gr.	2987	
	4198 37.4 gr.	2875	
	4895 50.7 gr.	2982	
	3031 45.6 gr.	3003	
	H-380 52.0 gr.	2991	
	H-335 49.0 gr.	3080	
150 gr.	4350 50.0 gr.	2661	
	4320 44.0 gr.	2643	
	4895 44.7 gr.	2580	
	4064 43.4 gr.	2700	
	4198 35.5 gr.	2441	
	3031 41.0 gr.	2670	
	H-380 47.0 gr.	2590	
	H-335 46.0 gr.	2783	
165 gr.	4350 48.0 gr.	2451	
	4320 42.2 gr.	2474	
	4895 42.6 gr.	2503	
	4064 41.4 gr.	2511	
	3031 38.3 gr.	2537	
	H-380 43.0 gr.	2444	
	H-335 42.5 gr.	2463	
180 gr.	4350 47.0 gr.	2383	
	4320 41.2 gr.	2378	
	4895 40.5 gr.	2303	
	4064 41.0 gr.	2350	
	3031 37.2 gr.	2361	
	H-380 44.5 gr.	2418	
	H-335 41.0 gr.	2400	
200 gr.	4350 44.5 gr.	2218	
	4320 40.2 gr.	2210	
	4831 47.1 gr.	2100	
	4895 39.0 gr.	2263	
	4064 39.0 gr.	2294	
	3031 35.3 gr.	2202	

(cont'd)

Bullet Weight	Powder Charge	Muzzle Velocity	Remarks
	H-380 41.0 gr.	2160	
110 gr.	2400 15.0 gr.	1936	Lyman G. C. 311316
	4227 17.3 gr.	1763	,,
	4759 14.0 gr.	1651	,,
	4198 18.0 gr.	1600	,,
	H-240 15.3 gr.	1926	,,
	Unique 9.3 gr.	1946	,,
150 gr.	2400 15.2 gr.	1426	Lyman G. C. 311466
	4227 16.1 gr.	1431	,,
	4759 14.3 gr.	1284	,,
	4198 23.0 gr.	1741	,,
150 gr.	H-240 15.1 gr.	1438	,,
	Unique 9.0 gr.	1388	,,
165 gr.	2400 15.1 gr.	1438	Lyman G. C. 311466 also 311413 G. C. 170 gr.
	4759 14.3 gr.	1452	,,
	4227 17.0 gr.	1520	,,
	4198 23.6 gr.	1530	,,
	H-240 15.4 gr.	1520	,,
205 gr.	2400 14.0 gr.	1402	Lyman G. C. 311467
	4759 16.0 gr.	1453	,,
	4198 22.0 gr.	1361	,,
	4227 14.6 gr.	1413	,,
	H-240 13.6 gr.	1322	,,
110 gr.	Factory load	3340	
125 gr.	Factory load	3100	
150 gr.	Factory load	2860	
180 gr.	Factory load	2610	
200 gr.	Factory load	2450	

.30-06

Bullet Weight	Powder Charge	Muzzle Velocity	Remarks
100 gr.	3031 47.0 gr.	2967	
	4198 37.8 gr.	3050	
	4759 16.0 gr.	1539	
	4895 55.4 gr.	3217	
110 gr.	4350 63.2 gr.	3251	
	4320 56.0 gr.	3206	
	4895 57.0 gr.	3251	
	4064 55.6 gr.	3247	
	3031 50.6 gr.	3249	
	BL-C(2) 52.0 gr.	3187	
	H-380 57.0 gr.	3160	
	H-335 52.0 gr.	3216	
	H-450 65.0 gr.	2931	Try Magnum primers in this caliber with H-450
130 gr.	4831 60.3 gr.	2673	
	4350 62.0 gr.	3000	
	4320 54.7 gr.	3150	
	4895 54.2 gr.	3047	
	4064 54.6 gr.	3019	
	3031 49.3 gr.	3006	
	BL-C(2) 54.0 gr.	3003	Max. load
	H-380 55.5 gr.	3116	
	H-335 55.0 gr.	3221	
	H-450 62.4 gr.	2800	CCI 250
150 gr.	4831 60.0 gr.	2739	
	4350 58.0 gr.	2889	
	4320 52.3 gr.	2887	
	4895 52.0 gr.	2900	
	4064 51.6 gr.	2862	
	3031 47.3 gr.	2817	
	H-450 63.2 gr.	2823	CCI 250
	H-380 53.6 gr.	2912	
	4831 59.6 gr.	2773	
165 gr.	4350 57.0 gr.	2830	

(cont'd)

GOOD STARTING LOADS

Bullet Weight	Powder Charge	Muzzle Velocity	Remarks
165 gr.	4320 50.6 gr.	2831	
	4831 61.5 gr.	2698	
	4895 50.3 gr.	2776	
	4064 48.3 gr.	2802	
	3031 45.0 gr.	2749	
	H-450 61.6 gr.	2763	CCI 250
	H-380 50.5 gr.	2676	
	H-335 48.0 gr.	2739	
180 gr.	4350 53.6 gr.	2581	
	4320 48.2 gr.	2623	
	4831 58.3 gr.	2572	
	4895 48.0 gr.	2640	
	4064 47.3 gr.	2603	
	3031 44.0 gr.	2560	
	H-450 59.6 gr.	2613	CCI 250
	H-335 46.0 gr.	2586	
	H-380 49.0 gr.	2630	
	H-570 58.0 gr.	2054	
	5010 59.0 gr.	2100	
200 gr.	4350 50.6 gr.	2440	
	4320 45.4 gr.	2431	
	4831 56.0 gr.	2415	
	4895 45.5 gr.	2432	
	4064 46.0 gr.	2500	
	3031 41.0 gr.	2316	
	5010 55.4 gr.	——	
	H-450 56.0 gr.	2460	CCI 250
	H-570 57.0 gr.	2123	
	H-380 46.5 gr.	2417	
	H-870 62.0 gr.	2311	
	H-335 43.6 gr.	2300	
220 gr.	4350 51.0 gr.	2418	
	4320 47.3 gr.	2307	
	5010 60.0 gr.	2130	
	H-570 57.0 gr.	2013	
	4831 55.0 gr.	2422	
	H-450 55.0 gr.	2282	CCI 250
150 gr.	4198 23.4 gr.	1817	Lyman G. C. 311440 or Lyman 311466.
	4227 17.3 gr.	1862	For #311241 use slightly reduced charges for lower velocities.
	H-240 19.6 gr.	1693	
	2400 23.6 gr.	1962	
165 gr.	4198 23.0 gr.	1581	Lyman G. C. 311413 Also try #311375 (170 gr.).
	4227 14.6 gr.	1670	
	H-240 19.4 gr.	1627	
	2400 23.5 gr.	1936	
175 gr.	4198 23.0 gr.	1580	Lyman G. C. 311329 or G. C. 311467, or plain base 31141.
	4227 15.0 gr.	1647	”
	H-240 19.2 gr.	1652	”
	2400 23.3 gr.	1965	
210 gr.	4198 24.3 gr.	1467	Lyman G. C. 311284 Try #311299 G. C. (205 gr.).
	4227 17.5 gr.	1351	”
	H-240 19.3 gr.	1427	”
	2400 23.6 gr.	1670	
110 gr.	Factory load	3420	
125 gr.	Factory load	3200	
150 gr.	Factory load	2970	
180 gr.	Factory load	2700	
220 gr.	Factory load	2410	

Bullet Weight	Powder Charge	Muzzle Velocity	Remarks
7.62 x 39mm			
130 gr.	4198 24.8 gr.	2420	Custom bolt action rifle.
	N-200 27.5 gr.	2420	Use 6.5x54 M-S brass.
	3031 27.0 gr.	2260	Max load
150 gr.	4198 23.5 gr.	2200	
	N-200 27.8 gr.	2300	
7.62 Russian (7.62 x 54R)			
130 gr.	3031 49.0 gr.	3000	Federal 210 primers used in all loads
	4895 50.0 gr.	2960	
	4064 49.5 gr.	2950	
150 gr.	3031 43.9 gr.	2750	
	4895 48.7 gr.	2830	
	4064 48.8 gr.	2810	Near max
165 gr.	3031 43.0 gr.	2600	Near max
	4895 48.0 gr.	2700	Near max
	4064 45.6 gr.	2600	Near max
180 gr.	3031 44.3 gr.	2650	
	4895 46.7 gr.	2620	
	4320 49.5 gr.	2720	
220 gr.	H-380 48.3 gr.	2460	
	760 51.3 gr.	2430	
	N-204 52.0 gr.	2440	
.30-338 (.30 Belted Newton)			
150 gr.	4350 74.0 gr.	3300	Use .338 brass necked down to .30 cal.
180 gr.	4831 72.0 gr.	3040	
.300 Apex Magnum			
125 gr.	4895 69.0 gr.	3650	Apex Rifle Co. data
150 gr.	4895 66.0 gr.	3341	
180 gr.	4350 69.0 gr.	3140	
220 gr.	4350 68.0 gr.	2885	
	4831 69.0 gr.	2780	
.300 H&H Magnum			
110 gr.	4350 72.8 gr.	3541	
	4320 63.4 gr.	3537	
	4064 61.6 gr.	3566	
	4831 77.0 gr.	3486	
	4895 62.5 gr.	3550	
	3031 57.4 gr.	3522	
	H-380 61.0 gr.	3379	
130 gr.	4350 70.4 gr.	3341	
	4320 62.5 gr.	3339	
	4064 60.8 gr.	3333	
	4831 75.3 gr.	3164	
	4895 61.6 gr.	3310	
	3031 57.7 gr.	3273	
	H-380 60.3 gr.	3221	
	H-450 71.0 gr.	—	
150 gr.	4350 67.4 gr.	3123	
	4320 58.2 gr.	3003	

(cont'd)

GOOD STARTING LOADS

Bullet Weight	Powder Charge	Muzzle Velocity	Remarks
150 gr.	4064 56.3 gr.	3027	
	4831 73.0 gr.	3100	
	4895 57.8 gr.	3080	
	3031 54.0 gr.	3050	
165 gr.	4350 64.6 gr.	3000	
	4320 56.4 gr.	2888	
	4064 54.6 gr.	2900	
	4831 70.0 gr.	3000	
	4895 55.7 gr.	2917	
	3031 51.5 gr.	2845	
180 gr.	4350 63.0 gr.	2900	
	4320 54.0 gr.	2748	
	4831 67.4 gr.	2879	
	4895 53.6 gr.	2761	
	4064 53.7 gr.	2751	
	5010 82.0 gr.	2843	
200 gr.	4350 60.0 gr.	2650	
	4320 52.5 gr.	2618	
	4831 65.3 gr.	2739	
	4895 52.0 gr.	2600	
	4064 51.3 gr.	2585	
	5010 79.0 gr.	2670	
150 gr.	2400 23.8 gr.	1900	Lyman G. C. 311440
	4198 23.5 gr.	1735	”
	4759 17.3 gr.	1482	”
	4227 19.6 gr.	1717	”
175 gr.	2400 24.0 gr.	1600	Lyman G. C. 31141; also try #'s 311467 G. C. and 311329 G. C.
	4198 23.3 gr.	1581	
	4759 21.4 gr.	1551	”
	4227 24.8 gr.	1849	”
205 gr.	2400 26.0 gr.	1445	Lyman G. C. 311299
	4198 24.6 gr.	1483	”
	4759 22.5 gr.	1515	”
	4227 24.0 gr.	1665	
150 gr.	Factory load	3190	
180 gr.	Factory load	2920	
220 gr.	Factory load	2620	

.300 Weatherby Magnum

Bullet Weight	Powder Charge	Muzzle Velocity	Remarks
130 gr.	4350 82.5 gr.	3636	
	4320 73.7 gr.	3500	
	4064 70.2 gr.	3465	
	4831 89.0 gr.	3503	
	4895 72.4 gr.	3500	
	3031 66.4 gr.	3425	
150 gr.	4350 80.0 gr.	3320	
	4320 71.0 gr.	3300	
	4064 68.6 gr.	3220	
	4831 86.0 gr.	3440	
	4895 70.5 gr.	3250	
	3031 64.0 gr.	3100	
165 gr.	4350 77.5 gr.	3200	
	4320 68.3 gr.	3100	
	4064 66.8 gr.	3100	
	4831 83.5 gr.	3200	
	4895 68.6 gr.	3110	
	3031 62.5 gr.	3020	
180 gr.	4350 76.0 gr.	3050	
	4320 67.0 gr.	3000	
	4831 80.5 gr.	3065	
	4895 67.3 gr.	3000	
	4064 65.0 gr.	2900	
	5010 94.0 gr.	2910	
200 gr.	4350 73.4 gr.	2950	

(cont'd)

Bullet Weight	Powder Charge	Muzzle Velocity	Remarks
200 gr.	4320 64.6 gr.	2865	
	4831 77.4 gr.	2920	
	4895 63.0 gr.	2740	
	4064 64.0 gr.	2800	
	5010 91.5 gr.	2860	
	H-380 65.0 gr.	2630	
	H-570 91.5 gr.	2900	
	H-870 95.0 gr.	2940	
150 gr.	Factory load	3545	
180 gr.	Factory load	3245	

.300 Winchester Magnum

Bullet Weight	Powder Charge	Muzzle Velocity	Remarks
130 gr.	4350 80.5 gr.	3540	Use magnum primers for this caliber.
	4320 67.6 gr.	3420	
	4831 86.0 gr.	3400	
	4895 68.4 gr.	3400	
	4064 68.2 gr.	3320	
	3031 64.0 gr.	3310	
150 gr.	4350 76.6 gr.	3380	
	4320 64.0 gr.	3200	
	4831 84.6 gr.	3352	
	4895 63.0 gr.	3240	
	4064 62.5 gr.	3215	
	3031 58.0 gr.	3123	
	H-450 78.7 gr.	3100	
165 gr.	4350 74.4 gr.	3210	
	4320 62.0 gr.	3100	
	4831 81.6 gr.	3229	
	4895 60.7 gr.	3100	
	4064 60.2 gr.	3085	
	3031 56.1 gr.	2920	
	H 450 75.6 gr.	3100	
	N 205 77.0 gr.	3170	
180 gr.	4350 72.2 gr.	3100	
	4320 59.4 gr.	2900	
	4831 78.6 gr.	3080	
	4895 59.3 gr.	2926	
	4064 59.5 gr.	2920	
	3031 56.0 gr.	2865	
	H-450 75.6 gr.	2900	
	N 205 75.0 gr.	3070	
200 gr.	4350 70.0 gr.	2905	
	4320 59.4 gr.	2708	
	4831 76.7 gr.	2900	
	4895 59.5 gr.	2700	
	4064 59.0 gr.	2683	
	H-450 72.0 gr.	2600	
220 gr.	4895 56.5 gr.	2510	
	4350 65.0 gr.	2550	
	4831 68.0 gr.	2586	
	H-450 70.0 gr.	2592	
	H-870 82.0 gr.	2576	
150 gr.	Factory load	3400	
180 gr.	Factory load	3070	

.308 Norma Magnum

Bullet Weight	Powder Charge	Muzzle Velocity	Remarks
130 gr.	4350 75.5 gr.	3400	
	4320 64.0 gr.	3350	
	4831 82.0 gr.	3400	
	4895 64.4 gr.	3300	
	4064 63.5 gr.	3400	
	3031 59.6 gr.	3310	
	H-450 80.6 gr.	3375	CCT 250 primer
150 gr.	4350 72.4 gr.	3290	
	4320 62.6 gr.	3200	

(cont'd)

Bullet Weight	Powder Charge	Muzzle Velocity	Remarks
150 gr.	4831 78.6 gr.	3250	
	4895 63.0 gr.	3150	
	4064 62.5 gr.	3215	
	3031 56.0 gr.	3050	
	H-450 77.0 gr.	3275	CCT 250 primer
165 gr.	4350 70.0 gr.	3100	
	4320 60.2 gr.	3020	
	4831 76.4 gr.	3125	
	4895 60.6 gr.	3000	
	4064 59.8 gr.	3045	
	3031 55.4 gr.	2950	
180 gr.	4350 69.0 gr.	3020	
	4320 57.7 gr.	2847	
	4831 74.5 gr.	3000	
	4895 56.8 gr.	2760	
	4064 56.1 gr.	2800	
	3031 52.4 gr.	2755	
	N 204 72.0 gr.	3114	Norma powder
	H-450 72.6 gr.	3000	CCT 250 primer
200 gr.	4350 67.0 gr.	2888	
	4320 56.6 gr.	2750	
	4831 72.5 gr.	2875	
	4895 55.4 gr.	2720	
	4064 55.5 gr.	2740	
	H-570 83.0 gr.	2750	
	H-450 70.5 gr.	2820	CCT 250 primer
180 gr.	Factory load	3100	

7.65 Mauser (7.65 x 53)

Bullet Weight	Powder Charge	Muzzle Velocity	Remarks
150 gr.	3031 40.8 gr.	2700	The M1891 cannot handle the same pressures as the M98. Hence, use caution when developing loads. Use .312" bullets; Federal 210 primers
	4895 43.0 gr.	2720	
	4064 43.6 gr.	2700	
180 gr.	3031 41.0 gr.	2490	Near max
	4895 43.0 gr.	2500	Near max
	4064 42.9 gr.	2490	

.303 British

Bullet Weight	Powder Charge	Muzzle Velocity	Remarks
150 gr.	3031 40.6 gr.	2610	Norma brass; use .311" bullets, Federal 210 primers
	4064 43.0 gr.	2540	Max load
	4895 41.5 gr.	2550	
174 gr.	3031 36.4 gr.	2340	
	4064 40.0 gr.	2400	
	4895 40.4 gr.	2400	
180 gr.	3031 38.0 gr.	2300	
	4064 39.5 gr.	2200	
	4895 40.0 gr.	2360	Max load

7.7 Japanese (7.7 Arisaka — 7.7 x 58mm)

Bullet Weight	Powder Charge	Muzzle Velocity	Remarks
150 gr.	3031 42.0 gr.	2500	Use .311" bullets
	4895 44.3 gr.	2600	
	4350 52.6 gr.	2500	
180 gr.	3031 40.0 gr.	2310	Max load
	4895 40.3 gr.	2240	
	4350 48.5 gr.	2280	

Bullet Weight	Powder Charge	Muzzle Velocity	Remarks
.32 Win. Special and .32 Rem.			
170 gr.	4350 35.0 gr.	1860	
	4320 34.5 gr.	2010	
	4895 34.0 gr.	2040	
	4759 23.2 gr.	2000	
	4198 24.2 gr.	2006	
	4064 33.5 gr.	2001	
	3031 31.0 gr.	2108	
135 gr.	4759 13.0 gr.	1449	Lyman G. C. 321427 NOTE: Lyman suggests sizing all .32 Win. Spl. bullets to .321.
	4227 14.5 gr.	1701	,,
	2400 13.7 gr.	1680	,,
	Unique 8.3 gr.	1526	,,
	H-240 15.0 gr.	1842	
160 gr.	3031 19.0 gr.	1487	Lyman G. C. 321317
	4198 18.3 gr.	1500	,,
	4759 16.0 gr.	1750	,,
	4227 17.3 gr.	1781	,,
	2400 17.0 gr.	1812	,,
	Unique 9.6 gr.	1326	,,
	H-240 17.0 gr.	1881	
180 gr.	3031 22.0 gr.	1462	Lyman G. C. 321297
	4198 18.3 gr.	1471	,,
	4759 13.6 gr.	1511	,,
	4227 17.3 gr.	1748	,,
	2400 13.4 gr.	1467	,,
	Unique 9.6 gr.	1300	,,
	H-240 16.7 gr.	1683	,,
170 gr.	Factory load (Rem.)	2220	
170 gr.	Factory load (Win.)	2280	
8 mm Mauser (8 x 57)			
125 gr.	4895 54.0 gr.	2953	Check your rifle for bore diameter—these data for .323 barrels! Stoeger Arms Corp. and Norma carry .318 bullets.
	4320 53.6 gr.	2963	
	4198 40.3 gr.	3000	
	4064 52.5 gr.	2963	
	3031 48.0 gr.	3047	
150 gr.	4350 56.3 gr.	2675	
	4320 51.2 gr.	2736	
	4895 51.5 gr.	2726	
	4198 40.0 gr.	2800	
	4064 50.5 gr.	2835	
	3031 46.7 gr.	2842	
170 gr.	4350 55.0 gr.	2610	
	4320 49.5 gr.	2553	
	4064 47.6 gr.	2561	
	4895 48.1 gr.	2560	
	3031 45.0 gr.	2706	
225 gr.	4350 53.5 gr.	2418	
	4320 46.0 gr.	2370	
	4831 55.0 gr.	2300	
	4895 46.3 gr.	2380	
	4064 45.6 gr.	2310	
	3031 43.0 gr.	2298	
135 gr.	H-240 15.2 gr.	1541	Lyman G. C. 321427
	4227 16.5 gr.	1485	,,
	4759 16.1 gr.	1668	,,

(cont'd)

Bullet Weight	Powder Charge	Muzzle Velocity	Remarks
160 gr.	4198 24.0 gr.	1583	Lyman G. C. 323470
	4759 18.0 gr.	1670	
	H-240 17.6 gr.	1762	
	4227 14.5 gr.	1550	
180 gr.	3031 24.0 gr.	1569	Lyman G. C. 323366 or 323481
	4198 22.6 gr.	1549	”
	4759 17.0 gr.	1600	”
	4227 15.6 gr.	1420	”
	2400 18.0 gr.	1560	”
	H-240 18.0 gr.	1600	”
210 gr.	3031 24.0 gr.	1475	Lyman G. C. 323471
	4198 24.0 gr.	1600	”
	4759 18.2 gr.	1575	”
	4227 16.2 gr.	1351	”
170 gr.	Factory load (Federal)	2570	

8mm/06

Bullet Weight	Powder Charge	Muzzle Velocity	Remarks
150 gr.	4350 57.6 gr.	2750	An excellent wildcat which ballistically is quite similar to the outstanding 8x64S Brenneke. Only rechambering and rethroating of a sound 8x57 military rifle is needed.
	4064 52.7 gr.	2980	
	4320 51.0 gr.	2830	
	4895 49.5 gr.	2900	
170 gr.	4350 57.5 gr.	2710	
	4064 51.6 gr.	2840	
	4320 51.0 gr.	2710	
	4895 48.0 gr.	2730	Max load
225 gr.	4350 52.9 gr.	2400	
	4064 44.7 gr.	2340	
	4831 54.1 gr.	2420	
	4895 39.6 gr.	2220	

8mm/338 Magnum

Bullet Weight	Powder Charge	Muzzle Velocity	Remarks
			Only relatively simple gunsmithing on a military 8mm rifle is needed to make this "poor man's magnum." Use .323" bullets.
150 gr.	4064 64.3 gr.	3120	
	H-380 68.6 gr.	3100	Magnum primer
	4320 65.5 gr.	3100	
170 gr.	4831 72.8 gr.	2930	Near max
	4064 63.6 gr.	2920	
	4350 70.6 gr.	2930	Near max
225 gr.	4831 65.6 gr.	2510	
	N-205 68.3 gr.	2500	
	4350 63.6 gr.	2470	

.30-333 O.K.H.

Bullet Weight	Powder Charge	Muzzle Velocity	Remarks
275 gr.	4831 57.0 gr.	2314	Odd-ball wildcat that can only be loaded with .333 bullets. Rifle bore diameter .325, groove diameter .333. (Speer data)
	4350 53.0 gr.	2250	
	4320 45.0 gr.	2154	
	4895 45.0 gr.	2202	
	4064 44.0 gr.	2141	

Bullet Weight	Powder Charge	Muzzle Velocity	Remarks
.338-06			
250 gr.	4831 62.0 gr.	—	Author's favorite big game wildcat. Fireform '06 brass in rifle, use .338 bullets
	4064 51.0 gr.	—	
	4320 55.0 gr.	2400	estimated
265 gr.	4320 52.0 gr.	2310	
275 gr.	4831 58.0 gr.	2357	
.338 Win. Mag.			
200 gr.	4350 72.0 gr.	2960	
	4320 60.5 gr.	2800	
	4831 77.3 gr.	2965	
	4895 61.0 gr.	2800	
	4064 59.4 gr.	2865	
	3031 54.0 gr.	2763	
275 gr.	4350 66.3 gr.	2500	
	4320 58.0 gr.	2400	
	4895 57.3 gr.	2365	
	4831 72.4 gr.	2530	
	4064 57.0 gr.	2400	
	4895 51.0 gr.	—	Reduced load
200 gr.	3031 30.0 gr.	1892	Lyman G. C. 338320
	4198 30.0 gr.	2000	”
	4759 24.0 gr.	1593	”
	4227 24.0 gr.	1589	”
250 gr.	3031 33.5 gr.	1879	Lyman G. C. 33889; for game, try this bullet with H.P.
	4198 31.2 gr.	1880	
	4759 23.4 gr.	1525	
	4227 23.0 gr.	1570	
200 gr.	Factory load	3000	
250 gr.	Factory load	2700	
300 gr.	Factory load	2450	
.340 Weatherby Magnum			
200 gr.	4350 83.0 gr.	3175	
250 gr.	4350 77.0 gr.	2785	
275 gr.	4350 73.0 gr.	2741	
300 gr.	4350 66.0 gr.	2600	
250 gr.	Factory load	2850	
.35 Rem.			
180 gr.	4320 42.5 gr.	2160	
	4198 33.6 gr.	2150	
	4064 41.4 gr.	2167	
	4895 41.2 gr.	2130	
	H-380 44.0 gr.	2100	
	3031 39.0 gr.	2222	
200 gr.	3031 36.5 gr.	2117	
	4198 27.0 gr.	1947	
	4895 38.0 gr.	2035	
220 gr.	4320 38.0 gr.	1901	
	4198 26.0 gr.	1667	
	4895 36.0 gr.	1841	
	4064 37.0 gr.	1840	
	3031 33.5 gr.	1800	
200 gr.	3031 29.8 gr.	1631	Lyman G. C. 358315
	4198 23.6 gr.	1700	”
	4759 14.3 gr.	1320	”
	4227 17.5 gr.	1600	”

(cont'd)

Bullet Weight	Powder Charge	Muzzle Velocity	Remarks
150 gr.	Factory load	2400	
200 gr.	Factory load	2100	

.350 Rem. Mag.

Bullet Weight	Powder Charge	Muzzle Velocity	Remarks
			With the obsolete short actions — M600 & M660 — bullets have to be seated deep so that rounds will feed from magazine. With these actions, use round or flat nose bullets. Pistol bullet loads can be used for plinking, small game and some varmint shooting.
158-160 gr. revolver bullets	Unique 17.0 gr.	---	Light load
	4064 54.0 gr.	---	Light load
180 gr.	4320 61.0 gr.	2760	Max load
	4895 59.4 gr.	2880	
	3031 57.5 gr.	2850	
	4064 60.0 gr.	2780	
200 gr.	4198 46.5 gr.	2540	Near max
	4320 60.0 gr.	2710	Near max
	3031 58.5 gr.	2725	Hot!
	N-201 55.0 gr.	2547	
220 gr.	4320 57.8 gr.	2500	
	4064 58.0 gr.	2630	Max load
	4895 56.0 gr.	2600	
	3031 55.8 gr.	2660	
250 gr.	4064 54.0 gr.	2320	
	4895 52.8 gr.	2330	Near max
	4198 44.1 gr.	2200	Max load
	3031 52.5 gr.	2410	Hot!
	4320 56.0 gr.	2456	Hot!
	N-201 50.0 gr.	2279	
275 gr.	N-201 48.2 gr.	2113	
200 gr.	Factory load	2725	
250 gr.	Factory load	2410	

.358 Win.

Bullet Weight	Powder Charge	Muzzle Velocity	Remarks
180 gr.	4064 49.0 gr.	2522	
	4198 41.0 gr.	2583	
	4320 51.0 gr.	2527	
	4895 51.2 gr.	2506	
	3031 48.0 gr.	2578	
200 gr.	4064 48.0 gr.	———	
	4320 50.0 gr.	2433	
	4895 49.0 gr.	2463	
220 gr.	4064 47.8 gr.	2431	
	4198 39.2 gr.	2403	
	4320 49.5 gr.	2437	
	4895 48.5 gr.	2400	
	3031 46.0 gr.	2414	
250 gr.	4064 45.0 gr.	2303	
	4198 36.3 gr.	2216	
	4320 46.0 gr.	2289	
	4350 45.0 gr.	1923	
	4895 46.0 gr.	2275	
	3031 43.2 gr.	2312	
	BL-C(2) 43.0 gr.	2241	

(cont'd)

Bullet Weight	Powder Charge	Muzzle Velocity	Remarks
200 gr.	4198 23.0 gr.	1575	Lyman G. C. 358315
	4759 21.2 gr.	1863	”
	4227 18.0 gr.	1520	”
250 gr.	3031 28.0 gr.	1463	Lyman G. C. 358318
	4198 23.2 gr.	1359	”
	4759 21.4 gr.	1766	”
	4227 20.0 gr.	1535	”
200 gr.	Factory load	2530	
250 gr.	Factory load	2250	

.358 Norma Magnum

Bullet Weight	Powder Charge	Muzzle Velocity	Remarks
180 gr.	3031 67.2 gr.	3113	
	4064 76.0 gr.	3342	
	4320 77.6 gr.	3290	
	4350 81.3 gr.	3000	
	4895 76.2 gr.	3201	
	H-380 77.0 gr.	3112	
220 gr.	3031 60.0 gr.	2800	
	4064 66.3 gr.	2875	
	4320 67.0 gr.	2864	
	4350 78.4 gr.	2893	
	4831 81.0 gr.	2704	
	4895 67.3 gr.	2880	
	H-380 67.5 gr.	2740	
250 gr.	3031 60.0 gr.	2790	
	4064 66.5 gr.	2859	
	4320 67.4 gr.	2850	
	4350 79.0 gr.	2888	
	4831 81.4 gr.	2700	
	4895 67.3 gr.	2853	
	H-380 67.0 gr.	2711	
250 gr.	Factory load	2790	

.375 H&H Mag.

Bullet Weight	Powder Charge	Muzzle Velocity	Remarks
235 gr.	4350 82.0 gr.	2755	
	4064 72.6 gr.	2888	
	4831 87.5 gr.	2728	
285 gr.	4320 71.5 gr.	2610	
	4350 82.3 gr.	2620	
	4064 70.0 gr.	2625	
	4831 81.6 gr.	2400	
	4895 71.6 gr.	2560	
300 gr.	4350 73.0 gr.	2441	
	4064 61.4 gr.	2330	
250 gr.	4198 23.0 gr.	1402	Lyman 375248
	4759 19.3 gr.	1269	”
	3031 40.6 gr.	1858	Lyman G. C. 375449
	4198 30.2 gr.	1650	”
270 gr.	Factory load	2740	
300 gr.	Factory load	2550	

.378 Weatherby Magnum

Bullet Weight	Powder Charge	Muzzle Velocity	Remarks
235 gr.	4064 83.0 gr.	2980	
	4895 79.6 gr.	2871	
	H-380 76.3 gr.	——	
300 gr.	4064 80.5 gr.	——	
	4895 74.2 gr.	——	
	H-380 74.0 gr.	——	
270 gr.	Factory load	3180	
300 gr.	Factory load	2925	

GOOD STARTING LOADS

Bullet Weight	Powder Charge	Muzzle Velocity	Remarks
.444 Marlin			
240 gr.	4198 49.0 gr.	2527	
240 gr.	Factory load	2400	
.44 Rem. Magnum			
225 gr.	4227 22.6 gr.	1619	These loads for
	2400 21.0 gr.	1623	rifles only.
240 gr.	4227 21.6 gr.	1558	
	2400 20.5 gr.	1600	
240 gr.	Factory load	1850	

.44-40 Winchester (.44 WCF)

Special care is essential in load development for this caliber since action strength varies a great deal between the various models. So, the M92 Winchester, Marlin's M94, Navy Arms import and the Euroarms rifle can withstand considerably higher pressures than the M73 Winchester action. Some .44-40 rifles were designed for black powder loads and special care in working up loads for such a rifle is essential.

Bullet Weight	Powder Charge	Muzzle Velocity	Remarks
140 gr.	2400 27.0-30.0 gr.	---	These loads were
	Unique 12.0-14.0 gr.	---	developed for the new
200 gr.	H-4227 15.0-18.0 gr.	---	Navy Arms replica of the
	H-110 15.0-17.6 gr.	---	Win. M73 lever action
	2400 25.0-27.0 gr.	---	rifle
	Unique 10.0-11.5 gr.	---	
210 gr.	Unique 9.0 gr.	---	Cast bullet, plain base

.45-70

An overwhelming variety of .45-70 rifles have become available in the past few years. Some rifles, such as the Ruger single-shot and the Mauser bolt-action guns, are capable of handling hotter loads than Springfield trapdoor or Winchester M86 rifles in good condition. As with the .44-40, work up loads slowly and carefully. Older guns should be checked by a competent gunsmith for soundness.

Loads for Springfield and M86 rifles

Bullet Weight	Powder Charge	Muzzle Velocity	Remarks
300 gr.	4198 31.0-33.0 gr.	---	
400 gr.	4895 39.0-50.0 gr.	---	
	4895 48.0-52.7 gr.	---	For Marlin 1895
	4198 28.0-30.0 gr.	---	
	4198 34.0-37.0 gr.	---	For Marlin 1895
	4064 52.0-55.8 gr.	---	For Marlin 1895
500 gr.	4198 25.0-27.7 gr.	---	
	H-4227 26.0-27.4 gr.	---	For M86

Bullet Weight	Powder Charge	Muzzle Velocity	Remarks

Loads for Ruger and Mauser rifles

300 gr.	4227 46.5-50.1 gr.	---	
	4198 52.0-54.3 gr.	---	
400 gr.	4064 60.0-63.8 gr.	---	
	3031 54.6-58.1 gr.	---	
500 gr.	3031 50.0-53.0 gr.	---	
	4198 45.0-47.5 gr.	---	

.458 Win. Magnum

500 gr.	3031 70.0 gr.	2166	Custom rifle
FMJ	83.0 gr.	---	
	4831 75.0 gr.	2146	
510 gr.	Factory load	2130	

GOOD STARTING LOADS

Table A
COMPARISON OF .30 CALIBER MAGNUM BALLISTICS

Cartridge & bullet weight	MV	V100	V200	V300	ME	E100	E200	E300
.300 Weatherby Mag., 180 gr.	3245	2960	2705	2475	4201	3501	2925	2448
.300 Win. Mag., 180 gr.	3070	2850	2640	2440	3770	3250	2790	2380
.308 Norma Mag., 180 gr.	3100	2881	2668	2464	3842	3318	2846	2427

Table B

U.S. RIM-FIRE PISTOL AND REVOLVER CARTRIDGES

Cartridge	Wt. Grs.	Barrel Length	Muzzle Velocity Ft. Per Sec.	Muzzle Energy Ft. Lbs.
22 Short High Velocity	29	6"	1035	69
22 Short Standard Velocity	29	6"	865	48
22 Long High Velocity	29	6"	1095	77
22 Long Rifle High Velocity	40	6"	1125	112
22 Long Rifle Standard Vel. & Match	40	6"	950	80
22 W.R.F. Magnum	40	6-1/2"	1550	210
22 Super Match for Pistol	29	6-3/4"	1020	67

Table C

U.S. CENTER-FIRE PISTOL AND REVOLVER CARTRIDGES

Cartridge	Wt. Grs.	Bullet	Style	Barrel Length	Muzzle Velocity Ft. Per Sec.	Muzzle Energy Ft. Lbs.	Penetration ⅞" Soft Pine Boards At 15 Ft.
22 Rem. Jet Magnum	40	S.P.		8⅜"	2460	535	
221 Fireball	50	S.P.		10½"	2650	780	
256 Win. Magnum	60	S.P.		8½"	2350	735	
25 Automatic	50	F.M.C.		2"	810	73	3
38 Automatic	130		F.M.C.	4½"	1040	312	9
For all 38 Automatic Pistols							
380 Automatic	95		F.M.C.	3¾"	955	192	5.5
38-40 Winchester	180		S.P.	5"	775	380	6
41 Long Colt	200	Lubaloy		6"	730	231	3
41 Magnum	210	Lead	Gas Ch.	6"	986	450	
41 Magnum	210		S.P.	6"	1342	836	
44 Magnum	240	Lubaloy			1450		
44 Magnum***	240	Lead	Gas Ch.	6"	1570	1313	
44 Smith & Wesson Special	246		Lead	6½"	755	311	4
44-40 Winchester	200		S.P.	7½"	975	422	6
45 Colt	255		Lead	5½"	855	405	6
45 Automatic	230		F.M.C.	5"	850	369	6
45 Automatic Match Cl. Cut.	210		Lead	5"	710	235	
45 Automatic Metal Piercing	230		F.M.C.	5"	945	456	11
45 Automatic	173		Spec.	5"	1140	500	
45 Automatic	185		F.M.C.	5"	875	314	
45 Auto Rim	230		Lead	5½"	805	331	6

*** Mid-range trajectory of .6 inch at 50 yds., 2.3 inches at 100 yds.

Table D

U.S. CENTER-FIRE CARTRIDGES
(Although made abroad, Weatherby ammunition is included here for the convenience of comparison)

Cartridge	Wt. Grs.	Velocity—Ft. Per Sec. Muzzle	100 Yds.	200 Yds.	300 Yds.	Energy—Ft. Lbs. Muzzle	100 Yds.	200 Yds.	300 Yds.	Mid-Range Trajectory 100 Yds.	200 Yds.	300 Yds.
218 Bee	46	2860	2160	1610	1200	835	475	265	145	0.7	3.8	11.5
219 Zipper	56	3110	2440	1940	1550	1200	740	465	300	0.6	2.9	8.3
22 Jet Center-fire Magnum	40	2460	1780	1280	1020	535	280	150	90	1.0	5.7	18.0
22 Hornet	45	2690	2030	1510	1150	720	410	230	130	0.8	4.3	13.0
22 Hornet	46	2690	2030	1510	1150	740	420	235	135	0.8	4.3	13.0
220 Swift	48	4110	3490	2930	2440	1800	1300	915	635	0.3	1.4	3.8
222 Remington	50	3200	2660	2170	1750	1140	785	520	340	0.5	2.5	7.0
222 Remington Magnum	55	3300	2800	2340	1930	1330	955	670	455	0.5	2.3	6.1
223 (5.56 mm)	55	3300	2800	2340	1930	1330	955	670	455	0.5	2.3	6.1
22-250 Rem.	55	3760	3230	2745	2305	1730	1275	920	650	0.4	1.7	4.5
224 Weatherby Magnum	50	3800	3200	2660	2170	1604	1135	786	523	0.4	1.7	4.7
225 Winchester	55	3650	3140	2680	2270	1630	1200	875	630	0.4	1.8	4.8
6 mm Remington	100	3190	2920	2660	2420	2260	1890	1570	1300	1.6	—	6.5
243 Winchester	80	3500	3080	2720	2410	2180	1690	1320	1030	0.4	1.8	4.7
243 Winchester	100	3070	2790	2540	2320	2090	1730	1430	1190	0.5	2.2	5.5
244 Remington Hi-Speed	75	3500	3070	2660	2290	2040	1570	1180	875	0.4	1.9	4.9
244 Remington Hi-Speed	90	3200	2850	2530	2230	2050	1630	1200	995	0.5	2.1	5.5
25-20 Winchester High Velocity	60	2250	1660	1240	1030	675	365	205	140	1.2	6.3	21.0
25-20 Winchester	86	1460	1180	1030	940	405	265	200	170	2.6	12.5	32.0

CARTRIDGE SPECIFICATIONS

Cartridge	Wt. Grs.	Velocity—Ft. Per Sec. Muzzle 100 Yds. 200 Yds. 300 Yds.	Energy—Ft. Lbs. Muzzle 100 Yds. 200 Yds. 300 Yds.	Mid-Range. Trajectory 100 Yds. 200 Yds. 300 Yds.
25-35 Winchester	117	2300 1910 1600 1340	1370 945 665 465	1.0 4.6 12.5
250 Savage	87	3030 2660 2330 2060	1770 1370 1050 820	0.6 2.5 6.4
250 Savage	100	2820 2410 2070 1770	1760 1290 950 695	0.6 3.0 7.7
256 Win. Mag.	60	2800 2070 1570 1220	1040 570 330 200	0.8 4.0 12.0
257 Roberts	87	3200 2840 2500 2190	1980 1560 1210 925	0.5 2.2 5.7
257 Roberts	100	2900 2540 2210 1920	1870 1430 1080 820	0.6 2.7 7.0
257 Roberts	117	2650 2280 1950 1690	1820 1350 985 740	0.7 3.4 8.8
257 Weatherby Magnum	87	3825 3290 2835 2450	2828 2087 1553 1160	0.3 1.6 4.4
257 Weatherby Magnum	100	3555 3150 2815 2500	2802 2199 1760 1388	0.4 1.7 4.4
257 Weatherby Magnum	117	3300 2900 2550 2250	2824 2184 1689 1315	0.4 2.4 6.8
6.5 Jap	139	2430 2280 2130 1990	1815 1600 1405 1225	0.6 2.9 7.7
6.5 Jap	156	2070 1870 1690 1530	1475 1210 990 810	0.6 4.4 11.9
6.5 x 54 MS	77	3120 2730 2370 2040	1660 1275 960 710	0.1 1.9 5.6
6.5 x 54 MS	139	2580 2420 2270 2120	2040 1805 1590 1390	0.2 2.5 6.9
6.5 x 54 MS	156	2460 2240 2030 1840	2995 1735 1430 1170	0.3 3.0 8.2
6.5 x 55	77	3120 2730 2370 2040	1660 1275 960 710	0.1 1.9 5.6
6.5 x 55	93	3150 2710 2290 1920	2035 1500 1080 760	0.1 1.9 6.0
6.5 x 55	139	2790 2630 2470 2320	2395 2130 1880 1650	0.1 2.0 5.6
6.5 x 55	156	2490 2270 2060 1870	2150 1785 1470 1205	0.3 2.9 7.9
264 Winchester Magnum	100	3700 3260 2880 2550	3040 2360 1840 1440	0.4 1.6 4.2
264 Winchester Magnum	140	3200 2940 2700 2480	3180 2690 2270 1910	0.5 2.1 4.9
270 Winchester	100	3580 3160 2770 2400	2840 2210 1700 1280	0.4 1.7 4.5
270 Winchester	130	3140 2850 2580 2320	2840 2340 1920 1550	0.5 2.1 5.3
270 Winchester	150	2800 2400 2040 1750	2610 1920 1380 1020	0.7 3.0 7.8
270 Weatherby Magnum	100	3760 3265 2825 2435	3140 2363 1772 1317	0.4 1.6 4.3
270 Weatherby Magnum	130	3375 3050 2750 2480	3283 2686 2183 1776	0.4 1.8 4.5
270 Weatherby Magnum	150	3245 2955 2675 2430	3501 2909 2385 1967	0.5 2.0 5.0
280 Remington	125	3140 2840 2550 2280	2740 2240 1800 1440	0.5 2.2 5.5
280 Remington	150	2810 2580 2360 2130	2630 2220 1850 1510	0.6 2.6 6.5
280 Remington	165	2770 2460 2180 1930	2810 2220 1740 1360	0.7 2.9 7.4
284 Winchester	125	3200 2880 2590 2310	2840 2300 1860 1480	0.5 2.1 5.3
284 Winchester	150	2900 2630 2380 2160	2800 2300 1890 1550	0.6 2.5 6.3
7 mm Mauser (7x57)	175	2490 2170 1900 1680	2410 1830 1400 1100	0.8 3.7 9.5
7 x 61 SH	160	3100 2927 2757 2595	3410 3040 2700 2385	0.1 1.5 4.3
7 mm Remington Magnum	150	3260 3070 2880 2690	3540 3140 2760 2410	0.5 1.8 4.7
7 mm Remington Magnum	175	3020 2660 2340 2050	3540 2750 2130 1630	0.6 2.5 6.2
7 mm Weatherby Magnum	175	3067 2790 2500 2270	3662 3024 2429 2002	0.4 1.4 5.0
30-30 Winchester	150	2410 2020 1700 1430	1930 1360 960 680	0.9 4.2 11.0
30-30 Winchester	170	2220 1890 1630 1410	1860 1350 1000 750	1.2 4.6 12.5
30-30 Winchester Express	160	2220 1870 1600 1370	1750 1240 910 665	1.0 5.0 13.0
30 US Carbine	110	1980 1540 1230 1040	960 580 370 265	1.4 8.5 24.5
30 US Carbine (Norma)	110	1970 1595 1300 1090	948 622 413 290	0.8 6.4 19.0
30 Remington	170	2220 1890 1630 1410	1860 1350 1000 750	1.2 4.6 12.5
30-40 Krag	180	2470 2250 2040 1850	2440 2020 1660 1370	0.8 3.5 8.5
30-40 Krag	220	2200 1990 1800 1630	2360 1930 1580 1300	1.4 4.4 11.0
30-06 Springfield	110	3420 2880 2400 1970	2850 2020 1410 945	0.4 2.1 5.6
30-06 Springfield	150	2970 2670 2400 2130	2930 2370 1920 1510	0.6 2.4 6.1
30-06 Springfield	180	2700 2470 2250 2040	2910 2440 2020 1660	0.7 2.9 7.0
30-06 Springfield	180	2700 2520 2350 2190	2910 2540 2200 1900	0.6 2.8 6.7
30-06 Springfield F.M.C.B.T.	180	2700 2520 2350 2190	2910 2540 2200 1900	0.6 2.8 6.7
30-06 Springfield	220	2410 2180 1980 1790	2830 2320 1910 1560	0.8 3.7 9.2
300 Savage	150	2670 2390 2130 1890	2370 1900 1510 1190	0.7 3.0 7.6
300 Savage	180	2370 2160 1960 1770	2240 1860 1530 1250	0.9 3.7 9.2
300 H. & H. Magnum	150	3190 2870 2580 2300	3390 2740 2220 1760	0.5 2.1 5.2
300 H. & H. Magnum	180	2920 2670 2440 2220	3400 2850 2380 1970	0.6 2.4 5.8
300 H. & H. Magnum	180	2920 2740 2550 2380	3400 3000 2600 2260	0.6 2.4 5.7
300 H. & H. Magnum	220	2620 2370 2150 1940	3350 2740 2260 1840	0.7 3.1 7.7
300 Weatherby Magnum	150	3545 3195 2890 2615	4179 3393 2783 2279	0.4 1.5 3.9
300 Weatherby Magnum	180	3245 2960 2705 2475	4201 3501 2925 2448	0.4 1.9 5.2
300 Weatherby Magnum	220	2905 2610 2385 2150	4123 3329 2757 2257	0.6 2.5 6.7
300 Winchester Magnum	150	3400 3050 2730 2430	3850 3100 2480 1970	0.4 1.9 4.8
300 Winchester Magnum	180	3070 2850 2640 2440	3770 3250 2790 2380	0.5 2.1 5.3
303 Savage	180	2140 1810 1550 1340	1830 1310 960 715	1.1 5.4 14.0
303 Savage	190	1980 1680 1440 1250	1650 1190 875 660	1.3 6.2 15.5
303 British	215	2180 1900 1660 1460	2270 1720 1310 1020	1.1 4.9 12.5
308 Winchester	110	3340 2810 2340 1920	2730 1930 1340 900	0.5 2.2 6.0
308 Winchester	150	2860 2570 2300 2050	2730 2200 1760 1400	0.6 2.6 6.5
308 Winchester	180	2610 2390 2170 1970	2720 2280 1870 1540	0.8 3.1 7.4

Cartridge	Wt. Grs.	Velocity—Ft. Per Sec. Muzzle 100 Yds. 200 Yds. 300 Yds.	Energy—Ft. Lbs. Muzzle 100 Yds. 200 Yds. 300 Yds.	Mid-Range. Trajectory 100 Yds. 200 Yds. 300 Yds.
308 Winchester	200	2450 2210 1980 1170	2670 2170 1750 1400	0.8 3.6 9.0
308 Norma Magnum	180	3100 2881 2668 2464	3842 3318 2846 2427	0.6 1.6 4.6
308 Norma Magnum	250	2790 2493 2231 2001	4322 3451 2764 2223	0.2 2.4 6.6
7.65 Argentine	150	2920 2630 2355 2105	2841 2304 1843 1476	0.1 2.0 5.8
7.7 Jap	130	2950 2635 2340 2065	2513 2004 1581 1231	0.1 2.0 5.9
7.7 Jap	180	2493 2292 2101 1922	2484 2100 1765 1477	0.3 2.8 7.7
7.7 Jap	215	2264 2023 1802 1603	2448 1954 1550 1227	0.5 3.0 10.4
32-20 Winchester High Velocity	80	2100 1430 1090 950	780 365 210 160	1.5 8.5 24.5
32-20 Winchester	100	1290 1060 940 840	370 250 195 155	3.3 15.5 38.0
32 Winchester Special	170	2280 1870 1560 1330	1960 1320 920 665	1.0 4.8 13.0
32 Remington	170	2220 1840 1530 1280	1860 1280 885 620	1.1 5.0 13.5
32-40 Winchester	165	1440 1250 1100 1030	760 570 445 390	2.4 11.0 28.0
8 mm Lebel Hi-Speed	170	2640 2260 1960 1700	2630 1930 1450 1090	0.7 3.4 8.9
8 x 56 MS	200	2190 1880 1630 1430	2130 1570 1180 905	1.1 4.9 12.7
8 mm Mauser (8x57; or 7.9)	170	2570 2140 1790 1520	2490 1730 1210 870	0.8 3.9 10.5
8 x 57 JR, JRS	159	2590 2240 1920 1640	2370 1770 1300 945	0.2 3.0 8.8
8 x 57 JR, JRS	196	2360 2045 1760 1515	2425 1820 1350 995	0.4 3.7 10.6
8 x 57 JS	123	2890 2515 2170 1860	2280 1730 1290 945	0.1 2.3 6.8
8 x 57 JS	159	2720 2360 2030 1735	2615 1965 1450 1060	0.2 2.6 7.9
8 x 57 JS	198	2630 2420 2215 2030	3020 2555 2150 1800	0.2 2.5 6.9
8 x 57 JS	227	2330 2085 1855 1650	2730 2180 1730 1370	0.4 3.4 9.5
338 Winchester Magnum	200	3000 2690 2410 2170	4000 3210 2580 2090	0.5 2.4 6.0
338 Winchester Magnum	250	2700 2430 2180 1940	4050 3280 2640 2090	0.7 3.0 7.0
340 Weatherby Magnum	200	3210 2905 2615 2345	4566 3748 3038 2442	0.5 2.1 5.3
340 Weatherby Magnum	210	3165 2910 2665 2435	4660 3948 3312 2766	0.5 2.1 5.0
340 Weatherby Magnum	250	2850 2580 2325 2090	4510 3695 3000 2425	0.6 2.7 6.7
348 Winchester	150	2890 2460 2060 1710	2780 2020 1410 975	0.6 2.9 7.9
348 Winchester	200	2530 2140 1820 1570	2840 2030 1470 1090	0.8 3.8 10.0
348 Winchester	250	2350 1970 1660 1410	3060 2150 1530 1100	0.9 4.4 11.5
35 Remington	150	2400 1960 1580 1280	1920 1280 835 545	0.9 4.6 13.0
35 Remington Express	200	2210 1830 1540 1310	2170 1490 1050 760	1.1 5.2 14.0
350 Remington Mag.	200	2725 2355 2025 1730	3290 2465 1820 1325	0.7 3.2 8.3
350 Remington Mag.	250	2410 2135 1885 1660	3220 2535 1975 1530	0.8 3.8 9.8
351 Winchester Self-Loading	180	1850 1560 1310 1140	1370 975 685 520	1.5 7.8 21.5
351 Winchester Self-Loading	177	1850 1560 1310 1140	1370 975 685 520	1.5 7.8 21.5
38-40 Winchester	180	1330 1070 960 850	705 455 370 290	3.2 15.0 36.5
38-55 Winchester	255	1320 1160 1050 1000	985 760 625 565	2.9 13.0 32.0
358 Winchester	200	2530 2210 1910 1640	2840 2160 1610 1190	0.8 3.6 9.4
358 Winchester	250	2250 2010 1780 1570	2810 2230 1760 1370	1.0 4.4 11.0
358 Norma Magnum	250	2790 2493 2231 2001	4322 3451 2764 2223	0.2 2.4 6.6
9.3 x 57	232	2329 2032 1763 1527	2795 2127 1602 1202	0.4 3.7 10.6
9.3 x 57	286	2067 1818 1595 1404	2714 2099 1616 1252	0.6 4.8 13.2
9.3 x 62	232	2625 2304 2009 1742	3551 2735 2080 1564	0.2 2.8 8.1
9.3 x 62	286	2362 2088 1837 1612	3544 2769 2144 1651	0.4 3.5 9.8
9.3 x 74 R	232	2625 2304 2009 1742	3551 2735 2080 1554	0.2 2.0 8.1
9.3 x 74 R	286	2362 2088 1837 1612	3544 2769 2144 1651	0.4 3.5 9.8
375 H. & H. Magnum	270	2740 2460 2210 1990	4500 3620 2920 2370	0.7 2.9 7.1
375 H. & H. Magnum	300	2550 2280 2040 1830	4330 3460 2770 2230	0.7 3.3 8.3
375 H. & H. Magnum	300	2550 2180 1860 1590	4330 3160 2300 1680	0.7 3.6 9.3
378 Weatherby Magnum	270	3180 2850 2600 2315	6051 4871 4053 3210	0.5 2.0 5.2
378 Weatherby Magnum	300	2925 2610 2380 2125	5700 4539 3774 3009	0.6 2.5 6.2
38-40 Winchester (Oilproof)	180	1330 1070 960 850	705 455 370 290	3.2 15.0 36.5
38-55 Winchester	255	1320 1160 1050 1000	985 760 625 565	2.9 13.0 32.0
44-40 Winchester (Oilproof)	200	1310 1050 940 830	760 490 390 305	3.3 15.0 36.5
44 Winchester Magnum	240	1750 1350	1630	1.8
444 Marlin Mag.	240	2400 1845 1410 1125	3069 1815 1060 672	1.0 — —
45-70 Government	405	1320 1160 1050 990	1570 1210 990 880	2.9 13.0 32.5
458 Winchester Magnum	510	2125 1840 1600 1400	5110 3830 2900 2220	1.1 5.1 13.2
458 Winchester Magnum	500	2125 1910 1700 1520	5010 4050 3210 2570	1.1 4.8 12.0
460 Weatherby Magnum	500	2700 2330 2005 1730	8095 6025 4465 3320	0.7 3.3 10.0

CARTRIDGE SPECIFICATIONS

COMPARATIVE BALLISTICS

Caliber	Bullet Weight	Vel 0	Vel 100	Vel 200	Vel 300	E 0	E 100	E 200	E 300	MRT 100	MRT 200	MRT 300
.220 Swift	48	4110	3490	2930	2440	1800	1300	915	635	0.3	1.4	3.8
.222 Rem.	50	3200	2660	2170	1750	1140	785	520	340	0.5	2.5	7.0
.222 Rem. Magnum	55	3300	2800	2340	1930	1330	955	670	455	0.5	2.3	6.1
.223 (AR-15)	55	3300	2800	2340	1930	1330	955	670	455	0.5	2.3	6.1
.224 Weatherby Magnum	50	3800	3200	2660	2170	1604	1135	786	523	0.4	1.7	4.7
.225 Win.	55	3650	3140	2680	2270	1630	1200	875	630	0.4	1.8	4.8

Table E

U.S. RIM-FIRE RIFLE CARTRIDGES

High Velocity

Cartridge	Bullet Weight Grains	Style	Velocity — Feet Per Second Muzzle	100 Yds.	Energy — Foot Pounds Muzzle	100 Yds.	Mid-Range Trajectory in. — 100 Yds.
22 Short	29	Lead	1125	920	81	54	4.3
22 Short	27	Hollow Point	1155	920	80	54	4.2
22 Short "Rocket"	15	Composition	1710	—	97	—	—
22 Long	29	Lead	1240	965	99	60	3.8
22 Long Rifle	40	Lead	1335	1045	158	97	3.3
22 Long Rifle	36	Hollow Point	1365	1040	149	86	3.3
22 W.R.F. (Remington Special)	45	Lead	1450	1110	210	123	2.7

Standard Velocity

Cartridge	Bullet Weight Grains	Style	Velocity Muzzle	100 Yds.	Energy Muzzle	100 Yds.	MRT
22 Short	29	Lead	1045	810	70	—	5.6
22 Short Gallery Special Spatter-Less	29	Lead	1045	—	70	—	—
22 Short Spatter-Less	29	Lead	1045	—	70	—	—
22 Short New & Improved Spatter-Less	15	Composition	1710	—	97	—	—
22 Long Rifle	40	Lead	1145	975	116	84	4.0
22 Winchester Automatic	45	Lead	1055	930	111	86	4.6
22 Remington Autoloading	45	Lead	920	—	84	—	5.5
25 Stevens	67	Lead	1130	985	184	140	3.8
32 Short	80	Lead	945	840	158	125	5.3
32 Long	90	Lead	945	850	178	144	5.3

Match

Cartridge	Bullet Weight Grains	Style	Velocity Muzzle	100 Yds.	Energy Muzzle	100 Yds.	MRT
22 Long Rifle	40	Lead	1145	975	116	84	4.0
22 Long Rifle Mark II	40	Lead	1145	975	116	84	4.0
22 Long Rifle EZXS	40	Lead	1145	975	116	84	4.0
22 Long Rifle Mark III	40	Lead	1105	970	108	84	4.1
22 Long Rifle L V EZXS	40	Lead	1105	970	108	84	4.1

Table I — DOMINION (C-I-L) AMMUNITION BALLISTICS

DESCRIPTION	BULLET Type	Weight Grains	VELOCITY Feet per Second Muzzle	100 Yds.	200 Yds.	300 Yds.	ENERGY Foot-Lbs. Muzzle	100 Yds.	200 Yds.	300 Yds.
RIFLE CARTRIDGES										
22 Hornet	PSP	45	2690	2030	1510	1150	720	410	230	130
22 Savage	PSP	70	2800	2440	2110	1840	1220	925	690	525
6.5 mm Mannlicher-Schoenauer	SP	160	2160	1950	1750	1570	1660	1350	1090	875
25-20 Winchester	Pneu	60	2250	1660	1240	1030	675	365	205	140
25-20 Winchester	SP	86	1460	1180	1030	940	405	265	200	170
25-20 Winchester	MC	86	1460	1180	1030	940	405	265	200	170
25-35 Winchester	SP	117	2300	1910	1600	1340	1370	945	665	465
250 Savage	PSP	100	2820	2460	2140	1870	1760	1340	1020	775
270 Winchester	PSP	130	3140	2850	2580	2320	2840	2340	1920	1550
7 mm Mauser	PSP	139	2900	2630	2370	2190	2600	2130	1730	1480
30-30 Winchester	Pneu	150	2410	2020	1700	1430	1930	1360	960	680
30-30 Winchester	KKSP	170	2220	1890	1630	1410	1860	1350	1000	750
30-30 Winchester	MC	170	2220	1890	1630	1410	1860	1350	1000	750
30 Remington	KKSP	170	2220	1890	1630	1410	1860	1350	1000	750
30-40 Krag	KKSP	180	2470	2120	1830	1590	2440	1740	1340	1010
30-06 Springfield	PSP	150	2970	2670	2400	2130	2930	2370	1920	1510
30-06 Springfield	KKSP	180	2700	2330	2010	1740	2910	2170	1610	1210
30-06 Springfield	KKSP	220	2410	2120	1870	1670	2830	2190	1710	1360
30-06 Springfield	CPE	180	2700	2480	2280	2080	2910	2460	2080	1730
300 Savage	PSP	150	2670	2390	2130	1890	2370	1900	1510	1190
300 Savage	KKSP	180	2370	2040	1760	1520	2240	1660	1240	920
303 Savage	KKSP	190	1980	1680	1440	1250	1650	1190	875	660
303 Savage	MC	190	1980	1680	1440	1250	1650	1190	875	660
303 British	PSP	150	2720	2440	2170	1930	2460	1980	1570	1240
303 British	KKSP	180	2540	2180	1880	1640	2580	1910	1420	1070
303 British	KKSP	215	2180	1900	1660	1460	2270	1720	1310	1020
303 British	CPE	180	2540	2320	2110	1920	2580	2140	1790	1470
8 mm Mauser	SP	170	2570	2140	1790	1520	2490	1730	1210	870
32-20 Winchester	SP	115	1480	1100	940	820	560	310	225	170
32 Winchester Special	KKSP	170	2280	1920	1630	1410	1960	1390	1000	757
32 Remington	KKSP	170	2220	1890	1610	1400	1860	1350	975	740
32-40 Winchester	KKSP	170	1540	1340	1180	1080	895	675	525	440
35 Remington	SP	200	2210	1830	1540	1310	2170	1490	1050	760
351 Winchester Self Loading	SP	180	1850	1560	1310	1140	1370	975	685	520
38-40 Winchester	SP	180	1330	1070	960	850	705	455	370	290
38-55 Winchester	SP	255	1600	1370	1190	1070	1450	1065	800	650
43 Mauser	Lead	385	1360	1150	1030	940	1580	1130	910	750
44-40 Winchester	SP	200	1310	1050	940	830	760	490	390	305

KKSP—KLING-KOR Soft Point; SP—Soft Point; PSP—Pointed Soft Point; Pneu—Pneumatic; MC—Metal Cased (Hard Point); CPE—Copper Point Expanding

Table J

COMPARABLE U.S. AND EUROPEAN CARTRIDGES
RIFLE CARTRIDGES

U.S.	Foreign
.22 Hornet	5.6x35R *
.22 Savage	5.6x52R
.25 Rem.	6.5x52
.25-35 Win.	6.5x52R
7 mm Mauser	7x57
.30-30 Win.	7.62x51R
.30-06	7.62x63

* R designates that the case is rimmed.

Table K

COMPARISON OF RIFLE CHAMBER PRESSURES OF U.S. CARTRIDGES

Cartridge	Bullet Wt.	Powder Charge	MV in fps	Chamber psi	Source
.218 Bee	46 gr.	9.0 gr. H-110	2294	38,800	H
.22 Hornet	45 gr.	11.5 gr. 4227	2575	41,000	D
	46 gr.	6.9 gr. H-110	2294	39,100	H
.220 Swift	48 gr.	factory	3861	50,000	H
	55 gr.	40.0 gr. 4064	3950	54,000	D
.222 Rem.	50 gr.	25.0 gr. BL-C(2)	3309	41,400	H
.222 Rem. Mag.	55 gr.	factory	3222	47,700	H
.225 Win.	55 gr.	factory	3590	49,966	H
.22-250	55 gr.	37.0 gr. 4895	3918	49,100	H
.243 Win.	80 gr.	41.0 gr. 4895	3384	50,400	H
	100 gr.	44.5 gr. 4350	3120	51,500	D
6 mm Rem.	100 gr.	40.0 gr. 4064	2935	51,800	D
.250 Sav.	87 gr.	35.5 gr. 3031	3100	44,000	D
	100 gr.	40.0 gr. H-450	2727	44,700	H
.257 Robt.	100 gr.	factory	3170	47,600	H
.264 Win. Mag.	100 gr.	70.0 gr. H-450	3642	51,400	H
	140 gr.	73.0 gr. H-870	3163	54,200	H
.270 Win.	130 gr.	factory	3120	52,000	H
.284 Win.	130 gr.	57.0 gr. H-450	2913	46,200	H
7 mm Rem. Mag.	150 gr.	factory	3263	55,100	H
.30-30 Win.	150 gr.	factory	2069	38,000	H
.308 Win.	180 gr.	factory	2584	48,400	H
.30-06	150 gr.	61.0 gr. 4350	3000	50,000	D
	180 gr.	60.0 gr. 4831	2737	46,600	H
.308 Norma Mag.	180 gr.	factory	3206	62,700	H
	180 gr.	60.5 gr. 4320	2885	54,000	D
.300 Win. Mag.	180 gr.	75.0 gr. H-450	3064	52,200	H
.338 Win. Mag.	200 gr.	factory	3020	52,820	H
.375 H. & H. Mag.	300 gr.	84.0 gr. H-450	2516	49,700	H
.458 Win. Mag.	510 gr.	77.8 gr. BL-C(2)	2117	43,800	H

Note: These are maximum loads and were selected only to show comparative pressures. Loading Data shown here are based on tables issued by B.E. Hodgdon, Inc., and by the Explosives Department of E.I. duPont de Nemours & Co., Inc. **Do Not Use** *the above table as loading data table. If you do work up loads based on the above data, you must reduce starting loads by 10 per cent. H—denotes data from Hodgdon, while D denotes DuPont data.*

CONVERSION TABLES FOR HANDLOADERS AND SHOOTERS

The following tables are particularly helpful when you work with European or metric cartridges. When the .223 Remington cartridge was introduced for Colt's AR-15, the cartridge was also designated as the 5.56 mm. It is understood that this might be the first step toward the introduction of the metric system by the military and by the U.S. ammunition makers.

Table 1

Metric Cartridge Conversion

Metric	Inches	Metric	Inches
4 mm	.157480	7.7 mm	.303149
4.3 mm	.169291	7.8 mm	.307086
4.5 mm	.177165	7.9 mm	.311023
5 mm	.196850	7.91 mm	.311416
5.5 mm	.216535	7.92 mm	.311809
5.6 mm	.220470	8 mm	.314960
6 mm	.236220	8.15 mm	.320855
6.35 mm	.249999	9 mm	.354330
6.5 mm	.255905	9.1 mm	.358267
7 mm	.275590	9.3 mm	.366141
7.5 mm	.295275	9.5 mm	.374015
7.56 mm	.297637	10.35 mm	.407479
7.6 mm	.299212	10.75 mm	.423227
7.62 mm	.299998	11.15 mm	.438965
7.63 mm	.300093	11.2 mm	.440940
7.65 mm	.301180	11.25 mm	.462201

Table 2

Conversion of Inches to Millimeters

In.	0	1/16	1/8	3/16	1/4	5/16	3/8	7/16	1/2	9/16	5/8	11/16	3/4	13/16	7/8	15/16
0	0.0	1.6	3.2	4.8	6.4	7.9	9.5	11.1	12.7	14.3	15.9	17.5	19.1	20.6	22.2	23.8
1	25.4	27.0	28.6	30.2	31.7	33.3	34.9	36.5	28.1	39.7	41.3	42.9	44.4	46.0	47.6	49.2
2	50.8	52.4	54.0	55.6	57.1	58.7	60.3	61.9	63.5	65.1	66.7	68.3	69.8	71.4	73.0	74.6
3	76.2	77.8	79.4	81.0	82.5	84.1	85.7	87.3	88.9	90.5	92.1	93.7	95.2	96.8	98.4	100.0
4	101.6	103.2	104.8	106.4	108.0	109.5	111.1	112.7	114.3	115.9	117.5	119.1	120.7	122.2	123.8	125.4
5	127.0	128.6	130.2	131.8	133.4	134.9	136.5	138.1	139.7	141.3	142.9	144.5	146.1	147.6	149.2	150.8
6	152.4	154.0	155.6	157.2	158.8	160.3	161.9	163.5	165.1	166.7	168.3	169.9	171.5	173.0	174.6	176.2
7	177.8	179.4	181.0	182.6	184.2	185.7	187.3	188.9	190.5	192.1	193.7	195.3	196.9	198.4	200.0	201.6
8	203.2	204.8	206.4	208.0	209.6	211.1	212.7	214.3	215.9	217.5	219.1	220.7	222.3	223.8	225.4	227.0
9	228.6	230.2	231.8	233.4	235.0	236.5	238.1	239.7	241.3	242.9	244.5	246.1	247.7	249.2	250.8	252.4
10	254.0	255.6	257.2	258.8	260.4	261.9	263.5	265.1	266.7	268.3	269.9	271.5	273.1	274.6	276.2	277.8
11	279.4	281.0	282.6	284.2	285.7	287.3	288.9	290.5	292.1	293.7	295.3	296.9	298.4	300.0	301.6	303.2
12	304.8	306.4	308.0	309.6	311.1	312.7	314.3	315.9	317.5	319.1	320.7	322.3	323.8	325.4	327.0	828.6
13	330.2	331.8	333.4	335.0	336.5	338.1	339.7	341.3	342.9	344.5	346.1	347.7	349.2	350.8	352.4	354.0
14	355.6	357.2	358.8	360.4	361.9	363.5	365.1	366.7	368.3	369.9	371.5	373.1	374.6	376.2	377.8	379.4
15	381.0	382.6	384.2	385.8	387.3	388.9	390.5	392.1	393.7	395.3	396.9	398.5	400.0	401.6	403.2	404.8
16	406.4	408.0	409.6	411.2	412.7	414.3	415.9	417.5	419.1	420.7	422.3	423.9	425.4	427.0	428.6	430.2
17	431.8	433.4	435.0	436.6	438.1	439.7	441.3	442.9	444.5	446.1	447.9	449.3	450.8	452.4	454.0	455.6
18	457.2	458.8	460.4	462.0	463.5	465.1	466.7	468.3	469.9	471.5	473.1	474.7	476.2	477.8	479.4	481.0
19	482.6	484.2	485.8	487.4	488.9	490.5	492.1	493.7	495.3	496.9	498.5	500.1	501.6	503.2	504.8	506.4
20	508.0	509.6	511.2	512.8	514.3	515.9	517.5	519.1	520.7	522.3	523.9	525.5	527.0	528.6	530.2	531.8
21	533.4	535.0	536.6	538.2	539.7	541.3	542.9	544.5	546.1	547.7	549.3	550.9	552.4	554.0	555.6	557.2
22	558.8	560.4	562.0	563.6	565.1	566.7	568.3	569.9	571.5	573.1	574.7	576.3	577.8	579.4	581.0	582.6
23	584.2	585.8	587.4	589.0	590.5	592.1	593.7	595.3	596.9	598.5	600.1	601.7	603.2	604.8	606.4	608.0

Table 3

Conversion of Inch Decimals to Millimeters

Hundredths of an Inch	0	1	2	3	4	5	6	7	8	9
	0	0.254	0.508	0.762	1.016	1.270	1.524	1.778	2.032	2.286
10	2.540	2.794	3.048	3.302	3.556	3.810	4.064	4.318	4.572	4.826
20	5.080	5.334	5.588	5.842	6.096	6.350	6.604	6.858	7.112	7.366
30	7.620	7.874	8.128	8,382	8,636	8.890	9.144	9.398	9.652	9.906
40	10.160	10.414	10.668	10.922	11.176	11.430	11.684	11.938	12.192	12.446
50	12.700	12.954	13.208	13.462	13.716	13.970	14.224	14.478	14.732	14.986
60	15.240	15.494	15.748	16.002	16.257	16.510	16.764	17.018	17.272	17.526
80	20.320	20.574	20.828	21.082	21.336	21.590	21.844	22.098	22.352	22.606
90	22.860	23.114	23.368	23.622	23.876	24.130	24.384	24.638	24.892	25.146

Table 4

Conversion of Millimeters to Inches

	.0	.1	.2	.3	.4	.5	.6	.7	.8	.9
0		.003937	.007874	.01181	.015748	.019685	.023622	.027559	.031496	.035433
1	.03937	.043307	.047244	.051181	.055118	.059055	.062992	.066929	.070866	.074803
2	.07874	.082677	.086614	.090551	.094488	.098425	.102362	.106299	.110236	.114173
3	.11811	.122047	.125984	.129921	.133858	.137795	.141732	.145669	.149606	.153543
4	.157480	.161417	.165354	.169291	.173228	.177165	.181102	.185039	.188976	.192913
5	.196850	.200787	.204724	.208661	.212598	.216535	.220472	.224409	.228346	.232283
6	.236220	.240157	.244094	.248031	.251968	.255905	.259842	.263779	.267716	.271653
7	.275590	.279527	.283464	.287401	.291338	.295275	.299212	.303149	.307086	.311023
8	.314960	.318897	.322834	.326771	.330708	.334645	.338582	.342519	.346456	.350393
9	.354330	.358267	.362204	.366141	.370078	.374015	.377952	.381889	.385826	.389763
10	.393700	.397637	.401574	.405511	.409448	.413385	.417322	.421259	.425196	.429133
11	.433070	.437007	.440944	.444881	.448818	.452755	.456692	.460629	.464566	.468503
12	.472440	.476377	.480314	.484251	.488188	.492125	.496062	.499999	.503936	.507873
13	.511810	.515747	.519684	.523621	.527558	.531495	.535432	.539369	.543306	.547243
14	.551180	.555117	.559054	.562991	.566928	.570865	.574802	.578739	.582676	.586613
15	.590550	.594487	.598424	.602361	.606298	.610235	.614172	.618109	.622046	.625983

Table 5
Conversion Factors for Metric Units

Grams (Gm.) to grains (gr.)	multiply by 15.43
Grains (gr.) to Grams (Gm.)	multiply by 0.0648
Kilogram Kg./cm^2 to psi	multiply by 14.223
psi to Kg/cm^2	multiply by 0.07031
Atmospheres to psi	multiply by 14.70
psi to Atmospheres	multiply by 0.06804
ft/lbs to Kg/m	multiply by 0.1383
Kg/m to ft/lbs	multiply by 7.233
Meters (m) to feet (ft.)	multiply by 3.281
Ft. to m	multiply by 0.3048
Inches to mm	multiply by 0.254
Millimeters (mm) to inches	multiply by 0.394

Table 6
Weight Equivalents

1 avoirdupois pound	7,000 grains
1 avoirdupois ounce	437.5 grains
1 Gram (Gm.)	15.43 grains
1 milligram (mgm)	0.015 grains
1 pound av.	453.5 Gm.

FORMULAS FOR HANDLOADERS

Case Capacity Determination

$$\text{Case Volume} = \frac{b - a}{c}$$

where a is the weight of the empty case
      b is the weight of the case filled with water
      c is the weight of one cubic inch of water, that is 252.8 grains.

Determination of Sectional Density of Bullet

$$\text{Sectional Density or SD} = \frac{W}{7000 \, D^2}$$

where W is the bullet weight expressed in grains
      D is the bullet diameter expressed in inches
      7000 is the number of grains in one one pound.

Physical Properties of Bullet Casting Metals

Metal	Spec. Gravity	Melting Pt. (Fahrenheit)	gr./in.^{3}
Lead	11.3	625	2880
Antimony	6.8	1160	1710
Tin	7.3	440	1840

Ballistics Graphs

The following graphs are reproduced here with the permission of Winchester-Western. Their inclusion in this book has a twofold purpose: First of all, they serve to demonstrate that calculated data are as accurate as those derived from actual measurements, and secondly, on hand of these graphs you can easily see how ballistics data, when plotted or when applied against a plot, can be used to develop the foregoing tables. You can also work up your own graphs for other cartridges. Having the bullet weight, range, velocity, and energy, you can plot any cartridge for which data have been published.

Some rather complex tables and curves are often plotted by wildcatters and ballistics engineers. Given the partial of complete ballistics performance of two related cartridges and the MV of an experimental cartridge, it is not too difficult to plot the anticipated bullet performance, especially if MV is close to the other two velocities and bullet weights are identical.

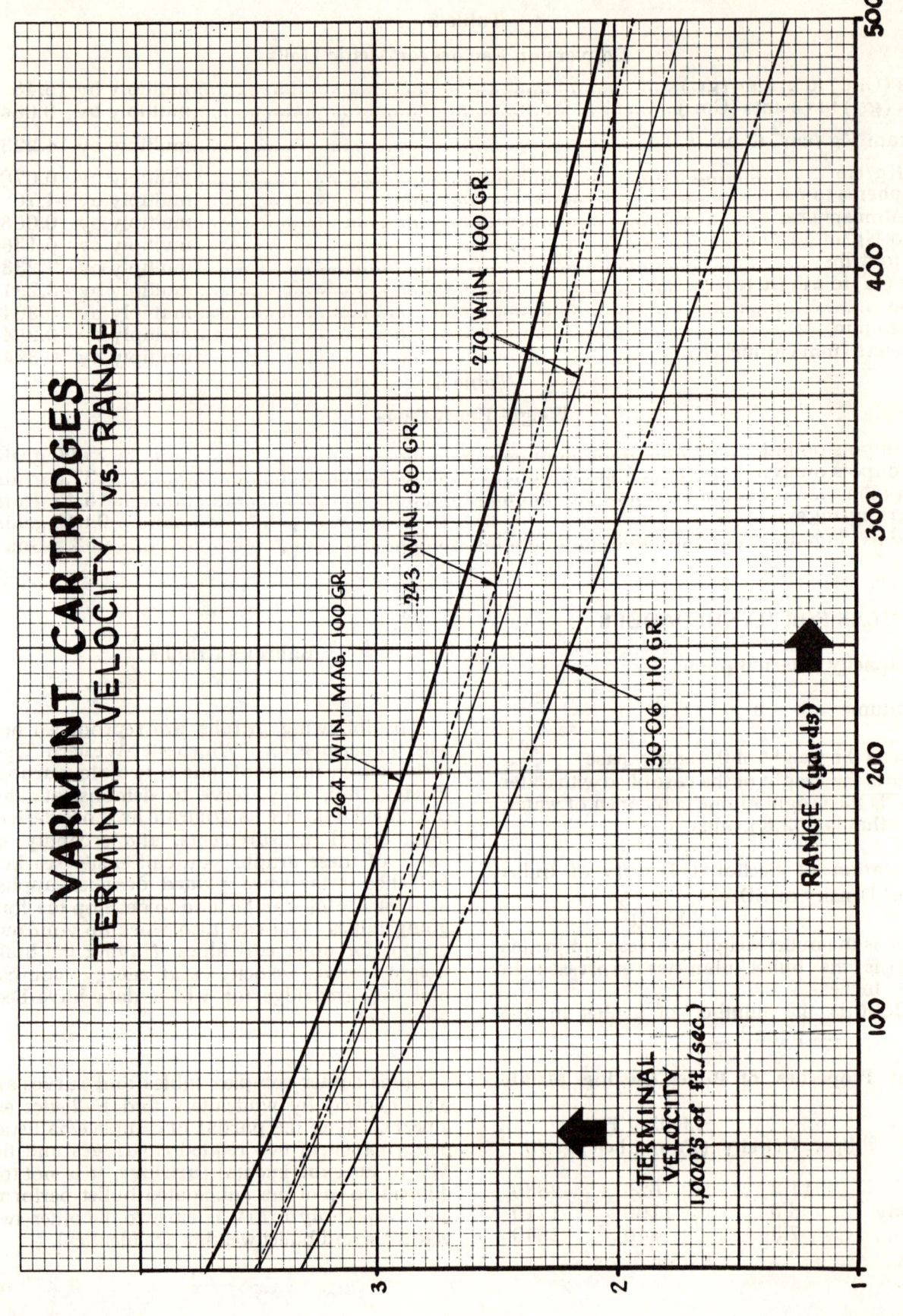
Courtesy of Winchester-Western

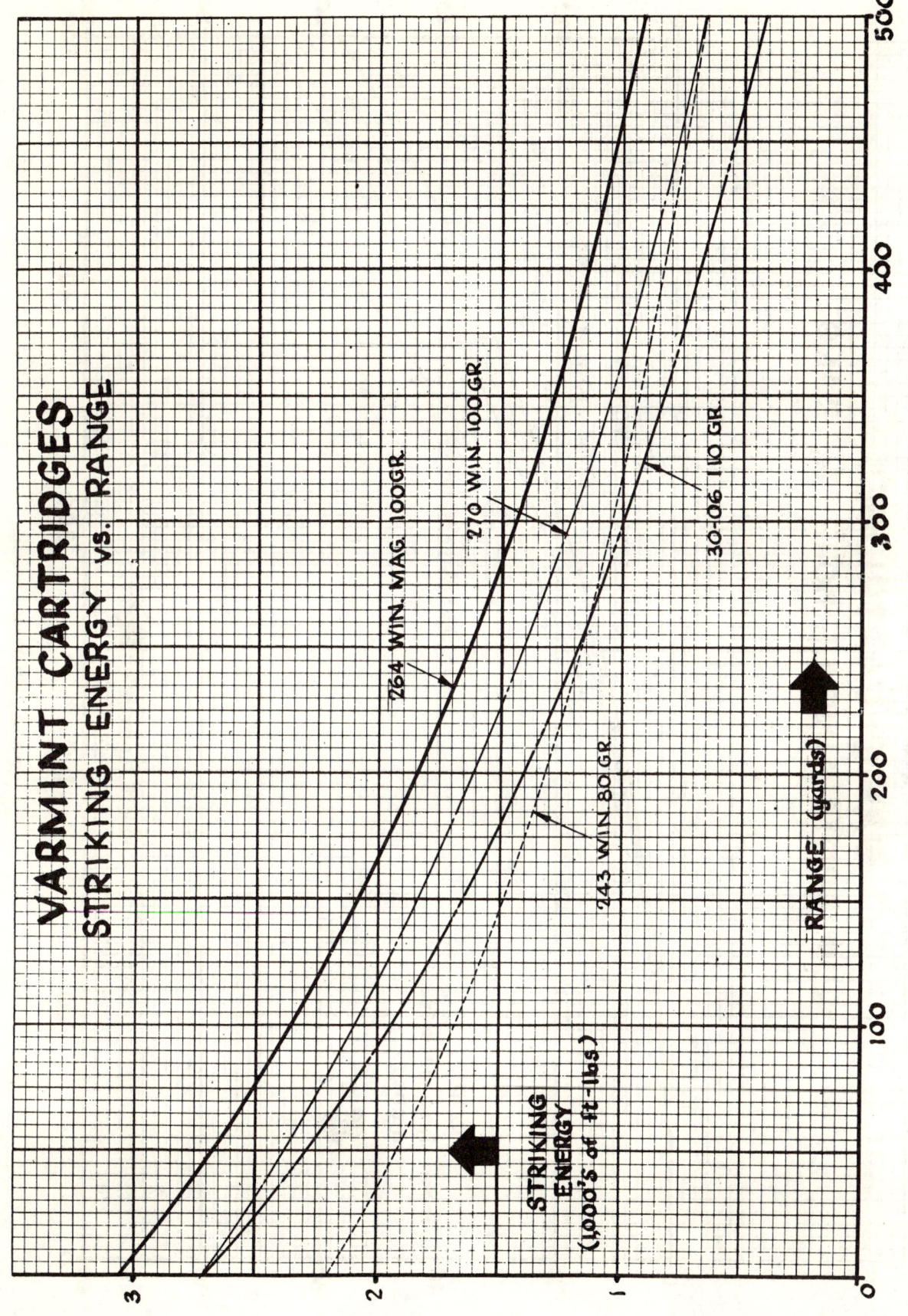
Courtesy of Winchester-Western

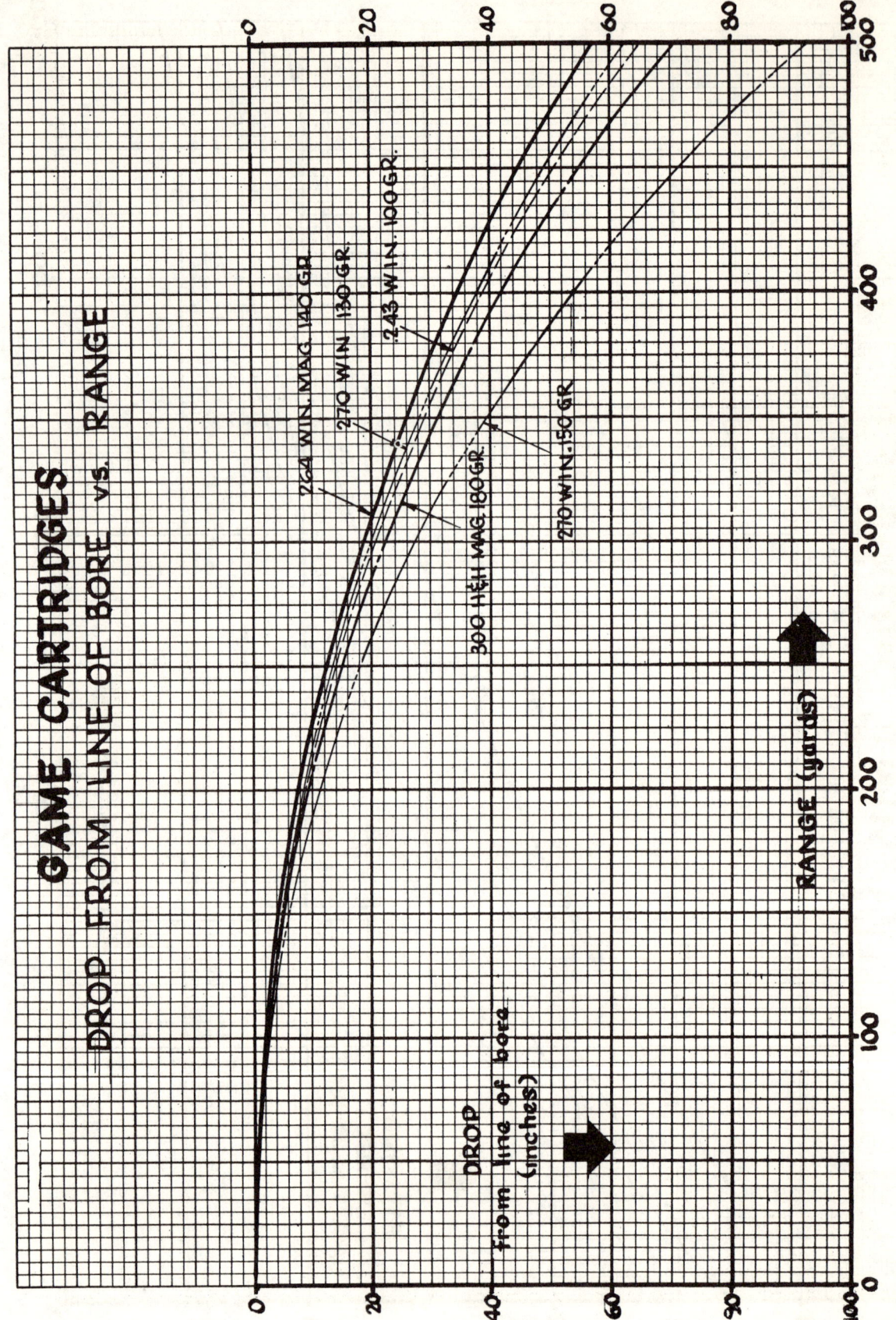

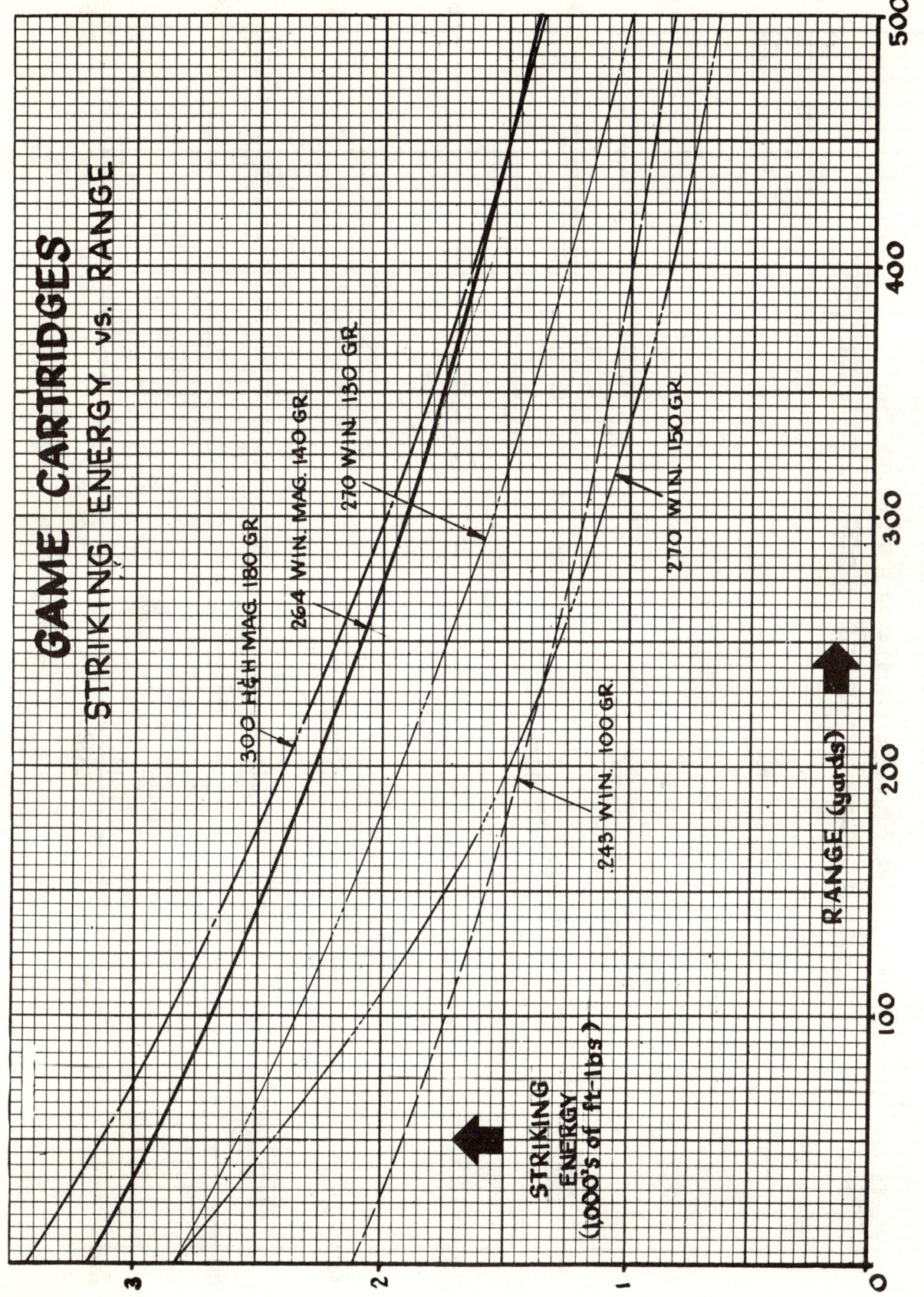

Courtesy of Winchester-Western

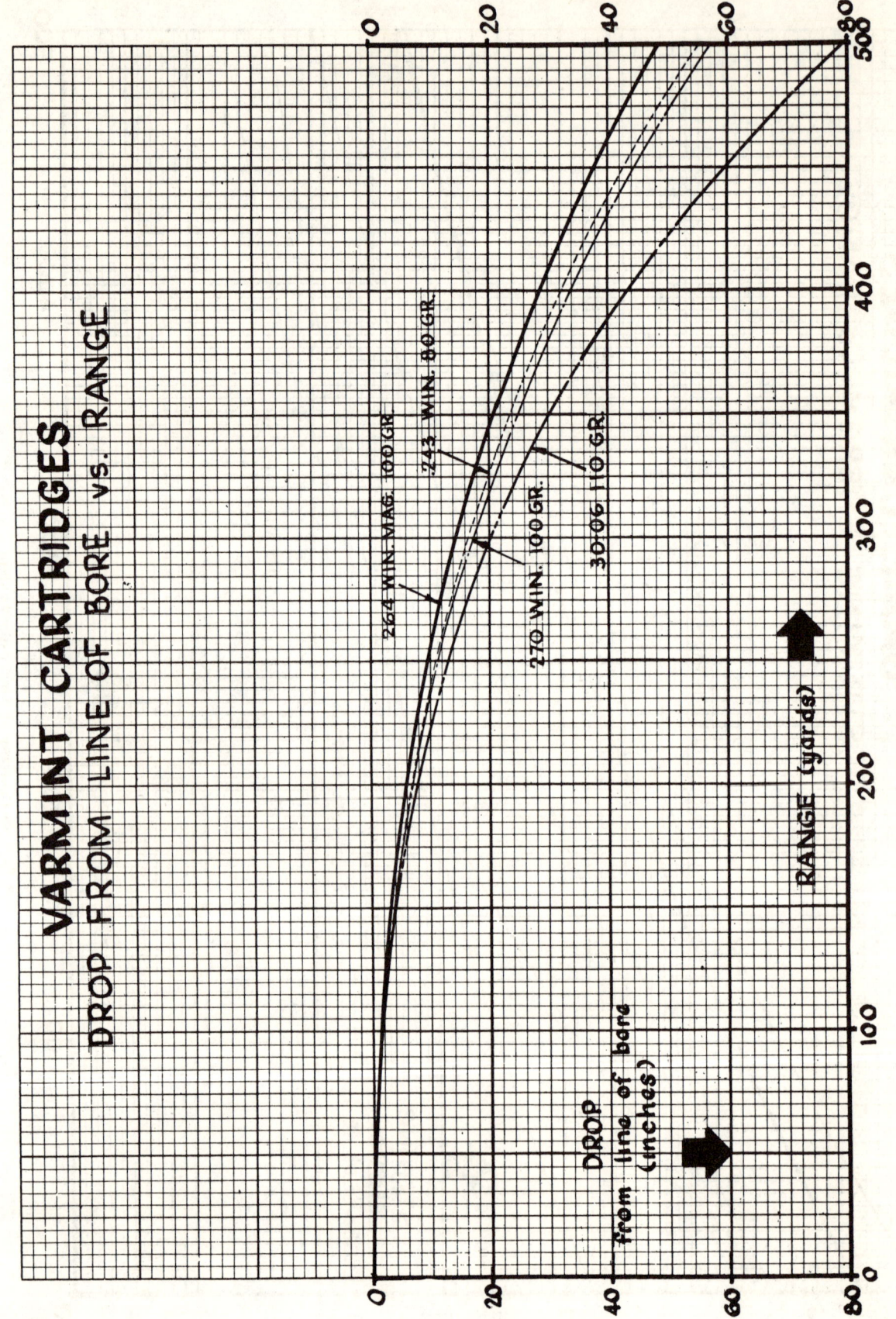

Index

accuracy, 14, 20, 134-35, 143, 157-59
action
    bolt-action, 33, 37
    combination, 41-44
    lever-action, 37-38
    match, 33
    Mauser, 36
    military, 224
    pump-action, 40
    selection of, 44
    semiautomatic, 38
    single-shot, 31-33
    takedown, 34
air gaging, 21
anchoring mounts, 174-75, 178
annealing, 131-34

ballistics
    external, 107
    formula, 103-4, 112
    graphs, 298-302
    internal, 101-3
    rifle, 99-116
barrel
    configuration, 22-23
    free-floated, 142-43
    stress, 20-21, 142
big-game calibers, 94
bolt-action rifles, 33-37, 63-65, 72-80
bore cleaning, 187-93
bore, line of, 107-8
bluing, 195, 207-8
bullet
    expansion, 114-15
    keyholing, 21, 25
    kinetic energy formula, 112
    nose battering, 134-35
    pullers, 237
    stabilization, 115-16
    swaging, 119
bullpups, 160-62

calibers
    big-game, 94-98
    choice of, 92
    discontinued, 46
    medium-game, 93-94
    metric designations, 85-87
    new, 44-46
    popular, 44-51
    varmint, 92-93
    wildcats, 86-90, 119, 134, 221-22, 233
caps, muzzle, 237-38
cartridge specifications, 288-97
case trimming handloads, 40-41, 123, 128-30
centerfire rifles, 68-82
chamber pressure, measuring, 109-12

checkering, 51, 150, 203
chronographs, 103-4
choice of calibers, 92
cleaning
    bore, 187-93
    how to, 187-93
    internal action parts, 191-92
    rifle, 187-93
    rust, 207
configuration, barrel, 22-23

dents in stocks, 203
discontinued calibers, 46

eye relief, 176-78
expansion, bullet, 114-15
external ballistics, 107

finishes, stocks, 203-7
formula, ballistics, 103-4, 112
fouling, metal, 188
free-floated barrels, 142-43
full-length sizing of handloads, 125

gaging, air, 21
glassbedding, 143, 200-2
graphs, ballistics, 298-302

handloads, 117-35, 236-37
    case-trimming, 40-41, 123, 128-30
    full-length sizing, 125
    how to, 125-28
    neck-sizing, 123
    resizing, 119-23, 125
    tools for, 119-23
hunting rifles, hints on, 231-40

internal action parts, cleaning of, 191-92
internal ballistics, 101-3
internal stress, 21

keyholing, bullet, 21, 25
kinetic energy formula, bullet, 112

lever-action rifles, 37-38, 61-62, 70-72
line of bore, 107
line of sight, 107
lock time, 56

match rifles, 33
medium-game calibers, 93
metal fouling, 188
metric designations, calibers, 85-86
midrange trajectory, 107-9
military rifles, 219-28
    ammunition for, 221-22, 224, 226
military sights, 167-68
minute of angle, 139
mirage, 109, 143
mounts, 173-78
    anchoring of, 174-75, 178
    eye relief, 176-78

    see-through, 176
    tip-off, 175
muzzle
    caps, 237-38
    velocity, 103-7

neck-sizing handloads, 123
new calibers, 44-46
nose battering, bullet, 134-35

open sights, 165-67

peep sights, 165-67
plinking, 55, 231
popular calibers, 44-51
pump-action rifles, 40, 56-61, 68-70
pressure, chamber measuring, 109-12
pullers, bullet, 237

rate of twist, 13-14, 22
recoil pad, installation of, 202-3
reseating, screw, 195
rifle
    ballistics, 99-116
    bolt-action, 33-37, 63-65, 72-80
    care, 187-94
    care afield, 192-93
    centerfire, 68-82
    cleaning, 187-93
    hunting, hints on, 231-40
    lever-action, 37-38, 61-62, 70-72
    match, 33
    military, 219-28
    pump-action, 40, 56-61, 68-70
    rimfire, 56-67
    single-shot, 31-33, 66-67, 80-82
    takedown, 34
    target, hints on, 240-43
    versatility, 90-91
riflings, 13-26
    types of, 14
    wear and tear on, 21
rimfire rifles, 56-67
Rule of Three, 181
rust, cleaning of, 207

scopes
    adjustment of, 171
    bases, 153-54
    covers, 154, 234-35
    hunting, 170-71
    installation of, 208-15
    selection of, 168
    shields, 154
    spotting, 183
    target, 168-71
    varmint, 170-71

screw reseating, 195
sealing, 195, 198
see-through mounts, 176
sight, line of, 107-8
sights, 165-83
   military, 167-68
   open, 165-67
   peep, 165-67
   target, 170
   telescopic, 168
   varmint, 168
sighting-in, 108-9, 178
   bore sighters, 178, 182
   how to, 178-80
   Rule of Three, 181
single-shot rifles, 31-33, 66-67, 80-82
solvents, 188
specifications of cartridges, 288-97
stabilization, bullet, 115-16

stocks, 147-51, 159-60
   bullpups, 160-62
   checkering, 51, 150, 203
   dents, repairing, 203
   finishes, 203, 205-7
   installing recoil pad, 202-3
   stripping, 205
stress, barrel, 20-21, 142
stress, internal, 20-21
swaging, bullet, 119

takedown rifles, 34
target rifles, hints on, 240-43
target sights, 170
telescopic sights, 168
tinkering, 194-215
tip-off mounts, 175-76
trajectory, 105-9
   midrange, 107

trigger pull
   extra-light, 151-52
   set triggers, 152-53
   two-stage, 224
   two-stage military, 151
   tuning, 238
twist
   for common cartridges, 24-25
   rate of, 13-14, 22

varmint calibers, 92-93
varmint sights, 168
velocity, muzzle, 103-7

wildcats, 86-90, 119, 134, 221-22, 233-34

yaw, 115-16